Acclaim for PAULINE MAIER's

American Scripture

"*American Scripture* offers Americans a fresh perspective on their most treasured national relic." —*The New York Times*

"A fascinating story. . . . Maier has written a deft intellectual achievement." —*Boston Globe*

"*American Scripture* is a timely reaffirmation that the Declaration of Independence is what Americans choose to make it. . . . A remarkable, readable intellectual history." —*USA Today*

"Maier has delivered a colorful study of our country's most important political document: the Declaration of Independence." —*The New York Post*

"Astute and accomplished. . . . Carefully researched and thoughtfully written." —*The New Republic*

"Outstanding. Employs superior historiography and political sensitivity to place the Declaration in its original context, and considers what it has become in the context of American political history." —*Kirkus Reviews*

PAULINE MAIER

American Scripture

Pauline Maier, William R. Kennan, Jr., Professor of American History at M.I.T., is the author of *From Resistance to Revolution* and *The Old Revolutionaries.*

ALSO BY PAULINE MAIER

*From Resistance to Revolution: Colonial Radicals and the Development of
American Opposition to Britain, 1765–1776*

The Old Revolutionaries: Political Lives in the Age of Samuel Adams

The American People: A History

American Scripture

American Scripture

Making the Declaration of Independence

PAULINE MAIER

Vintage Books
A Division of Random House, Inc.
New York

FIRST VINTAGE BOOKS EDITION, JULY 1998

Copyright © 1997 by Pauline Maier

All rights reserved under International and Pan-American Copyright
Conventions. Published in the United States by Vintage Books, a division of
Random House, Inc., New York, and simultaneously in Canada by Random
House of Canada Limited, Toronto. Originally published in hardcover in the
United States by Alfred A. Knopf, Inc., New York, in 1997.

The Library of Congress has cataloged the Knopf edition as follows:
Maier, Pauline.
American scripture: making the Declaration of Independence/
Pauline Maier.
p.   cm.
ISBN 0-679-45492-6
1. United States. Declaration of Independence.
2. United States—Politics and government—1775–1783.
I. Title.
E221.M24   1997
973.3'13—dc21   97-2769
CIP
Vintage ISBN: 0-679-77908-6

Author photograph © Inspired Images

Random House Web address: www.randomhouse.com

Printed in the United States of America

For Charles,

my Jeffersonian

Contents

Introduction:
Gathering at the Shrine

FEBRUARY 14, 1995. "Speck-by-Speck," said the headline, "the Nation's Vital Documents Get Checkups." After years of preparation, the National Archives was wheeling out the big guns of modern conservation technology to preserve what it calls "the Charters of Freedom"—the Declaration of Independence, the Constitution, and the Bill of Rights. Normally those documents are encased in massive, bronze-framed, bulletproof glass containers filled with inert helium gas "to displace damaging oxygen" and with water vapor to keep the parchment from becoming brittle. During most days the "Charters of Freedom" are on display at the "Shrine" in the National Archives' rotunda, but at night the containers are lowered into a vault of reinforced concrete and steel that, according to a National Archives brochure, is twenty-two feet deep, weighs fifty-five tons, and was built (by the Mosler Safe Company of Hamilton, Ohio) in 1952, when the Cold War was beginning to make bomb shelters something of a fashion. Once the documents are inside the vault, the brochure says, "the massive doors on top . . . swing shut, and the documents are safe." But in February 1995, at a time of year when the stream of visitors slows, they were removed from protective custody and scrutinized scientifically for the slightest sign of deterioration.[1]

A senior conservator carefully moved a fiber-optic light source over the surface of the Declaration, noting evidence of old bends and of earlier, amateurish repairs. She also took photographs of the document with a 35-millimeter camera, then placed sheets of plastic film over the case and traced the locations of tears, bends, repairs, glue spots, even scars from the animal skins used to make the parchment, confident that her "painstaking work" would produce "invaluable" information. Meanwhile, a physicist and, I assume, other conservators examined the Bill of Rights with a computerized imaging system capable of discovering the disappearance, or even the fading, of the tiniest flakes of eighteenth-century black, iron-based ink, which, it turns out, fades to brown with age, particularly if exposed to light. (That was news to me. For decades I've read handwritten eighteenth-century documents assuming that brown ink was the style of the time. Even the colors of the past, it seems, can no longer be observed directly.)

The computerized imaging system, the jewel in the crown of the Archives' conservation program, was developed after 1981, when experts suggested that new and better ways be found than those then available to monitor the documents' condition. The Archives turned for help to the National Aeronautics and Space Administration, which, in turn, had engineers at the Jet Propulsion Laboratory in Pasadena, California, design a system for taking precise pictures of the documents that was based in part on equipment being created for the Hubble Space Telescope. The "Charters Monitoring System" that they proposed was built for $3.3 million (by what is now Hughes Optics in Danbury, Connecticut) and set up in 1987 at the Archives, which used it to generate a series of "baseline" images to which those of February 1995 were compared. Essentially the system consists of a computer-guided electronic camera that scans sample sections of the documents, measuring each dot or "pixel" of light on a scale of 1 to 1,000 and recording its results. The equipment is mounted on a 6,000-pound granite table that sits on a floor of reinforced concrete.[2]

The discovery of haze where the Bill of Rights had touched glass prompted consultations with a microbiologist and a glass chemist. The problem seemed worse than when the document was examined in 1988, perhaps because the fiber-optic light source was more sensitive than the incandescent bulb used in the earlier examination. Or was there a real physical change, and, if so, was it caused by some chemical reaction between the parchment and glass or by a living organism capable of surviving without oxygen? The 1995 evaluation confirmed earlier observations of tiny white flakes in the document enclosures that could be sodium coming from the glass or perhaps the result of other structural changes in the glass. All these phenomena were noted, measured, evaluated, and recorded for future reference.[3]

·   ·   ·

"THE NATION'S VITAL DOCUMENTS" have not always been regarded with such reverence, or, for that matter, given much regard of any kind. In 1776 the Declaration of Independence was not even copied onto a particularly good sheet of parchment, just an ordinary type of colonial manufacture that could be easily found on sale in Philadelphia and was perhaps "improvidently selected, being improperly cured and sized." The Declaration then went on to become "one of the most abused documents in the history of preservation . . . battered and bandaged since its birth."[4] The Continental Congress probably hauled the document—rolled up, as was the custom with parchment scrolls—with its other papers as it moved from place to place in the course of the revolutionary war. Later the Declaration found resting places with the national government at New York, Philadelphia, and, in 1800, at the nation's new capital in Washington, D.C. The Department of State received custody when the Declaration of Independence was still a teenager, but even so it was continually transferred from building to building, or from home to home. When the British invaded in August 1814, a government clerk managed to save the document from destruction. By the time it returned to Washington from its hiding place in Leesburg, Virginia, curiosity seekers found its text, and particularly the signatures, which were written in various qualities of ink, already in bad shape. The wet-pressing process used to make a facsimile in 1823 did further damage, and the fading continued after 1841 when the State Department grew tired of pulling the document out to show visitors and put it on public display for the first time—on a wall in the new Patent Office opposite a large window, where it remained for thirty-five years. The document traveled to Philadelphia's Independence Hall for six months during the centennial celebrations of 1876, and was subsequently put on display in the State Department's library.

By its hundredth year, however, the Declaration's decay had become so obvious that the first of many "scientific" committees was appointed to decide what to do. Generally the experts recommended keeping the document out of light and, in 1903, "as dry as possible," but their advice was not always followed. That was perhaps just as well, since extreme dryness makes parchment crack. Custodians continually sought to protect the document from fire, but no other serious efforts at preservation were made until the State Department transferred the

Declaration of Independence to the Library of Congress in 1921—but by later lights even its efforts seem positively backward. The Library set out to display the Declaration with the Constitution in a safe repository "that every visitor to Washington would wish to tell about when he returned," and that would be regarded "as a sort of 'shrine.' " Designed by Francis H. Bacon, whose brother, Henry, served as architect for the Lincoln Memorial, and installed on the Library's west wall, that first "shrine" was opened for visitors in 1924. It was made of marble, except that the Declaration was shown, tipped slightly forward, in an upright frame or case with gold-plated bronze doors made to resemble "a conventional altar piece." Below and in front lay five sheets of the Constitution in a larger case with a sloped top. Around the assemblage was a marble balustrade "suggesting the chancel rail before an altar," which "pilgrims" could enter, single-file, for a close look at the charters.[5]

Enormous care was taken to preserve the documents. They were covered with double panes of plate glass between which a gelatin film filtered damaging light rays, and a continuous guard kept watch for thieves and other evil-minded people as well as for the "silverfish" someone reported seeing in the Constitution's case, causing near-panic.[6] After Pearl Harbor, the Library carefully packed the Declaration and the Constitution in an elaborate container (or "reliquary") and sent them to the Bullion Depository at Fort Knox in a Pullman car accompanied by armed Secret Service agents, a Library officer, and, through the last lap of its journey, troops of the Thirteenth Armored Division. The Declaration nonetheless suffered greatly from its natural enemies, the great swings in Washington's humidity and temperature before the days of air-conditioning and climate control. When restorers examined it in 1942, the parchment was already cracked, a corner had split off, and its edges were curled. Worse yet, earlier efforts to repair damage had included pasting the Declaration to its mounting with "copious glue" and "fixing" a crack with cellophane tape that turned the color of molasses and had itself to be carefully removed. The modern method of repair, it seems, consisted in part of "luting" or cementing the cracks "with fibers from Japanese tissue moistened with rice paste." Before returning the documents to their container, their surfaces were protected by another covering of "Japanese tissue."[7] Did anyone appreciate the irony of using Japanese materials after taking such extreme measures to put our "vital national documents" beyond the reach of the Japanese and other wartime enemies? The documents were finally placed in their current airtight thermopane containers with an electronic device to detect helium loss in September 1952, a few months before they were transferred from the Library of Congress to the National Archives.

Modern "scientific" document conservation is obviously a very recent development, and it has not advanced equally on all fronts. "Our ability to detect problems is growing faster than our ability to solve them," according to a professor of conservation associated with the monitoring program. "What to do if we find something becomes the more difficult question."[8] And an important one, it seems. The original, signed texts of the Declaration of Independence and, to a lesser extent, the Constitution have become for the United States what Lenin's body was for the Soviet Union, a tangible remnant of the revolution to which its children can still cling. What we are struggling to preserve from time is, however, not a physical body but a physical document that was written to perform a constitutional function. That, too, involves some irony. The heroic efforts invested in conserving the document by which the United States declared its Independence from Britain testify to the powerful and enduring influence of English constitutional tradition on American political culture.

JULY 24, 1995. A meeting at the Woodrow Wilson International Center for Scholars adjourns for lunch, giving me a chance to have my first look at our nation's "vital documents." Historians seldom need to see the original texts of those documents anymore. Their words are reprinted in every American history textbook and in hundreds of other places; indeed, facsimile reproductions can be bought in many National Park Service gift shops. The various drafts of the Declaration have also been published, with all the little scribblings on them studied and charted with such care that virtually every piece of information scholars need can be found in a good research library. Curiosity more than anything sent me rushing though the hot summer air across the mall to the National Archives.

The lines in the rotunda were fortunately short. As I waited my turn, a family behind me discussed the mural above and to the left. Painted in the 1930s, it showed members of the Second Continental Congress, including a cluster of men at the far end that clearly

consisted of the committee that drafted the Declaration of Independence—Benjamin Franklin, John Adams, Roger Sherman, Robert R.
Livingston, and Thomas Jefferson. But what interested the family
members was George Washington. Where was he in the picture?
"That's him; I'm sure that's him," a boy said, referring to a figure "in
green." Should I tell them Washington wasn't at the Congress? That
he was with the Continental Army in New York? "This really makes
all that history you read about in school come alive, doesn't it," commented a woman whom I took to be the mother. Would I have killed
the fun by correcting their error?

To me the vital documents themselves seemed pretty dead. In fact,
the spectacle had the air of a state funeral. Guards stand at either side
of the "shrine" dressed in black and with an air of suppressed deep
emotion, breaking silence mainly to ask the line of tee-shirted, sneak-
ered tourists to keep moving. In 1944, when the Declaration and Constitution went back on display at the Archives, its honor guards were
drawn in succession from the Marines, Army, and Navy,[9] and almost
certainly consisted predominantly if not exclusively of white men. On
the day I went both guards, a woman and a man, were African Americans, which reflected contemporary Washington's civilian work force,
but also contributed to the sense of heavy symbolism. By their presence and attitude of reverence the guards witness the triumph of Abraham Lincoln's view that the guarantee of freedom in the Declaration
of Independence extended literally to "all men." These documents
were their "Charters of our Freedom," too, not just those of white
Americans, as Stephen Douglas had insisted in the 1850s, and to
women as well as men, as feminists of 1848 had argued.

The "shrine" itself resembles the awesome, gilded, pre–Vatican II
altars of my Catholic girlhood, raised three steps above where the wor-
shippers assembled. The Declaration is its centerpiece, held above the
Constitution and the Bill of Rights in what looks like a tabernacle, or
perhaps a monstrance, the device used to display the host on special
days of adoration. The Constitution and Bill of Rights are spread out
beneath, on the altar's surface. Off to the left as visitors leave they can
see another important document, a version of England's Magna Carta
of 1215 that was probably issued in 1297, and that has been lent to the
National Archives for an indefinite period by its owner, the Dallas
businessman Ross Perot. As the Archives explains, the fundamental

constitutional documents of the United States emerged from an old English tradition, and some rights mentioned in our Bill of Rights were asserted, or at least foreshadowed, in the Magna Carta five centuries earlier. But it's easy to walk past the Magna Carta without noticing it. It seems not like an ancestor but a sideshow to the main attraction at the rotunda's far end.

The Bill of Rights especially intrigued me. What could the Archives have on display? I wondered. The Declaration and Constitution were complete, formal documents, copied onto parchment by order of the Second Continental Congress in 1776 or the Constitutional Convention of 1787. But the Bill of Rights consists of those first ten amendments to the Constitution that the states chose to ratify from twelve that Congress had proposed in September 1789. When would those amendments have been put on parchment to take their place among our "vital national documents"? The text on exhibit, I knew, had joined the Declaration and Constitution relatively recently, and not much is known about its history as a physical artifact. The first photograph of the "Bill of Rights" was taken during its Sesquicentennial, in 1941, and it was among the documents carried across the land on the "Freedom Train" from September 1947 through January 1949.[10] It turned out that the document at the foot of the Constitution is Congress's official copy of the twelve amendments it proposed, not the ten that were ratified. In other words, the "Bill of Rights" on exhibit is not the Bill of Rights passed into law. The whole assemblage came to seem part and parcel of the 1940s and 1950s, an assertion of American values—religion, free enterprise (naming the companies that contributed to the display), liberty—against fascist and communist enemies and, with the vault and its massive closing doors, an assurance to the fearful that those values could not be destroyed. The 1960s and 1970s had also left their mark in the changing identity of the guards. The "shrine," in short, is an eloquent monument to the struggles and values of the American people in the mid- and late twentieth century.

Before leaving I asked one of the attendants whether the documents had been removed from display during "the recent preservation evaluation." She seemed shocked at the question. "The documents," she announced slowly with a deep, dramatic Southern drawl, "have been untouched by human hands for forty-three years."

. . .

I BEGAN this book against my better judgment. At first, if I recall correctly, I dismissed the suggestion that I write a "modern history of the Declaration of Independence." There's already too much written on the subject, I remember saying, and I have no particular interest in adding to the pile. I also thought that the document had been "hyped" out of all proportion to what was justified, and that more attention would only exacerbate the problem. But what book on the subject would I assign to my students? None, I replied, having concluded after a quick survey that most of the books in print at that time were antiquarian, dated, downright wrong on critical points, or too specialized for undergraduates. So I lost the argument and set out to write what was supposed to be a small book for advanced high school and college students that would tell them what I already knew—but I ended up writing something different, about things I never knew or hadn't thought much about before.

This is not the place to discuss earlier studies of the Declaration of Independence—they and their authors will come up at their proper places in this story—except to say that most of them since Carl Becker's delightful (but now dated) *The Declaration of Independence* (1922) have examined the Declaration for the political ideas it expressed, and then jumped from its text to the more systematic treatises of eighteenth-century European writers. Academics, I think, are generally more comfortable there, in the transatlantic world of ideas, than in the grubby world of eighteenth-century American politics where, for better or worse, I've spent much of my adult working life. More recently, and without abandoning their taste for the history of ideas and for the European origins of things American, historians (with a few notable exceptions) have also studied the draft that Thomas Jefferson composed for Congress's drafting committee, not the official Declaration as Congress approved it, and with an ever more narrow focus. For example, Jay Fliegelman's *Declaring Independence* (1993) spends considerable time analyzing "Jefferson's pauses"—the "diacritical quotation marks" that Jefferson apparently inserted into his text of the Declaration, and which mistakenly made their way into an early printed version, to show where a speaker should pause, and for how long.[11]

I had better be as clear as I can on this. I have no doubt that political ideology was critical to the American Revolution, and spent some time a quarter century ago sorting through the "revolution principles" that shaped American resistance to Britain. To me, however, the historical significance of the Declaration did not lie in the principles it stated except insofar as it restated what virtually all Americans—patriot and Loyalist alike—thought and said in other words in other places. And that was exactly what the Declaration was meant to do: it was, according to Jefferson, "to be an expression of the American mind, and to give that expression the proper tone and spirit called for by the occasion."[12] As a statement of political philosophy, the Declaration was therefore purposely unexceptional in 1776. No doubt the document was affected by contemporary rhetorical theory, as Fliegelman and also Stephen E. Lucas argue, and I would be the first to agree that the "associationalist psychology" of the early nineteenth century played a role in the esteemed position the document assumed as the fiftieth anniversary of American Independence approached. Those subjects are interesting and have a place in the Declaration's story, but they are not the whole of the story, or the most important aspects of it for us to understand.

Perhaps I should also explain that I bear no animus toward Jefferson. True, I once nominated him as the most overrated person in American history for an *American Heritage* survey, but only because of the extraordinary adulation (and, sometimes, execration) he has received and continues to receive. The mythology of Jefferson, and the way interpretations of him have reflected Americans' feelings about themselves, as if he were an incarnation of the American nation, has itself been the subject of some wonderful books and essays.[13] It does strike me as odd, however, that historians' obsession with Jefferson continues unabated at a time when studying the history of "great white men" has become unfashionable in the profession. As this book makes plain, I dissent from any suggestion that Jefferson was alone responsible for the Declaration of Independence, or that the document most worth studying and admiring is his draft, or that the full story of the Declaration can be told apart from that of the Independence it declared and the process that led to it.

My real problem with most studies of the Declaration of Independence is, in fact, less with what they say than with what they leave out. In a sense, I have written the book Becker was criticized for not writing and whose value he acknowledged, a book on the Declaration of Independence "regarded as an event, as the culmination of a series of revolutionary activities,"[14] and I also, like Becker, trace the document's development, which, in part because new evidence has come to light, looks different today than it did seventy-five years ago. The tortuous process by which Americans arrived at Independence, the political maneuvers that finally allowed Congress to make that decision, the mass of popular resolutions on Independence that those maneuvers produced (most of which have gone unnoticed over the past two centuries), the way the Declaration was drafted, the circumstances under which the Continental Congress considered it, how Congress changed the version recommended by its drafting committee—all seem to me part of a story worth repeating. That story is not of a solo performance or even, to extend the metaphor, a performance of chamber music with a handful of players. What I had in mind was more the Boston Symphony Orchestra or, better yet, the Mormon Tabernacle Choir, a production with a cast of hundreds, many of whom must remain nameless since we know them only for what they did. Certain characters in the story are, in fact, not people at all but documents with distinctive personalities, texts in which people (many obscure and unremembered) poured out their deepest convictions and emotions, sometimes assuming as if by instinct a form that was well defined in English history and tradition. I set out, in short, to tell the stories of Independence and of the Declaration of Independence when the Declaration was a workaday document of the Second Continental Congress, one of many similar documents of the time in which Americans advocated, explained, and justified Independence, the most painful decision of their collective lives.

Then, after throwing overboard all pretense of producing a pamphlet-sized "teaching book," I went on to tell another story, one that has been told only in fragments, about how, after a period in which the Declaration of Independence was all but forgotten, it was remade into a sacred text, a statement of basic, enduring truths often described with words borrowed from the vocabulary of religion. In the decade or so after 1815, I discovered, the document began to assume the quasi-religious attributes later institutionalized without a shadow of subtlety at the "shrines" in the Library of Congress and, more recently, the National Archives. I confess that I have long been and remain uncomfortable with the use of religious words and images for what are, after all, things of this world. That practice strikes me as idolatrous, and also curiously at odds with the values of the Revolution. As the heirs of a political tradition shaped by radical seventeenth-century English Protestants, most American revolutionaries were suspicious of Roman Catholicism and its iconographic traditions. Many went further and opposed the use of religion to reinforce the power of the state in any way: indeed, separation of church and state was one of the most radical innovations of the American Revolution. It also struck me that the Declaration of Independence itself was peculiarly unsuited for the role it came to play, essentially as a statement of basic principles for the guidance of an established society which, after all, had a Bill of Rights that was supposed to perform that function. How and why did the Declaration of Independence come to assume the role it has assumed in American society—a statement of values that more than any other expresses not why we separated from Britain, and not what we are or have been, but what we ought to be, an inscription of ideals that bind us as a people but have also been at the center of some of the most divisive controversies in our history? The book, then, tells two different but related stories—that of the original making of the Declaration of Independence and that of its remaking into the document most Americans know, remember, and revere.

All stories have endings, and the ending of this story, or as much of it as I want to tell in some detail, was, I learned, with Abraham Lincoln at Gettysburg. Again, I have chosen not to belabor my differences with people like Willmoore Kendall, Mel Bradford, or Garry Wills, who have written on Lincoln and his "inventive" interpretation of the Declaration. For them the questions I address in the final chapter of the book—on how the "remaking" of the Declaration occurred—are easily answered. Lincoln did it. Single-handedly, they claim, he foisted his personal understanding of the Declaration of Independence on the nation and, as Bradford suggested, through the biblical allusions in his oratory established the "quasi-religion of Equality." Wills described Lincoln's Gettysburg Address as perpetrating a "giant (if benign) swindle," as "one of the most daring acts of open-air sleight-of-hand ever witnessed by the unsuspecting," one that revolutionized the Revolution, "giving people a new past to live with that would change their future indefinitely."[15] Historians, I realize, have a way of wearying people by insisting that virtually any subject is too complex for simple answers, but here surely that objection is warranted. Rather than argue with these formidable opponents, however, I prefer to tell the story as I see it, with all its peculiar twists and turns. My answer to Kendall and Bradford and Wills is in a theme that goes through the book and can at least be stated simply: the remaking of the Declaration of Independence no less than its original creation was not an individual but a collective act that drew on the words and thoughts of many people, dead and alive, who struggled with the same or closely related problems. The eloquence of Jefferson's and Lincoln's texts depended in part on the resonances they captured, and their messages were convincing because the hearts of their audiences had been—to adopt the language of Lincoln's early New England ancestors, on which he drew so heavily in the dark years of the Civil War—"prepared" to receive it. The act of reinterpreting the Declaration, moreover, did not stop with Lincoln; it goes on today, expanding the story's cast from hundreds to millions. You, I, and less attentive members of the American public are participants. And the story has a moral.

Deciding where to end was one thing; settling on where the story begins was even more difficult. Should it start in 1763, a century before Lincoln's address at Gettysburg, when the British forced the French from North America and assumed financial obligations that led them to try to raise more revenue from the American colonists? Or perhaps in 1765, when the Stamp Act, Parliament's first effort to lay a direct tax on the Americans, provoked massive colonial opposition? It could begin in 1767–68, when Parliament's Townshend Acts attempted to raise money through duties on trade and provoked another wave of colonial resistance, or, better yet, with the Tea Act of 1773. After the "Indians" at the Boston Tea Party of December 1773 threw newly imported tea into Boston harbor rather than allow the import taxes on it to be paid, the British finally decided to knock the Americans (and especially those in Massachusetts) back in line with a series of "Coercive Acts." They closed the port of Boston, revised the Massachusetts charter to undercut popular power and enhance that of the Crown, allowed English officials charged with murder for killing colonists while repressing riots or enforcing British revenue laws to be tried in England (which, colonists said, meant they would be acquitted), and allowed military commanders to quarter troops where needed to control the civilian population. Americans throughout the Continent quickly called those laws the "Intolerable Acts," and most colonies sent delegates to a Continental Congress, later known as the "First Continental Congress," to coordinate their opposition. It met at Philadelphia in September and October 1774, and dumbfounded the King's ministers, who considered the colonists incapable of acting together.

I have chosen, however, to begin with the assembling of that first Congress's successor, known as the Second Continental Congress, which convened on May 10, 1775. It quickly became the first government of the United States, and no doubt the strangest government we have ever had. Its oddities explain the kinds of maneuverings that were made on behalf of Independence in 1776, and inevitably left their mark on what is today the Congress's most famous child, the Declaration of Independence.

It is late April of 1775. Samuel Adams and John Hancock have narrowly escaped the British at Lexington, and are setting out for Congress in great confusion and with great fear . . .

Pauline Maier
Cambridge, Massachusetts
August 15, 1996

American Scripture

CHAPTER I

Independence

THE DELEGATES' LONG, slow journey from Massachusetts to Pennsylvania need not have been made. Before adjourning in October 1774, the First Continental Congress called for the convening of another congress at Philadelphia on May 10, 1775, only if Britain had not redressed the Americans' grievances. Its members still believed that the imperial conflict could be settled at any time. Over and over the Congress had insisted that Americans remained loyal to Britain. Like their English ancestors, however, they would not endure violations of their "most sacred" rights and privileges. The First Continental Congress commended the people of Massachusetts for resisting Parliament's "Intolerable Acts" and declared that if Britain tried to execute those laws by force, "all America ought to support them in their opposition." But it also urged the people of Massachusetts to remain "peaceably and firmly . . . on the defensive," carefully avoiding incidents that might involve "all America in the horrors of a civil war" before George III could respond to its pleas. Peace and harmony would immediately return, Congress assured the King, if the colonies were returned to their situation in 1763, at the end of the French and Indian War.[1] But no news of redress arrived during the winter and spring after the first congress closed. Finally, three weeks before the new congress met, war broke out in the farming towns of Lexington and Concord some twenty miles north and west of Boston.

Two of the Massachusetts delegates, Samuel Adams and John Hancock, were in Lexington during the night of April 18–19, 1775, before the battle. Warned by Paul Revere, a Boston silversmith and experienced express rider, that British troops were coming, they fled first to the nearby towns of Woburn and Billerica, then moved westward, arriving at Worcester on April 24. There they expected to find the

other members of the Massachusetts delegation to the Second Continental Congress—Samuel's short-tempered country cousin John
Adams, Robert Treat Paine, and Thomas Cushing—and a military
guard to protect them along the route to Pennsylvania. No such luck.
All they met up with in Worcester were rumors that four more British
regiments were expected to arrive in Boston at any time. Frantically
Hancock wrote the Massachusetts Committee of Safety, which was
then meeting outside Boston at Watertown, for assistance, recent
news, and, above all, information on the events of five days earlier. "I
beg, by the return of this express [rider], to hear from you," he said;
"and pray furnish us with depositions of the conduct of the [British]
troops, the certainty of their firing first, and every circumstance relative to the conduct of the troops, from the 19th instant to this time,
that we may be able to give some account of matters as we proceed, especially at Philadelphia."[2] Clearly Hancock expected to be called to account by colonists elsewhere who might well blame the hotheaded
people of Massachusetts for the unwelcome opening of hostilities. If
the people of Massachusetts had failed to act defensively on the 19th,
as the First Continental Congress requested, would the other colonies
refuse to support them and leave Massachusetts to face the wrath of
Britain alone?

Hancock also wanted to know what the Committee of Safety had
done since the 19th, its plans for the immediate future, "what prisoners
we have, and what they have of ours; who of note was killed on both
sides; who commands our forces, &c. Are our men in good spirits?" he
asked. "For God's sake, do not suffer the spirit to subside . . ." He fired
off one suggestion after another in a mad tumble—drive the British
troops from Boston ("Our friends are valuable, but our country must
be saved. I have an interest in that town: what can be the enjoyment of
that to me, if I am obliged to hold it at the will of general Gage or any
one else?"); seize Castle William in the bay; prevent large ships from
entering the harbor. But what was the point of these frantic orders?
Hancock wrote from the desperation of ignorance: he had no idea
what had happened since he and Adams began their flight, and confessed that the members of the Committee of Safety "know better
what to do than I can point out." Immediately he began pouring out
more questions, more complaints. Where was Cushing? "Are Mr.
Paine and Mr. John Adams to be with us? What are we to depend
upon? We travel rather as deserters, which I will not submit to. I will

return and join you, if I cannot travel in reputation. I wish to hear from you. Pray spend a thought upon our situation." How was the Provincial Congress going? Who was its president? Were its members "hearty" in the cause? Then he ended: "Pray remember Mr. S. Adams and myself to all friends. God be with you."

A few days later, without, it seems, receiving a reply, that odd couple—Adams, a short, stocky man in his mid-fifties, unconcerned with wealth, social rank, or appearances, an old Puritan in many ways who went into politics as a kind of ministry; and Hancock, over a decade younger, tall and rich, something of a dandy, and ambitious to a fault—set out together for Philadelphia, meeting the other Massachusetts delegates before entering New York. By then Connecticut's delegates had joined the group, which, as it grew in size, gradually took on the character of a triumphal procession, which must have gone far to quiet Hancock's fears. The delegates' movement south had been preceded by the news of Lexington and Concord, which spread through the country as "on the wings of the wind," reaching New York in four days, Philadelphia in five, and, by the time Congress assembled, was already in Savannah. Now everywhere the delegates went their presence brought moving manifestations of sympathy and support for the people of Massachusetts. Starting in Connecticut, members of local militia companies came out to protect the delegates, then yielded that responsibility to others from towns further along the route. At first twelve armed men accompanied the delegates; by the time the procession left Manhattan, where New York's delegates joined in, perhaps two hundred militiamen accompanied the congressmen. When they first crossed onto Manhattan island, its roads were lined with thousands of spectators wrapped, Connecticut's Silas Deane noted, in a "cloud of dust" stirred up from the unseasonably dry earth by a torrent of wheels and feet. On May 6, when the parade arrived in New York City, still nestled at the southern end of the island, a cacophony of bells rang out and another "amazing concourse of people" gathered, whether by horse, carriage, or foot, "trudging and sweating thro' the dirt" for an opportunity to shout "huzzah" at the Massachusetts representatives: "the doors, the windows, the stoops, the roofs of the plazas, were loaded with all ranks, ages and sexes." A crowd of equal size bid them farewell two days later, after what seems to have been a quiet Sabbath.[3]

The "march in state" continued, with further outpourings of

popular support, through Newark, Elizabethtown, Woodbridge, Brunswick, Princeton, and Trenton, New Jersey, until finally the parade, "rolling and gathering like a Snowball," arrived at Philadelphia on May 10—the day Congress was scheduled to meet. Some two hundred "principal Gentlemen, on Horseback, with their Swords Drawn," who met the delegations six miles outside the city, led the way into Philadelphia. Behind them came the city's new militia officers, two by two, also with swords drawn, then Hancock and Samuel Adams in an open four-wheeled carriage, or phaeton (Hancock looking, one account suggested, somewhat sick), John Adams and Cushing in a two-wheeled "chaise," Robert Treat Paine, the New York and some Connecticut delegates—and, finally, a mass of additional participants in perhaps a hundred more horse-drawn carriages. Philadelphia itself, Deane reported, was "full of people, and the Crowd, as great as at New York; the Bells all ringing, and the air rent with Shouts and huzza's." The Massachusetts delegates' entrance into the city was "verry grand," Delaware's Caesar Rodney reported, "and Intended to show [the public's] approbation of the Conduct of the good people of that Government, in the distressing situation of Affairs there."[4]

How different the situation was from that when the First Continental Congress convened in September 1774 and Massachusetts delegates found themselves "obliged to act with great Delicacy and Caution" and to keep "out of sight," letting others speak their sentiments for them. Many members of the First Continental Congress, Samuel Adams observed, had at first considered Massachusetts "intemperate and rash," and even suspected it of aiming at "a total independency." As a result, both the colony and its delegates were forced to act with conspicuous moderation or risk losing the support they needed from other colonies and, more generally, undermining colonial unity, which was critical if the Americans were to hold their own against the power of Britain. In September 1774, Samuel Adams had asked Joseph Warren to "implore every Friend in Boston by every thing dear and sacred to Men of Sense and Virtue to avoid Blood and Tumult" because the other provinces needed time "*to think and resolve.*" If Boston could remain "on the defensive" against the British troops stationed in its midst, "the liberties of America, which that town has so nobly contended for, will be secured." There were, then, good reasons for Hancock's anxiety at Worcester. But the "Blood and

Tumult" at Lexington and Concord did not divide the colonies; it brought them closer together. As members of the Second Continental Congress assembled, the Virginian Richard Henry Lee observed that there had "never appeared more perfect unanimity among any sett of Men than among the Delegates," and that "all the old Provinces not one excepted are directed by the same firmness of union, and determination to resist by all ways and to every extremity."[5]

Circumstances determined that the new Congress would be different in character from its predecessor. Not for it the luxury of a single brief session, less than two months in duration, dedicated to debating major issues of policy and adopting grand statements of American rights and grievances. The Second Continental Congress would have to take charge of a country at war; it would become a government, the sole government of the emerging nation until 1781, when, in the final year of the war with Great Britain, the Articles of Confederation were finally ratified. Only in moments stolen from the daily work of wartime administration could it discuss broader issues, like the colonies' future, or consider documents of significance, such as the Declaration of Independence. Its decision to separate from Britain was one of the most important Congress made; and no other so seriously strained the sense of community with which the Congress began.

I. Congress

The delegates had hardly assembled when they received an address from the Massachusetts Provincial Congress reporting that it had taken steps during Congress's recess to raise 13,600 soldiers from its people and to secure additional men from New Hampshire, Connecticut, and Rhode Island. "The sudden Exigency of our public Affairs," the Massachusetts Congress explained, "precluded the possibility of waiting for your direction in these important measures." Reinforcements of the British Army in Boston were "daily expected," so "we are now reduced to the sad alternative of defending ourselves by arms, or submitting to be slaughtered." With the "greatest deference," the Bay Colony's Congress suggested that a powerful American army was the only way left to restrain "the rapid Progress of a tyrannical Ministry. Without a force, superior to our Enemies," it said, "we must reasonably expect to become the Victims of their relentless fury." With such a force, however, there was hope that the "inhuman Ravages of mercenary Troops in America" would end, and that those responsible for America's misery would be brought to "condign punishment . . . by the just Indignation of our Brethren in Great Britain."[6]

Not even in Massachusetts were hopes of reconciliation dead. A series of depositions on the events of April 19 and other papers sent to Philadelphia by the Massachusetts Provincial Congress included a letter it had written to the British people on April 26. In an effort to secure their support, it told how "the Regulars . . . first began Hostilities" at Lexington by firing on a company of townsmen that had already begun to disperse. Again at Concord, the redcoats "fired . . . before the provincials fired on them." During their retreat to Charlestown, British troops plundered and burned private houses; "Women in child bed were driven, by the Soldiery, naked into the Streets"; old men, "peaceably in their Houses, were shot dead; and such Scenes exhibited as would disgrace the annals of the most uncivilized Nation." All these vicious acts were explained as "Marks of ministerial Vengeance" against Massachusetts "for refusing, with her Sister Colonies, a Submission to Slavery." The colonists nonetheless remained "loyal and dutiful Subjects" of the King, ready "to defend his person, Family, Crown and Dignity" with their "Lives and Fortunes." They hoped for support from the "Honour, Wisdom, and Valour of Britons," especially since the ministry's campaign of oppression "must end in the ruin and Slavery of Britain, as well as the persecuted American Colonies." Six months earlier, the First Continental Congress had adopted a similar address to the People of Great Britain, asking their help in saving the empire "from the devices of wicked Ministers and evil Counsellors."[7] The outbreak of war seemed to have changed remarkably little; it had not, at any rate, destroyed the colonists' desire to remain subjects of the British Crown.

Reconciliation was still the American dream: most colonies' written instructions to their delegates gave them "full power . . . to concert, agree upon, direct and order" measures that the members of Congress found "best calculated for the recovery and establishment of American rights and Liberties, and for restoring harmony between Great-Britain and the Colonies" (Massachusetts, December 5, 1774) or simply "to obtain a redress of American grievances" (Maryland, December 12, 1774). On March 16 the Delaware Assembly authorized its delegates "to concert and agree upon such further measures, as shall appear to them best calculated for the accommodation of the unhappy differences between Great Britain and the Colonies, on a constitutional foundation," and then, for emphasis, added "which the House most ardently wish for."[8] These instructions predated Lexington and Concord; but if, as Massachusetts insisted, an army had become an essential prerequisite of reconciliation, the only way to hold off the King's ministers until right-thinking Britons could set things straight, then Congress could assume military responsibility without exceeding its powers. On that even the most moderate members of Congress seemed to agree, since they found it perfectly consistent to support a "vigorous" military effort and to propose initiatives for settling the Anglo-American conflict. In any case, the First Continental Congress had long since resolved that "all America" should support the inhabitants of Massachusetts Bay if Britain attempted to execute recent acts of Parliament by force.[9] And so, in a remarkably short period of time, parades and celebrations gave way to the hard work of guiding and governing a nation at war.

ON MAY 9, the day before Congress assembled, provincial troops seized the British-held Fort Ticonderoga, a fortress at the juncture between Lake George and Lake Champlain in northern New York, then rounded out their victory by taking the nearby British post at Crown Point. The conquerors—two contingents of troops under the fiery Ethan Allen, one of the founders of Vermont, and Colonel Benedict Arnold, an able and ambitious merchant from New Haven, Connecticut—had not been set to their task by Congress: the Connecticut men under Allen acted on their own initiative, and the Massachusetts Committee of Safety set Arnold and his soldiers, most of whom came from western Massachusetts, to work. It took a week before news of their victory arrived in Philadelphia. No doubt Ticonderoga would be a critical post in an Anglo-American war, as it had been in the French and Indian War. It guarded a major waterway that ran from a point on the mighty St. Lawrence River midway between Montreal and Quebec down the Richelieu River to Lake Champlain, Lake George, the Hudson River, and New York City.

After learning of the American victory and being briefed on Ticonderoga's military importance, Congress did its best to describe its capture as an act of defense. According to a set of resolves it adopted on May 18, there was "indubitable evidence" that the British Ministry planned to invade the colonies from Quebec. As a result, several inhabitants of the northern colonies who lived near Ticonderoga, "impelled by a just regard for the defence and preservation of themselves and their countrymen," had seized the post and a set of cannon and other military stores "that would certainly have been used in the intended invasion." Congress went on to recommend that committees at New York and Albany see to it that those supplies were moved to the southern end of Lake George and secured with the help, if necessary, of additional forces from New Hampshire, Massachusetts, and Connecticut. It specified, however, that a careful inventory should be taken of the cannon and military stores so they could be "safely returned when the restoration of the former harmony between great Britain and these colonies so ardently wished for by the latter shall render it prudent and consistent with the overruling law of self preservation."[10] But to British eyes, the American capture of Ticonderoga seemed an act of aggression, exacerbating doubts about the sincerity of American professions of loyalty, and making a peaceful reconciliation more unlikely.

Even before the news from Ticonderoga had arrived, military matters assumed a prominent place on Congress's agenda. The delegates had barely elected their president and secretary (the same people who had served the first Congress, Virginia's venerable Peyton Randolph, who would later be replaced as president by John Hancock, and, as secretary, Charles Thomson, a straitlaced Pennsylvania teacher and student of the classics), reviewed the delegates' credentials, and resolved to keep their proceedings secret when the city and county of New York asked for advice on how to receive the British troops expected to arrive there at any time. Congress recommended that New Yorkers act defensively as long as possible, but be ready to defend their lives and property with force. Then it debated which posts should be occupied in New York, how many men were needed to take and hold them, and under what terms those men should be recruited.[11]

On June 2, Congress received an official request from Massachusetts that Congress assume responsibility for the soldiers assembling in

Cambridge to defend the rights of America. Congress concurred not by passing a resolution to that effect, but by adopting a series of measures that brought the troops in Massachusetts under its control. The next day it began arranging the purchase of gunpowder "for the use of the Continental Army," and thereafter devoted a regular and substantial part of its attention to the army. Congress defined the army's command structure and appointed officers. On June 15 it chose one of its members, George Washington, as general and commander in chief of the army. Selecting a Virginian to head the troops gathered in Massachusetts made clear that they were not a regional force but a genuinely continental army. Congress also set the pay of both officers and their men, defined soldiers' rations, secured supplies, and found ways to pay for them or get others to pay for them. It drafted rules and regulations for the American army and later the navy, and took steps to provide them with medical care. It also directed troops to posts in New York or in Massachusetts, where the fledgling American army, swollen with angry militiamen from near and far who poured into the camp at Cambridge after Lexington and Concord, had confined the King's troops to Boston and put it under siege. Eighteenth-century Boston sat on a peninsula linked to the mainland by an easily guarded narrow neck of land, but it was vulnerable to artillery attacks from nearby highlands. On June 16, 1775, the provincials built an entrenchment on the Charlestown peninsula to Boston's north. The next day—still two weeks before Washington arrived to assume command—they inflicted some of the heaviest losses of the entire war on British forces that tried to seize the fortification. The Battle of Bunker Hill was nominally a victory for the King, but he lost 42 percent of the 2,500 men engaged in the operation.[12]

Ticonderoga and Bunker Hill made it abundantly clear that Congress faced a formidable task in controlling the popular military enthusiasm let loose with the outbreak of war. The creation of an American military command structure was a step in that direction. Congress, however, had no intention of founding a military establishment independent of its supervision: it continued not only to define the shape of the army and to appoint its officers, but also to determine as best it could where the troops would fight, and how. Early in its first session, Congress faced one of its most important strategic (and also political) decisions: should it use military force to take Canada, which, in hostile hands, would pose a major threat to the security of New England and New York? The First Continental Congress had petitioned the inhabitants of the Quebec colony to join the other American provinces in their struggle against British oppression, and, on May 29, 1775, its successor renewed the invitation. The 1775 petition described the government organized under Parliament's Quebec Act of 1774, which included no elected assembly, as a tyranny, and insisted that "the fate of the protestant and catholic colonies" was "strongly linked." Neither petition won Canadian support, however, in part because other Congressional pronouncements revealed the profound anti-Catholicism that had, in fact, provided the old Protestant colonies with one of their first common bonds.[13]

What if Canada refused to join the union voluntarily? Congress at first acted to prevent its being forcefully seized in the way Ticonderoga had been taken. On June 1, 1775, it voted that, "as this Congress has nothing more in view than the defence of these colonies, . . . no expedition or incursion ought to be undertaken or made, by any colony, or body of colonists, against or into Canada." Within the month, however, both Benedict Arnold and Ethan Allen urged Congress to push the war into Canada, which, they insisted, was weak and easily conquerable. Finally, four days after Allen and his fellow Green Mountain Boy, Seth Warner, told Congress "some things of importance," it reversed its course. On June 27 Congress instructed General Philip Schuyler immediately to proceed north through Lake Champlain, and to take St. Johns on the Richelieu River as well as Montreal and "any other parts of the country" if he found those measures "practicable" and "not . . . disagreeable to the Canadians." Schuyler was also told to "pursue any other measures in Canada, which may have a tendency to promote the peace and security of these Colonies."[14]

How an invasion could be agreeable to the Canadians or promote peace, except perhaps by scaring the British into making concessions, was not altogether clear. Congress again asserted that Quebec's Governor Guy Carleton was preparing to invade the colonies and instigating Indians "to take up the Hatchet" against them, but this time made no pretense that the attempted conquest was a simple act of defense. The war had its own powerful logic, which drew the delegates, like their constituents, into a contest for strategic positions, and perhaps also swept them up in Ethan Allen's dream that America might "rise on eagles' wings . . . to glory, freedom and immortal honour" if she would but "exert her strength." However, news of the Canadian campaign, which reached Britain in the fall, dissolved many lingering doubts about Americans' intentions. The effort to conquer Canada made even England's traditionally tax-shy country gentlemen ready, at least for the moment, to increase the land tax so the war could be continued and the colonists forced back into obedience.[15]

Meanwhile, other issues demanded the attention of Congress: before it had met two weeks John Adams noted that "such a vast Multitude of Objects, civil, political, commercial and military, press and crowd upon us so fast, that We know not what to do first." Some of the most urgent resulted from the collapse of royal governments, which began in Massachusetts. The governor and provincial council appointed under the Massachusetts Government Act of 1774 quickly lost all prospect of exercising their offices with effectiveness, if at all. Instead, power settled on extra-legal institutions, which seemed insufficient to guarantee the superiority of civil over military authority once the war began. Finally, on May 16, 1775, the Massachusetts Provincial Congress requested Congress's "most explicit advice" on how civil government should be reconstituted. Elect an assembly and council under the provisions of the Massachusetts Charter of 1691, Congress proposed on June 9, and conduct government as if the royal governor and lieutenant governor were absent until officials appear who "consent to govern the colony according to its charter." Five months later the same question arose over the governments of New Hampshire and South Carolina, and, in early December, Virginia. Each colony was told to "call a full and free representation of the people" to establish "such a form of government, as, in their judgment, will best produce the happiness of the people" while the dispute between the colonies and Great Britain continued.[16]

In the meantime, Congress established a Continental Post Office, took charge of Indian affairs, and provided directions for the treatment of Loyalists. It regulated American trade, supervising execution of the nonimportation and nonexportation association adopted by the First Continental Congress and, sometimes, modifying its provisions to allow exports in exchange for arms. Congress's oversight of trade allowed it to suggest improvements in internal communications and even to recommend how Americans should dress. On October 2, 1775, for example, it considered a report from its committee on trade that asked provincial conventions and assemblies to "put their Roads in good Repair, and particularly the great Roads that lead from Colony to Colony," and proposed that colonists get into the practice of wearing leather waistcoats and breeches, with Congressmen setting the example, since the supply of American-made wool was unlikely to satisfy the country's clothing needs. To Congress also fell the task of resolving internal disputes, including the violent conflict between Connecticut and Pennsylvania claimants to lands in the Wyoming Valley of Pennsylvania, or of the settlers of Vermont ("the New Hampshire Grants") with New York.[17]

The range of responsibilities that Congress assumed transformed it into what was for all practical purposes a national government. It was not, of course, a national government like those that followed it, whose powers were clearly defined in the Articles of Confederation or the Constitution of 1787. Instead its range of authority was limited by the written instructions issued by the various colonies to their Congressional delegates, who presented those credentials when they took their seats. In short, Congress could do nothing beyond what a majority of delegations were authorized to approve, and was generally unwilling to make major policy decisions without virtually unanimous agreement. The execution of its decisions was frequently delegated to local committees organized under the Continental Association of 1774, or to the governments of the various colonies, which in late 1775 consisted of extra-legal congresses or conventions that had assumed control after royal government collapsed, quasi-legal institutions such as those of Massachusetts, and, in Rhode Island, Connecticut, and Pennsylvania, the still-standing legal governments of the colonial past. In organizing, regulating, or directing the army, however, Congress exerted authority directly. It could not impose taxes, but it could borrow money, and found another independent if unstable source of financial support in the summer of 1775 when it decided to issue a continental currency. Moreover, even the most prominent colonies turned to it for directions on how they should proceed in political crises, which powerfully suggests that Congress had in its opening years an authority and even an eminence above and beyond that of any separate colony and, indeed, far beyond what the colonists conceded to Parliament.

The basic institutional structure of this first American national government was extremely simple. It consisted of a unicameral representative assembly with a presiding officer. Because there was no separate judiciary, Congress itself acted at times in a judicial capacity: appeals from state courts in cases concerning the seizure of British vessels and cargoes under Congressional resolves of November 25, 1775, for example, went to Congress itself "or such person or persons as they shall appoint for the trial of appeals."[18] More important, in 1775 the Congress exercised both legislative and executive responsibilities of ever-increasing scope with a staff that consisted late that year of Secretary Charles Thomson and two "treasurers" appointed when Congress decided to issue paper money. Soon Congress began hiring clerks; but the day-to-day work of government was entrusted not to bureaucrats but to Congressional committees whose number multiplied as new issues came before Congress.[19] During the winter of 1775–76, Congress attempted to establish a system of standing committees to oversee major policy areas, but even then it continued to depend upon ad hoc committees to perform a broad range of administrative and legislative tasks. Congress also regularly resolved itself into a Committee of the Whole, which allowed it to discuss issues with freedom since no official minutes of committee proceedings were kept. The reports of all such committees, including the Committee of the Whole, were submitted to the regular Congress for action. As a result, Congress decided not only major questions of general policy, but those of mundane administration that in a settled government would be the work of a relatively low-level civil servant, such as whether to pay the bill submitted by a doorkeeper for his services, or to dispense $6.90 to one Rebecca Reynolds "for horse hire."[20]

The toll on individual Congressmen was sometimes overwhelming. They might serve on committees in the early morning, attend the deliberations of Congress until late afternoon, and then "retire" to still more committee meetings. Congress met, moreover, from Monday through Saturday. Such long and rigorous hours were hardly familiar: "industrial work habits" had yet to replace a more leisurely pace of life in 1775, and the rush of work took delegates by surprise. "My time is all taken up," Connecticut's Silas Deane complained in early June 1775, when the Second Continental Congress was less than a month old; Congress "leaves me no spare time, and tires me effectually. Well as I love the busy scenes of politics, . . . I had rather not be appointed to committees quite so often as I am."[21]

A recess from early August to mid-September gave delegates a brief respite. But thereafter, as the crisis deepened and Congress's responsibilities expanded, the pressure on delegates increased. The amount of work per delegate also necessarily grew whenever attendance at Congress dropped. Not all of the sixty-five delegates who served in the second session of the Second Continental Congress were present at any one time. Why, after all, should the colonies maintain large delegations when, according to the rules of Congress, each colony could cast only a single vote? Some colonies sent one or two representatives at a time; Massachusetts sent five, and Virginia elected seven delegates, but the Virginians—like other delegations—seem to have practiced an informal rotation system by which some Congressmen went home when others arrived. New York named twelve delegates, five of whom could act, but so few attended that in October 1775 its delegation suggested that three members should be able to cast New York's vote "when the rest are absent." Overall absenteeism in the fall of 1775 pushed at times to over 30 percent of the delegates.[22] Always, however, a handful of especially responsible and capable men seem to have assumed a lion's share of the burden. "I can scarsely find time to write you even a Love Letter," Samuel Adams, an assiduous committeeman, wrote his wife in early 1776. (But then he seems to have sent her no love letters in less demanding times. Politics was his love no less than Deane's, and so, more true to himself, he proceeded to send Mrs. Adams "a Political Anecdote.") The following July, Joseph Hewes described his Congressional service over the previous two or three months, when he alone represented North Carolina, as "too severe." He sometimes attended meetings for eleven or twelve hours at a stretch "without eating or drinking." His health suffered, but still he "obstinately persisted in doing my duty to the best of my Judgment and abilities, and attended Congress the whole time, one day only excepted."[23]

The inefficiency of Congress's deliberations strained men's patience as effectively as its schedule drained their physical stamina. To accomplish anything of significance in Congress was extraordinarily cumbersome, Deane explained, because "no motion or resolution can be started or proposed but what must be subject to much canvassing before it will pass with the unanimous approbation of Thirteen Colonies whose situation and circumstances are various. And Unanimity is the basis on which we mean to rise. . . ."[24] Under the circumstances, that strategy made sense: against the power of Britain, colonial strength lay in colonial unity. But it gave an obstructionist power to timid or recalcitrant minorities that continually irritated those who were—or were confident they ought to be—in the majority.

John Adams understood the nature of Congressional politics as well as any man, although the delays and compromises it demanded warred with his temperament. In time, that scrappy Massachusetts delegate, as ambitious for fame as Hancock but, as the child of an obscure family from the town of Braintree, with no inherited advantages in that pursuit except for his intelligence, would become one of the country's most vigorous and effective advocates for Independence. Adams's impulse from the earliest years of the Second Continental Congress was to rush forward, dissolve all governments under the Crown, set up democratically elected state governments "like that of Connecticut," form an "indissoluble" confederation for mutual defense, close the King's customshouses and open American ports to all nations—but he knew the colonies were "not yet ripe" for such measures. "America is a great, unwieldy body," he wrote on June 17, 1775. "Its progress must be slow. It is like a large fleet sailing under convoy. The fleetest sailors must wait for the dullest and slowest. Like a coach and six, the swiftest horses must be slackened, and the slowest quickened, that all may keep an even pace. . . ."[25]

2. Independence?

Could such a system of labored coordination and mutual concession survive when, after the journey had begun, the fleet's home port—or the destination of Adams's coach and six—came into dispute? And when decisions to hold back the swift and wait for the slow had to be made by men whose equanimity was stretched to capacity by the rigors of Congressional service?

The issue of Congress's purpose—and the end for which the Americans were struggling—came under consideration early in its first session. On May 16, when Congress resolved itself into a Committee of the Whole to discuss "the state of America," South Carolina's John Rutledge interrupted a debate over raising an army to say he wanted other issues settled first. According to private notes kept by Silas Deane, Rutledge asked, "do We aim at independency? or do We only ask for a Restoration of Rights & putting of Us on Our old footing?" No one, it seems, favored separation from Britain, although delegates differed on the likelihood of reconciliation, on how best to seek it, and on what terms would be minimally acceptable.[26]

Rutledge's question, however, would not go away. Congress confronted it anew each time that it commissioned, considered, then rewrote drafts of addresses and other official statements that explained why the Americans were opposing the British government and what they sought to accomplish. Those formal, public pronouncements were meant to make known, from "obligations of respect to the rest of the world, . . . the justice of our cause," and so to recruit support and encourage opposition to Britain's repression of its "rebellious" colonists. Each document characteristically reviewed the events that had provoked colonial resistance, providing what the First Continental Congress once called a "catalogue of American Oppressions." But throughout 1775 every Congressional petition, address, or declaration insisted that, despite those provocations, the colonists sought a settlement of their differences with the Mother Country, not Independence.[27]

Congress recruited its best writers for the committees that drafted its public pronouncements. John Dickinson, a Philadelphia lawyer and author of *Letters from a Farmer in Pennsylvania,* a series of widely reprinted newspaper essays that had rallied colonial opposition to the Townshend Acts in 1767 and 1768, and had then been republished as a pamphlet, remained the best-known and most celebrated American political writer. The First Continental Congress had made good use of his talents—perhaps even before he officially took a seat in that body[28]—and the Second Congress followed its example. On June 26, 1775, after considering a hastily written proclamation for General Washington to issue when he took command of the American army, Congress returned the manuscript to the drafting committee and added Dickinson to its membership along with a lanky young Virginia delegate, Thomas Jefferson, who had taken his seat only five days earlier. Not having attended the First Continental Congress, Jefferson was new to the fellowship of delegates. He was, however, the author of *A Summary View of the Rights of British America* (1774), a spirited appeal to the King. Before leaving Virginia, Jefferson had also drafted the reply to a Conciliatory Proposal from the British Minister, Lord North, that the House of Burgesses adopted on June 10, 1775. Lord North's proposal was one of several schemes for settling the Anglo-American dispute that Parliament considered in early 1775, but the only one it accepted. Under its terms, Parliament would desist from taxing any colony that granted sufficient, permanent funds for defense and the support of civil government. The colonists saw the proposal as an attempt to divide the colonies without conceding that Parliament had no right to tax Americans. Virginians refused to take the bait: the Burgesses said that they would consider reconciliation with the Mother Country "the greatest of all human blessings" except for the possession of liberty, but after careful consideration concluded "with pain and disappointment" that Lord North's proposal "only changes the form of oppression, without lightening its burden." Jefferson later recalled that he carried the Virginia reply with him to Philadelphia and "conveyed to Congress the first notice they had of it." Congress must have been impressed: later, when it decided to issue its own reply to Lord North's proposal, Jefferson would again be the draftsman.[29]

In June, however, Jefferson took up his first writing assignment for Congress, and prepared a new version of what became its "Declaration . . . Seting [*sic*] forth the CAUSES and NECESSITY of their taking up ARMS." Dickinson, the senior man, offered various criticisms of Jefferson's manuscript. Then, after that headstrong Virginian—Jefferson's pride in authorship made its appearance early— rejected most of his suggestions, Dickinson prepared another extensively revised draft, which Congress approved with minor changes on July 6, 1775. In later years, Jefferson claimed that his composition had been "too strong for Mr. Dickinson," who "retained the hope of reconciliation with the mother country, and was unwilling it should be lessened by offensive statements." He forgot that in mid-1775, he, too, had hoped for reconciliation. Jefferson's version of the Declaration on Taking Up Arms assured the colonists' friends in Britain and other parts of the Empire that the Americans "mean not in any wise to affect that union with them in which we have so long & so

happily lived, and which we wish so much to see again restored," and
expressed continued faith in the "good offices" and "friendly dispositions" of "our fellow subjects beyond the Atlantic." Dickinson, in fact,
had made Jefferson's draft stronger, more assertive, even threatening.
He expanded the list of oppressions that, as the document said, forced
colonists to choose between "an unconditional submission to the
Tyranny of irritated Ministers, or Resistance by Force," and inserted a
statement that necessity had "not yet" driven the colonists to disrupt
the empire, which raised the possibility of Independence more explicitly than Jefferson had done. But Independence, the Declaration on
Taking Up Arms emphasized, was not what the colonists wanted.
"We have not raised armies with ambitious designs of separating from
Great-Britain, and establishing Independent states," Congress declared. The Americans were willing to lay down their arms "when
Hostilities shall cease on the part of the Aggressors, and all danger of
their being renewed shall be removed," but, the Declaration added,
"not before" that occurred.[30]

In different words, by different authors, for different audiences,
Congress again and again repeated the same message. An address "to
the Inhabitants of Great-Britain" adopted on July 8, 1775, insisted that
the Americans acted as the "Descendants of *Britons*" in defense of
"glorious Privileges" for which their "gallant and virtuous Ancestors"
had "fought, bled, and conquered." Charges that they were "aiming at
Independence" were but "the Allegations of your Ministers," dis-
proven by American actions—by their petitions for redress and their
failure to seek "the Aid of those foreign Powers, who are the Rivals of
your Grandeur." A written "speech" for presentation to the Iroquois
Confederacy, which Congress approved on July 13, described the conflict as one "betwixt the Counsellors of King George and the Inhabitants and Colonies of America," and insisted that the Americans
wanted only to retain "the covenant chain" that had bound their fathers with the British. Though the colonists had been forced to "take
up the hatchet" to defend their government and privileges, their fight
with Britain remained a "family quarrel." Two weeks later, in an address to the Inhabitants of Ireland, Congress insisted that the ministers called the Americans rebels for "asserting the very rights which
placed the crown of Great Britain on the heads of three successive
Princes of the House of Hanover." Although "insulted and abused,"

the colonists "wish for reconciliation. Though defamed as seditious, we are ready to obey the laws. And though charged with rebellion, [we] will cheerfully bleed in defence of our Sovereign in a righteous cause. What more can we say? What more can we offer?"[31]

Division continued to come not over what Americans wanted, but over what steps should be taken toward reconciliation, and how likely they were to get it. Even the most radical members of Congress professed a strong preference for remaining in the empire. So late as August 25, 1775, Jefferson wrote in a private letter that he sincerely wished for reunion and "would rather be in dependance on Great Britain, properly limited, than on any nation on earth, or than on no nation." He added, however, that rather than submit to the unlimited power that Parliament claimed over the colonies, which, as recent experience demonstrated, it would exercise with cruelty, he would lend his hand "to sink the whole island in the ocean." At that time the colonists sought, as a Virginia newspaper essayist later put it, not a "total separation from *Britain*," but a "constitutional Independence, founded on the ancient Charters and original contracts of the Colonies, and warranted by the laws of nature," which would give "a total exemption from Parliamentary Government, under the allegiance of the Crown of *England*."[32]

Was there any realistic prospect of such a settlement? By 1775 Jefferson and others in the vanguard of colonial resistance had moved beyond any desire to return to the situation of 1763. The Lords and Commons, they decided, had no right either to impose taxes or to make laws for the internal government of the colonies and, in fact, had never held that right, though the impropriety had long gone unrecognized. For Americans to be bound by the edicts of a Parliament in which they were unrepresented was demeaning: it put them under the control of a House of Commons elected by voters in Britain and so made them the subjects of subjects; it denied them the right to participate in making the laws that bound them, which the First Continental Congress called "the foundation of English liberty and of all free government." Nor could the problem be simply solved by admitting colonial representatives into the House of Commons, which the colonists' Stamp Act Congress had ruled out already in 1765. Parliament would never admit colonial representatives in proportion to their population (indeed, it never suggested any inclination toward accepting American representatives), and, if it did, the cost of maintaining those delegates in London would be prohibitive. Moreover, colonial representatives' knowledge of their constituents would become ever weaker the longer they remained abroad. It was obviously better to confine legislative authority to provincial assemblies whose members knew Americans and their circumstances intimately. But then what, if any, authority could Parliament justly exercise over America? In 1774 Congress was willing to let Parliament regulate trade for the good of both colonies and mother country, but colonists such as Jefferson or Pennsylvania's James Wilson rejected even that. They saw the empire as consisting of several independent political communities, each with its own legislature, bound together under the Crown—a concept which foreshadowed the British Commonwealth of the nineteenth century.[33]

The British ministry and members of Parliament—King, Lords, and Commons—instead looked back to the seventeenth century and the "Glorious Revolution" of 1689. After decades of turmoil and bloodshed, Englishmen had then firmly yoked the King to Parliament, denying him the powers of raising taxes and maintaining an army ("the purse and the sword") without the consent of the Lords and Commons, and so reduced substantially the sphere within which the Crown could act independently. From that perspective, Wilson's suggestion that the regulation of trade could be made part of the King's prerogative was absurd and dangerous. To make the King the linchpin of empire, and to cut him free from the restraining hand of Lords and Commons in imperial government, was a leap not toward the future but backwards, toward royal absolutism.

So confident were Britain's leaders of their position that they were unable to take seriously the colonists' efforts to devise a way of establishing traditional English liberties within an imperial context. To be sure, the Americans differed on some points among themselves, and their position shifted over time, which was natural enough given the novelty and complexity of the problem they were trying to resolve. Changes in their arguments were, however, taken as proof of insincerity, evidence that the colonists' spokesmen were working not for the aims they professed, but for some secret, unavowed ambition. How could anyone who understood English history do anything but support the supremacy of Parliament? For members of Britain's ruling class, moreover, parliamentary supremacy implied, as the Declaratory Act of 1766 had put it, that Parliament could bind the colonies "in all cases whatsoever." It was all or nothing: the colonists were entirely under Parliament, or they were outside the British system. Independence from Parliament, in short, meant independence from Britain.

No one agreed more heartily than George III, who never wavered in supporting the rights of Parliament. The King was stubborn, not especially imaginative, and temperamentally disinclined to think through the careful arguments colonists posed, which he quickly dismissed as the work of a few troublemakers; it was safer, he thought, to take a hard line than to make concessions to such nonsense. He also turned a deaf ear to petitions from the colonists' sympathizers in England, particularly from the City of London, urging that he intervene on behalf of his American subjects. The First Continental Congress's petition to the King met no better fate: as the Declaration on Taking Up Arms complained, it was "huddled" into Parliament "amongst a bundle of American papers, and there neglected." By the time he received that petition, and months before the outbreak of war, the King had already made up his mind. "The New England Governments," he wrote Lord North on November 18, 1774, "are in a state of rebellion," and "blows must decide whether they are to be subject to this country or independent."³⁴

The First Continental Congress had also urged the British people to choose members of Parliament "of such wisdom, independance and public spirit, as may save the violated rights of the whole empire from the devices of wicked Ministers and evil Counsellors." But the House of Commons elected in the fall of 1774 proved no better than its predecessors. In opening the new Parliament on November 30, the King spoke of a "most daring spirit of resistance and disobedience to law" in Massachusetts, which was being supported by other colonies, and he reaffirmed his "firm and steadfast resolution to withstand every attempt to weaken or impair the supreme authority of this Legislature over all the Dominions of my Crown." Both Lords and Commons dutifully endorsed his position by comfortable majorities. Then, in February 1775, Parliament declared that Massachusetts was in a state of rebellion supported by illegal combinations in other colonies, and it endorsed the King's intention to take "the most effectual measures to enforce due obedience to the laws and authority of the Supreme Legislature." It went on to adopt the New England Restraining Act, which denied New Englanders access to the North Atlantic fisheries and restricted their external trade. Later Parliament imposed the same commercial restraints on Pennsylvania, New Jersey, Maryland, Virginia, and South Carolina, which were considered sympathetic to Massachusetts and supporters of the Continental Congress. The same Parliament accepted Lord North's Conciliatory Proposal, trying, like Congress, to enlist simultaneously the instruments of coercion and of accommodation. The proposal went as far as Parliament was willing to go toward a settlement of the conflict, but nowhere far enough to meet the minimal demands of even moderate colonists, who thought that at least some exemptions from the overriding power of King, Lords, and Commons were essential. The gap between the still-loyal colonists and those who ruled the Mother Country was essentially unbridgeable; and "harsh measures" were more likely to harden the lines than to shorten the span.[35]

In the face of so dismal a history, it was an open question whether the Second Continental Congress should again petition the King. George III's hostile speeches, as John Dickinson continually affirmed, could be attributed to the ministers who prepared them. Perhaps further pleas could get to the King himself and persuade him to act like the father of his people. Radicals such as the Adamses thought it demeaning to submit yet another "humble and dutiful petition" to a monarch who had answered earlier pleas for redress with worse grievances. On the other hand, to agree to a petition would mollify Dickinson and other Congressional moderates, who were desperate for a settlement. If the new petition was again rejected, its supporters might be persuaded that more extreme measures had become necessary. Dickinson drafted the "Olive Branch Petition" to the King that Congress adopted on July 8, 1775, signed, and sent to England under the care of Richard Penn, a former governor of Pennsylvania, who arrived at Bristol in mid-August. A week later Penn and the colonial agent, Arthur Lee, sent a copy of the petition to Lord Dartmouth, the King's Secretary for the American Colonies, and on September 1 ("the first moment that was permitted us") personally delivered the original. Dartmouth promised to give the petition to George III, who had refused to receive it in person. But when Penn and Lee urged Dartmouth to get a reply, they were told that, since the King would not formally receive the petition on the throne, no answer would be given.[36]

In fact, for all practical purposes George III had already answered the petition. On August 23, the King issued a proclamation that said the Americans had "proceeded to open and avowed rebellion," and that they were encouraged by persons within the Mother Country whose "traitorous conspiracies" would be suitably punished.[37] Two months later, in a speech to Parliament on October 26, 1775, that would have an enormous impact on colonial opinion, the King asserted that the American rebellion was "manifestly carried on for the purpose of establishing an independent Empire." The "authors and supporters" of that "desperate conspiracy," he insisted, "meant only to amuse, by vague expressions of attachment to the parent State, and the strongest protestations of loyalty to me, whilst they were preparing for a general revolt." Proof lay in actions that "openly avow their revolt, hostility, and rebellion": their raising troops and building a naval force, and the fact that they "seized the publick revenue, and assumed to themselves legislative, executive, and judicial powers. . . ." The time had come, the King said, "to put a speedy end to these disorders by the most decisive exertions." As a result, he had strengthened his naval and land forces and was also considering "friendly offers of foreign assistance."[38]

Members of pro-American minorities in the Lords and Commons protested that the colonists had not, as the King charged, openly avowed their revolt and rebellion. Congress explicitly denied any desire for Independence; in fact, its petition to the King offered a splendid opportunity for "extricating this country from the ruinous situation in which the folly of Administration has involved us." Was it the government's intention, asked the Earl of Shelburne in the House of Lords, by "perpetually sounding independence in the ears of the *Americans*, to lead them to it, or by treating them, upon suspicion, with every possible violence, to compel them in that, which must be our ruin?"[39] The majority in both houses nonetheless approved the King's speech, and later, after further debates, passed a "Prohibitory Act" that replaced previous restrictions on American trade. The new and more severe law prohibited all commerce with the thirteen North American colonies "during the continuance of the present Rebellion." It put the Americans outside the King's protection, declaring colonial vessels and their cargoes, whether in harbor or at sea, forfeit to the Crown "as if the same were the ships and effects of open enemies." The Act also allowed the impressment of those vessels' officers and crews into the Royal Navy, where, the Americans complained, they might be forced to fight against their countrymen. George III gave his approval on December 22, 1775, and American ships, ports, and seamen became the prey of the British Navy.[40]

In truth, however, they already were, since the Prohibitory Act essentially ratified and extended a policy already in effect. On November 25, 1775, a Congressional committee reported that orders in the King's name had been issued to the commanders of the Royal Navy "to proceed as in the case of actual rebellion against such of the sea port towns and places being accessible to the king's ships, in which any troops shall be raised or military works erected." On the basis of those orders, the British captain Henry Mowatt had assembled the people of Falmouth (now Portland), Maine, accused them of rebellion, and given them two hours—later extended until the next morning—to leave the town, which, on October 17, he brutally bombarded from 9:30 a.m. until sunset, driving "hundreds of helpless women and children" from their homes in a manner long since abandoned by "civilized nations."[41] Nor, it seemed, was the King content to set British forces against British subjects. Already in the Declaration on Taking Up Arms, Congress had complained that Governor Guy Carleton of Quebec was attempting ("by orders of the ministry," the Dickinson draft said) to raise Indians against the Americans.[42] Then, on November 7, Lord Dunmore, the Royal Governor of Virginia, issued a proclamation offering freedom to slaves who would join him and fight their masters, and so won more Virginians to the idea of Independence, as the historian Merrill Jensen put it, "than all the acts of Parliament since the founding of the colonies." By the end of that month Jefferson concluded that it was "an immense misfortune to the whole empire to have a king of such a disposition at such a time. We are told and every thing proves it true that he is the bitterest enemy we have." To destroy the empire, he added, George III had only to learn "that after colonies have drawn the sword there is but one step more they can take. That step is now pressed upon us by the measures adopted as if [the British] were afraid we would not take it. . . . We want neither inducement nor power to declare and assert a separation. It is will alone which is wanting and that is growing apace under the fostering hand of our king."[43]

Congress received news of George III's October speech to Parliament on January 8, 1776. It also learned that a British fleet had set sail with 5,000 troops ("some think this premature," the diarist Richard Smith noted) and that "Ld. Dunmore has Destroyed the Town of Norfolk in Virginia." Norfolk was burned in the opening days of January, which, with the burning of Charlestown, Massachusetts, by the King's army during the Battle of Bunker Hill, and the destruction of Falmouth, Maine, in the fall of 1775, seemed to show how harshly George III was prepared to repress his American subjects.[44] On January 9, the day after receiving these pieces of news, James Wilson—who, despite his advanced views on the constitutional structure of the empire, was one of Congress's great foot-draggers on Independence—moved that the Continental Congress "expressly declare to their Constituents and the World their present Intentions respecting an Independency, observing that the Kings Speech directly charged Us with that Design." He had precedent on his side: just a month earlier, Congress had issued an answer to the King's proclamation of August 23, 1775, denying his charge that they were engaged in a rebellion. Now, however, the proposal that Congress again disavow Independence provoked dissent. "The motion alarmed me," Samuel Adams wrote; "I thought Congress had already been explicit enough, and was apprehensive that we might get ourselves upon dangerous ground." The opposition managed to postpone the issue; and on February 13, when Wilson brought in an address to the people that Richard Smith described as "very long, badly written and full against Independency," he discovered that "the Majority did not relish his Address and Doctrine" and "never thought fit to stir it again."[45] Moreover, several members had noticed the reference to "friendly offers of foreign assistance" in George III's October speech to Parliament. If the King sent foreign soldiers to fight in America, those delegates said, they would be "willing to declare the Colonies in a State of Independent Sovereignty [*sic*]."[46]

News of the Prohibitory Act arrived in February, further dimming the prospects for settlement. As John Hancock put it, "the making all our Vessels lawful Prize don't look like a Reconciliation." The law should be called the "Act of Independency," John Adams proposed, because by passing it "King, Lords and Commons have united in Sundering this Country and that I think forever. It is a compleat Dismemberment of the British Empire. It throws thirteen Colonies out of the

Royal Protection . . . and makes us independent in Spight [*sic*] of our supplications and Entreaties." Even Robert Morris, a "conservative" Pennsylvanian of English birth, reported that the seizing of American ships and burning of colonial towns along "with numerous acts of wanton barbarity & Cruelty perpetrated by the British Forces has prepared Men's minds for an Independency, that were shock'd at the idea a few weeks ago."[47] Some, clinging desperately to anything that could sustain hope, noted that the Prohibitory Act empowered the King to send commissioners to America. Unfortunately, Joseph Hewes observed, they were authorized only to receive "submissions and grant pardons . . . I see no prospect of a reconciliation," he wrote, "nothing is left now but to fight it out, and for this we are not well provided, having but little ammunition, no Arms no money, nor are we unanimous in our Councils."[48]

The strain from seeking a reconciliation that became increasingly improbable, from practicing a politics of mutual accommodation among men with different capacities to accept a future outside the British fold, had taken a toll. Congressmen, Hewes observed, no longer treated each other with the "decency and respect" of earlier days. "Jealousies, ill natured observations and recriminations take place of reason and Argument, . . . some among us urge strongly for Independency and eternal separation, others wish to wait a little longer and to have the opinion of their Constituents on that subject. . . ."[49]

3　　*Common Sense*

Why was the decision for Independence so difficult? Fear played a role. Could the colonists stand up against the power of Britain? A full-scale war would bring more death and devastation; and an alliance with France, which would help the colonies hold out militarily, itself seemed extremely dangerous. For most colonists, France was an old enemy whose defeat in the French and Indian War had freed North America from the threat of Catholic absolutism. Was France any more trustworthy in 1776 than it had been fifteen or twenty years earlier? Louis XVI would not help America for reasons of benevolence, or from any dedication to the cause of freedom: France would act only to serve its own best interests. Suppose, then, that Britain, once it despaired of keeping all its colonies, offered to partition them, much as

Poland had been partitioned in 1772, returning Canada to France and Florida to Spain, if they kept out of the Anglo-American conflict. Would France refuse? Or suppose that France and America did form an alliance and succeeded in defeating Britain. Who would then protect America from French domination? "We shall weep at our victories," John Dickinson predicted. Even British tyranny seemed preferable to French rule.[50]

Americans with special ties to the British government often planted themselves most firmly in the opposition: British officeholders, from royal governors of colonial birth down through justices of the peace, became Loyalists well out of proportion to their incidence in the population. But virtually all colonists, some recent European immigrants excepted, found the prospect of Independence troubling because they thought of themselves as British, and their pride in that identity, which had risen to a feverish height with Britain's victory in the French and Indian War, remained strong. Even in opposing British policies, colonists saw themselves as following in the footsteps of their English ancestors who had resisted the tyranny of Charles I and James II, which the Americans considered no different from Parliament's attempt to rule the colonies "in all cases whatsoever." So deep a bond could not be cut without pain that was almost physical: "torn from the body, to which we are united by religion, liberty, laws, affections, relations, language, and commerce," Dickinson had written in his *Farmer's Letters,* "we must bleed at every vein." In May 1776, a newspaper essayist who argued against Independence used almost the same words, but with a fear not just of loss, but of chaos. To sever the ligaments that Dickinson had listed, he suggested, would destroy all social order. Separation from Britain would dissolve "the bands of religion, of oaths, of laws, of language, of blood, of interest, of commerce," in short, "of all those habitudes . . . which hold us united among ourselves, under the influence of the common parent." Such a "rending to pieces" would necessarily "reach the entrails, the heart, the very life of the Colonies."[51]

Americans took particular pride in being governed under Britain's unwritten constitution, which they considered the most perfect form of government ever invented "by the wit of man"—a judgment with which, they often added, every major writer on politics agreed. Power in Britain was entrusted not to any one man or group of men, but was divided and balanced among King, Lords, and Commons, which curbed the ambitions of rulers and so preserved freedom. Under the "mildness and equity of the *English* Constitution," members of the Maryland Convention recalled on January 12, 1776, they and their ancestors had experienced a remarkable state of happiness because "of all known systems" British government was "best calculated to secure the liberty of the subject." Their felicity had lapsed when the "grounds of the present controversy were laid by the Ministry and Parliament of *Great Britain*," but Maryland wanted above all else to recover the remembered peace and freedom of times past. Even the news of early January failed to shake that desire: the Convention instructed its Congressional delegates to do all they could to secure reconciliation with the Mother Country, and also explicitly precluded their voting for Independence or for measures that might lead toward Independence without its previous consent.[52]

In the closing months of 1775 and early 1776, as the crisis mounted, several other provincial assemblies, congresses, and conventions, particularly those in the "middle colonies" between New England and Virginia, also adopted instructions that prohibited their Congressional delegates from consenting to separation from the Mother Country or, as Pennsylvania and New Jersey added, any change in the form of American government.[53] In part those instructions reflected strategic maneuvers on the part of moderate delegates, particularly Dickinson, to strengthen their position in Congress. But resistance to political change was by no means confined to the middle colonies: everywhere reverence for the inherited institutions of British government inhibited the movement toward separate nationhood. Throughout their conflict with Britain, colonists had rarely questioned the British system of government, but directed their suspicions toward particular men within it. The King's governors and other agents in America, his ministers, members of Parliament, even the King himself, came under suspicion of causing the Crown's ruinous American policy. Such men supposedly sought to accumulate power or support an accumulation of power that would destroy the balance of Britain's constitution, and so its freedom. To resist such an effort was conservative since it sought to preserve Britain's historic system of governance. That a movement whose "primary object . . . was a restoration of [the British] Constitution" might end by removing America from the British system seemed paradoxical, even perverse. By 1776, one moderate after another protested that the colonists were moving in a direction altogether different from that upon which they had originally agreed.[54] Soon, however, Americans throughout the Continent would be reading a powerful treatise that challenged assumptions deeply bound up with the colonists' pride in being British.

On January 9, the same day James Wilson proposed that Congress once again disavow any desire for Independence, the Philadelphia press of Robert Bell distributed the first copies of *Common Sense*. The pamphlet was published anonymously, but in time it became known as the work of Thomas Paine, a largely self-educated Englishman of no particular previous distinction, who had first arrived in America on November 30, 1774.[55] Earlier colonial pamphlets and essays, including Dickinson's, had presented carefully reasoned arguments sprinkled with references to Tacitus, Montesquieu, or a familiar list of English and Scottish political and legal writers of the seventeenth and eighteenth centuries, and often assumed an almost scholarly character. Not *Common Sense*. Paine wrote in a knock-about language, as John Adams later put it, "suitable for an Emigrant from New Gate [the English jail], or one who had chiefly associated with such Company," with references to " 'The Royal Brute of England,' 'The Blood upon his Soul,' and a few others of equal delicacy."[56]

American freedom would never be secure under British rule, Paine argued, because "the so much boasted Constitution of England" was deeply flawed. The problem lay in two major *"constitutional errors"*—monarchy and hereditary rule. To prove the point he cited, with more passion than order, one kind of evidence after another. The Bible, he insisted, condemned monarchy as "one of the sins of the Jews." Nature also disapproved of monarchy, which was why it so often presented capable kings with inept sons, or gave mankind *"an ass for a lion."* Monarchy and hereditary rule made bad rulers even of capable individuals by breeding arrogance, and by separating them from the rest of mankind whose interests they needed to know well. Moreover, the ambitions of kings and those who would be kings caused civil and foreign wars that had laid both Britain and "the world in ashes."[57] The problem, then, was not just that evil persons were exercising power. It was systemic, in the very design of British government, which, like all governments, was incapable of constraining the power of hereditary rulers. The only way to solve that problem was to redesign the machine of government, eliminating monarchy and hereditary rule and expanding the "republican" element of British government which derived power not from birth but from the ballot. The solution, in short, was revolution.

Americans were afraid to embrace Independence, Paine said, not only because they thought better of the old regime than it deserved, but also because they had no plans for a new one. So he offered some suggestions guided by a "maxim" that "the more simple any thing is, the less liable it is to be disordered, and the easier repaired when disordered," which remains today a basic principle of engineering. Out went the complex divisions and balancing of the British constitution. State governments, he suggested, should consist of annually elected assemblies with a president or presiding officer—not altogether unlike the extra-legal provincial congresses and conventions of the time— and be "subject to the authority of a Continental Congress." To assure that the people were adequately represented, Paine proposed that Congress consist of 390 members. He sketched his plan of government in broad strokes with little detail, as "hints" offered in the hope that they might "be the means of giving rise to something better." The precise institutions of the American republic could be determined only through debate and experimentation. Paine promised, however, that by eliminating monarchy and hereditary rule and founding government entirely on popular choice, the Americans could "form the noblest, purest constitution on the face of the earth," one free of errors that had dogged mankind for centuries. "We have it in our power to begin the world over again," he wrote; and what the Americans did would affect the future of "all mankind."[58]

Paine confronted the fears that kept many colonists from embracing Independence. Could the Americans hold out against Britain? Yes, since they had sufficient men and materials, a strength that came from political unity, and the prospect of foreign aid. Could America's economy thrive outside the British trade system? American products, he said, "will always have a market while eating is the custom of Europe." He cited the King's use of Indians and slaves against the Americans and his rejection of their petitions for redress and reconciliation. Later editions noted that news of the King's speech of October 26, 1775, had providentially arrived in America just as *Common Sense* was first published, such that "the bloody-mindedness of the one" showed "the necessity of pursuing the doctrine of the other." Above all, however, Paine insisted that the war made Independence necessary. "No man was a warmer wisher for reconciliation than myself, before the fatal nineteenth of April, 1775," he wrote, "but the moment the event of the day was made known, I rejected the hardened, sullen-tempered Pharaoh of England for ever; and disdain the wretch, that with the pretended title of FATHER OF HIS PEOPLE can unfeelingly hear of their slaughter, and composedly sleep with their blood upon his soul." War bred feelings of resentment and hatred that God had planted in peoples' hearts "for good and wise purposes," and that made reconciliation "a fallacious dream." The "blood of the slain, the weeping voice of nature cries, 'TIS TIME TO PART." Any settlement would be "mere patchwork" with no prospect of "lasting felicity," a temporary solution purchased at an enormous price in blood and treasure when by going "a little more, a little further," the Americans could have "rendered this continent the glory of the earth."[59]

Three decades later John Adams, riled by Paine's claims of responsibility for American Independence, said *Common Sense* presented no argument that had not already been made repeatedly in Congress. Perhaps so. Certainly much of Paine's case against monarchy had been made in the colonial press or pulpits at one point or another over the previous six years.[60] *Common Sense*, however, gathered those arguments together and used them not to persuade Congress, which was already moving apace toward Independence, but the people whose support Congress needed. Within days of the pamphlet's publication, the New Hampshire delegate Josiah Bartlett reported that it was "greedily bought up and read by all ranks of people." Further editions soon issued from rival presses in Philadelphia and then in other cities until Paine estimated that some 150,000 copies had been sold in America alone, which he proudly described as "the greatest sale that any performance ever had since the use of letters." A contemporary, the Reverend Ashbel Green, was nearer the mark when he suggested it had a greater run than any other pamphlet "published in our country." Advertisements appeared in newspapers, taverns, "and at every place of public resort, . . . and very generally in these words, 'Common Sense for eighteen pence,'" a price that facilitated its broad circulation. The pamphlet's style also contributed to its popularity, and it appeared just as breaking news—of the burning of Norfolk, the King's speech of October 1775, and soon also the Prohibitory Act—seemed to close off alternatives to Independence. *Common Sense* "struck a string which required but a touch to make it vibrate," Green testified. "The country was ripe for independence, and only needed somebody to tell the people so, with decision, boldness, and plausibility."[61]

The pamphlet's usefulness was recognized by Congressmen, who sent copies to their home constituencies. Bartlett, for example, hoped that *Common Sense* would convince the people of Portsmouth, New Hampshire, who seemed terrified by "the frightful word *Independence*," that it would not perhaps be so bad as they feared. Rhode Island's Congressional delegate Samuel Ward went so far as to suggest that *Common Sense* should be "distributed throughout all the Colonies . . . even at the Public Expence. It has done immense Service." He was told on good authority that two-thirds of the people of Pennsylvania, a colony which was officially dead set against Independence, "are now full in his Sentiments; in the Jerseys & Maryland &c they gain ground daily." Two months later, on April 20, John Penn, a delegate who had recently returned to North Carolina, reported (according to John Adams) that he "heard nothing praised in the Course of his Journey, but Common sense and Independence. That this was the Cry, throughout Virginia."[62]

Paine's plans of government awoke more opposition than his arguments for Independence. By its "crude, ignorant Notion of a Government by one assembly," *Common Sense* would "do more Mischief, in dividing the Friends of Liberty, than all the Tory Writings together," John Adams lamented. Paine was "a keen Writer, but very ignorant of the Science of Government." Adams expressed his own views in *Thoughts on Government* (1776), which advocated the retention of complexity and balance in American republican institutions. However, Adams's challenge to *Common Sense* served to confirm that pamphlet's success. Paine wanted to shift the focus of public debate from evaluations of British rulers and the prospects for reconciliation to deciding how an independent America should be governed. And that he did.[63]

4. A Republic?

Among those still hesitant on Independence, the idea of founding a republic gave another good reason for delay. In 1776, there were no regular, "republican" governments of the sort Paine advocated, in which all authority rested on popular choice and none on hereditary title. The best-known republics of past times—Athens and Rome, for example, or England's own Commonwealth of the 1650s—had not survived, and in general republics were said to be so short-lived that the wisdom of founding another was questionable. Carter Braxton, a member of Virginia's Congressional delegation, pointed out that one republic after another had come to a bad end: that of the Netherlands, he claimed, became "as unhappy and despotick as the one of which we complain," and Venice "is now governed by one of the worst of despotisms." Since no nation remained a republic for long, or with any greatness, Braxton concluded that "the principle contended for is ideal, and a mere creature of a warm imagination." The advantages of republics existed "only in theory, and were never confirmed by the experience, even of those who recommend them." Public order and political stability required rulers who held office for long terms—life, for example—and on a more stable basis than popular election. If the people rule, who will be ruled?[64]

Republics, in short, were "fraught with all the tumult and riot incident to simple Democracy." The problem was evident in Connecticut and Rhode Island, provinces whose "purely democratical" governments were established under royal charters by which all officials were elected. They had always lived in a "restless state" under British monarchy, Braxton said. The other New England colonies, Massachusetts and New Hampshire, had less popular governments—they at least had royal governors—but still were so near a democratic form "that Monarchical Influence hung very heavy on them." The "eastern colonies," Braxton charged, "do not mean to have a Reconciliation" with Britain. They now had "the best opportunity in the World . . . to throw off all Subjection & embrace their darling Democracy," and they were determined to seize the chance.[65] John Adams, of course, saw things differently. He attributed Americans' reluctance to accept from Britain the "gift" of Independence to "a single source— the Reluctance of the Southern Colonies to Republican Government." The creation of constitutions for the states and a confederation for the whole could only be accomplished, he wrote, on "popular Principles and Maxims," which were "abhorrent to the Inclinations of the Barons of the South, and the Proprietary Interests in the Middle

Colonies. . . ." But "thirteen Colonies under such a Form of Government as that of Connecticutt, or one not quite so popular, leagued together in a faithfull Confederacy, might bid Defiance to all the Potentates of Europe if united against them. . . ."[66]

In truth, those who held back had reason to fear that Independence would bring "Intestine Wars and Convulsions" and so leave the Americans worse off than they were under a hostile King and Parliament. They saw a republican future in the threat of rebellion by poor whites, Loyalists, and slaves on Maryland's eastern shore; restive slaves elsewhere who read their own meaning into the cause of liberty; mobs that freed debtors from jail, or the ordinary people who claimed seats in Virginia's provincial convention, one of whom, Landon Carter reported, defined independency as "a form of Government that, by being independent of the rich men, every man would then be able to do as he pleased." And what about the acrimonious and sometimes bloody disputes over land rights in the western reaches of Virginia and Pennsylvania or between New York and the settlers of Vermont? Surely such conflicts should be resolved, or at least a firm confederation formed to replace the supervising power of Britain, before Independence was declared.[67] New Englanders were by no means free of such doubts. Not even Adams expected that new governments founded on the authority of the people would be "so quiet as I could wish," or "that harmony, confidence, and affection" would bind the colonies before a "long time" had passed. Independence would require "toil and blood and treasure" more surely than it would bring "happiness and halcyon days." In the end, he could only pray that "Heaven prosper the new-born Republick, and make it more glorious than any former Republicks have been!"[68]

Unfortunately for the proponents of delay, indecision itself brought threats of anarchy. In Maryland, officials who had been appointed under the Crown were refusing to exercise their duties, "alleging scruples to take the usual oaths to Government." The provincial convention could dispense with oaths[69]—itself an extraordinary and even treasonable act by British standards, but that was at best a stopgap measure. The problem remained of reestablishing governments capable of maintaining order under the tumultuous circumstances of 1776 and assuring the superiority of civil over military authority. Congress had recommended the establishment of new, ad hoc constitutional governments in a handful of colonies, but now the problem of reestablishing civil authority had become general, and fading dreams of reconciliation made it unclear why new state constitutions should be temporary, like those adopted by New Hampshire and South Carolina, for the duration of the conflict with England only.

Finally, on May 10, 1776, the Continental Congress recommended to "the respective assemblies and conventions of the United Colonies, where no government sufficient to the exigencies of their affairs has been hitherto established," that they "adopt such government as shall, in the opinion of the representatives of the people, best conduce to the happiness and safety of their constituents in particular and America in general." Then it appointed a committee consisting of John Adams, Richard Henry Lee, and Edward Rutledge to compose a preface for the resolution. Three days later the committee proposed a draft that Adams had written. It was even more radical than the resolution it introduced:[70]

> Whereas his Britannic Majesty, in conjunction with the lords and commons of Great Britain, has, by a late act of Parliament, excluded the inhabitants of these United Colonies from the protection of his crown; And whereas, no answer, whatever to the humble petitions of the colonies for redress of grievances and reconciliation with Great Britain, has been or is likely to be given; but, the whole force of that kingdom, aided by foreign mercenaries, is to be exerted for the destruction of the good people of these colonies; And whereas, it appears absolutely irreconcileable to reason and good Conscience, for the people of these colonies now to take the oaths and affirmations necessary for the support of any government under the crown of Great Britain, and it is necessary that the exercise of every kind of authority under the said crown should be totally suppressed, and all the powers of government exerted, under the authority of the people of the colonies, for the preservation of internal peace, virtue, and good order, as well as for the defence of their lives, liberties, and properties, against the hostile invasions and cruel depredations of their enemies; therefore, resolved, &c.

Congress approved the preface on May 15, but only after two days of acrimonious debate and—despite its practice of seeking consensus on important issues—by a divided vote, with six or seven colonies in favor, four opposed, and at least one and perhaps two states abstaining.[71] New York's instructions, as James Duane made clear, prevented its delegates from approving anything that did not further a restoration of harmony between Great Britain and its colonies, and the Pennsylvania delegation, James Wilson noted, was under a similar restraint. Maryland's delegates in fact left Congress once the preface was passed and returned only later, after their provincial convention reaffirmed the instructions it had passed the previous January, which prevented the delegates from approving anything that might lead to Independence. The meaning of a call for the total suppression of Crown authority was, it seems, abundantly clear. For all practical purposes, Adams wrote his wife, Abigail, the preface and resolution together effected "a total, absolute Independence" of America not only from Britain's Parliament but from her Crown. The document was not, however, a formal Declaration of Independence, which Adams understood would still be necessary.[72]

In the preface of May 15 Congress for the first time publicly assigned responsibility for American grievances to the King. That was highly significant. In British politics, accusations of misgovernment were customarily leveled against the King's ministers even if there was strong reason to think that the King was personally responsible for the actions of his government. The King remained above politics, an incarnation of the state and its continuing legitimacy. Accusations were extended to the King only when grievances had become so general, and evidence of his complicity so unmistakable, that the authority of his government had come into dispute. To attack the King was, in short, a constitutional form. It was the way Englishmen announced revolution.

The specific charges that Congress brought against the King on May 15 were few but powerful: he had consented to the Prohibitory Act, which formally removed the Americans from his protection; refused to answer their petitions for redress; and was bringing against them "the whole Force of the Kingdom, aided by foreign Mercenaries." The reference to "foreign mercenaries" was new. Early in the year Congress had received reports that the King was attempting to hire troops from other countries, but only in early May did it learn, from a Cork newspaper, that Britain was sending some 40,000 additional soldiers to America, including substantial numbers of "Hessians, Hanoverians, Mechlenburghers, Scotch Hollanders, & Scotch Highlanders. . . . Their destination [was] uncertain," Richard Henry Lee wrote a correspondent, but it was said to be "N. York, New England, Canada, & 2 expeditions more South." On May 16, John Hancock wrote Massachusetts that "the best Intelligence from Europe" indicated that "the British Nation have proceeded to the last Extremity, and have actually taken into pay a Number of foreign Troops," who were probably "on their Passage to America at this very Time." Five days later Congress received—through a mysterious emissary who came from London with documents sewn in his clothes—copies of the treaties George III had concluded with the Duke of Brunswick, the Landgrave of Hesse Cassel, and the Count of Hanau, each of which specified the terms on which German-speaking soldiers would be supplied for the King's service in America. Within a week the treaties were published in Pennsylvania newspapers.[73]

The effect was electrifying, in part because the treaties' arrival coincided with alarming news from Canada. The American campaign there had gone poorly from the start: the invasion under General Schuyler was slow to begin, then, in the fall of 1775, moved northward at a snail's pace, investing some fifty-five days laying siege to St. Johns on the Richelieu River before that British post surrendered. General Richard Montgomery, who took over Schuyler's command, finally crossed the St. Lawrence on November 12, and within a matter of days took Montreal. By then another contingent of troops under Colonel Benedict Arnold had reached the St. Lawrence after an extraordinarily arduous and costly six-week march through the backwoods of Maine. Montgomery and Arnold together put Quebec under siege, and then, on December 30, initiated an attack that ended in disaster: Montgomery was killed, Arnold wounded, and the Continental forces suffered some sixty casualties to the defenders' eighteen and gave up over four hundred prisoners. Arnold rallied the remnants of the American forces about a mile from the city, called for reinforcements, and attempted to continue blockading Quebec, but his efforts were hampered by an acute lack of supplies and the ravages of smallpox among his men. Finally, in May 1776, when a British fleet of fifteen ships brought reinforcements to Quebec, the siege collapsed and the sick, hungry colonists retreated in total disorder, more a mob than an army.[74]

Accounts of the unfolding catastrophe provoked enormous concern. If American troops were forced to evacuate that province, John Hancock wrote General John Thomas in late May, not only would Canada be lost, but the northern frontiers of New York and New England would be exposed to the "ravages" of both Indians and the British forces. Congress sent more troops to salvage the situation, but all efforts to reverse the downward spiral failed. A planned second offensive against Quebec ended on June 8 at Trois-Rivières, midway between Montreal and Quebec, when a vastly outnumbered American army met defeat and began another desperate retreat through swamps and forests, stalked by Indians and Canadians, and afflicted by hunger, disease, and "Musketoes of a Monstrous size and unnumerable numbers." Before long even Arnold, who bore some responsibility for initiating the Canadian fiasco, understood that there was no point in going on, that it was best to leave the northland "and secure our own country before it is too late."[75]

In fact, the colonies' home territory needed all the defenders it could gather. After finally evacuating Boston on March 17, 1776, the British Army had regrouped at Halifax, Nova Scotia, from which it was expected to mount a major offensive somewhere along the Atlantic coast in the spring or summer of 1776. If the British were recruiting German and Scottish soldiers to reinforce that campaign, surely the Americans would have to solicit foreign aid on their own behalf. But would any European power consent to support a people who remained subjects of the British Crown? Hopes of help from imperial France were specious in any case, the opponents of Independence insisted; why should Louis XVI help sustain the struggle of a revolutionary republican America? Their argument that the friendship of Catholic France was a worse danger to American freedom than the enmity of George III made some sense to colonists for whom France had long been the enemy and an incarnation of absolutism.

Once again events in England undercut the arguments of those colonists most committed to preserving the empire. In late May, colonists learned that the King had rejected a petition from the City of London that asked him to define the terms of a just and honorable peace before turning the full force of British arms against the colonists. In reply, George III expressed regret for the miseries his American subjects had "brought upon themselves by an unjustifiable resistance to the constitutional authority of this Kingdom," and said he would be "ready and happy to alleviate those miseries, by acts of mercy and clemency, whenever that authority is established, and the now existing rebellion is at an end. To obtain these salutary purposes," he added, "I will invariably pursue the most proper and effectual means." In other words, there would be no peace until the British military had forced the colonists back into subjection. By June 5 even Robert Morris, who had done his best to hold off a decision for separation, conceded that George III's response to London "totally destroyed all hopes of reconciliation" and made a "declaration of Independency" inevitable. For that event, he said, Great Britain could thank only herself.[76]

5. Decision

The Continental Congress had a full schedule on Friday, June 7. It began by agreeing to compensate a Mr. Charles Walker for a sloop and other goods taken by Esek Hopkins, commodore of the continental fleet. Next it considered a committee report on resolutions passed by the convention of South Carolina concerning battalions raised in that colony, which it recommitted to the committee, received complaints about the quality of gunpowder manufactured at a Mr. Oswald Eve's Mill, and set up a committee to investigate those complaints and, if necessary, devise a means to remedy the problem. Then "certain resolutions" were moved by Richard Henry Lee on the instructions of the Virginia Convention and seconded by John Adams:

> That these United Colonies are, and of right ought to be, free and independent States, that they are absolved from all allegiance to the British Crown, and that all political connection between them and the State of Great Britain is, and ought to be, totally dissolved.
>
> That it is expedient forthwith to take the most effectual measures for forming foreign Alliances.
>
> That a plan of confederation be prepared and transmitted to the respective Colonies for their consideration and approbation.

Since Congress was "obliged to attend at that time to some other business," according to notes kept by Jefferson, it put off debate on Lee's resolutions until the next morning. Then it received the report of a committee charged with investigating an attempt to counterfeit Congressional bills of credit.[77]

When Congress returned to Lee's motion on June 8, it resolved itself into a Committee of the Whole and—again according to Jefferson's notes—"passed that day & Monday the 10th. in debating on the subject." One group of Congressmen, including Pennsylvania's Dickinson, his colleague James Wilson, Edward Rutledge of South Carolina, and New York's Robert R. Livingston, admitted that it was impossible for the colonies "ever again [to] be united with Gr[eat] Britain" and said they were "friends" to Lee's resolutions, but opposed adopting them at that time. In the past, Congress had followed the "wise & proper" policy of "deferring to take any capital step till the voice of the people drove us into it" since "they were our power, & without them our declarations could not be carried into effect." At present, however, the delegates of several colonies, including Maryland, Pennsylvania, Delaware, New Jersey, and New York, had not been empowered by their home governments to vote for Independence. If the vote was taken immediately, those delegates would necessarily "retire" from Congress, and "possibly their colonies might secede from the Union," which would hurt the American cause more than a foreign alliance would help it. Division, in fact, would make foreign powers less willing "to join themselves to our fortunes," or allow them to insist on hard terms for their help. Delaying the decision would avoid that contingency since opinion in the middle colonies was "fast ripening & in a short time [the people there] would join in the general voice of America." The proponents of putting off Independence also questioned whether France or Spain would help the Americans, concerned as those nations were for the continued subjection of their own colonies. It was more likely, they argued, that France would form an alliance with Britain to divide the North American colonies between them. Little would be lost, in any case, by waiting until more concrete information on the inclination of the French court arrived from Paris and the terms of a possible alliance were decided, since "the advance of the season and distance of our situation" made it impossible for France to provide assistance in the 1776 military campaign. Indeed, American negotiators were likely to win an alliance on better terms before than after Congress adopted Independence.[78]

The proposition's supporters—particularly Lee, John Adams, and Virginia's George Wythe—responded that Lee's first resolution called on Congress only to "declare a fact which already exists." The Americans had always been independent of the British people and Parliament, they argued, and were now absolved from their obligation of allegiance to the King by his own act in declaring them out of his protection and waging war against them. Until the colonists declared their Independence, no European power could negotiate with them, receive an ambassador, or even allow American ships to enter their ports. It was surely in France's interest to help sever the connection between the American colonies and Britain; but if, as their opponents alleged, France proved unwilling to support the Americans, "we shall be but where we are; whereas without trying we shall never know whether they will aid us or not." On the other hand, France could be of considerable help in the coming military campaign, if only by interrupting the shipment of British military supplies, or by obliging Britain to divert some of its forces to the protection of its possessions in the West Indies. The surest way to prevent a partition treaty by which the American colonies would be divided among European powers much as Poland had been partitioned was to declare Independence and secure an alliance with France before Britain could raise that possibility. As for opposition to Independence in the middle colonies, only Pennsylvania and Maryland seemed serious problems. Pennsylvania's instructions had been passed long ago, "since which the face of affairs has totally changed: . . . it had become apparent that Britain was determined to accept nothing less than a carte blanche, and . . . the king's answer to the Lord mayor Aldermen & common council of London, which had come to hand four days ago, must have satisfied every one of this point." The people were in favor of Independence; on that issue, the state assemblies and conventions, especially those in the middle colonies, lagged behind their constituents. If necessary, however, the supporters of Lee's resolutions were willing to abandon Congress's longstanding struggle for consensus, as they had on May 15 in pushing through Adams's call for the repression of all authority under the Crown. It would be "vain to wait either weeks or months for perfect unanimity," they said, "since it was impossible that all men should ever become of one sentiment on any question."[79]

This time Congress was more prudent. It decided to give the laggard colonies time to accept Independence, and postponed the question for three weeks, until the first of July. So no time would be lost if Congress then approved Lee's motion, on June 11 it appointed a committee to prepare a declaration of Independence. That committee had five members: Thomas Jefferson, John Adams, Benjamin Franklin, Roger Sherman of Connecticut, and Robert R. Livingston of New York. Seventeen days later, on June 28, the committee presented its draft to Congress, which promptly tabled the report. By then only Maryland and New York had failed to allow their delegates to vote for Independence. That night Maryland fell into line.[80]

The war did not wait for Congress's decision. On June 9, according to intelligence Washington received, a British fleet of 132 ships sailed from Halifax under General William Howe. Two days later President Hancock urged Massachusetts, Connecticut, New York, and New Jersey to send their militias as soon as possible to New York City, which Howe was expected to attack within the next ten days. Howe's voyage took longer than Congress anticipated, but on June 29 Washington reported the arrival of some fifty British ships of sail at Sandy Hook on the New Jersey shore near the entrance to New York harbor. Their number doubled within a few days. Washington was making "every preparation" for the impending attack, but reported that the American army was "extremely deficient in arms . . . and in great distress for want of them." By July 1 Congress also learned that another fifty-three British ships were outside Charleston, South Carolina, and that the American army had been forced to evacuate Canada.[81] Urgent military issues consequently competed for the delegates' attention and haunted their deliberations as Congress turned again to Lee's resolution. The outcome of the war, they understood, would decide whether they would be remembered as the founders of a nation or be hanged by the British as traitors. Even if Britain conquered America, argued a newspaper letter signed "Republicus" and dated June 29, "I would . . . choose rather to be conquered as an independent State than as an acknowledged rebel." The time had come for Americans "to call ourselves by some name," he said, for which he proposed "the *United States of America*." That new nation could only be helped by Independence, "and every man that is against it is a traitor."[82]

On July 1, Congress again resolved itself into a Committee of the Whole "to take into consideration the resolution respecting independency." The debates went on through most of the day, but they were, John Adams claimed, a waste of time, since nothing was said "but what had been repeated and hackneyed in that Room before an hundred Times, for Six Months past." Details survive only of an impassioned but hopeless speech by John Dickinson, who indeed recapitulated much of what had been said in the debates of June. Finally, "at the request of a colony," the delegates agreed to delay their final decision until the following day. Jefferson told the story: nine colonies had voted in favor of declaring Independence (the four New England states, New Jersey, Maryland, Virginia, North Carolina, and Georgia); South Carolina and Pennsylvania opposed the motion; Delaware's two delegates split, and New York's delegates abstained because their twelve-month-old instructions allowed them to do nothing that would impede reconciliation. Then Edward Rutledge of South Carolina asked that the final Congressional decision be put off until July 2 because he thought his delegation, though it disapproved of the motion, would then vote in favor "for the sake of unanimity."[83]

When Congress reconvened on July 2, it received correspondence from Washington and others, mostly relating to the military situation. It ordered the publication of one letter, from Lieutenant Colonel Campbell to General Howe, and referred others to the "Board of War and Ordnance," a five-member committee that had been set up in June, except for the paymaster general's weekly account, which it submitted to the "Board of Treasury." Congress then received from the Committee of the Whole the resolutions Richard Henry Lee had first proposed almost a month earlier. When the vote was put, the nine affirmative votes of the previous day had grown to twelve: not only South Carolina voted in favor, but also Delaware—the arrival of Caesar Rodney broke the tie in that delegation's vote—and Pennsylvania. Because John Dickinson and Robert Morris abstained on July 2, the four-to-three vote of Pennsylvania delegates against Independence on the previous day became a three-to-two vote in favor of Independence. A week later New York's Provincial Congress convention allowed its delegates to add the colony's approval to that of the other twelve colonies. The politics of patience—of slackening the pace of the "fleetest sailors" until they kept pace with "the dullest and slowest," that all might arrive at their destiny together—had triumphed. Public unanimity disguised differences of judgment on timing but not on Independence itself. In the end, there was no alternative; even the most hesitant agreed on that.[84]

With Independence itself adopted, Congress again resolved itself into a Committee of the Whole to consider the document written to "declare the causes" of the colonies' separation from Britain. Other issues kept interrupting the Committee's discussions. On July 3, the

British landed on Staten Island, and, while New Jersey militiamen were helping defend New York, threatened the Jersey coast. Congress asked Pennsylvania's Committee of Safety to send as many troops as it could to help defend Monmouth, New Jersey, and ordered a circular letter written to county committees in Pennsylvania requesting them to raise troops and send them to Philadelphia "as fast as raised" (except for those from Bucks, Berks, and Northampton counties, which were sent to New Brunswick, New Jersey). Congress also authorized its Marine Committee to hire shipwrights to go to Lake Champlain on terms that Congress defined (each man would get "34 dollars and two-thirds per month" and rations that included a half pint of rum per day).[85] And yet, as the British began to bring the greatest fleet and the largest army ever assembled in North America into action against the Americans, Congress devoted the better part of two days to revising the draft declaration of Independence. Wars, it understood, were not won by ships and sailors and arms alone. Words, too, had power to serve the cause of victory.

CHAPTER II

The "Other" Declarations of Independence

THOMAS JEFFERSON left Congress in December 1775 and remained in Virginia through the winter. His mother's death and then his own illness, which seems to have been a peculiarly persistent headache, delayed his return to Philadelphia. In the best of all worlds, Jefferson would have preferred to stay home at Monticello with his wife of three years, watching over his family, his farm, the work on his house. But he dutifully set out in the spring, taking a western route that offered splendid views of the mountains, and arrived at Philadelphia on May 14, 1776, when Congress had already approved a resolution calling on the states to adopt new governments where none "sufficient to the exigencies of their affairs" were already in place. The next day it adopted John Adams's radical preface calling for the suppression of all authority under the Crown.

Jefferson knew immediately that he was in the wrong place. Now Virginia would establish a new government and he, recently turned thirty-three and still to leave his mark on the world, wanted to be in Williamsburg, taking part. Other colonies had recalled their Congressional delegates when designing new governments, leaving perhaps one or two delegates to cast their vote in Congress. Virginia could do the same thing. The creation of a new government, he wrote Thomas Nelson on May 16, two days after his arrival in Philadelphia, was "a work of the most interesting nature" in which every individual would wish to have a voice. In fact, he went on, "it is the whole object of the present controversy; for should a bad government be instituted for us. . . it had been as well to have accepted at first the bad one offered to us from beyond the water without the risk and expence of contest."[1]

Two members of the Virginia delegation did go home to participate in the Convention but, no doubt to his deep disappointment, Jefferson was not among them. As the most recently arrived Virginia delegate, he had to remain in Philadelphia, take up the slack the others left, and do the work of Congress. Nonetheless, he remained determined to have a say in designing Virginia's future government. On June 13, when Jefferson's fellow delegate and onetime teacher George Wythe left Philadelphia for Williamsburg in the company of Richard Henry Lee, he had tucked away in his baggage the third draft of a constitution for Virginia on which Jefferson had labored for several weeks.[2] Then Jefferson turned his attention to another writing project. He had been asked to draft Congress's Declaration of Independence.

By the time Wythe delivered Jefferson's proposal to the Virginia Convention it was close to accepting another plan of government that it had disputed "inch by inch," and was unwilling to reconsider what it had accomplished with so much pain. The Convention did, however, make a few changes in the body of the document on the basis of Jefferson's proposals and, more important, added to the new constitution a preamble that Jefferson had written.[3] That preamble charged George III with trying to establish "a detestable and insupportable Tyranny" and provided a bill of particulars to prove the point. The final, amended version that the Virginia Convention adopted on June 29 said that, as a result of those "several Acts of Misrule," the old government of Virginia under the Crown of Great Britain was "totally dissolved." The preamble, in short, was Virginia's declaration of Independence.[4] And Jefferson's first draft of that preamble, which remained among his papers in Philadelphia, became the first draft of Congress's Declaration of Independence.

But before we see how Congress's drafting committee and the committee's designated draftsman put together the Declaration that Congress took up on July 2, it's worth our while to stop and examine the other "declarations of Independence" that Americans in colonies (or, as they soon became, states) and localities adopted between April and July 1776, of which Virginia's was one among many. There are, in fact, at least ninety documents in that category, and perhaps still more waiting to be found. Most have been forgotten under the influence of our national obsession with "the" Declaration of Independence, although the bulk of them were published almost a century and a half ago, scattered through the pages of Peter Force's voluminous *American Archives*.

In truth, those state and local "declarations of Independence," only a select few of which were called "declarations" at the time, are a some-what miscellaneous set of documents written for a variety of related purposes. Some officially ended the old regime within a state. Virginia and New Jersey formally concluded British rule with provisions that opened their first state constitutions, which were adopted before Congress declared Independence. Rhode Island passed a separate law that served the same purpose, and Maryland—as if to fulfill John Adams's prediction that Maryland would "go beyond every body else, when they begin to go"—adopted its own, separate "Declaration" on July 6, 1776. The list of "declarations of Independence" also includes instructions that authorized states' Congressional delegates to approve Independence. Those carefully drafted, formal statements proclaimed a state's commitment to separate nationhood and almost always summarized the events that had provoked and justified that position. Moreover, in Massachusetts, Virginia, and Maryland, substantial numbers of towns or counties instructed their state representatives to work for Independence, and, again, often explained why. Elsewhere other groups, such as New York's mechanics, militia units in Pennsylvania, or grand jurymen in South Carolina, announced their support for Independence and reflected on its causes or, sometimes, its benefits.[5]

Only a small part of the American people participated in writing and approving these state and local "declarations of Independence." Given the political situation in the spring of 1776, efforts to mobilize popular support for Independence concentrated on a handful of states, particularly those whose Congressional instructions barred their delegates from consenting to Independence, or Massachusetts, which hoped to lead the way to the promised land and produced a disproportionate part of the ninety "declarations." Even where communities did speak out, the number and representativeness of participants varied from place to place. What they said was, however, everywhere remarkably alike. Despite their shortcomings, the state and local "declarations of Independence" offer the best opportunity to hear the voice of the people from the spring of 1776 that we are likely to get. Nothing—certainly not the Declaration of Independence Congress set about editing on July 2—provides a better explanation of why the American people finally chose to leave the British Empire and to take up the reins of government themselves.

That these documents exist at all is surprising—until we realize that their creation continued, with a peculiar American twist, an English tradition that had been in place since at least the fourteenth century.

I.   In English Ways

The milestones of English history are marked not so much by stone monuments as by parchment documents, including an abundance of addresses, petitions, and declarations. Members of the Continental Congress were imitating their English ancestors, as they readily acknowledged, when they sent addresses or letters to the people of England, Ireland, and Quebec, submitted petitions to the King, issued a declaration on taking up arms, and commissioned another on Independence.

Each type of document had a distinct usage that the colonists knew from study if not by instinct. The term "address" covered a wide variety of written presentations. Parliament or a group of subjects might, for example, send an address to the King to congratulate him on some happy event, such as a victory or the birth of a child, or to express regret, support, or gratitude. On occasion, addresses could also make policy suggestions. Petitions were addresses that asked for something, and one specific type, petitions of right, had a particularly important place in English practice. They gave subjects a way of seeking redress of wrongs done under the authority of the King, whom they could not sue in the regular courts. Petitions of right asked for the recognition of undoubted rights, not mercy, and were directed to the King as the font of justice. The famous Petition of Right of 1628, for example, asserted that the Crown had violated the laws of the land by forcing subjects to make loans and pay other levies that Parliament had not authorized, billeting soldiers in private homes, and proceeding in improper ways against persons accused of crimes, and it asked that all such violations of English "laws and liberties" cease. Once Charles I accepted the petition with certain prescribed words, as he did to the immense relief of Parliament, he bound himself to recognize the rights it asserted.[6]

Declarations were still different, and had their own rich history. A declaration was a particularly emphatic pronouncement or proclamation that was often explanatory: from the fourteenth century "declaration" implied "making clear" or "telling." Occasionally a declaration announced and, for all practical purposes, enacted a new policy. For example, James II's Declarations of Indulgence granted liberty of conscience to Catholics and dissenters. Declarations were always meant to command broad public support, and both kings and Parliament issued them during their protracted seventeenth-century struggles. But the word "declaration" also referred to a legal instrument, a written statement of claims served on the defendant at the commencement of a civil action. Such summaries of wrongs were supposed to be presented in a "plain and certain" manner.[7]

Often declarations conformed to several of these definitions, bringing charges of wrongdoing in an emphatic way while appealing for public support. The Continental Congress's Declaration on Taking Up Arms is an example: it summarized the injuries America had suffered at Parliament's hand in an effort to demonstrate "the justice of our cause" to "the rest of the world."[8] Similarly, town and county resolutions on Independence often summarized the events that led them to advocate separation from Britain. Then they were published in newspapers, which was obviously done to convince others. Those local documents therefore qualify in fact if not in name as "declarations" in the English tradition.

By far the best-known and most influential English declaration among Americans was the Declaration of Rights of 1689, which formally ended the reign of James II and inaugurated that of William and Mary. It became for the colonists a sacred text, a document which, although not celebrated with religious imagery, provided a statement of established, fundamental political and legal truths. Like all such documents in English and American history, the Declaration of Rights was itself built on a substantial body of precedents. On five occasions between 1327 and 1485, then twice again in the seventeenth century, Englishmen brought the reign of a living king to an end. English kings were never disposed of lightly or silently; official statements of one sort or another always explained and justified the change of regime. Those justifications served over time to limit the legitimate deposition of a monarch to cases in which he was blatantly incompetent (*rex inutilis*) or bad in the sense of having violated established laws, customs, and moral standards, whether on his own initiative or by stubbornly following (as was said of Edward IV in 1484) "the counsel of persons insolent, vicious, and of inordinate avarice, despising the counsel of good, virtuous, and prudent persons." But who could judge a king? God, of course, and the language of the fourteenth and fifteenth centuries suggested that the community of the governed could also decide whether a reigning king was incompetent or evil and who would replace him on the throne, although in practice a small number of high-placed men made the critical decisions. Gradually, however, the right to speak for "the whole community of the kingdom" became invested in Parliament, which included the King, Lords, and Commons, and so in theory represented all the "estates" or social classes within the realm.[9]

It remained possible, of course, to dispute the legitimacy of a Parliament, or the extent of its rights. In 1649, the House of Commons alone—without the Lords and King—established a special "High Court of Justice" to try King Charles I for attempting "to subvert the ancient and fundamental laws and liberties of this nation" and establish in their place "an arbitrary and tyrannical government." The court brought detailed charges against him, but Charles denied its jurisdiction. The Commons could not make laws or create such a court without the consent of the Lords and King, he said, nor could it claim the right to try a king "without the consent of every man in England of whatsoever quality or condition." He was nonetheless tried, convicted, and executed. The Commons went on to abolish monarchy and the House of Lords and to establish a short-lived "Commonwealth" in which power was exercised by "the representatives of the people in Parliament, and by such as they shall appoint."[10]

In January 1689, Englishmen again faced the problem of ending one regime and establishing another. This time there were no court proceedings. King James II had fled to France, having canceled writs for a parliamentary election and tossed the Great Seal into the Thames. Elections were nonetheless held on the basis of an informal call from William of Orange. On February 12, the newly elected House of Commons and the House of Lords—which together constituted an imperfect or "convention" Parliament because no king was on the throne—adopted a Declaration of Rights, which they presented to William and Mary the next day. After the new king and queen were settled on the throne and Parliament became a regular, legal body, it revised the Declaration of Rights and, on December 16, 1689, reenacted that document as the Bill of Rights.[11]

The opening section of the Declaration of Rights had a particular significance for Americans in 1776 because it formally closed the reign of James II. It began with a "Whereas" clause that said "the late King James the second"—late not because he was dead but because he was no longer King—with "the Assistance of divers Evil Counsellors, Judges, and Ministers, imployed by him did endeavour to Subvert and extirpate the Protestant Religion, and the Lawes and Liberties of this Kingdome." Then, in thirteen clauses, it cited specific instances of the King's misconduct in an appropriately plain and certain manner. He was charged, for example, with raising money without the consent of Parliament, "raiseing and keeping a standing army within this Kingdom in time of Peace without Consent of Parliament and quartering of Souldiers contrary to Law," requiring excessive bail of accused criminals, and inflicting "illegall and cruell punishments." All of these acts were pronounced "utterly contrary to the knowne Laws and Statutes and freedome of this Realme." Then a second "Whereas" clause said that, the "late King James the second having abdicated the Government," the throne was "thereby vacant."[12]

That concluding statement raised as many issues as it resolved. Which of the King's acts had left the throne vacant? His flight from England, which was otherwise unmentioned? Or had James abdicated his office by the illegal actions that the document listed? Moreover, if James had forfeited his right to rule, why didn't the Crown pass to his infant son? An earlier version of the Declaration of Rights left fewer unanswered questions. It said that James II had endeavored to "subvert the constitution of this kingdom by breaking the original contract between king and people," had "violated the fundamental laws," and, "having withdrawn himself out of the kingdom, has abdicated the government; and that the throne is thereby vacant." But phrases such as "original contract" and "fundamental laws" were unacceptable to conservative Tory members of Parliament, and the more radical Whigs were unwilling to say that James's withdrawal from the kingdom—and, implicitly, that of his son—alone left the throne vacant. The resulting compromises in wording left the Declaration of Rights "most unsatisfactory as a statement of political principles."[13]

Having disposed of the previous king, the Declaration described William of Orange's summoning the Lords and Commons to meet at Westminster on January 22, 1689, to set up "such an establishment [of government] as that their Religion Lawes and Libertyes might not againe be in danger of being subverted." For that purpose, the Lords and Commons, "assembled in a full and free representative of this nation," went on to declare, "as their Ancestors in like Case have usually done," thirteen "undoubted Rights and Liberties." Some they stated in direct, positive terms: "levying of money . . . without Grant of Parliament . . . is illegall." Others were asserted with language that seems strangely tentative to the modern ear: "excessive Bayle ought not to be required nor excessive fynes imposed nor cruel and unusuall Punishments inflicted." Then, after expressing confidence that the Prince of Orange would "preserve them from the violation of their rights which they have here asserted and from other attempts upon their Religion Rights and Liberties," the Lords and Commons resolved that William and Mary should be declared King and Queen of England, defined the future succession to the throne, and specified new forms of the oaths of allegiance and supremacy. After William accepted the Declaration, promising to support "your Religion Laws and Liberties" and "doe all that is in My Power to advance the Welfare and Glory of the Nation," he and his wife were declared King and Queen.

The colonists indicated their respect for the English Declaration by adopting their own "Bills" or "Declarations of Rights" even before 1776. In October 1765, for example, the Stamp Act Congress issued a document of "declarations . . . respecting the most essential rights and liberties of the colonists, and of the grievances under which they labour," and seven years later Boston issued a more elaborate statement of the colonists' rights as men, Christians, and subjects, with a list of violations of those rights.[14] The "Bill of Rights" adopted in 1774 by the First Continental Congress was more closely modeled on its English predecessor. It began with four "whereas" clauses that summarized the "arbitrary proceedings" of Parliament and ministry that violated colonial rights. Where the English Declaration went on to describe the calling of the convention Parliament, Congress's Bill of Rights told of the colonies' sending deputies to Congress "to obtain such establishment, as that their religion, laws, and liberties may not be subverted," an awkward phrase memorable only because it was taken from the English Declaration of Rights. The Congressmen went on, "as Englishmen their ancestors in like cases have usually done"—another borrowed phrase—to "DECLARE" a list of ten rights, some of which echoed the English Declaration ("the keeping a standing army in these colonies, in times of peace, without the consent of the legislature of that colony in which such army is kept, is against law"), although others were entirely new (the colonists were entitled to "all the rights, liberties, and immunities of free and natural born subjects, within the realm of England"). Finally, Congress's Bill of Rights listed with great specificity those acts of Parliament and the King's government that violated their rights. Then it abruptly ended without drawing any grand conclusions, or founding a new "establishment" that would better protect their rights.[15] The 1774 colonial Bill of Rights was not a revolutionary document: unlike its English predecessor, it did not mark the end of an old regime and the beginning of a new. Instead it sought, like a petition of right, justice under the standing order.

By the late spring of 1776 the situation had changed, but not the references swimming around in American heads. When Jefferson began writing the preamble of his constitution for Virginia—the part the Virginia Convention used—he turned to the opening section of the English Declaration of Rights. And why not? It provided an entirely appropriate model of how to proclaim the end of an old regime. The English document could stand some improvement, of course, but it was a beginning. Jefferson's draft started, like the English Declaration, with a "Whereas" clause:

> Whereas George Guelf king of Great Britain and Ireland and Elector of Hanover, heretofore entrusted with the exercise of the kingly office in this government[,] hath endeavored to pervert the same into a detestable and insupportable tyranny

The statement that George III had "endeavored" to establish a tyranny links Jefferson's paragraph with its English model, but he clearly could not use all the English language. He substituted the long, somewhat cumbersome phrase "heretofore entrusted with the exercise of the kingly office in this government" for the English Declaration's simpler "late King James" because George III remained king in Britain, and so was not a "late King." Only his authority "in this government," that is, in Virginia, was at issue. Next Jefferson listed, again like the English

Declaration of Rights, a series of policies and acts by which the King had attempted to pervert his kingship of Virginia into a tyranny. Those charges were organized into sixteen clauses, three more than in the English Declaration, and were introduced, as in the English Declaration, with the word "by."[16]

As a consequence of these "several acts of misrule," Jefferson's draft preamble went on, George III "has forfeited the kingly office and has rendered it necessary for the preservation of the people that he should be immediately deposed from the same, & divested of all it's privileges, powers, & prerogatives." That was new: Jefferson's use of the word "forfeited" suggested that the relationship of rulers and subjects was contractual, and that a violation of their contract led to the King's loss of authority. The contractual nature of authority was assumed rather than asserted; nonetheless, the connection between the King's actions and his loss of power was more explicit than in the English Declaration, which fudged the issue. Finally, Jefferson's draft preamble rejected clearly and unequivocally—as the English Declaration of Rights had not—all claims of George III *and his heirs* to power in Virginia:

> Be it ... enacted by the authority of the people that the said George Guelf be, and he hereby is deposed from the kingly office within this government and absolutely divested of all it's rights, powers and prerogatives; and that he and his descendants and all persons claiming by or through him, and all other persons whatsoever shall be & for ever remain incapable of the same; and that the said office shall henceforth cease and never more either in name or substance be re-established within this colony.

The Virginia Convention chose to substitute for these passages a shorter and more restrained statement that linked the opening "Whereas" clause and the subsidiary "by" clauses with the body of the new constitution. As a result of these "several Acts of Misrule," the Virginia constitution of 1776 said, "the Government of this Country, as formerly exercised under the Crown of Great Britain, is totally dissolved." Having officially closed the old regime, the "Delegates and Representatives of the good People of Virginia" could logically proceed to "ordain and declare the future Form of Government of Virginia," one that effectively disposed of George III's heirs by denying office to anyone by right of birth.[17]

Several weeks before enacting the new constitution and its preamble, Virginians had adopted a separate document that was specifically called a "Declaration of Rights." It listed a series of rights that constituted "the basis and foundation of government," and so corresponded to the middle section of the English Declaration. Again, the similarity between the English and Virginia document went beyond their name: the Virginia provision against excessive bail, for example, was identical with that in the English Document except in punctuation and spelling, and certain borrowed phrases, such as the injunction against "cruel and unusual punishments," passed unchanged into Virginia's and then into American law.[18] Other provisions were new; and Virginia's adoption of a Declaration of Rights separate from its constitution was itself an auspicious innovation. The way Virginia went about its business began an American practice of delegating each of the three distinct functions served by the English Declaration of Rights to separate families of documents. The opening provisions ending the reign of James II became in America declarations of Independence, which were sometimes the opening sections of the first state constitutions but could also be separate documents (as in Maryland, or with the Congressional Declaration of Independence). The middle section of the English Declaration corresponded to what Americans called "Bills" or "Declarations" of Rights, like that of Virginia, and, after an initial period of some confusion, they became part of the legal code in states that adopted them and later of the American federal government's fundamental laws. The final section of the English Declaration, which established the reign of William and Mary, corresponded to the American constitutions. They, too, created a new "establishment" designed, as the English Declaration had said, so the people's "Religion Lawes and Libertyes might not againe be in danger of being subverted," although the texts of the American constitutions were of course longer and more complex.

How conscious of these debts were members of the revolutionary generation? Educated persons, particularly those who, like Jefferson, had studied law, were no doubt fully conscious of the link between English precedent and American practice. How else can we explain the persistence of phrases, including the First Continental Congress's careful reference to acting "as Englishmen their ancestors in like cases have usually done"? The question is more difficult to answer for the ordinary and frequently uneducated people in towns and counties, the farmers, militiamen, and jury members who felt compelled not only to announce their decision for Independence, but often also to justify it. Did those obscure colonists explain themselves so carefully in an effort to persuade others, to set the record straight, to release some of the emotions that their decision involved, or for all of those reasons? The effect, in any case, was familiar. Their justifications made clear that governments were not to be overthrown casually. To explain was to limit, to define the extraordinary circumstances in which so extreme an act could be done rightfully. And so, whether consciously or not, they acted as their ancestors had "usually done" over several centuries.

It is also worth asking why ordinary people in towns and counties were involved at all in deciding the fate of the old British Empire. Nowhere in English history had any similar effort been made to win consent to a change of regime from, as Charles I had said, "the major part of every man . . . of whatsoever quality or condition." But then nowhere in America was there an institution that, like Parliament, could claim the right to speak for the "whole community" without its specific authorization. Surely the Continental Congress had no such right: it was new and wholly dependent on grants of power from the states, where the effective authority of government was in all but a handful of cases exercised by extra-legal congresses or conventions that were themselves obliged to measure their acts against the will of those who elected them. For good reason, then, some delegates argued in June 1776 that Congress should adopt Independence only when "the voice of the people drove us into it" because the people "were our power, & without them our declarations could not be carried into effect."[19] If Congress moved forward too quickly, it might find itself alone, like some comic general in an old movie, issuing pompous orders to a nonexistent army.

Those "radical" delegates who advocated Independence did not disagree. They, too, understood the importance of Congress's acting only when the people's convictions had, as the phrase went, "ripened," as if that development would come in the natural course of things, like fruit maturing on a tree. But they thought the fruit was already ripe. The people, they said in the debates of early June, were in favor of Independence, but, particularly in the middle colonies, their state representatives lagged behind them.[20] If so, there was an obvious way to advance the harvest. Mobilize the people; bring their voices to bear upon the members of their provincial assemblies, congresses, or conventions, and in that way secure new instructions that would allow Congressmen from those colonies to approve Independence.

By the time Congress first took up Richard Henry Lee's resolutions on Independence, that strategy was already in place. As a result, the struggle for Independence became a complex political war, fought on many local fronts between April and July 1776, over the instructions that critical colonies issued to their Congressional delegations.

2. Mobilizing the People

On May 10, 1776, the Massachusetts assembly asked the inhabitants of each town in the colony to debate, "in full Meeting warned for that Purpose," an extraordinary topic: if the honorable Continental Congress should decide that, for the safety of the United Colonies, it was necessary to declare them independent of Great Britain, would "they the said Inhabitants . . . solemnly engage with their Lives and Fortunes to Support the Congress in the Measure"?[21] The assembly put the question in an unusually personal way, and chose its words carefully. In British law, death and the forfeiture of estate were the punishment for treason.

The towns were also asked to "advise" their representatives to the next General Court how they stood on the above proposition, as the warrants for their meetings sometimes indicated.[22] In fact, the exercise was meant to build support for a revision of Massachusetts's instructions to its Congressional delegation, which might seem strange since the instructions in place were fully sufficient to let them vote for Independence. The five Congressmen Massachusetts elected in December 1775—Hancock, the two Adamses, Robert Treat Paine, and Elbridge Gerry, who replaced the more moderate Thomas Cushing—were "fully impowered" to "direct and order," with other members of Congress, whatever measures seemed "best calculated for the Establishment of Right and Liberty to the *American* Colonies upon a Basis permanent and secured against the Power and Arts of the *British* administration."[23] The idea of revising the instructions so they specifically endorsed Independence began not in Boston but in Philadelphia, among Massachusetts Congressmen, who hoped to spark a movement whose effects would be felt far beyond the Bay Colony. On March 26, 1776, Gerry wrote James Warren, the speaker of the province's House of Representatives, that the Massachusetts legislature should "originate instructions, expressed with decency and firmness—your own style—. . . in favour of independency. I am certain it would turn many doubtful minds," Gerry said, "and produce a reversal of the contrary instructions adopted by some Assemblies."[24]

To judge by Warren's letters, there should have been no problem implementing Gerry's suggestion. The "Sighing after Independence," Warren wrote John Adams on April 3, was "Universal" in Massachusetts. "The Harvest is Mature, . . . Nothing remains of that Prudence Moderation, or Timidity with which we have so long been plagued. . . . All are United in this question." Still, nothing happened, and in fact it proved surprisingly difficult to get the Massachusetts instructions changed. On April 22, John Adams again wrote Warren that, if Massachusetts was so unanimously in favor of Independence, "now is the proper Time for you to instruct your Delegates to that Effect . . . Such an Instruction at this Time would comfort and cheer the Spirits of your Friends, and would discourage and dishearten your Enemies."[25] Finally, on May 9, the colony's lower house proposed that the various towns debate the wisdom of Independence and instruct their representatives to the next assembly on that issue. However, the Council, or upper house, refused to go along with the idea. Enmity between the Council's head, Thomas Cushing, and the more radical members of the Massachusetts Congressional delegation, who had worked against his reelection to Congress, probably influenced that decision.[26]

The Council's opposition meant that the lower house of assembly alone asked townsmen to decide if they were willing to support Independence with their "lives and fortunes." The request—or, more exactly, a resolution that in the "opinion" of the House such debates should be held—was sent to the towns through newspaper notices, which proved unsatisfactory. By June 6, a week after the newly elected House had reconvened, a great majority of the members—some two-thirds, according to one account—said their towns had expressed support for Independence. But others had failed to take up the issue, supposedly because they were not "seasonably favored" with the appropriate newspapers. The assembly therefore called on towns that had not already acted, whether represented in the legislature or not, to hold meetings "as soon as may be" and debate Independence so "their sentiments may be fully known to this House," and it printed some 150 handbills to announce its request. Not even that did the trick. Massachusetts towns continued to debate Independence on through the month of June and into early July. Not until July 3—when Congress, unknown to the people in Boston, had already approved Independence and was hard at work editing Jefferson's draft declaration— did the Massachusetts House of Representatives vote, unanimously, that it would approve a decision by Congress to declare Independence.[27]

Why were the towns so slow to act? Enthusiasm, for one thing, was less universal than Warren indicated. On June 25, Barnstable on Cape Cod voted 36–30 against supporting Independence "at the hazard of life and estate," which provoked a vigorous protest by the town's substantial minority. In general, however, surviving returns suggest that townsmen took up the issue with seriousness and even a certain awe, and came to agreement without deep divisions. Independence was "the greatest and most important question that ever came before this town," the Topsfield town meeting observed on June 21, as it undoubtedly was for many towns more accustomed to dealing with wandering hogs and fallen fences. Sometimes towns explained that they had failed to act earlier, as the legislature assumed, because they never saw the original resolution of the House of Representatives asking townsmen "to express their minds" on Independence, but, as Acton said on June 14, having finally received it, the town "cheerfully" embraced the opportunity.[28]

There were some good reasons not to bother asking localities what they thought about the issue. In May 1776, the lower house of the Rhode Island legislature considered surveying the colony's people on the question of Independence, but decided against it. As Governor Nicholas Cooke explained, members of the colony's upper house argued that, "although a very great majority of the Colony were perfectly ripe for such a question, yet, upon its being canvassed, several towns would vote against it" and "the appearance of disunion would be injurious to the common cause." To take the "sense of the Colony in the proposed way" and transmit the results to Philadelphia would also take time, and in the interim Rhode Island's delegates would remain unable to vote for Independence if Congress took up that topic. Finally, on May 4, without any further consultations, the legislature adopted new instructions that gave its Congressmen ample power to approve Independence without using that word. Independence, Governor Cooke observed, "with many honest and ignorant people" still carried the "idea of eternal warfare," a prospect with little appeal anywhere, and even less in a colony with a large number of Quakers. The legislature also repealed an earlier law for securing allegiance to the King and changed the form of commissions and writs. That act began with two "whereas" clauses that explained and justified the termination of British authority, and decreed that henceforth official documents would be issued not in the name of the King but in the name of "the Governor and Company of the English Colony of Rhode Island and Providence Plantations." Even in separating itself from the British Crown, Rhode Island held tightly to its English identity.[29]

Massachusetts and Rhode Island might be safe for Independence, but the tardiness of many Massachusetts towns in debating that issue and the Rhode Island legislature's anxious caution kept them from inspiring other assemblies—particularly those of the wayward middle colonies—to change their positions. That role went instead to Virginia. There again the freeholders and other inhabitants of several counties debated Independence and came to "plain and certain" conclusions in the spring of 1776. Instructions signed by a majority of freeholders in James City County on April 24 told their representatives to exert their "utmost abilities, in the next Convention, toward dissolving the connection between *America* and *Great Britain*, totally, finally, and irrevocably," although a parenthetical phrase, "provided no just and honorable terms are offered by the King," detracted somewhat from the instruction's decisiveness. Two days earlier Cumberland County had been even more forceful, telling its delegates "positively to declare for an Independency, . . . solemnly abjure any Allegeance to his Britannick Majesty, and bid him a good night forever." Landon Carter, a crotchety Virginia planter for whom life was generally filled with annoyances, took strong exception to the apparent flowering of popular power: "Papers it seems are every where circulating about for poor ignorant Creatures to sign, as directions to their delegates to endeavour at independency," he complained on the 9th of May.[30]

Such expressions of popular convictions encouraged the Virginia Convention to adopt, on May 15, two resolutions, with a long explanatory preface, whose impact went far beyond that state. The second resolution called for the preparation of a Declaration of Rights and "such a plan of government as will be most likely to maintain peace and order in this Colony, and secure substantial and equal liberty to the people." The first told Virginia's delegates at Philadelphia to propose that Congress "declare the United Colonies free and independent States; absolved from all allegiance to, or dependance upon, the Crown or Parliament of Great Britain," and that they approve that measure as well as the forming of foreign alliances and a formal American Confederation. Virginia's were not the first state instructions that specifically endorsed Independence: almost a month earlier, on April 12, 1776, North Carolina had "empowered" its delegates to concur with other members of Congress in declaring Independence. But both North Carolina's and Virginia's instructions were laid before Congress on the same day, May 27, and North Carolina did not, like Virginia, order its delegates to propose Independence. In conformity with Virginia's instructions of May 15, and echoing its words, Richard Henry Lee made his motion that "these United Colonies are, and of right ought to be, free and independent States, . . . absolved from all allegiance to the British Crown," which Congress adopted on July 2.[31] Virginia, moreover, added to the influence of its resolutions by carefully sending them to other states, where they inspired imitators.

After receiving the Virginia resolves, Connecticut's assembly also changed the instructions given to its Congressional delegates. The Connecticut resolutions, which were adopted on June 14, began with a long "whereas" clause summarizing the ways in which the King and Parliament had "claimed and attempted to exercise powers incompatible with and subversive of the ancient, just, and constitutional rights of this and the rest of the *English* Colonies in *America.*" Then, like Virginia, Connecticut asked its delegates to "propose" that Congress "declare the United *American* Colonies free and independent States, absolved from all allegiance to the King of *Great Britain,*" and authorized their assent to the establishment of foreign alliance and a colonial Confederation. The assembly also changed the form of all oaths that expressed any duty or obligation to the King, and altered commissions and legal documents so they were issued in the name of the governor and people of the state. With those measures, Connecticut became, for all practical purposes, independent of Britain.[32]

The next day both New Hampshire and Delaware adopted new instructions for their Congressional delegates. New Hampshire, after observing that it had "the example of several of the most respectable of our sister Colonies before us," instructed its representatives "to join with the other Colonies in Declaring the thirteen United Colonies, a free & independent State" and pledged to support that measure "with our lives and fortunes." Delaware was less direct. Like Rhode Island, it avoided the word "Independence," authorizing its delegates to "concur" with other members of Congress in forming further compacts among the colonies, concluding treaties, and "adopting such other measures as shall be judged necessary for promoting the liberty, safety, and interests of America."[33]

The New Jersey legislature read and filed the Virginia instructions on June 12, then—whether influenced by Virginia, Congress's resolutions of May 10 and 15, or, more likely, the increasingly threatening military situation—took one radical step after another. It arrested the colony's royal governor, William Franklin, the Loyalist son of Benjamin Franklin. Then it voted to form a new state government, elected a new slate of Congressional delegates favorably disposed toward Independence, and, on June 22, adopted instructions for its Congressmen that were briefer and more equivocal than those of Virginia. New Jersey's Congressmen were directed and empowered to join with delegates from other colonies "in the most vigorous measures for supporting the just rights and liberties of *America*," including, if they considered it "necessary and expedient for this purpose, . . . declaring the United Colonies independent of *Great Britain*, entering into a Confederacy for union and common defence, making treaties with foreign nations for commerce and assistance," and taking "such other measures as . . . appear necessary for these great ends." In arresting Franklin and taking steps to change the state government, New Jersey seemed to commit itself inextricably to Independence. Yet its decision against simply telling its Congressional delegates to vote for separation from Britain suggests that New Jersey—no less than the freeholders of James City County, Virginia—still hoped that some unexpected development might make that step unnecessary.[34]

Pennsylvania was more difficult to change. There the old colonial assembly remained in place and under the control of a conservative elite that adamantly refused to repeal or alter its instructions of November 9, 1775, which told the colony's Congressional delegates to "dissent from, and utterly reject, any propositions . . . that may cause or lead to a separation from our Mother Country." To the advocates of Independence, Pennsylvania came to seem the source of all opposition to that measure: the Pennsylvania instructions, Elbridge Gerry wrote James Warren on May 20, "induced the middle colonies and some of the southern to backward every measure which had the appearance of independency." Those instructions were therefore responsible for "the delay of congress in agitating questions of the greatest importance, which long ere now must have terminated in a separation from Great Britain" and for "the disadvantages we now experience for want of a full supply of every necessity for carrying on the war. Alliances might have been formed, and a diversion been given to the enemy's arms in Europe or the West Indies, had these instructions never appeared." And yet "the spirit of the people" was "great, if a judgment is to be formed by appearances. They are well convinced of the injury their assembly has done to the continent by their instructions."[35]

The voters of Pennsylvania had not, however, seen fit to shift the political character of the assembly's membership in a by-election held on May 1, 1776. Within the next week news that the King had hired German soldiers for service in America, the appearance of a British warship, the *Roebuck*, in the Delaware River, and its subsequent engagement with Pennsylvania gunboats increased popular support for Independence; but the damage was done. The only way to bring Pennsylvania into line, it seemed, was to replace the established government, which was still controlled by conservative Quakers and wealthy proprietary leaders, with another that would reflect more accurately the convictions of rural supporters of Independence, including Germans, and, above all, Philadelphia's radical mechanics. Congress's resolution of May 10, calling on the states to found new governments, was chiefly designed to bring that about. However, it proved insufficient since John Dickinson—who had drafted the November instructions to buttress his own position within Congress—and his conservative colleagues on Pennsylvania's Congressional delegation argued that the resolution did not apply to Pennsylvania. The standing government of the colony, they said, was fully adequate "to the exigency of their affairs," because the governor of Pennsylvania, unlike those of most other colonies, had no power to prorogue or dissolve the assembly. Adams's preamble of May 15 answered Dickinson's argument: if it was "absolutely irreconcilable to reason and good conscience, for the people of these colonies now to take oaths and affirmations . . . for the support of any government under the crown of Great Britain" and therefore "necessary that the exercise of every kind of authority under the said crown . . . be totally suppressed," the proprietary government of Pennsylvania was as much in need of replacement as any other.[36]

Within hours Philadelphia radicals caucused and used "the resolve of Congress of the fifteenth instant" as the basis for securing a public meeting on May 20 that, in turn, began with the Moderator reading Congress's statement of May 15 "with a loud Stentorean Voice that might be heard a Quarter of a Mile 'Whereas his Britannic Majesty &c.'" As soon as he was done, the "wett" people—the day was very rainy—"rendered the Welkin with three Cheers, Hatts flying as usual &c." The meeting went on to condemn the assembly's instructions of November 9, affirm that the colony's current government was inadequate for the exigencies of its affairs, and call a conference of committee representatives from throughout the colony to arrange the election of a constitutional convention. Two days later, the assembly met and tried to recover its authority. It withdrew its old instructions and, on June 8, authorized Pennsylvania's Congressional delegates to approve whatever measures seemed necessary "for promoting the Liberty, Safety and Interests of America." But the assembly's day had passed: rising absenteeism robbed it of the necessary quorum to conduct business, and on June 14 it dissolved for good. The Provincial Conference of Committees met at Carpenter's Hall four days later and called a constitutional convention whose members would be chosen under rules that expanded the electorate by as much as 50 to 90 percent. Finally, on June 24, the Conference issued a "Declaration on the subject of Independence" by which its members, "in behalf of ourselves, and with the approbation, consent, and authority of our constituents," unanimously declared their "willingness to concur in a vote of the Congress declaring the United Colonies free and independent states." In the end, then, Pennsylvania had two sets of new instructions that endorsed Independence—the assembly's and that of the Conference of Committees.[37]

The unenviable animosity Pennsylvania attracted among the supporters of Independence is somewhat surprising considering that Maryland was equally recalcitrant. Perhaps inconsistency saved it: Maryland was "so excentric [*sic*] a Colony—some times so hot, sometimes so cold—now so high, then so low—that I do not know what to say about it or expect from it," John Adams wrote on May 20. It was then he predicted that "when they get agoing I expect some wild extravagant Flight or other from it. To be sure they must go beyond every body else, when they begin to go." Maryland "got agoing" the very next day, but apparently in the wrong direction. On May 21, the colony's provincial convention resolved unanimously "that reunion with *Great Britain* on constitutional principles would most effectually secure the rights and liberties, and increase the strength and promote the happiness of the whole empire," and reaffirmed its instructions of the previous January, which precluded Maryland's Congressional delegates from assenting to "any proposition to declare the Colonies independent," establish foreign alliances, or to form "any union or confederation of these Colonies which may necessarily lead to a separation from the mother country" without the previous consent of the provincial convention.[38]

Congressional advocates of Independence were convinced that the Maryland convention was out of touch with its people, and set out to rectify the problem. On June 11, Maryland's delegates wrote the state's Committee of Safety that Congress had delayed its vote on Independence by three weeks "to give an Oppertunity to the Delegates from those Colonies, which had not yet given Authority to adopt this decisive Measure, to consult their Constituents." It was therefore necessary that the Maryland Convention reassemble "as soon as possible." Moreover, since Maryland's Congressional delegates wanted to have "the fair and uninfluenced Sense of the People" on Independence, members of the Convention should "endeavour to collect the opinion of the people at large in some Manner or other" before meeting. The same day, Samuel Chase, a close associate of the Adamses, returned from a Congressional mission to Canada and began working in Maryland on behalf of Independence. The people, he wrote John Adams on June 21, were generally displeased with their convention's position on that issue. "County after county" was writing instructions to their representatives in the provincial convention, and those in favor of Independence from Frederick County, which had appeared in newspapers, spoke "the Sense of many Counties." Resolutions or instructions in favor of Independence survive from several other counties, including Anne Arundel, Charles, and Talbot. On June 28, when Chase could finally report that the Convention had voted unanimously for Independence, he attributed the change to "the glorious Effects of County Instructions."[39]

Popular pressure did not always succeed in shifting a colony's position. In late May the General Committee of the Mechanics in Union of New York City and County urged the New York Provincial Congress to instruct its delegates in Philadelphia to support Independence, but its petition failed. The Provincial Congress replied that the mechanics were only a "voluntary association" without "any authority whatsoever in the public transactions of the present times," and added that it saw no reason to make a pronouncement on Independence until the Continental Congress took up that issue and solicited New York's opinion. On June 24 the inhabitants of King's District and Spencer-Town in Albany County, both of which were settled by New Englanders, also approved resolutions in favor of Independence and apparently used them, in the Massachusetts way, to instruct their representatives to the next Provincial Congress. Nonetheless, true to its word, the New York Congress waited until July 9, a week after Congress acted, before agreeing to support Independence "at the risk of our lives and fortunes," lamenting still "the cruel necessity which has rendered that measure unavoidable."[40]

The effort to build an Independence movement "from the bottom up," and to topple the standing government of Pennsylvania when it got in the way, is often attributed to master political strategists in the Massachusetts Congressional delegation, and particularly to Samuel Adams, that "éminence grise" of the Revolution whom many historians have used to explain anything they found otherwise inexplicable. Here there is at least some evidence to support the argument. The technique of mobilizing the people was strikingly like that implemented by Adams in Massachusetts four years earlier, when, under his leadership, Boston called for the establishment of town committees of correspondence throughout the colony, and in that way broadened the base of opposition to Britain. Moreover, Christopher Marshall, one of Philadelphia's revolutionary leaders, regularly consulted both Samuel and John Adams in the spring of 1776, and Marshall worked closely with Thomas Young, who had served a political apprenticeship under Samuel Adams in Boston.[41] On the other hand, it was John Adams, not Samuel, who drafted Congress's radical preface of May 15 that led to the overthrow of Pennsylvania's government and opened the way for that state's consent to Independence; it was to John Adams, not Samuel, that Samuel Chase reported on the progress of county instructions in Maryland; and it was John Adams and Elbridge Gerry, not Samuel Adams, who encouraged James Warren to mobilize Massachusetts towns on behalf of Independence, just as it was John Adams who openly and repeatedly argued for Independence on the floor of Congress, not Samuel, who had a speech impediment and tended to make his contributions in other ways. Moreover, the Massachusetts delegates' strategy of using their home state to lead a cascading movement toward Independence utterly failed. Instead Virginia prompted one state after another to revise its Congressional instructions, and no one—not even the most conspiratorial-minded chronicler of the Revolution—has suggested that Samuel Adams, or his cousin John, for that matter, controlled Virginia.

The timing of the effort to mobilize popular support was, in any case, more important than who promoted it. A similar attempt six months earlier would have failed since the "ripening" of opinion on Independence was, in the spring of 1776, a recent occurrence. On that the declarations themselves offer direct and powerful evidence.

3. Declaring Independence

William Henry Drayton, the Chief Justice of South Carolina, understood that the opening of the Court of General Sessions of the Peace, Oyer and Terminer, Assize and General Jail Delivery held at Charlestown—which would soon become Charleston—on April 23, 1776, was an historic event. When the colony remained under the British Crown, juries had been assembled, but then, he said, they were "silently and arbitrarily dismissed . . . whereby, in contempt of *Magna Charta*, justice has been delayed and denied." It was finally possible to impanel a jury because, less than a month earlier, South Carolina had adopted a new state constitution "independent of Royal authority." The occasion seemed sufficiently important that, rather than simply brief the jury in an ordinary way, Drayton used his charge to explain for the benefit of the jury, his associate justices, and all who would later read his words, the principal causes that led to "the late revolution of our Government" as well as "the law upon the point, and the benefits resulting from that happy and necessary establishment." At the end of his disquisition, Drayton took it upon himself to declare South Carolina independent of Great Britain.[42]

That conclusion was something of a surprise, since Drayton began by telling stories—stories that began in 1719, when Carolinians cast off their original proprietary government and called upon the English king to rule them directly. Drayton then moved forward to the period since 1763. The British King and Parliament, he said, had "made the most arbitrary attempts to enslave America." Then he listed "some of the most weighty" examples from an enormous "catalogue of . . . oppressions" the colonists had suffered, beginning each instance—as in the English Declaration of Rights—with the word "by." Some of the grievances he mentioned went back to the 1760s, when Parliament first claimed the right "to bind the Colonies 'in all cases whatsoever.'" However, Drayton described with particular indignation events of the previous year. The colonists, faced with ruin, petitioned the King for redress, but their "dutiful petition" was answered at Lexington and Concord, where British troops "by surprise drew the sword of civil war, and plunged it into the breasts of the *Americans!*" Another petition "on the part of millions, praying that the effusion of blood might be stayed, was not thought worthy of an answer!" Instead the war continued.

Drayton recalled "the ruins of *Charlestown* [Massachusetts], *Falmouth*, and *Norfolk*," which marked "the humane progress of the Royal arms" as much as "the ruins of *Carthage*, *Corinth*, and *Numantium*, proclaimed to the world that justice was expelled from the *Roman* Senate!" He complained of British efforts to turn Indians and slaves against white colonists. He also described the Prohibitory Act of December 1775—a law that would "make prize of all vessels trading in, to, or from the United Colonies," enslave their crews by impressing them into the British navy, and "compel them to bear arms against their conscience, their fathers, their bleeding country"—as "so atrocious" that it had "no parallel in the registers of tyranny." When the English King first agreed to rule the Carolinians, Drayton argued, he "thereby indisputably admitted the legality" of the "Revolution" by which they had overthrown the proprietors, and "vested in those our forefathers, and us their posterity, a clear right to effect another revolution, if the government of the House of *Brunswick* should operate to the ruin of the People." By then the point of his story seemed obvious. What more did the Chief Justice need to explain and justify the recent "revolution of our Government"?

But suddenly Drayton dipped back further into the past, to "the famous Revolution in *England*, in the year 1688," whose foundations Drayton thought "much inferior" to those behind the recent change of government in South Carolina, but which provided an "illustrious precedent." He strangely quoted an early draft of the English Declaration of Rights, not the revised version that Parliament finally presented to William and Mary.[43] The Lords and Commons resolved, Drayton said, that James II,

> having endeavoured to subvert the Constitution of the Kingdom, by breaking the original contract between King and People, and by the advice of *Jesuits* and other wicked persons, having violated the fundamental laws, and having withdrawn himself out of this Kingdom, has abdicated the Government, and that the Throne is thereby vacant.

Then Drayton proceeded to compare, point by point, the charges against James II in the Declaration of Rights with the record of George III. King James "broke the original contract by not affording due protection to his subjects," but was not charged with seizing their towns, or laying them in ruins, or seizing their vessels, or pursuing the people "with fire and sword" or declaring them rebels "for resisting his arms levelled to destroy their lives, liberties, and properties," all of which "*George* the Third had done . . . against *America*." If James II "violated the fundamental laws" by levying taxes, interfering with the freedom of elections, keeping a standing army in time of peace, suspending the operation of laws, and quartering soldiers contrary to law and "without consent of the Legislative Assembly chosen by the personal election of that People over whom such doings were exercised," so had George III. He had even, like James II, abdicated government in South Carolina through the action of his representative, the colony's "late" royal governor, Lord William Campbell, who had "carried off the great seal" and "withdrawn" from the colony.

To determine the implications of this "great precedent in constitutional law," Drayton turned not to the writings of political theorists such as John Locke, but to "the learned Judge" William Blackstone for a statement that James's abdication of government affected not only him but his heirs and "rendered the throne absolutely and completely vacant." Then, "on the foot of the best of authorities," Drayton pronounced his own version of the Declaration of Rights, much as Thomas Jefferson would do a month later. Since "*George* the Third, King of *Great Britain*, has endeavoured to subvert the Constitution of this country, by breaking the original contract between King and People; by the advice of wicked persons has violated the fundamental laws, and has withdrawn himself, by withdrawing the constitutional benefits of the Kingly office and his protection out of this country," the Chief Justice said, "the law of the land authorizes me to declare, and it is my duty boldly to declare the law, that *George* the Third, King of *Great Britain*, has abdicated the Government, and that the throne is thereby vacant; that is, he has no authority over us, and we owe no obedience to him."

Drayton's "declaration of Independence" was unusual in that it took the form of a judgment in law on which he, as Chief Justice, could—indeed, he said, was obliged to—make a pronouncement. His use of an early, "Whig" draft of the Declaration of Rights made his task easier, since the official version included no reference to an "original contract between King and People" or "fundamental laws." A selective reading of Blackstone's *Commentaries on the Laws of England* also helped. Blackstone did say that the precedent of 1689 provided a limited "*law* of redress against public oppression." If some future King endeavored to subvert the constitution by breaking the original contract between King and people, violated the fundamental laws, and withdrew from the kingdom, that is, if he precisely replicated the conduct of James II, that precedent, Blackstone said, authorized a judgment that the King had abdicated and the throne was vacant. But the *Commentaries* did not authorize an ordinary judge like Drayton to make such a decision. Conflicts between society at large and the rulers to whom it entrusted authority, Blackstone said, "must be decided by society itself: there is not upon earth any other tribunal to resort to."[44]

Elected provincial legislatures or conventions had a far better claim than Drayton to speak for "society itself," at least that part of

American society within their jurisdictions. So, too, did many of the towns and counties that adopted instructions on Independence, although from place to place different bodies approved those resolutions, some of which were more representative of the local population than others. On the high end of the scale were the votes of Massachusetts town meetings and of James City County, Virginia, where a majority of resident freeholders signed the instructions on Independence; on the other were places like Talbot County, Maryland, whose instructions came from a group that openly described itself as "part of the freemen of said County." Some instructions were the work of an elected committee that felt free to speak for its constituents. For example, the instructions of Charlotte County, Virginia, issued "by the unanimous approbation and direction of the whole freeholders, and all the other inhabitants of this County," were adopted at a meeting of the county committee with the chairman and fifteen members present. A meeting of freeholders probably approved the instructions of Buckingham County, Virginia, which were then signed by a clerk. Even when approved by large and representative bodies of people, such documents were not necessarily simple and spontaneous expressions of popular sentiment: on some occasions, county meetings were probably called and instructions drafted in whole or in part by the persons being instructed.[45]

The various resolutions and instructions on Independence differed from one another in form and style. Some state instructions adopted in the critical period between April and July of 1776 were short, consisting of a paragraph or two (Delaware, New Jersey, and Maryland). Most states, however, adopted more elaborate documents that followed historic models such as the English Declaration of Rights and also a certain logical order by listing various acts of the King and his government, drawing a conclusion on the basis of those acts, and culminating with a resolution or declaration on behalf of Independence. The instructions of North Carolina, Virginia, Connecticut, New Hampshire, and both sets of Pennsylvania instructions (those of the Assembly and of the Conference of Committees) followed that pattern. So did the "Declaration of the Delegates of Maryland" issued on July 6 and the preambles to the new constitutions of Virginia (June 29) and New Jersey (July 2).

Several town and county instructions similarly consisted of a series of propositions beginning "whereas" or "resolved," but, for the most part, local resolutions tended to be more informal than those of states. Some communities did little more than announce the conclusions of their debates, while others explained themselves at length, occasionally, like Drayton, by telling stories. One of the longest local instructions came from Buckingham County, Virginia. It went back to the beginning of the Anglo-American conflict to trace, step by step, the bewildering process by which Britain and the colonists became increasingly "incensed" at each other until the separation neither wanted became unavoidable. The people of Wrentham, Massachusetts, set their decision for Independence within the history of their colony, which they summarized in a few paragraphs that went back a century and a half to recall how "tyranny and oppression" had forced their ancestors to seek asylum "in this distant land, amidst a howling wilderness. . . ." Even brief local resolutions could catch the distinctive voice of a people. Consider the resolutions of Greenwich, a small farming town in western Massachusetts that met "at the Public House" on Monday, July 1, at three in the afternoon. There the townsmen voted, in good Yankee English, "for independence on *Great Britain* if the honourable American Congress thinks fit, and most for the interest and safety of the Colonies; it being a unanimous vote," then added, as if that wasn't clear enough, "not one dissenting." Short resolutions could also be eloquent. Like many other towns, Ashby, a small rural community in north-central Massachusetts, simply rephrased the assembly's call for debate in composing its resolution on Independence, but managed to do so with striking effect: "should the honourable Congress, for the safety of the Colonies, declare them independent of *Great Britain*," it said, "the inhabitants of *Ashby* will solemnly engage with their lives and fortunes to support them in the measure." There was no false humility there, no suggestion that their decisions were insignificant; these colonists understood that the Revolution depended on the people, that is, on themselves, and that without their commitment it could not succeed.[46]

In the end, however, the differences that distinguished one set of instructions or resolutions from another proved relatively insignificant. For all practical purposes, the contents of the various state and local resolutions on Independence are virtually identical.[47] Among other common attributes, they were universally deferential toward the Continental Congress. Even the most decisive supporters of separation, such as the townsmen of Topsfield, Massachusetts, who argued for a declaration of Independence "as soon as may be," took care to add that they meant not to dictate, but left the final decision on "that momentous affair to the well-known wisdom, prudence, justice, and integrity, of that honourable body the Continental Congress, under whose direction it more immediately belongs." Since there was a Congress "of wise and good men" who sat "at the helm of affairs, consulting measures which will be most for the safety and prosperity of the whole, and have the means of intelligence and information in their hands," it made sense, as the town of Palmer, Massachusetts, put it, to "submit the whole affair to their wise consideration and determination." Wrentham, Massachusetts, went so far as to say it placed in "the honourable *American* Congress ... the highest confidence under God"! Less euphorically, the associators of Anne Arundel County, Maryland, expressed their "thorough conviction that the true interests and substantial happiness of the United Colonies in general, and this in particular," were "inseparably interwoven and linked together, and essentially dependant upon a close Union and Continental Confederation."[48]

Instructions from the separate states to their Congressional delegates also explicitly acknowledged the importance and superior authority of Congress. They characteristically "empowered" their representatives to "concur with the Delegates of the other Colonies in declaring Independency," as North Carolina put it, or in such measures as "shall be judged necessary" by Congress "for promoting the liberty, safety, and interests of America" in Delaware's words. Even Connecticut, which, like Virginia, told its delegates actively to propose a declaration of Independence, allowed Congress substantial latitude in deciding when a declaration would be "expedient and best" and what other measures were "proper and necessary." And when provincial assemblies or conventions took it upon themselves to declare their states independent from Britain, they did so in ways that avoided any indication that they were acting apart from or with disrespect toward Congress. Such declarations were issued as part of new state constitutions established under the explicit direction of Congress or, in the case of Maryland, stressed that the state had empowered its deputies in Congress to join with "a majority of the United Colonies in declaring them free and independent States" and that it was concerned with not only its own freedom but that of its "sister Colonies."[49]

No less than their Congressmen, in short, these state and local constituencies understood the importance of American unanimity, which, in turn, required acting under Congress's direction. Everywhere those who opposed adopting state instructions on behalf of Independence were charged with breaking the American union. That was the accusation the minority in Barnstable, Massachusetts, hurled at their fellow townsmen, that radicals in Pennsylvania leveled at their assembly, that Marylanders raised against their provincial convention. The committee of Frederick County condemned all votes of the Maryland Convention that tended to separate Maryland from a majority of the Colonies as "destructive to our internal safety, and big with publick ruin"; and members of militia battalions in Chester County, Pennsylvania, condemned that state's instructions against Independence as "calculated to break an important middle link in the grand Continental chain of Union" and declared their readiness to exert the "most strenuous efforts to support and strengthen the Continental Union." Only colonial unanimity, Anne Arundel County said, could "render our opposition to the establishment of a Parliamentary tyranny glorious."[50] These enthusiastic affirmations of Congressional authority and American unity suggest that the society that adopted Independence was national to a remarkable extent considering that before 1764 the North American colonies had no connection with each other except through Britain. A sense of shared grievances and the repeated efforts to coordinate opposition and to secure redress helped establish this common identity, but it also owed much to the colonists' experience of belonging to an entity larger than their separate provinces, the British Empire. As affection for the Mother Country faded, it was transferred to that jerry-built institution, the Second Continental Congress, and the fledgling nation it struggled to lead.

The similar ways the states and local bodies explained their conversion to Independence are no less striking. One after another cited the same brief set of events to make their point, and drew much the same conclusions from them. To find such consistency in resolutions regardless of whether they came from New England or the Chesapeake, from the "backward" Pennsylvania Assembly or the "radical"

Pennsylvania Conference of Committees, from Rhode Island legislators, militiamen in Pennsylvania, or New York mechanics gives reason to suspect that, had other communities spoken out, they, too, would have said much the same thing. It is likely, in short, that the observations and reasonings in these documents were shared by other Americans who had made their peace with leaving the British Empire.

State and local resolutions on Independence rarely looked back over the entire sweep of the Anglo-American conflict. If they referred to grievances that predated 1775, they generally did so in a summary manner. Connecticut, for example, said the King and Parliament had "claimed and attempted to exercise powers incompatible with and subversive of the ancient, just, and constitutional rights of this and the rest of the *English* Colonies in *America.*" It made no effort to restate the extensive chronicle of grievances in Congress's 1774 Bill of Rights and List of Grievances, Declaration on Taking Up Arms of July 1775, or petitions to the British people, in part because those earlier documents had done a fine job of summarizing Americans' complaints. As Topsfield, Massachusetts, put it, "the whole conduct of the Court of *Great Britain*, and the fallacious conduct of their Governors appointed and sent into these Colonies," was "so well known, and have been, by much abler hands, set forth in such a clear, plain, and true light," that "we think it needless to enumerate any further particulars."[51]

In its Declaration on Taking Up Arms, Congress had, in any case, suggested that there was no need to "enumerate our injuries in detail" because one statute—the Declaratory Act of 1766—had summarized the whole by asserting Parliament's right to "make laws to bind us IN ALL CASES WHATSOEVER." In 1776, that phrase was repeated in one set of resolutions after another. The resolves of the Elk Battalion Militia of Chester County, Pennsylvania, signed by 660 men, began, "Whereas the King, Ministry and Parliament of *Great Britain*, have declared their right of making laws to bind the inhabitants of these Colonies in all cases whatsoever. . . ." In claiming a right to "force us, and take away our substance from us, and that at any time, or for any use, that they please, without our consent" (Topsfield), the British Parliament seemed to undercut all property rights since Americans could not "justly call that our own which others may, when they please, take from us against our will" (Palmer). It was "to enforce an unconditional submission" and so to establish its claim to "an uncontrollable right of binding these Colonies in all cases whatsoever" that, according to Maryland's Declaration of July 6, the "Legislative and Executive powers" of the British state had "invariably pursued for these ten years past a studied system of oppression."[52]

In explaining their conversion to Independence, state and local "declarations" usually focused on a handful of events of 1775 and 1776. Those they cited were essentially the same that William Henry Drayton emphasized in his charge to the Charlestown grand jury. Some instructions, particularly those of the states, constructed a case for Independence by bringing charges against the King that were "plain and certain," referring back to specific acts that remain readily identifiable; and they, again like Drayton, were eager to show that the King's government had violated several established rights of Englishmen. But the resolutions of many towns and counties were more historical and personal than legal in character. That is, they sought to explain how, why, and even when the men who drafted and adopted those resolutions had become converted to Independence, which they again explained as a response to a finite number of relatively recent events.

Among the developments that had "greatly altered" public affairs, even Pennsylvania's conservative assembly gave prominent attention to the "contempt" with which the King had received Congress's "Olive Branch Petition" of 1775. The colonists had begged "as children to a father to be heard and relieved," the townsmen of Palmer, Massachusetts, observed, "but all to no purpose." Despite "every peaceable endeavour of the United Colonies to get redress of grievances, by decent, dutiful, and sincere petitions and representations to the King and Parliament, giving every assurance of our affection and loyalty, and praying for no more than peace, liberty and safety under the *British* Government," the freemen of Charles County, Maryland, recalled, they had "received nothing but an increase of insult and injury" or, as Virginia's instructions put it, "increased insult, oppression, and a vigorous attempt to effect our total destruction." "For the prayer of peace," Boston asserted, the King had "tendered the sword; for liberty, chains; and for safety, death." How, asked New York's Mechanics in Union, could the Americans "contentedly continue the subjects of . . . a Prince, who is deaf to our petitions for interposing his Royal authority in our behalf, and for redressing our grievances, but . . . seems to take pleasure in our destruction?"[53]

The war itself, over a year old by the time Congress decided on Independence, made continued expressions of allegiance to the King absurd. The fleets and armies of George III were "daily employed in destroying the people, and committing the most horrid devastations on the country" (North Carolina). They had been sent to America in the hope that "they might awe us into submission" and so "enlarge the influence of the Crown as to enable it to rivet their shackles upon the people of *Great Britain.*" The plan came to a crisis, the town of Malden, Massachusetts, asserted, on the "ever memorable 19th of *April.* We remember the fatal day! The expiring groans of our countrymen yet vibrate on our ears. . . . We hear their blood crying to us from the ground for vengeance; charging us . . . to have no further connection with a King who can"—and the following words were adapted from *Common Sense*—"unfeelingly hear of the slaughter of his subjects, and composedly sleep with their blood upon his soul!"⁵⁴

The way the British prosecuted the war confirmed this view. In the course of the struggle, "the lives of hundreds" had been destroyed; "flourishing towns burnt down and demolished; property seized and taken, secretly and openly," and "thousands reduced from easy and affluent circumstances to poverty and distress" (Buckingham County, Virginia). The British, moreover, had "excited the savages of this country to carry on a war against us, as also the negroes to imbrue their hands in the blood of their masters, in a manner unpractised by civilized nations" (Pennsylvania's Conference of Committees). The charge that the British were instigating Indians and slaves to fight the colonists had appeared in Congress's Declaration on Taking Up Arms, but it took on new force from the Crown's use of Indian allies against colonial forces in Canada, and from Lord Dunmore's proclamation of November 1775. Nor was the fear of slave insurrection confined to Virginia: North Carolina's instructions claimed that royal governors in other colonies had also offered protection to slaves who murdered their masters.⁵⁵

Parliament's Prohibitory Act, which took force when the King signed it on December 22, 1775, assumed a prominent place in all the state and many local resolutions on Independence except for those from Massachusetts, where the war itself received more attention. "By a late act," Virginia's instructions asserted, "all these Colonies are declared to be in rebellion, and out of the protection of the *British* crown;

our properties subject to confiscation, our people, when captivated, compelled to join in the murder and plunder of their relations and countrymen; and all former rapine and oppression of *Americans* declared legal and just." The Pennsylvania Assembly also included among a short list of critical developments "the late act of Parliament declaring the just resistance of the Colonists against violences actually offered, to be rebellion, excluding them from the protection of the Crown, and even compelling some of them to bear arms against their countrymen," as did the Pennsylvania Conference of Committees, North Carolina, Connecticut, and Maryland, as well as several Chesapeake counties and Pennsylvania battalions.[56]

George III's hiring of German soldiers to fight the colonists was cited almost everywhere and seems to have been decisive in alienating large numbers of colonists from the Crown. "The treaties of the King of *Great Britain* for engaging foreign mercenaries to aid the forces of that kingdom in their hostile Enterprises against America" appeared on the Pennsylvania Assembly's select list of critical events along with the Prohibitory Act; and Boston (like Maryland) linked that development with the King's use of Indians and slaves, charging that George III had "invited every barbarous nation whom he could hope to influence, to assist him" in realizing his "inhuman purposes."[57] The colonies would be hard-pressed to hold their own against the King's "formidable fleet of *British* ships, with a numerous army of foreign soldiers, in *British* pay" that were "daily expected on our coast" (Charles County, Maryland). But if they "bid the last adieu" to Britain, the freeholders of Buckingham County, Virginia, said, perhaps "some foreign power may, for their own interest, lend an assisting hand . . . and enable us to discharge the great burthens of the war, which otherwise may become intolerable."[58]

Occasionally states or local groups mentioned other events that struck them as relevant. Charlotte County, Virginia, said that the Prohibitory Act and "a late letter from the Secretary of State to Governour *Eden*" of Maryland had dispelled any doubts about Britain's intentions for America and demonstrated that it sought to establish only "the most abject slavery." The colonists had intercepted letters from Lord George Germain, the King's new Secretary for the American Colonies, to Eden, who still exercised the office of governor and was, in fact, popular among Marylanders. Two of the letters were dated

December 23, 1775, and had accompanied a copy of the Prohibitory Act. They indicated that Eden had sent confidential information to England. More significant, the letters said that the King was determined, "in concurrence with Parliament, to pursue the most vigorous measures for reducing his rebellious subjects in *North America* to obedience," and announced that seven regiments and a fleet of frigates and small ships were being sent to restore "legal Government" in the Southern colonies. Those forces would go first to North Carolina, then to South Carolina or Virginia "as circumstances of greater or less advantages shall point out," and Germain told Eden to work with Virginia's Governor Dunmore in assisting their operations.[59]

The Pennsylvania Assembly, Maryland's Convention, and the freemen of Talbot County, Maryland, also cited the King's reply to the petition presented to him by the City of London on March 22, 1776, news of which had arrived in Philadelphia during the early days of June. In refusing the Londoners' request that he announce the terms of a just and honorable peace before using British armed power to crush the Americans and saying he would alleviate the Americans' miseries only when their "rebellion" was over, the King finally destroyed many colonists' desperate hopes for a peaceful settlement. In his reply to London, the Maryland Convention said, "the unrelenting Monarch of *Britain* . . . at length avowed, his determined and inexorable resolution of reducing these Colonies to abject slavery." The same piece of news probably prompted a statement by the Pennsylvania Conference of Committees that George III "hath lately insulted [i.e., exacerbated] our calamities, by declaring that he will show us no mercy until he has reduced us." Even for the Pennsylvania Assembly, the King's response to the City of London, like the contempt with which he received the Congress's petition, the Prohibitory Act, and the treaties he had negotiated for engaging foreign mercenaries, manifested "such a determined and implacable resolution to effect the utter destruction of these Colonies, that all hopes of a reconciliation, on reasonable terms, are extinguished."[60]

"Our enemies denounce [i.e., announce] our ruin," Buckingham County said, "from the whole of their conduct," and the consistency of the King's speeches with the addresses, resolutions, and acts of Parliament meant that only "the ignorant, credulous, and unwary" could still hope for a settlement. That "general confidence . . . necessary to the support of every kind of Government" seemed "entirely annihilated, without a prospect of reunion of affections sufficient to restore it." Reconciliation and a return of the colonists to British rule came to seem not just impossible, but dangerous. The memory of past injuries would "perpetually keep alive the flame of jealousy," provoking new impositions and then new acts of resistance such that "the whole body-politick" would constantly be subject to "civil commotions" (Boston). Moreover, if the British regained the powers they had held in 1763, "the life of every man who has been active in the cause of his country would be endangered" (Malden).[61]

In their emphasis on particular events, the news of which had sometimes arrived in the colonies only recently, these documents reveal an American people that was well informed and adopted Independence after analyzing the implications of specific recent developments. From the beginning of the Anglo-American conflict, in fact, colonists had scoured newspapers for news of events that might reveal who exactly was responsible for their grievances and what that implied for them. The events of 1775–76 implicated the King, but some of the instructions, particularly those passed earlier in the spring, held back from putting exclusive responsibility on George III. North Carolina (April 12) referred to "the usurpations and violences attempted and committed by the King and Parliament," who acted "pursuant to the plan concerted by the *British* Ministry for subjugating *America*," as if the Ministry was mainly responsible. Virginia's instructions of May 15 similarly referred to "an imperious and vindictive Administration." New Hampshire (June 15) identified "the *British* Ministry, arbitrary and vindictive," as the villain without so much as mentioning the King.[62] Except perhaps for those of North Carolina, which at least mentioned the King, these instructions continued the standard British practice of attributing wrongdoing to the King's advisors because the king could "do no wrong." Even Connecticut's instructions of June 14 began by blaming "the King and Parliament of *Great Britain*" for attempting to exercise powers "incompatible with and subversive of the ancient, just, and constitutional rights of this and the rest of the *English* Colonies in *America*," although it went on to renounce allegiance to the King alone.[63]

By late June and early July, when Virginia and New Jersey inaugurated the first permanent state constitutions, and as states began to adopt documents that were formally labeled "Declarations" rather than instructions or resolutions, the American declarations of Independence arrived at their mature, revolutionary form. Pennsylvania's "Declaration on the subject of the Independence of this Colony of the Crown of *Great Britain*"—the title the Conference of Committees gave the instructions on Independence it adopted on June 24—placed responsibility firmly on the King, as had the English Declaration of Rights. It began:

> Whereas, *George* the Third, King of *Great Britain*, &c., in violation of the principles of the *British* Constitution, and of the laws of justice and humanity, hath, by an accumulation of oppression unparalleled in history, excluded the inhabitants of this, with the other *American* Colonies, from his protection. . . .

The Pennsylvania Declaration then went on, in another "whereas" clause, to cite other offensive acts of the King. The preamble Jefferson drafted for the Virginia constitution (adopted on June 29) and the opening section of the New Jersey constitution (July 2) also blamed the King. So did the "DECLARATION of the Delegates of MARYLAND" on Independence (July 6): "We the Delegates of *Maryland* in Convention assembled," it said, "do declare, that the King of *Great Britain* has violated his compact with this people, and that they owe no allegiance to him." By blaming the King, these documents announced that the authority of the British state had, as a consequence of its actions, dissolved, and that the legitimate exercise of power had reverted to the sovereign people.[64]

That narrowed attribution of responsibility was not simply formulaic. To blame the King was, of course, the way Englishmen announced revolution, but local resolutions and instructions testify that Americans also blamed the King because they had become convinced that he was personally responsible for their grievances, and they found that realization painful. The address of the New York Mechanics in Union (May 29) described their discovery of the King's responsibility in a highly rhetorical manner:

> When we cast a glance upon our beloved continent, where fair freedom, civil and religious, we have long enjoyed, whose fruitful fields have made the world glad, and whose trade has filled with plenty of all things, sorrow fills our hearts to behold her struggling under the heavy load of oppression, tyranny, and death. But when we extend

our sight a little farther, and view the iron hand that is lifted up
against us, behold it is our King; he who, by his oath and station, is
bound to support and defend us in the quiet enjoyment of all our glorious rights as freemen, and whose dominions have been supported
and made rich by our commerce.

After mentioning George III's inattention to the Americans' petitions
for redress and his apparent pleasure in the destructiveness of a war
protracted by a "cruel Ministry" and in which colonial towns were
burned, vessels seized, and "sons of liberty" murdered, leaving "weeping widows" and "helpless orphans to bemoan the death of an affectionate father," the Mechanics concluded they "would rather choose to
separate from, than to continue any longer in connection with such
oppressors."[65]

Others spoke directly of the distress that decision involved. With
"sorrow of heart" the freemen of Talbot County, Maryland, beheld
"the King of *Great Britain* inexorably determined upon the ruin of our
liberties." George III was "the Prince we once adored" (Wrentham,
Massachusetts); he was "the Prince . . . in support of whose Crown
and dignity, not many years since, we would most cheerfully have ex-
pended life and fortune" (Boston). "When dissensions first arose," the
freeholders of Buckingham County, Virginia, recalled, "we felt our
hearts warmly attached to the King of *Great Britain* and the Royal
family . . . At that time we wished to look upon the Ministry and Parliament as the only fountain from which the bitter waters flowed, . . .
considered the King as deceived and misguided by his counsellors,"
and hoped "he might, in proper time, open his eyes, and become a mediator between his contending subjects." But "now the case is much altered"; the measures "still pursued against *America* leave no room to
expect such an interposition from motives of goodness and affection."
"King George the Third . . . has manifested deliberate enmity towards
us," the committee of Charlotte County, Virginia, said, "and, under
the character of a parent, persists in behaving as a tyrant," and so
it renounced allegiance not to Britain but to him, personally, "forever."[66]

Were these professions sincere? The question arose because, in his
October 1775 speech to Parliament, George III asserted that American
statements of loyalty and desire for reconciliation were meant "only to
amuse," that is, to conceal their ambition for Independence. As if to

refute him—and so to set the record straight—one set of local resolutions after another emphasized how profound a change their commitment to Independence involved. "A few years ago, sir," the town of Topsfield, Massachusetts, said in instructing its representative to the General Court, the question of Independence

> would have put us into a surprise, and, we apprehend, would have been treated with the utmost contempt. We then looked on ourselves happy in being subjects of the King of *Great Britain*. It being our forefathers' native country, we looked up unto them as our parent State; and we have always looked upon it as our duty, as well as our interest to defend and support the honour of the Crown of *Great Britain*, and we have always done it . . . counting ourselves happy when in the strictest union and connection with our parent State.

"But the scene is now changed," they said; "our sentiments are altered." The townsmen of Malden, Massachusetts, also recalled the time when they "loved the King and the people of *Great Britain* with an affection truly filial," when they "felt . . . interested in their glory," shared "their joys and sorrows," and "cheerfully" spent their blood and treasure in the British cause. While Britain "continued to act the part of a parent state" they were "happy in our connection with her, nor wished it to be dissolved; but our sentiments," they said, in words like those of both Topsfield and Buckingham County, Virginia, "are altered. It is now the ardent wish of our souls that *America* may become a free and independent State."[67]

Sometimes these statements embellished the past. When, for example, had the people of Malden, as they claimed, "cheerfully poured the fruits" of "all" their labor into the lap of the mother country? No doubt affection for the King finally gave way in the course of 1775 and 1776, but criticisms of George III had begun in the early 1770s. By the spring of 1776, states and localities also expressed disillusionment with the British people, and that was new. Both the First and Second Continental Congresses had petitioned the British people, and it was to them that Massachusetts appealed after Lexington and Concord. A sense of common interest sustained hope in their "friendly dispositions": once the Americans were successfully subdued, the colonists argued, the British administration would impose the same arbitrary rule within the British Isles. As Jefferson put it in his draft of Congress's Declaration on Taking Up Arms, the British people had "nothing more to expect from the same common enemy than the humble favor of being last devoured."[68]

What precisely the British people could do was another issue. Since the electorate had returned essentially the same Parliament to power in the general election of 1774, and no further election had to be held for another seven years, popular insurrection seemed their only recourse. At least some Americans had hoped that Congress's nonimportation program would awaken the British people, or that they would follow the colonists' example in taking up arms. But such expectations were no sooner raised than they collapsed: "I Believe the account of the rising in England is not to be depended on," Congressman Josiah Bartlett wrote his wife in December 1775;[69] and by May 1776 the town of Boston concluded that the British people had passed over "the most pathetick and earnest appeals to their justice with an unfeeling indifference," that "the hopes we placed on their exertions have long since failed. In short," the town said, "we are convinced that it is the fixed and settled determination of the King, Ministry, and Parliament . . . to conquer and subjugate the colonies, and that the people there have no disposition to oppose them." The freemen of Charles County, Maryland, also concluded that "nothing virtuous, humane, generous, or just" could be expected from the British King "or nation," and so declared that their "affection for the people" as well as allegiance to George III was "forfeited on their part." Even Pennsylvania's Conference of Committees noted that there was "reason to believe" that "too many of the people of *Great Britain*" had "concurred in the . . . arbitrary and unjust proceedings against us."[70]

The conclusion drawn from these considerations was comforting because it seemed utterly clear. Unlike New York's Mechanics, who said they "chose" to separate from their oppressors, most states and localities insisted they had no choice at all. In the current "state of extreme danger," the Virginia instructions said, the colony had "no alternative left but an abject submission to the will of . . . overbearing tyrants, or a total separation from the Crown and Government of *Great Britain*." Appealing to "the Searcher of hearts for the sincerity of former declarations, expressing our desire to preserve the connection with that nation," Virginia insisted that it had been "driven from that inclination by their wicked counsels, and the eternal laws of self-preservation." North Carolina similarly said that the colonies' efforts to achieve reconciliation "on constitutional principles" had failed, and "no hope remains of obtaining redress by those means alone which have been hitherto tried." Connecticut also referred to the Americans' "state of extreme danger" in which "no alternative is left us but absolute and indefinite submission to such claims as must terminate in the extreme of misery and wretchedness, or a total separation from the King of *Great Britain*." After insisting on the sincerity of its earlier wishes for reconciliation, Connecticut added that it was "compelled . . . to use such means as God, in his providence, hath put in our power for our necessary defence and preservation." Or, as William Henry Drayton put it in his charge to the Charlestown Grand Jury, once British government attempted the destruction of America, "Nature cried aloud, self-preservation is the great law; we have but obeyed."[71]

To justify revolution by "the eternal laws of self-preservation" or, as others sometimes said, "the first law of nature," drew upon a politicized religious literature that equated the laws of God with the laws of nature and described self-preservation as "an instinct by God implanted in our nature."[72] That justification was distinct from another that emphasized the contractual origins of government and the right of the people to judge their rulers—in a word, on the "Whig" principles that were conveniently stated in John Locke's *Second Treatise of Government* and by many other seventeenth- and eighteenth-century English and Scottish writers. Colonists encountered those principles in the press and from the pulpit; even Blackstone's *Commentaries on the Laws of England* cited "the principles of Mr. Locke" in interpreting the English Revolution of 1689. By the late eighteenth century, "Lockean" ideas on government and revolution were accepted everywhere in America; they seemed, in fact, a statement of principles built into English constitutional tradition.[73] Sometimes those principles were explicitly stated—as when the Committee for the Lower District of Frederick County, Maryland, resolved unanimously

> That all just and legal Government was instituted for the ease and convenience of the People, and that the People have the indubitable right to reform or abolish a Government which may appear to them insufficient for the exigency of their affairs.[74]

Men could, of course, have both a contractual right and a God-given obligation to resist rulers attempting to destroy them; indeed, Locke himself and other secular English political writers referred at times to men's natural right and duty of self-preservation. Drayton, like many others, used both arguments, and obviously saw no conflict between them, although his "declaration of Independence" emphasized the King's breaking the "original contract" between King and people and his violation of fundamental law. But several other "declarations," particularly those adopted relatively early in the spring of 1776, which might be described as "first cut" efforts to explain Independence, tended to ground their position primarily upon "the first law of nature." Take Rhode Island's revolutionary law of May 4, 1776, which ended that colony's allegiance to the Crown. It began by asserting, in good Whig fashion, that "in all states, existing by compact, protection and allegiance are reciprocal; the latter being only due in consequence of the former." But after citing chapter and text to show that George III was attempting to destroy "the good people of this colony," and so was obviously not protecting them, it did not simply say that the King had thereby forfeited all claim to Rhode Islanders' allegiance. Instead it invoked a quasi-religious obligation of self-preservation. As a result of the King's acts, it said

> we are obliged, by necessity, and it becomes our highest duty, to use every means, with which God and nature have furnished us, in support of our invaluable rights and privileges; to oppose that power which is exerted only for our destruction.[75]

The emphasis on necessity did offer a cogent justification for Independence. It said, in effect, that separation was a last resort, undertaken only when all alternatives had failed. But it gave the state and local instructions and resolutions a tone of disappointment and desperation that was not altogether appealing. A people fighting for survival with their backs to the wall can inspire sympathy—but are they inspiring? Once the colonists began adopting documents formally labeled "Declarations," which, in the old English manner, sought broad support for their cause, they expanded their appeal beyond self-preservation and expressed "Whig" ideas with none of the compromises that had made the English Declaration of Rights so unsatisfactory as a statement of political principle. The Declaration issued by Pennsylvania's Conference of Committees asserted in a straightforward manner that "the obligations of allegiance (being reciprocal between a King and his subjects) are now dissolved on the side of the Colonists, by the despotism of the said King." Maryland's Declaration of July 6 proclaimed that the King had "violated his compact with this people, and that they owe no allegiance to him." Both states, moreover, said that they were "driven" to Independence not only for their own survival but to preserve their liberties and those of their children, which changed the spirit of the documents, committing those who approved them to a higher cause than saving their own necks, and so making the Declarations more inspirational than their predecessors.

Neither the Pennsylvania nor the Maryland Declaration was secularized. Both cited "the first principles of nature" and called on God to witness the justice of their cause. After announcing their willingness and that of their constituents to concur with Congress in declaring the colonies free and independent states, the Pennsylvania Conference went on to

> call upon the nations of *Europe*, and appeal to the great Arbiter and Governour of the Empires of the World, to witness for us that this declaration did not originate in ambition, or in an impatience of lawful authority, but that we were driven to it, in obedience to the first principles of nature, by the oppressions and cruelties of the aforesaid King and Parliament, of *Great-Britain*, as the only measure left to us to preserve and establish our liberties, and to transmit them inviolate to posterity.

Maryland said it was "compelled by dire necessity either to surrender our properties, liberties, and lives, into the hands of a *British* King and Parliament, or to use such means as will most probably secure to us and our posterity those invaluable blessings," and later insisted that

> No ambitious views, no desire of independence, induced the people of *Maryland* to form an union with the other Colonies . . . To maintain inviolate our liberties, and to transmit them unimpaired to posterity, was our duty and first wish; our next, to continue with, and dependant on, *Great Britain*. For the truth of these assertions, we appeal to that Almighty Being who is emphatically styled the Searcher of hearts, and from whose omniscience nothing is concealed.

Relying on God's "divine providence . . . and trusting to the justice of our cause," Maryland exhorted "every virtuous citizen to join cordially in defence of our common rights, and in maintenance of the freedom of this and her sister Colonies."[76]

Whatever principles they cited, and with whatever eloquence they made their appeal, the various state and local "declarations" all described the Americans' situation and the need for Independence in the same way. From their perspective, the colonists faced a King who stood resolutely behind the right of Parliament to pass laws for the colonies "in all cases whatsoever," who would not so much as receive their carefully drafted and explicitly loyal petitions for redress of grievances with graciousness, who had approved an act of Parliament that removed them from his protection and consigned their ships to be seized like those of open enemies, whose government authorized efforts to raise Indians and slaves against the colonists, who had carried on a war against them for a year and was at the time preparing a major military expedition, including hired German soldiers, to subdue them, and, despite early suggestions that he was sending peace commissioners, had publicly refused to state clearly the terms by which the dispute might be honorably settled. And their fellow subjects in Britain were unwilling or unable to help. Under the circumstances, American affection for Britain gave way, which made it even more unlikely that the conflict could be resolved by a negotiated settlement that involved the reestablishment of British rule.

The conflict, then, would be settled by arms, and the Americans had to do everything possible to avoid losing the contest on the battlefield. If the colonists were defeated and reduced to an "unconditional dependance" on the Crown, as a Virginia newspaper essayist said in early April of 1776, "many who have engaged in this business are irrevocably destined to the cord." Independence, with the possibility of foreign alliances, which most states authorized their delegates to negotiate as part of their instructions on Independence, was a step toward military survival and perhaps victory. And so the sooner the colonies declared their Independence, "the sooner they will be able to make effectual opposition, and establish their liberties on a firm and permanent basis."[77]

4.   Founding a Republic

The case was tightly argued and essentially convincing. It was not, however, the argument of Thomas Paine. State and local resolutions on Independence said nothing about the flaws of the British constitution, or the future of mankind, or the birthday of a new world. They suggest, in fact, that Paine's influence was more modest than he claimed and than his more enthusiastic admirers assume. *Common Sense* helped provoke public debate on Independence, as did the news from England that arrived at the time of its publication. But thereafter the argument for separation from Britain among Americans turned, as it always had, on what the Mother Country did, who was responsible for its actions, and what implications those considerations carried for the American future. Paine also influenced the language in which Independence was justified, but even there colonists used his words to comment on George III, the acts of his government, and their implications. Malden, Massachusetts, for example, borrowed Paine's words to condemn an "unfeeling" king, not monarchy; and James City County, Virginia, echoed *Common Sense* when it said "the blood of those fallen in our cause cries aloud, 'It is time to part.' "[78]

If there was no viable alternative to Independence by the spring of 1776, a substantial number of Americans were nonetheless discovering that the choice they made out of necessity had some real advantages. For one thing, an independent America would be isolated from what the town of Malden called "the contagion of venality and dissipation" that had spread through the British nation and explained its docility before "lawless domination." Pennsylvania's Conference of Committees also said "the publick virtue of this Colony (so essential to its liberty and happiness)" would be "endangered" by a future political union with the British king and nation. But concern for American "virtue," so much emphasized by recent historians, was a distinctly minor theme.[79]

The most commonly mentioned benefits were more concrete, and economic advantages finally appeared among them. Americans from the first had denied Parliament's right to bind them in "all cases whatsoever." They were, however, willing through much of the Anglo-American conflict to accept Parliament's regulation of trade if regulations served the interests of the British empire as a whole. By April 1776, however, William Henry Drayton observed that the British had constrained American manufacturing, while the new government of South Carolina actively encouraged it. British policy had also restricted colonial trade to make it "subservient to their commerce, our real interest being ever out of the question," while South Carolina's new government sought to extend trade with foreign nations and enabled merchants to make their purchases wherever they could do so on the most advantageous terms. Clearly these were "great benefits" that flowed from the revolution in government. The town of Malden also noted that, if the colonies returned to Crown rule as it had existed in 1763, their "arts, trade, and manufactures would be cramped." Despite such references, however, the promise of economic freedom and expansion was never powerfully yoked to the cause of Independence.[80]

The strongest advantage Independence brought was political, in the founding of new governments based entirely on popular choice. Paine had made a powerful case for eliminating hereditary rule and founding a "republic," but the idea was not new with him. On December 26, 1775, before *Common Sense* was published, the inhabitants of Pittsfield in the far western reaches of Massachusetts called for the founding of a new state government whose offices would be filled by popular choice. If "the right of nominating to office is not invested in the people," they said, "we are indifferent who assumes it whether any particular persons on this or on the other side of the [wa]ter." The experience of self-government under the ad hoc institutions of the revolution itself provided a powerful argument for republicanism. In late January 1776 the Massachusetts General Court congratulated the people of that colony for having acquired, in the makeshift arrangements prescribed by Congress, "a Form of Government" entirely under the "Influence and Controul of the People, and therefore more free and happy than was enjoyed by their Ancestors." Occasionally, however, the merits of self-government took people by surprise. In explaining its commitment to Independence, the town of Natick, Massachusetts, began, like others, by citing various acts of Parliament. Then, as if the idea had just occurred to them, the townsmen went on to denounce "the glaring impropriety, incapacity, and fatal tendency, of any State whatever, at the distance of three thousand miles, to legislate for these Colonies, which . . . are so numerous, so knowing, and capable of legislating," or to exercise a veto on laws that the colonists had approved through their representatives.[81] In that historic moment of late June 1776, the inhabitants of Natick realized, as other colonists did at other moments of revelation, that they were far more capable of governing themselves than Britain was or could ever be.

Some of the most moving and powerful arguments for self-government came from those who had just begun to experience it.

South Carolina's constitution of March 1776 was not, like Virginia's, a permanent government; it was supposed to last only until the "unhappy differences" between Britain and America were settled. Even so, William Henry Drayton argued, it gave South Carolinians a mode of government "in every respect preferable" to that under Britain. The Crown had sent royal governors who were utterly ignorant of the colonists, their laws and interests, men who were answerable to the King's ministry, and against whose misgovernment redress was impossible to secure "by any peaceable means." Now the people could choose governors from among themselves, raising even "the poorest man" to "the highest dignity" because of his "virtue and merit." They could elect persons who knew them and the state intimately, who were disposed to defend them and promote their happiness, and who "without the least difficulty" could be removed from office "and blended in the common mass." Why would anyone abandon such a constitution and return to royal government?[82]

Members of the Charlestown grand jury readily accepted as "sacred" the duty Drayton impressed upon them to understand, explain, and defend the new constitution to others. They lamented the necessity that had forced the people to resume the powers of government, but expressed the "most unfeigned joy" in the state's new constitution, whose benefits were "not confined or limited to any ranks or degrees of men" but extended "generally, equally, and indiscriminately to all, from the richest to the poorest."[83] Another grand jury for the Cheraws District in the remote north-central part of the state was even more enthusiastic. Independence had come, it testified, by acts of Great Britain, and was "unsought for and undesired." But "what every one once dreaded as the greatest misery, they now unexpectedly find their greatest advantage. . . . We now feel," the jurymen testified, "every joyful and comfortable hope that a people could desire in the present Constitution and form of Government established in this Colony," a constitution by which "the rights and happiness of the whole, the poor and the rich, are equally secured." With an evangelical fervor they went on "most earnestly" to

> recommend it to every man, as essential to his own liberty and happiness, as well as that of his posterity, to secure and defend with his life and fortune a form of Government so just, so equitable, and promising; to inculcate its principles to their children, and hand them down

to them unviolated, that the latest posterity may enjoy the virtuous fruits of that work, which the integrity and fortitude of the present age had, at the expense of their blood and treasure, at length happily effected.[84]

Soon several towns in Massachusetts called upon their representatives to endorse not just Independence but a revolution in government. The conduct of Great Britain, said the townsmen of Acton, "confirm us in the opinion that the present age will be deficient in their duty to God, to their posterity, and themselves, if they do not establish an *American* Republick. This is the only form of Government we wish to see established." Others simply assumed that, with Independence, "a Republic or Commonwealth will be our Form of Government." The explanation for ending monarchy, if any was offered, was simple: "we can never be willingly subject to any other King than He, who, being possessed of infinite wisdom, goodness, and rectitude, is alone fit to possess unlimited power."[85]

Nowhere was the ending of the old regime an end in itself; everywhere it was intimately connected with the founding of new governments that marked a more dramatic departure from the past than what Parliament achieved in 1689. John Adams assumed that Independence and the founding of new governments were so closely tied that they amounted to the same thing. Congress's resolutions of May 10 and 15, 1776, linked them, and so did state instructions that authorized their Congressional delegates to vote not only for Independence and foreign alliances—which they assumed were necessary for survival but impossible without Independence—but also for a more permanent American Confederation. In granting those powers, however, state after state explicitly reserved to itself, as North Carolina put it, "the sole and exclusive right of forming a Constitution and Laws for this Colony." Those reservations of state power to define their domestic institutions were important, and would be recalled time and again in the nineteenth century, when Americans again debated the division of authority between local and central governments.[86]

Even before the issue of Independence had been decided, discussion was under way on what rules and practices should prevail in a self-governing republic. In Maryland, county meetings that endorsed Independence also demanded that members of their provincial convention vote individually, not by county, that the convention's meetings be open to the public, and that all votes be recorded and published "with the proceedings, for the information of the publick respecting the behaviour of their Representatives." Meanwhile, coastal towns in Massachusetts argued that, since every man should have equal liberty and an equal right to representation in the legislature, the allocation of seats in the General Court should be tied more closely to population. "But care should be taken that the Assembly be not unwieldy," Boston added, since "the largest bodies of men do not always despatch business with the greatest expedition, nor conduct it in the wisest manner." Whatever the details, however, the task of designing institutions, even the "privilege of choosing Deputies to form a Government," was awesome since, as the Pennsylvania Conference of Committees reminded the people of that state, "your liberty, safety, happiness, and everything that posterity will hold dear to them, to the end of time, will depend upon their deliberations." And so the people helped turn a colonial rebellion into a revolution. As Paine observed years later in *The Rights of Man*, "the independence of America, considered merely as a separation from England, would have been a matter of but little importance." Independence acquired broad historical significance because it was "accompanied by a revolution in the principles and practise of governments."[87]

The many Americans who debated Independence did not need Thomas Jefferson to remind them that the "whole point" of the controversy that had absorbed their lives lay not in the ending of an old regime but in the founding of a better one, or that their future would be bound up with that powerful but ambiguous word, equality. Their resolutions and instructions on Independence provided together an eloquent expression of the American mind, which the Congressional Declaration of Independence was also meant to do, and they gradually captured "the proper tone and spirit called for by the occasion." The most moving of the state documents, the Declarations of the Pennsylvania Conference of Committees and of Maryland, did not provide models for Congress's draftsman to follow since they were issued after his work was done. By June 1776, however, it had become clear that in announcing their separate nationhood, Americans had to do more than demonstrate that the British Crown had forced them to the measure. They needed to overcome fear and the sense of loss, to link their cause with a purpose beyond survival alone, to raise the vision of a better future so compelling that in its name men would sacrifice even life itself.

Congress's Declaration of Independence had to meet the same challenge, which it did in a somewhat different way, and under circumstances that were less than ideal for the creation of a political masterpiece.

CHAPTER III

Mr. Jefferson and His Editors

THE COMMITTEE Congress appointed to draft a declaration of Independence left no minutes of its proceedings, and the account of its work written nearest the event, Thomas Jefferson's "Notes of Proceedings in the Continental Congress," is succinct to a fault. Members of the committee, Jefferson said, "desired" or asked him to prepare it; "it was accordingly done, and being approved by them, I reported it to the house on Friday the 28th. of June when it was read and ordered to lie on the table."[1] Both Jefferson and John Adams later helped flesh out that bare-bones story. However, most of their testimony on the drafting process was written between a quarter and a half century later, which even at the time raised questions about its accuracy, and, it turns out, for good reason. What they said contains one mistake after another.

Fortunately, Adams's statements can be compared to Jefferson's, and both can be measured against shards of evidence that have survived from the 1770s. Piecing together the story demands sifting through contradictory clues with the care of a shrewd detective; indeed, a good part of the story involves evaluating evidence. So do detective stories, but they at least reveal by their endings exactly who did what and when, which is not the case here. Learning how the Declaration of Independence was written is more like assembling an immensely complex jigsaw puzzle in which some pieces are "teases," serving only to mislead, while others necessary to complete the picture have probably been lost forever. Whenever a new piece of the puzzle does appear, as still happens occasionally, it fills out the picture, adding or changing some details, which can affect interpretations of the document.

Despite those problems, the picture's subject—or the story of how the Declaration was written—is reasonably clear. It includes not a single talented writer but a group of men working under tight time constraints to complete this one of many assignments the Continental Congress gave them. Adams and Jefferson dominate the scene in part because they lived long enough to tell the story to a generation of interested younger Americans, but also because they in fact played central roles in the Declaration's development. They were a curious team, the short, stocky, feisty New Englander, who spoke his mind even more openly on paper than he did in Congress (which is one reason why Adams is eternally quoted), a doer who was well read, particularly on law and politics, and the somewhat younger Virginian, tall and slim, as shy and reserved as Adams was frank and open, and probably more thin-skinned than Adams, with whom he shared a love of reading, but on a broader range of topics. Both were deeply caught up in the controversy between Britain and its American colonies because it raised intrinsically interesting and important issues, and also gave capable young men a chance to earn a place in history, which Adams and Jefferson craved. In ordinary times, their lives would probably have been ordinary, their minds preoccupied with the mundane problems of practicing law or running a plantation; but they lived in an extraordinary time which made extraordinary achievements possible. Adams's main accomplishment was Independence itself; Jefferson wrote the Declaration with the encouragement of Adams, who later fought for its adoption. But the other committee members, particularly Connecticut's Roger Sherman and Robert R. Livingston of New York, also contributed to the creation of the Declaration. So did Benjamin Franklin, although his involvement was late and brief. In the end, the efforts of these five men produced a workable draft that the Congress itself, sitting as the Committee of the Whole, made into a distinguished document by an act of group editing that has to be one of the great marvels of history.

What Jefferson did and how he worked remains a critical part of the story not only because he composed most of the draft, but because the chronicle of his labor shows what familiar human strategies he used in producing what would later seem a remarkable literary accomplishment. He was no Moses receiving the Ten Commandments from the hand of God, but a man who had to prepare a written text with little time to waste, and who, like others in similar circumstances, drew on earlier documents of his own and other people's creation, acting within the rhetorical and ethical standards of his time, and producing a draft that revealed both splendid artistry and signs of haste. In the end, considering its complex ancestry and the number of people who actively intervened in defining its text, the Declaration of Independence was the work not of one man, but of many.

I. The Drafting Committee

According to the Continental Congress's official journal, the drafting committee was appointed on June 11. It probably met soon thereafter, either that day or the next, perhaps with Jefferson as its head.[2] In his autobiography, written in 1805, John Adams said that the committee had "several meetings, in which were proposed the Articles of which the Declaration was to consist, and minutes made of them." In other words, it outlined the document, dividing it into sections or "Articles," probably decided in at least general terms what its various parts should say, and committed those conclusions to paper as "minutes" or instructions to its draftsman. Then the drafting committee—or "Committee of Five," as it came to be called—had to decide who would write the document. As Adams told the story, the committee

appointed Mr. Jefferson and me, to draw them [i.e., the "Articles"] up in form, and cloath them in a proper Dress. The Sub Committee met, and considered the Minutes, making such Observations on them as then occurred: when Mr. Jefferson desired me to take them to my Lodgings and make the Draught. This I declined and gave several reasons for declining. 1 That he was a Virginian and I a Massachusettensian. 2. that he was a southern Man and I a northern one. 3. That I had been so obnoxious for my early and constant Zeal in promoting the Measure, that any draught of mine, would undergo a more severe Scrutiny and Criticism in Congress, than one of his composition. 4thly and lastly that would be reason enough if there were no other, I had a great Opinion of the Elegance of his pen and none at all of my own . . . He accordingly took the Minutes and in a day or two produced to me his Draught . . .[3]

Adams repeated the story in a letter to Timothy Pickering on August 6, 1822. The committee met, he said, "discussed the subject, and then

appointed Mr. Jefferson & me to make the draught." Adams also restated the arguments by which he persuaded Jefferson to do the writing, including his insistence that " 'You can write ten times better than
I can.' 'Well,' said Jefferson, 'if you are decided I will do as well as I
can.' 'Very well, when you have drawn it up we will have a meeting.' A
Meeting we accordingly had, and conned the paper over."[4]

The next year Pickering quoted passages from the Adams letter
in a Fourth of July oration at Salem, Massachusetts. Pickering's talk
was subsequently published and came to Jefferson's attention. In
several details, Jefferson wrote his friend James Madison in August
1823, Adams's memory was mistaken, which, "at the age of eighty-
eight and forty-seven years after the transactions of Independence, . . .
is not wonderful." At the time Jefferson was himself eighty years old,
but, he claimed, he had "written notes, taken by myself at the moment
and on the spot." The Committee of Five met, he said, and "unanimously pressed on myself alone to make the draught. I consented; I
drew it; but before I reported it to the committee, I communicated it
separately to Dr. Franklin and Mr. Adams, requesting their corrections, because they were the two members of whose judgments and
amendments I wished most to have the benefit, before presenting it to
the committee. . . . Their alterations were two or three only, and
merely verbal. I then wrote a fair copy, reported it to the committee,
and from them, unaltered, to Congress."[5]

Whether or not Jefferson really had in hand notes he had taken "at
the moment and on the spot"—and it seems likely that he did not[6]—
his account was right on some points, wrong on others. An entry in
John Adams's diary for June 23, 1779, which was, of course, much
nearer the event, supports the assertion that Jefferson alone was appointed to draft the Declaration. It said that the committee "appointed [Mr.] Jefferson a subcommittee" to draw up a declaration,
with no suggestion that Adams was also on that subcommittee.[7] The
drafting committee probably gave Jefferson responsibility for all the
reasons Adams stated. The political advantages in having the Declaration written by a Virginian and a Southerner rather than a New Englander, and above all one from Massachusetts, were powerful: it would
demonstrate that support for Independence went far beyond the "radical" children of the Puritans, who were sometimes accused of pulling
the country in their preferred "democratical" or "anti-monarchical" di-

rection. Adams, moreover, had in fact been an outspoken defender of Independence in Congressional debates, perhaps to the point of obnoxiousness, while Jefferson, a notoriously weak speaker, remained silent. It could well be that the exchange Adams recalled between himself and Jefferson occurred as the committee debated who should be given responsibility for producing a draft—not later, within a subcommittee of two members, as Adams indicated in 1805 and 1822. Of all the writers in Congress, moreover, Jefferson was the best available. John Dickinson's opposition to Independence disqualified him from this particular assignment (though Dickinson was appointed to the committee to draft the Articles of Confederation as well as that to propose model treaties with foreign nations), and Benjamin Franklin was suffering from a fit of gout so severe that he stopped attending Congress about a week before the drafting committee was appointed. As late as June 26—two days before the committee submitted its draft—he wrote a friend that he hoped "in a few days to be strong enough to come to town and attend my Duty in Congress."[8]

Franklin's illness did more than disqualify him as a possible draftsman of the Declaration. It meant that only four people attended most and perhaps all meetings of the Committee of Five, a detail neither Adams nor Jefferson seems to have remembered. Jefferson did, however, submit his draft to Adams and Franklin, as he said in 1823. Part of the evidence that he did so lies in what Jefferson later called "the original rough draft" of the document. It was in fact not an "original rough draft," but a copy Jefferson made from earlier compositional fragments to show members of the drafting committee. He then used that copy to record all subsequent revisions in the Declaration of Independence, including those Congress made in early July. The manuscript is therefore heavily interlined, incorporating several "generations" or layers of revisions. Some of the editorial changes seem to be in Adams's and Franklin's handwriting, although most were made by Jefferson. We also know that Jefferson submitted the manuscript to Adams because Adams made a copy for himself, which he kept. It shows the text at an early stage in its development.[9]

Moreover, when Jefferson sent the draft to Franklin on a "Friday morn" in June, he attached a note whose significance seems to have gone virtually unnoticed, although it was published by Julian Boyd in the first volume of the modern *Papers of Thomas Jefferson* and again thirty-two years later, in 1982, by the editors of the *Papers of Benjamin Franklin*. "The inclosed paper has been read and with some small alterations approved of by the committee," it began. "Will Doctr. Franklin be so good as to peruse it and suggest such alterations as his more enlarged view of the subject will dictate? The paper having been returned to me to change a particular sentiment or two, I propose laying it again before the committee tomorrow morning, if Doctr. Franklin can think of it before that time."[10] That description of the drafting procedure contradicts Jefferson's 1823 account, by which he showed the draft to Adams and Franklin before submitting it to the committee, and the committee did nothing between appointing him draftsman and approving the text he submitted with two or three "verbal" adjustments suggested by Adams and Franklin. In fact, the committee met not only at the beginning and end of the drafting process, but in between. It took responsibility for the overall design of the Declaration if Adams was right, and, as Jefferson told Franklin, requested other revisions that seem to have gone beyond simple adjustments in wording (i.e., it asked him to change "a particular sentiment or two," that is, some of the ideas it stated). Those revisions were probably recorded on the "original rough draft"—in Jefferson's handwriting—before Franklin received it.

Not that the committee members had nothing else to do. On June 11, Congress put John Adams on both the committee to draft a declaration of Independence and another "to consider of a compensation to the secretary for his services." The next day it placed Adams and Franklin—despite his illness—on a committee to prepare "a plan of treaties to be proposed to foreign powers," and appointed Robert Livingston and Roger Sherman to the committee charged with preparing articles of confederation. On June 13 it also elected Adams and Sherman members of a committee "to form a Board of war and ordnance," which was a major assignment since the board was created to bring order to the administration of the army. It assumed responsibility for supplies and personnel, including appointments and promotions, and also for prisoners. Adams was probably delighted that Jefferson agreed to write the Declaration since Adams's other assignments, particularly the creation of draft treaties and the "Board of war," seemed substantively more important and so more worth the investment of his precious time.[11]

Not even Jefferson—who, by Julian Boyd's calculations, served on some thirty-four Congressional committees in a six-month period during 1775 and 1776[12]—was given respite. On Saturday, June 15, Congress put him on a committee of four to "digest and arrange" a long list of resolutions concerning the Canadian campaign and to evaluate a complicated set of papers regarding a cartel for the exchange of prisoners that General Benedict Arnold had entered into at the Cedars, a point on the St. Lawrence above Montreal. On Monday, June 17, that committee submitted two reports, both in Jefferson's hand. Their completion no doubt claimed one of the only two Sundays between the appointment of the Committee of Five and the submission of its draft Declaration of Independence, and Sunday was the one day of the week on which Congress did not regularly meet.[13] As it happened, on the afternoon of Friday, June 21, Congress adjourned until Monday morning, giving Congress two days "off." But if, as seems likely, that was the "Friday morn" on which Jefferson sent Franklin his manuscript of the Declaration to review, he had by then not only completed his draft but submitted it to Adams and other committee members for comments. By then, too, he had been appointed to another committee to draw up rules and regulations for Congressional debates (June 20), and on Monday, June 24, he and Sherman were made members of a committee "to enquire into the causes of the miscarriages in Canada," which was granted the power to send for persons and papers to facilitate its inquiry.[14]

Did Jefferson perhaps skip some Congressional sessions to get extra writing time? Normally the nonattendance of one delegate would have been of little consequence. However, after June 13, when Wythe and Lee left Congress, the Virginia delegation was relatively thin, which put more responsibility on those who remained. No surviving document records daily attendance at the Continental Congress. But anxiety over the fate of the Canadian campaign, which deeply concerned Jefferson, and the possibility that news of the British fleet's movements might arrive and demand immediate attention probably kept him at his seat—perhaps with his "original rough draft" on the table before him so he could poke at it in dull moments, eliminating words and phrases, substituting others in their place. His physical presence at Congress might, in fact, help explain his appointment to so many committees.

In 1823 Jefferson took no exception to Adams's statement to Pickering—which Jefferson saw, since it appeared in the published version of Pickering's oration—that "We were all in haste; Congress was impatient." That statement makes sense considering the many obligations members of the drafting committee had to acquit simultaneously. Because he worked in the midst of so harried a situation, Jefferson did not have the luxury of, say, sixteen or seventeen days to write the Declaration, as one might assume considering the time between the appointment of the drafting committee and its submission of a draft to Congress. He had to sandwich that job in among his various other duties. Fortunately, Jefferson could write quickly. Adams claimed that he produced a draft in a day or two and, considering the rapidity with which Jefferson completed the two reports submitted to Congress on June 17, the statement is believable.[15]

Jefferson was fortunate in other ways, too. Writers forced to complete an assignment under great time pressure often look around for texts they can adapt for their purposes, and Jefferson managed to find two. One was the draft preamble for the Virginia constitution that he had just finished and which was itself based upon the English Declaration of Rights; the other, a preliminary version of the Virginia Declaration of Rights, had been drafted for the convention sitting in Williamsburg by George Mason, an older man whom Jefferson knew and respected. By modern lights, Jefferson's use of texts by other authors might be considered to detract from his achievement. In the eighteenth century, however, educated people regarded with disdain the striving for novelty. Achievement lay instead in the creative adaptation of preexisting models to different circumstances, and the highest praise of all went to imitations whose excellence exceeded that of the examples that inspired them. Young men were taught to copy and often to memorize compelling passages from their readings for future use since you could never tell when, say, a citation from Cicero might come in handy. Jefferson had not only a good memory but, as his biographer Dumas Malone observed, "a rare gift of adaptation": he creatively used Palladian models in designing his house at Monticello and struggled mightily to achieve the impression of an English landscape in the very un-English climate of Virginia. He applied the same gift in drafting the Declaration of Independence, which was as much in keeping with the values of his time as it facilitated the completion of his task under the constraints he faced in June 1776.[16]

In the end, the draft Declaration of Independence submitted to Congress by the Committee of Five was so much the work of Thomas Jefferson that it can justly be called "Jefferson's draft." But within the committee and, above all, later, when Congress let loose its collective editorial talent on Jefferson's prose, other men made more substantial and constructive contributions to the Declaration of Independence than pleased Jefferson at the time, and far more than he remembered in the 1820s.

2. Jefferson's Draft: The Charges Against the King

Whatever written directions or "minutes" the Committee of Five gave Jefferson have long since disappeared. There is nonetheless good reason to think that the "articles of which the Declaration was to consist," as Adams described them, included a set of charges against the King. The English Declaration of Rights and previous colonial documents of a similar sort had included such a set of claims, and it would have been difficult to justify American Independence without citing its causes. And so, when Jefferson took up his responsibility as draftsman of the Declaration of Independence, he turned to the preamble of his constitution for Virginia, numbering and then rearranging its charges against the King.[17] Items in that list were meant to show how George III had endeavored to "pervert" the government of Virginia "into a detestable & insupportable tyranny." In the Declaration of Independence, the various charges had essentially the same purpose: to demonstrate that the King had inflicted on the colonists "unremitting injuries and usurpations," all of which had as a "direct object the establishment of an absolute tyranny." Specific accusations catalogued those "injuries and usurpations"; they were the "facts" that the Declaration of Independence "submitted to a candid world." Independence was justified only if the charges against the King were convincing and of sufficient gravity to warrant the dissolution of his authority over the American people. They were therefore essential to the Declaration's central purpose, not subordinate to an assumed premise, as Carl Becker argued in one of the more tortured passages in his book on the Declaration.[18]

At the time, no one doubted the importance of the charges against the King. British and Loyalist critics of the Declaration, like good defense lawyers, turned immediately to that part of the document, and had a field day ripping it apart. But first they had to figure out exactly what events lay behind the charges. Today most Americans, including professional historians, would be hard put to identify exactly what prompted many of the accusations Jefferson hurled against the King, which is not surprising since even some well-informed persons of the eighteenth century were perplexed. Thomas Hutchinson, a Loyalist historian and ex-governor of Massachusetts, began a pamphlet criticizing the Declaration by recalling the statement of a "Noble Lord"—Philip Yorke, the second Earl of Hardwicke—that he was "utterly at a loss [as] to what facts many parts of the Declaration of Independence published by the Philadelphia Congress referred, and . . . wished they had been more particularly mentioned" so he could "better judge of the grievances, alleged as special causes of the separation of the Colonies from the other parts of the Empire."[19] Hutchinson proceeded to explain the more ambiguous of Jefferson's charges, many of which, he argued in his *Strictures upon the Declaration of the Congress at Philadelphia* (1776), were "false and frivolous." Many "facts . . . alledged to be the evidence of injuries and usurpation" were purposely stated in an obscure manner, he said, because if they were clear they would reveal the criminality of the American revolt rather than justify it. A writer in the *Scots Magazine* similarly remarked that the Americans' effort to cite "some justifiable reasons of their separating themselves from G[reat] Britain" suffered for lack of "truth and sense" and so reflected "no honour" on their "erudition or their honesty." John Lind's *An Answer to the Declaration of the American Congress* (1776) again focused almost exclusively on the charges against the King, and came to much the same conclusion.[20]

Hutchinson and Lind were closely connected with the British ministry, which helps explain why they wrote the two most sustained criticisms of the Declaration of Independence. That they opposed American Independence and the arguments advanced to justify it was therefore predictable, but not the way they criticized the Declaration. The charges of frivolousness and obscurity could hardly have been brought against most state and local declarations on Independence, which for the most part cited a few prominent events of undoubted seriousness—the King's failure to respond to the colonists' petitions, his consent to the Prohibitory Act, his use of slaves, Indians, and, finally, German "mercenaries" against them. Jefferson chose instead to

construct a much longer and less selective list of accusations. His preamble to the Virginia constitution included sixteen charges against the
King, one of which cited his consent to six different "pretended acts
of legislation." And in revising that document for the Declaration of
Independence, Jefferson made an already long list even longer: the
draft submitted to Congress included twenty-one charges against the
King, and increased to nine the "pretended acts of legislation" in what
became the thirteenth of those charges.[21]

The accusations Jefferson leveled against George III fell into three
general groups.[22] The first, which is by far the most obscure and prob-
lematic, includes the first eight "by" clauses in the Virginia preamble.
The King had attempted to establish a tyranny, they said,

1.   by putting his negative on laws the most wholesome &
necessary for the public good
2.   by denying to his governors permission to pass laws of immediate and pressing importance, unless suspended in their operation for
his assent &, when so suspended, neglecting to attend to them for
many years:
3.   by refusing to pass certain other laws, unless the persons to be
benefited by them would relinquish the inestimable right of
representation in the legislature:
4.   by dissolving legislative assemblies repeatedly & continually for
opposing with manly firmness his invasions on the rights of the
people:
5.   when dissolved, by refusing to call others for a long space of
time, thereby leaving the political system without any legislative
head.
6.   by endeavouring to prevent the population of our country & encouraging the import[atio]n of foreigners & raising the conditions
of new appropriations of lands: . . .[23]
7.   by keeping among us in times of peace standing armies & ships
of war:
8.   by affecting to render the military independant of & superior to
the civil power:[24]

In preparing the committee's draft Declaration of Independence,
Jefferson rewrote these clauses, eliminating here, as in subsequent
charges against the King, the "by" construction—and so distancing the
American Declaration from its grandparent, the English Declaration

of Rights—and substituted a series of independent statements beginning "he has" that drummed home the King's iniquity by attributing
direct responsibility to him, point after point. He also added words or
phrases to the spare language of the Virginia preamble in an effort to
emphasize further the King's infamy (i.e., he had neglected "utterly" to
attend to American laws; the right of representation was a formidable
danger "to tyrants only"; in refusing to call new legislatures George III
had left the state "exposed to all the dangers of invasion from without,
& convulsions within"). Four new charges against the King were inserted in this first part of the Declaration of Independence, which are
numbers four and eight through ten below:

[1] he has refused his assent to laws the most wholesome and necessary for the public good:

[2] he has forbidden his governors to pass laws of immediate &
pressing importance, unless suspended in their operation till his
assent should be obtained; and when so suspended, he has neglected
utterly to attend to them.

[3] he has refused to pass other laws for the accommodation of large
districts of people unless those people would relinquish the right of
representation in the legislature;[25] a right inestimable to them, &
formidable to tyrants only:

[4] he has called together legislative bodies at places unusual,
uncomfortable, & distant from the depository of their public
records, for the sole purpose of fatiguing them into compliance with
his measures:

[5] he has dissolved Representative houses repeatedly & continually,
for opposing with manly firmness his invasions on the rights of the
people:

[6] he has refused for a long time after such dissolutions to cause
others to be elected, whereby the legislative powers, incapable of annihilation, have returned to the people at large for their exercise, the
state remaining in the meantime exposed to all the dangers of invasion from without, & convulsions within:

[7] he has endeavored to prevent the population of these states; for
that purpose obstructing the laws for naturalization of foreigners; refusing to pass others to encourage their migrations hither; & raising
the conditions of new appropriations of lands:

[8] he has suffered the administration of justice totally to cease in

some of these states, refusing his assent to laws for establishing judiciary powers:

[9] he has made our judges dependent on his will alone, for the
tenure of their offices, and the amount and payment of their salaries:

[10] he has erected a multitude of new offices by a self-assumed
power, & sent hither swarms of officers to harrass our people, and
eat out their substance:

[11] he has kept among us, in times of peace, standing armies and
ships of war without the consent of our legislatures:

[12] he has affected to render the military independent of & superior
to the civil power:[26]

In his critique of the Declaration, Hutchinson noted that the first
of these accusations was "general . . . without any particulars to support it," which made it "fit enough to be placed at the head of a list of
imaginary grievances." In fact, the way Jefferson presented his charges
suggests a continuing influence of the English Declaration of Rights,
which also presented its charges in general terms. But when the Lords
and Commons accused James II of "assuming and exercising a Power
of dispensing with and Suspending of Lawes, and the Execution of
Lawes without Consent of Parliament," there was no doubt what they
meant because the accusation rested on conspicuous public events,
such as the King's grant of toleration to Catholics without Parliament's consent. That was not the case with Jefferson's statement that
George III had "refused his assent to laws the most wholesome and
necessary for the public good." What did he mean? Hutchinson
guessed that the charge was inspired by laws restricting colonial legislatures from issuing paper currency, which did cause considerable distress. But this was only a guess.

There's a real issue, of course, whether anyone should have to
think hard about what Jefferson meant. Declarations in English law
were supposed to be "plain and certain." And some charges no doubt
were—in specific colonies. The problem with this opening set of
charges against the King, in short, was not just in the language with
which they were stated, but in the fact that they referred to controversies over the King's use of his executive powers that had often been
played out on the provincial level, within individual colonies. The accusations Jefferson added to those in his Virginia preamble are partic-

ularly good examples; indeed, they were probably included because certain delegates wanted their province's pet complaint put on the list. If a delegate was on the drafting committee he could make his point during its deliberations; others had to buttonhole Jefferson or some other committee member privately. John Adams almost certainly suggested the fourth charge, that the King had "called together legislative bodies at places unusual, uncomfortable, & distant from the depository of their public records." It recalled the royal governor's moving the Massachusetts House of Representatives to Cambridge in 1768 when, as Hutchinson said, the recent arrival of British troops and a "riotous, violent opposition to Government" in Boston seemed to make it unwise for the assembly to meet there. The eighth charge, that the King had "suffered the administration of justice totally to cease in some of these states," was inspired by an extended controversy in North Carolina. The superior courts there were finally closed in 1773 because the assembly absolutely refused to exclude from its court bill a clause allowing the attachment of nonresidents' property in prosecutions for debt, which the Crown considered contrary to the substance and spirit of English law.[27]

The ninth charge rested upon a broader base. Controversies over the independence of the colonial judiciary raged in Pennsylvania and New York beginning in the 1750s, then "exploded" in the next decade after an order of December 1761 from the King in Council permanently forbade the issuance of colonial judicial commissions for any term except "the pleasure of the Crown." In England, judges had enjoyed tenure on good behavior since 1701, and in 1761 George III himself described the independence of the judiciary as "one of the best securities of the rights and liberties of his subjects." Fears that the Crown sought to control the judiciary increased after the Townshend Act of 1767 suggested that it would soon begin paying judges' salaries, as it did in Massachusetts six years later.[28] The tenth accusation, that George III had sent "swarms of officers to harrass our people, and eat out their substance," was probably prompted by the American Board of Customs Commissioners, which was located in Boston, and its dependents—clerks, surveyors, tide waiters and the like—whom the Bible-reading folk of Massachusetts considered much like an Old Testament plague of locusts.

There was good reason for referring to some of these cases in only the most oblique way. To examine them more closely confirms the adage that there are two sides to every story, and the colonists weren't always clearly on the side of the angels. In North Carolina, for example, the royal governor, acting on instructions from the Crown, had tried to reestablish the courts, but the assembly refused to recognize his authority to do so or to pay the judges. Who, then, "suffered the administration of justice totally to cease"? The assembly's intransigence might well have been justified; still, the situation was complex. The less said the better. As for the American Board of Customs Commissioners, could it honestly be alleged, Hutchinson asked, that "thirty or forty additional officers in the whole Continent" were "the Swarms which eat out the substance of . . . three millions of people"? And how outrageous was it that the governor moved the Massachusetts assembly to Cambridge? Harvard College had convenient public rooms in which the legislature could assemble, Hutchinson noted, and representatives could lodge in private houses, so Cambridge was "not *uncomfortable*." Moreover, it was "within four miles of the Town of Boston, and less *distant* than any other Town fit for the purpose." The assembly had in fact voluntarily adjourned to Cambridge when smallpox raged in Boston. To include this "unimportant dispute between an American Governor and his Assembly" as "a ground to justify Rebellion" seemed absurd to Hutchinson. John Lind found the allegation so "truly ridiculous" that "at first blush it looks as if inserted by an enemy . . . to throw an air of ridicule on the declaration in general." To find it "gravely alleged" among the justifications of revolt "that the members of an assembly happened, once upon a time, to be straitened in their apartments, and compelled to sit on strange seats, and to sleep in strange beds," Lind said, was "unexampled in the history of mankind."[29]

But what of the other eight of this first group of charges—that is, those that Jefferson took from his Virginia preamble? It remains possible—as several historians have proven—to rummage through colonial history in search of events that could give substance to Jefferson's charges, some of which are so buried in the remote history of colonies other than his own that Jefferson probably never heard of them.[30] The question remains what Jefferson meant when he said, for example, that the King had "refused his assent to laws the most wholesome and necessary for the public good," or neglected to give his consent to "laws of immediate & pressing importance," or attempted to retard American population growth by discouraging immigration. Luckily, Jefferson left important clues to the meaning of his opening charges against the King in a still earlier document of his composition, a set of draft instructions for Virginia's delegates to the First Continental Congress that he wrote in 1774.

Jefferson had not been asked to draft those instructions—he had a way of producing documents in the hope they might be adopted, which in this case did not happen. His friends nonetheless published his text as *A Summary View of the Rights of British America* (1774). Jefferson proposed, in short, that Congress send an appeal to the King "penned in the language of truth, and divested of those expressions of servility which would persuade his majesty that we are asking favors and not rights." A "freedom of language and sentiment," one free of subterfuge, seemed to him fitting for a free people: "Let those flatter, who fear: it is not an American art." Because Jefferson refused to be constrained by the conventions of British politics, including that which insisted "the king can do no wrong," *A Summary View* became the first sustained piece of American political writing that subjected the King's conduct to direct and pointed criticism. Jefferson not only raised all of the first eight charges against the King that he would later include in his draft preamble to the Virginia constitution, but discussed them *in the same order* they appeared in that document.[31]

The criticisms of the King in *A Summary View* were founded upon a theory of empire that was becoming ever more widely shared among Americans in 1774, and an understanding of early American history that remained controversial since it conveniently overlooked considerable conflicting evidence. The first colonists of British North America, Jefferson insisted, settled the country at their own expense and—despite the charters and patents for which they applied before leaving England—were as free of British authority as the Saxon migrants to England had been of German rule. After a time, however, the settlers decided to adopt the legal system of their mother country and to establish a continuing union with it by submitting themselves to "the same common sovereign." But while the King thereby became "the central link connecting the several parts of the empire," the colonists remained outside the jurisdiction of Parliament, whose power was confined to the British Isles. It followed that all exertions of Parliamentary power over the Americans were improper, and in *A Summary*

View Jefferson called upon George III to reclaim the power of vetoing acts of Parliament—which the Crown had lost early in the eighteenth century—"to prevent the passage of laws by any one legislature of the empire" that violated "the rights and interests of another." He then went on to argue that in other ways, too, the King's exercise of power was open to criticism.[32]

"For the most trifling reasons, and sometimes for no conceivable reason at all," Jefferson asserted in *A Summary View*, "his majesty has rejected laws of the most salutary tendency," which some two years later became the first item in his preamble to the Virginia constitution. He gave one example: the King had blocked the efforts of colonial legislatures to discourage the slave trade "by imposing duties which might amount to a prohibition." Royal governors had vetoed acts to tax slave imports (which was not the same as ending slavery) in Virginia and several other colonies, including New Jersey and Massachusetts.[33] *A Summary View* went on to criticize the King for having "permitted our laws to lie neglected in England for years," and condemned instructions to royal governors that allowed them to "pass no law of any moment" unless it had a suspending clause "so that, however immediate may be the call for legislative interposition, the law cannot be executed till it has twice crossed the Atlantic, by which time the evil may have spent it's whole force" (charge two). Without providing more detail, Jefferson went on to attack at some length "a late instruction to his majesty's governor of . . . Virginia, by which he is forbidden to assent to any law for the division of a county, unless the new county will consent to have no representative in the assembly." That provided a basis for the third charge against the King in the Virginia preamble and, later, fortified by similar controversies over the extension of representation in New York, New Jersey, and New Hampshire, in the Declaration of Independence.[34]

Two long paragraphs in *A Summary View* covered the next two charges, that the King had dissolved representative bodies, as the Virginia preamble put it, "repeatedly & continually" for opposing invasions of their rights, and had refused to call others "for a long space of time," but, again, Jefferson gave no concrete examples from the colonial past.[35] Next he discussed "an error in the nature of our landholdings," arguing that American land titles were allodial, like those of their Saxon ancestors, since "America was not conquered by William the Norman, nor it's lands surrendered to him or any of his successors," and so remained free of the feudal duties William the Conqueror had introduced into Britain. Unfortunately, the first settlers were "laborers, not lawyers," and were persuaded to accept as real the "fictitious principle that all lands belong originally to the king." While the Crown continued to grant lands for small sums and on reasonable rents, there was little reason to "arrest the error and lay it open to the public view." But the King, he said, had lately increased the terms of purchase and the fees to which lands were subject, "by which means the acquisition of lands being rendered difficult, the population of our country is likely to be checked." That became the charge in the Virginia preamble that the King had "endeavoured to pervert" the government of that colony into a tyranny "by endeavouring to prevent the population of our country & for that purpose . . . raising the conditions of new appropriations of lands" as well as by "obstructing the laws for the naturalization of foreigners," and, in the Declaration of Independence, "refusing to pass [laws] to encourage [foreigners'] migrations hither."[36]

Finally, *A Summary View* charged that "his majesty has from time to time sent among us large bodies of armed forces, not made up of the people here, nor raised by the authority of our laws." The King's grandfather, George II, had asked Parliament's permission before bringing Hanoverian troops into England, and George III was similarly bound, Jefferson argued, to get the permission of colonial legislatures before sending troops into their territories. "To render these proceedings still more criminal against our laws," he continued, "instead of subjecting the military to the civil power, his majesty has expressly made the civil subordinate to the military." Again, he did not state when or where or how that was done. These assertions became clauses seven and eight in the Virginia constitution's charges against the King, and then eleven and twelve in the committee's draft Declaration of Independence.[37]

The fact that in 1774 Jefferson had raised eight of the first twelve charges against the King that subsequently appeared in the Declaration of Independence is itself a sign of how different the Declaration was from state and local resolutions on Independence. In 1774, the colonists had not yet been converted to Independence: indeed, Jefferson's *Summary View* was an overtly loyal document that urged George III to redress the colonists' grievances, remove fears of "future incroachment" on American freedom, and "establish fraternal love and harmony thro' the whole empire."[38] Clearly, then, the grievances in the Declaration were not meant to identify, as did the state and local declarations, precisely which events had reconciled Americans to separate nationhood. The grievances in the Declaration served a different purpose—not to explain the Americans' change of heart but to justify revolution by proving that George III was a tyrant.

Jefferson's statement of grievances in *A Summary View* was, of course, only slightly more specific in content than the Virginia preamble and the Declaration of Independence. But his failure to cite concrete examples to support the charges against the King did not mean they lacked historical foundation. The King had, for example, approved a suspension of the New York and Massachusetts assemblies for opposing Acts of Parliament (charge 5); British troops were sent to Boston in 1768 and again in 1774, when the Crown established military government there (charges 11 and 12). To have cited chapter and verse for charge after charge in the preamble and the Declaration would have been tedious in the extreme. In fact, from a literary point of view, Jefferson's decision to cite his charges in general terms, as they had been stated in the English Declaration of Rights, was probably wise. Even his inclusion of grievances that sometimes pertained to a single colony in the Declaration of Independence is defensible: that all Americans felt aggrieved by the oppression of any among them testified to a sense of fellowship that confirmed their identity as a people.

Many of the charges in this opening section of the Declaration had, however, played a relatively inconspicuous part in the imperial controversy, which is why the Declaration left observers, then and now, scrambling to figure out what it was talking about. Thomas Hutchinson suggested as much when he asked whether the colonists had ever petitioned the King

—To give his Assent to these wholesome and necessary Laws to which he had refused it?

—To allow his Governors to pass laws without a su[s]pending clause, or without the people's relinquishing the right of Representation?

—To withdraw his instructions for calling legislative bodies at unusual, uncomfortable and distant places?

—To allow Assemblies, which had been dissolved by his order, to meet again?

—To pass laws to encourage the migration of foreigners?

—To consent to the establishment of judiciary Powers?

—To suffer Judges to be independent for the continuance of their offices and salaries?

—To vacate or disannul new erected offices?

—To withdraw his troops *in times of peace*, until it appeared that the reason for it was to give a free course to Rebellion?

In fact, individual colonies had submitted petitions or remonstrances against the acts that prompted some of these complaints, and the final three charges mentioned by Hutchinson had appeared as grievances in the First Continental Congress's address to the King of October 1774. It remains nonetheless significant that all the allegations Hutchinson singled out for comment and described as "grossly misrepresented," or founded on events "so trivial and insignificant as to have been of no general notoriety . . . , or mere contests between Governors and Assemblies, so light and transient, as to have been presently forgot," came from the first group of charges against the King. Those that followed referred to far more familiar and widely contested events of the revolutionary era.[39]

NO ONE WOULD DESCRIBE as trivial or insignificant the next group of charges against the King, which was based upon the ninth clause in Jefferson's preamble to the Virginia constitution. The King had endeavored to establish a tyranny, the preamble said,

by combining with others to subject us to a foreign jurisdiction giving his assent to their pretended acts of legislation

[1] for quartering large bodies of armed troops among us:

[2] for cutting off our trade with all parts of the world:

[3] for imposing taxes on us without our consent:

[4] for depriving us of the benefits of trial by jury:

[5] for transporting us beyond seas to be tried for pretended offenses:

[6] for suspending our own legislatures & declaring themselves invested with power to legislate for us in all cases whatsoever[40]

With a rewritten opening statement and the addition of three new subsidiary "for" clauses (numbers two, seven, and eight below), this became the thirteenth accusation in the Declaration of Independence as it emerged from the drafting committee:

he has combined with others to subject us to a jurisdiction foreign to
our constitutions and unacknowledged by our laws; giving his assent
to their acts of pretended legislation,

[1] for quartering large bodies of armed troops among us;

[2] for protecting them by a mock-trial from punishment for any
murders which they should commit on the inhabitants of these
states;

[3] for cutting off our trade with all parts of the world;

[4] for imposing taxes on us without our consent;

[5] for depriving us of the benefits of trial by jury;

[6] for transporting us beyond seas to be tried for pretended offenses;

[7] for abolishing the free system of English laws in a neighboring
province, establishing therein an arbitrary government, and
enlarging it's boundaries so as to render it at once an example & fit
instrument for introducing the same absolute rule into these states;

[8] for taking away our charters, abolishing our most valuable laws,
and altering fundamentally the forms of our governments;

[9] for suspending our own legislatures, & declaring themselves
invested with power to legislate for us in all cases whatsoever:[41]

The "others" with whom the King had combined were the members of Parliament. By the mid-1770s, Jefferson's conception of the
Empire as a set of separate political communities bound together
under the King was shared by many other leading Americans, for
whom the British Parliament was therefore a "foreign jurisdiction"
with only a "pretended" power of legislation over the colonies. The
framers of the Declaration, as Carl Becker noted, made it "a point of
principle not on any account to pronounce the word Parliament"—
and, in fact, the final version of that document did not use the word
even once. We seem to hear the framers say, Becker went on, "Of
course, our British brethren have their legislature, as we have ours. But
with their legislature we have nothing to do, God forbid! The very
name of the thing escapes us!"[42] From the British point of view, that
position was ridiculous, but since the colonists had repeatedly and vo-
ciferously contested acts of Parliament from the beginning of the
Anglo-American controversy, these charges recalled conspicuous and
readily identifiable public events.

The order in which Jefferson listed the charges was, however, not altogether obvious. The Stamp Act of 1765, by which Parliament proposed to levy a direct tax on the colonists, provoked the first general wave of opposition by colonists, who insisted they could be taxed only by representatives whom they had chosen, that is, by those in their provincial legislatures. Jefferson seems to have considered beginning the list of "pretended acts of legislation" in the Virginia constitution with the phrase "for imposing taxes on us without our consent." However, he crossed out the phrase there and inserted it further down the list. The order of the "pretended acts of legislation" in the committee's draft Declaration of Independence bore no relationship whatsoever to the order in which they occurred: the first recalled the Quartering Acts of 1765 and 1774, the second the Administration of Justice Act of 1774, the third the New England Restraining and Prohibitory Acts of 1775. The next item, on taxes, was based on several Parliamentary enactments including the Sugar Act (1764), Stamp Act (1765), and Townshend Acts (1767) and possibly the Tea Act of 1773. Colonists' right to trial by jury was injured by Parliament's extending the jurisdiction of Admiralty Courts, which lacked juries, to cover offenses against the Stamp Act. The right to trial by juries "of the vicinage" was also threatened by an act of 1772 "for the better securing and preserving His Majesty's Dock Yards, Magazines, Ships, Ammunition and Stores" and the Administration of Justice Act of 1774, under which colonial offenders could be tried in England, and by Parliament's encouraging the King to apply against the colonists an old statute of Henry VIII that allowed trials in England for treason or misprision of treason committed outside the realm (35 Hen. VIII, c.2). Even the most assiduous efforts have, however, identified no colonists of the revolutionaries' generation who were actually transported "beyond seas to be tried for pretended offenses." The seventh provision referred to the Quebec Act of 1774, the eighth to the Massachusetts Government Act of 1774, the ninth to the New York Restraining Act of 1767 and the Declaratory Act of 1766.[43]

Jefferson's arrangement of grievances may seem random, but it was in fact carefully considered. He had listed Parliament's violations of American rights in roughly the same sequence in his draft of Congress's Declaration on Taking Up Arms, although there he began with Parliament's efforts to tax colonists without their consent and listed two subsequent complaints in reverse order.⁴⁴ His purpose, it seems, was to arrange this set of grievances in order of increasing political atrocity, and so to build rhetorical momentum, ending with the suspension of colonial legislatures—about as extreme an outrage as one independent legislature could commit on another—and the assertion of power to bind the colonists in "all cases whatsoever." Those two acts alone, he observed in his draft of the Declaration on Taking Up Arms, formed "a basis broad enough whereon to erect a despotism of unlimited extent."⁴⁵

IN THE THIRD and concluding group of charges against the King, Jefferson finally arrived at those recent events that were repeatedly and often exclusively cited in state and local resolutions on Independence. His first draft of the Virginia constitution charged that the King had attempted to erect a tyranny

[10] by plundering our seas, ravaging our coasts, burning our towns, & destroying the lives of our people:

[11] by inciting insurrections of our fellow subjects with the allurements of forfeiture & confiscation

[12] by prompting our negroes to rise in arms among us; those very negroes whom by an inhuman use of his negative he hath refused us permission to exclude by law:

[13] by endeavoring to bring on the inhabitants of our frontiers the merciless Indian savages whose known rule of warfare is an undistinguished destruction of all ages, sexes, & conditions of existence.

[14] by transporting at this time a large army of foreign mercenaries to compleat the works of death, desolation, & tyranny already begun with circumstances of cruelty & perfidy so unworthy the head of a civilized nation

[15] by answering our repeated petitions for redress with a repetition of injuries:

[16] and finally by abandoning the helm of government & declaring us out of his allegiance & protection.⁴⁶

Jefferson rearranged these provisions in preparing the Declaration of Independence, numbering the charges in his draft Virginia constitution, then inserting numbers between clauses to indicate that the

sixteenth charge would open rather than close this sequence, and that
the fourteenth and thirteenth charges would come after the tenth. He
also added a new charge after the eleventh, and radically expanded
what was originally the twelfth:

[14] he has abdicated government here, withdrawing his governors,
& declaring us out of his allegiance & protection:

[15] he has plundered our seas, ravaged our coasts, burnt our towns
& destroyed the lives of our people:

[16] he is at this time transporting large armies of foreign mercenaries to compleat the works of death, desolation & tyranny, already
begun with circumstances of cruelty & perfidy unworthy the head of
a civilized nation:

[17] he has endeavored to bring on the inhabitants of our frontiers
the merciless Indian savages, whose known rule of warfare is an
undistinguished destruction of all ages, sexes, & conditions of
existence:

[18] he has incited treasonable insurrections of our fellow citizens,
with the allurements of forfeiture & confiscation of property:

[19] he has constrained others taken captives on the high seas to bear
arms against their country, to become the executioners of their
friends & brethren, or to fall themselves by their hands.

[20] he has waged cruel war against human nature itself, violating
it's most sacred rights of life & liberty in the persons of a distant
people who never offended him, captivating & carrying them into
slavery in another hemisphere, or to incur miserable death in their
transportation thither. this piratical warfare, the opprobrium of *infidel* powers is the warfare of the *Christian* king of Great Britain.
determined to keep open a market where MEN should be bought &
sold, he has prostituted his negative for suppressing every legislative
attempt to prohibit or to restrain this execrable commerce and that
this assemblage of horrors might want no fact of distinguished die,
he is now exciting those very people to rise in arms among us, and to
purchase that liberty of which *he* has deprived them, by murdering
the people upon whom *he* also obtruded them; thus paying off
former crimes committed against the *liberties* of one people, with
crimes which he urges them to commit against the *lives* of another.
in every stage of these oppressions, [21] we have petitioned for redress
in the most humble terms; our repeated petitions have been answered
only by repeated injury.[47]

These changes gave Jefferson's draft Declaration of Independence a character or feeling different from that of his preamble to the Virginia constitution or, for that matter, the body of state and local resolutions on Independence that had emphasized so many of the same events. There was much to be said for concluding with the King's formally putting the Americans out of his protection by approving the Prohibitory Act, as Jefferson had done in the Virginia preamble. Like Parliament's assertion of power to bind the colonies "in all cases whatsoever," with which Jefferson concluded his list of "pretended acts of legislation," that act seemed to encapsulate the tendency of all the charges that preceded it. For John Adams and others, the Prohibitory Act provided a wholly sufficient justification for Independence since the Americans had no obligation of allegiance to a King who publicly promised to treat them like enemy aliens. Here, however, the King's abdication of government and declaring the colonists out of his protection seems to introduce the charges that follow, which list positive acts of an increasingly heinous character—the burning of colonial towns, turning slaves, Indians, and German mercenaries against them, making American seamen fight against their countrymen.

Some dispassionate observers might object that royal governors were sometimes forced from office, not withdrawn by the King, as the fourteenth charge said, or ask whether any Americans had actually been forced "to become the executioners of their friends & brethren," which the Prohibitory Act made theoretically possible. Still more profound questions were raised by the elaborate charge at the end of the list, which not only denounced George III for turning slaves against their masters and blocking provincial efforts to tax the importation of slaves (which Jefferson had, of course, already condemned in the very first charge), but imposed upon him entire responsibility for the slave trade, an accusation that one seeks in vain elsewhere in the literature on behalf of Independence.

Jefferson obviously invested considerable effort in the passage and meant it to be the emotional climax of his case against the King. But his effort failed. The charge leaves a sense of "labored effort, of deliberate striving for an effect that does not come."[48] The problem is not, I think, that Jefferson lacked passion, as Becker argued;[49] a subsequent section of the draft Declaration revealed passion in abundance. Jefferson did, however, have difficulty expressing emotion. In his long passage on the slave trade, he described a form of "piratical warfare" that he had personally witnessed, and attempted to convey its iniquity and that of the King by enlisting strong words such as "prostituted," "murdering," "execrable," "assemblage of horrors." The attempt foundered in part because the image of King George personally "captivating and carrying" innocent Africans into slavery was patently unbelievable. This complex passage, with its "twisted language and logic," also invites misinterpretation. It does not call for the abolition of slavery, but, in its closing lines, actually condemns the King for opening the prospect of manumission to slaves if they supported his cause.[50]

And yet, curiously, John Adams liked what he called the "high tone" and "flights of oratory" in Jefferson's draft, and particularly in the passage "concerning negro slavery," which, however, he said in his 1822 letter to Pickering, "I knew his Southern brethren would never suffer to pass in Congress." Adams then volunteered that "there were other expressions which I would not have inserted if I had drawn it up, particularly that which called the king tyrant. I thought this too personal; for I never believed George to be a tyrant in disposition and in nature; I always believed him to be deceived by his courtiers on both sides of the Atlantic, and in his official capacity only, cruel. I thought the expression too passionate, and too much like scolding, for so grave and solemn a document." However, since the manuscript was still to be submitted to other committee members, Adams "thought it would not become me to strike it out," and he "consented to report it, and do not now remember that I made or suggested a single alteration." (In fact, Adams probably inserted two changes and Franklin five, all of which were essentially verbal.) Nor did he recall that the committee made any changes in Jefferson's draft. It was then that he noted, "We were all in haste. Congress was impatient,"[51] and, what he did not say, the members of the committee perhaps failed to spend more time than they did editing a document that seemed generally acceptable because they had their plates full with other business. For all those reasons, and, unless Adams's memory failed, from an uncharacteristic diffidence on his part (and Adams could well have been the committee's most cantankerous member), the draft Declaration presented to Congress was for the most part Jefferson's work.

Adams's criticism of the document remains striking. That Thomas Hutchinson, the Loyalist ex-governor of Massachusetts, or John Lind, a ministerial hack, was unconvinced by the Declaration of

Independence was to be expected. John Adams, on the other hand, was the foremost advocate of Independence in the Continental Congress, a man who would defend Jefferson's text through the difficult debates of early July with the determination of a prizefighter. If even he remained unconvinced that George III was a tyrant, then Jefferson's draft declaration had failed to prove a point central to its very purpose.

From a comparative perspective, it is difficult to avoid the conclusion that the states and localities had offered a more effective case for Independence by concentrating on a handful of specific events of 1775 and 1776 and arguing that they left Americans with no good alternative to separate nationhood. Jefferson agreed with that description of the Americans' position.[52] But in the Declaration of Independence he tried to show that Independence had become necessary—which implies that there was no reasonable alternative—in a different way. Groups of related documents, like the members of human families, can have different features and do similar things in different ways. The Declaration of Independence was distinguished from its American and English relatives in part by its effort to prove that George III was a tyrant,[53] which led to other distinctions such as the extraordinarily large number of grievances it listed. The key to the document's approach lies in the paragraphs that preceded and introduced the charges against the King and which were, in fact, themselves part of the document's distinctiveness.

3. Jefferson's Draft: A Revolutionary Manifesto

"Of the preamble [to the Declaration of Independence] I have taken little or no notice," John Lind wrote in 1776. "The truth is, little or none does it deserve." Hutchinson gave it scarcely more attention, devoting less than a paragraph to the Declaration's opening paragraphs before moving on to "the facts which are alleged to be the evidence of injuries and usurpations."[54] Most prominent modern studies have taken the opposite course, devoting little serious attention to the charges against the King, whose origins too often lay in the obscure quarrels of provincial politics, and focusing instead on the document's preface, or on words or phrases within it. From there they jump to the more familiar and perhaps more congenial intellectual world of eighteenth-century Europe. Carl Becker's landmark book of 1922, *The Declaration of Independence*, was subtitled *A Study in the History of Political Ideas*. Morton White's *The Philosophy of the American Revolution* (1978) used phrases from the opening section of the Declaration to examine the "epistemology, metaphysics, philosophical theology, and ethics upon which the revolutionaries rested their claim to independence." We cannot understand the revolutionaries' use of concepts such as self-evident truths, or the equal creation of men, inalienable rights, or happiness, White said, "without detailed probing of their writings and of those writings from which they borrowed."[55] And in *Inventing America: Jefferson's Declaration of Independence* (1978), Garry Wills again used phrases from the preface and also the closing paragraphs of Jefferson's draft as chapter headings in a book that attempted to demonstrate the critical contributions of Scottish philosophers to Jefferson's political thought.

The observation that Jefferson borrowed ideas from other writers was not original to the twentieth century. Richard Henry Lee, Jefferson recalled, said the Declaration had been "copied from Locke's treatise on government," and John Adams, in his 1822 letter to Timothy Pickering, asserted that there was "not an idea in it, but what had been hackneyed in Congress for two years before." But then Jefferson had been appointed not as an author in the modern sense but as a draftsman to realize on paper a declaration outlined in general terms by the Committee of Five. It would, however, be a strangely inept politician who failed to seize such an opportunity to express his own deep-felt convictions, even those that were not yet generally shared, and attempt to secure their endorsement by the committee and then by Congress. Jefferson had tried unsuccessfully, for example, to write his historical views into Congress's Declaration on Taking Up Arms, but then he had John Dickinson to contend with, which was no longer true, at least not in the drafting committee. In any case, Jefferson told Madison in 1823 that he "did not consider it part of my charge to invent new ideas altogether, and to offer no sentiment which had ever been expressed before." Whether he had gathered his ideas from reading or reflection, he added, "I do not know. I know only that I turned to neither book nor pamphlet while writing it."[56]

There his memory was probably accurate. Words and phrases remembered from past readings could easily have made their way into his text, where they might or might not have carried the implications expressed in the more systematic treatises from which they originally came. Resemblances between Jefferson's draft declaration and his own earlier writings could also have been produced from memory or from persisting patterns of thought. Access to a library might have been useful: according to Jefferson's autobiography, in May 1774, after news of the Boston Port Act arrived in Williamsburg, he and a set of fellow insurgent members of the House of Burgesses met in the council chamber "for the benefit of the library in that room" and "rummaged over" John Rushworth's *Historical Collections* of English documents from 1618 to 1648 "for the revolutionary precedents and forms of the Puritans of that day." They then "cooked up a resolution, somewhat modernizing [the Puritans'] phrases," for a day of fast and humiliation.[57] In June 1776, Jefferson could easily have visited the Library Company of Philadelphia, which was near the Pennsylvania State House where Congress met, but Jefferson seems to have had little time, and perhaps little need, for such "rummaging." Even echoes of the English Declaration of Rights in Jefferson's constitution for Virginia, which, in turn, fed into his draft Declaration of Independence, could have been recalled from what Douglass Adair described as his "careful, and, one might say, professional, study of English seventeenth-century history." The man obviously kept a wealth of words "stored . . . away in his head": Jefferson's famous statement that "the mass of mankind has not been born with saddles on their backs, nor a favored few booted and spurred to ride them legitimately by the grace of God," written in 1826 within weeks of his death, faithfully recalled the dying speech of England's Colonel Richard Rumbold, "an old one-eyed Cromwellian soldier" executed for treason in 1685. In his last speech, delivered from the scaffold, Rumbold said he was "sure there was no Man born marked of God above another; for none comes into the World with a Saddle on his Back, neither any Booted and Spurr'd to Ride him."[58] Access to so formidable an internal lexicon was a substantial asset to a man forced to write a declaration of Independence "in haste."

Jefferson did have in hand two texts that he used in drafting the Declaration of Independence, neither of which qualified as a book or a pamphlet. One, of course, was his draft constitution for Virginia, which was particularly important for the charges against the King, and the other, which fed into the document's opening paragraphs, was a draft of Virginia's Declaration of Rights as written by George Mason and modified by a committee of the Virginia Convention. the committee version of Virginia's Declaration of Rights appeared in the *Pennsylvania Gazette* on June 12, 1776, the day after the Committee of Five was appointed, and possibly the same day it first met. The document might have caught the approving eyes of committee members, who asked their draftsman to incorporate language like Mason's into the Declaration of Independence; or perhaps Jefferson decided to do that on his own.[59] In any case, his use of those particular texts suggests that the Declaration of Independence should be understood first and foremost not as a philosophical but, in the language of the day, as a constitutional document, that is, one that concerned the fundamental authority of government. The Committee of Five had been asked to compose a declaration "to the effect of [Richard Henry Lee's] first resolution, . . . 'That these United Colonies are, and of right ought to be, free and independent states; that they are absolved from all allegiance to the British Crown: and that all political connexion between them and the state of Great Britain is, and ought to be, totally dissolved.'" Such a declaration would, as John Hancock later put it, provide "the Ground & Foundation of a future Government."[60]

Both Jefferson's draft preamble to the Virginia constitution and Mason's draft Declaration of Rights were direct descendants of another constitutional document, the English Declaration of Rights. The lineage is obvious in Mason's case since the child bore its ancestor's name, and a few other features as well. But Jefferson's preamble corresponded to the first part of the English Declaration, which formally ended the reign of James II, while Mason's Declaration fulfilled the second function of the English document in stating "which rights do pertain to us and our posterity, as the basis and foundation of government." Mason's Declaration was far more radical than its parent, which set out simply to reaffirm "antient rights and Liberties." It began with three clauses that would preserve it forever from criticism as an unsatisfactory statement of political principle:

    1. That all men are born equally free and independant, and have certain inherent natural rights, of which they cannot, by any compact, deprive or divest their posterity; among which are the en-

joyment of life and liberty, with the means of acquiring and possessing property, and pursuing and obtaining happiness and safety.

2. That all power is vested in, and consequently derived from the people; that magistrates are their trustees and servants, and at all times amenable to them.

3. That government is, or ought to be instituted for the common benefit, protection, and security of the people, nation or community. Of all the various modes and forms of government, that is best, which is capable of producing the greatest degree of happiness and safety, and is most effectually secured against the danger of maladministration; and that, whenever any government shall be found inadequate or contrary to these purposes, a majority of the community hath an indubitable, unalienable and indefeasible right to reform, alter or abolish it, in such manner as shall be judged most conducive to the public weal.[61]

The draft Virginia Declaration of Rights also included provisions denouncing hereditary office-holding, affirming separation of powers and the importance of "frequent recurrence to fundamental principles," and asserting a series of more specific rights and principles. Some of those specific provisions, such as that calling for "the fullest toleration in the exercise of religion," went far beyond anything in its English ancestor. (And before ratifying the document, the Virginia Convention revised that provision so it asserted an even more radical right to "the free exercise of religion, according to the dictates of conscience.") Family resemblances, however, remained. The draft Virginia Declaration of Rights included eighteen provisions, which the Virginia Convention later cut to sixteen, only a few more than the thirteen in the English document. Moreover, the wording of several provisions resembled others in the English Declaration, and its assertion "That excessive bail ought not to be required, nor excessive fines imposed, nor cruel and unusual punishments inflicted," which Mason added to the text during committee deliberations, was exactly the same except in spelling and punctuation. Mason also retained the English Declaration's use of the verb forms "should" and "ought to," as, for example, in the provision on bail. There was, of course, nothing in the English Declaration of Rights like Mason's opening clauses. Nonetheless, the ideas and even language resembling Mason's most memorable phrases were familiar to colonial readers. For example, the fifty-ninth number of *Cato's Letters*, a set of newspaper essays published in England in the early 1720s and widely reprinted in America, asserted that "All men are born free. . . ."[62]

Jefferson began composing his draft Virginia constitution at about the same time that Mason and the committee of the Virginia Convention were laboring at their assignment. They were, of course, unaware of each other's work, and Jefferson, who acted on his own mandate, unlimited by instructions from the Virginia Convention, also wrote a statement of "Rights Private and Public" that was essentially a bill or "declaration" of rights for Virginia. In fact, his composition did everything the English Declaration of Rights had done: the preamble ended the old regime; a subsequent section declared the basic rights of Virginians, and the constitution itself established a new regime, much as the English document had done in giving the Crown to William and Mary. Jefferson's draft statement of rights was, moreover, even more radical than Mason's. Jefferson boldly proposed, for example, that "no person hereafter coming into this country shall be held within the same in slavery under any pretext whatsoever" and that in "descents" or inheritances "females shall have equal rights with males." Moreover, he abandoned the weak verb forms that Mason's Declaration shared with the English Declaration of Rights. Where Mason had written that "standing armies, in time of peace, should be avoided," Jefferson's draft constitution said, for example, that "There shall be no standing army but in time of actual war." Nowhere in Jefferson's draft constitution, however, was there a statement of those "fundamental principles" that Mason asserted in the first three provisions of his draft Declaration of Rights, and which found their way into the opening section of the Declaration of Independence.[63]

But why did the Declaration of Independence need a preface? It could have begun, like the English Declaration of Rights and Jefferson's preamble to his draft Virginia constitution, with a simple "whereas" clause stating that George III had endeavored to establish a tyranny or that he had violated Americans' fundamental rights and liberties, then gone on to present examples to substantiate that proposition, assert that by those acts he had forfeited authority over the Americans, and, finally, declare that the United Colonies were free and independent states. Many states followed that formula. Instead

Jefferson, whether under the direction of the Committee of Five or on his own inspiration, composed those first paragraphs that have attracted enduring attention and almost entirely explain descriptions of the Declaration of Independence as a document of "transcendent importance," "the foundation of American political philosophy," a statement of "immortal" principles, "the most sacred of all American political scriptures."[64]

He—or they—might have had in mind a previous "Declaration" issued by Congress. The Declaration on the Causes and Necessity of Taking Up Arms had begun with a preface drafted by John Dickinson that was, however, extraordinarily cumbersome. It opened with a long sentence that remains almost unreadable:

> If it was possible for Men who exercise their Reason to believe, that the Divine Author of our Existence intended a Part of the human Race to hold an absolute property in, and an unbounded Power over others, marked out by his infinite Goodness and Wisdom, as the Objects of a legal Domination never rightfully resistible, however severe and oppressive, the Inhabitants of these Colonies might at least require from the Parliament of Great-Britain some Evidence, that this dreadful Authority over them has been granted to that Body.[65]

Old Colonel Rumbold had said much the same thing much more effectively. In 1775 Jefferson also improved on Dickinson, but not by much. His draft Declaration on Taking Up Arms started with an assertion that

> The large strides of late taken by *the legislature of Great Britain* towards establishing over these colonies their absolute rule, and the hardiness of the present attempt to effect by force of arms what by law or right they could never effect, *render* it necessary for us also to change the ground of opposition, and to close with their last appeal from reason to arms. And as it behoves those, *who are called to this great decision*, to be assured that their cause is approved before supreme reason; so is it of great avail that it's justice be made known to the world, whose affections will ever take part with those encountering oppression.[66]

He had not yet mastered the genre, but was on the right track.

A well-written preface should command the attention of its audience and begin to win them over to its message. But who was the intended audience? The Declaration of Independence claimed to be written from "a decent respect to the opinions of mankind," and submitted its "facts to a candid world," which has generally been taken to mean that it was intended for persons outside British North America and, given the need for foreign aid that made Independence urgent, was probably meant to enlist French support. If that was the case, Congress acted in a most curious way after it finally adopted the document. To be sure, on July 8 a committee of Congress sent the Declaration to the American emissary in Paris, Silas Deane, with instructions that he should "immediately communicate the piece to the Court of France, and send copies of it to the other Courts of Europe," and also suggested that "it may be well . . . to procure a good translation of it into French, and get it published in the gazettes." It wrote Deane again on August 7, enclosing a copy of the earlier letter and another copy of the Declaration of Independence, which had by then been copied onto parchment and signed. But the original letter of July 8 was lost, and the later one arrived only on November 17, when news of American Independence, Deane said, "had been circulated thro' Europe for two months before," which made his "pretending" to inform the French Court of that development a somewhat awkward formality. To make matters worse, "two or three Lines from the Committee of Congress in a Letter" that was not even sealed seemed to Deane an embarrassingly cursory manner of announcing to "old and powerfull States" the arrival of the United States of America among the established powers of the earth. To make up for the gaffe he told the French that, since the original letter was dated July 8, "the honorable Congress, had taken the earliest Opportunity of informing this Court, of the declaration of their Independencey and that the variety of important affairs before the Congress with the Critical situation of the Armies, in their Neighborhood, & the Obstructions of their Commerce had prevented that Intelligence which had been wished for. . . ."[67]

In fact, on July 4, after finally approving the Declaration and ordering it "authenticated and printed," Congress voted that copies "be sent to the several assemblies, conventions and committees, or councils of safety, and to the several commanding officers of the continental troops; that it be proclaimed in each of the United States, and at the head of the army." France and the other nations of Europe were not mentioned.[68] The situation in 1776 also gives strong reason to think that the Declaration of Independence was designed first and foremost for domestic consumption. Independence itself was critical to securing support from the French government, but the purposes of Independence and of the Declaration of Independence must be distinguished. The willingness of the French court to back the Americans was founded on its rivalry with Britain, not on any commitment to the justice of their cause. No American had any doubt about that; like the freeholders of Buckingham County, Virginia, they expected foreign nations to support the American cause only if it served "their own interest."[69] A document that cited the right of revolution in justifying American Independence and formally marked the end of monarchical authority could hardly have been designed primarily to awaken enthusiasm among the political servants of King Louis XVI. Within the United States, however, the Declaration of Independence had many practical uses: it provided a vehicle for announcing Independence to the American people, and, if properly framed, might evoke a deeply felt and widespread commitment to the cause of nationhood and, above all, inspire the soldiers who would have to win the Independence that Congress proclaimed. For those purposes Congress specifically directed that the Declaration should be sent not only to the state assemblies, congresses, and conventions that were its immediate constituents and to their Committees of Safety, but to the commanders of the Continental Army, and that it be proclaimed not only in all the states, but at the head of the army.

The Declaration was, moreover, to be disseminated by print—the printer John Dunlap produced a broadside version the day after it was adopted—and also read aloud at public gatherings.[70] Whether or not, as Jay Fliegelman has argued, Jefferson "was expected to rise to the oratorical task of reading the text of the Declaration of Independence aloud" when it was presented to the Continental Congress on June 28, 1776—the Congress's journal says only that the committee "brought in a draught, which was read," and Jefferson's notes on Congress's proceedings are no more specific[71]—he was clearly conscious of how the document would sound when read aloud, as it would be, before large public bodies. He inserted otherwise mysterious marks into the Declaration to indicate where a speaker would pause, which Dunlap at first mistakenly printed as if they were part of the text. Such attention to the cadences of language was natural for Jefferson, a committed violinist fascinated with music. He had also studied classical oratory and rhetorical theory, employed several known rhetorical strategies in composing the Declaration, and wrote "for the ear as well as for the eye," above all in the document's eloquent preamble. He was, however, a poor orator, who probably added the markings to the Declaration to help him get through a public reading of the document; and, to this reader at least, Fliegelman's rendition of how the Declaration would sound given Jefferson's directions suggests how mightily he worked to be even a plodding speaker.[72] But then a good playwright need not be an actor.

And no piece of prose written to be spoken aloud was likely to begin with a "whereas" clause, however appropriate that might be for instructions passed silently from meetings or assemblies to their representatives, or in a Declaration of Rights read aloud to a future King and Queen who had been consulted as the document evolved, and whose assent was no longer in doubt. The Virginia Convention, whose resolutions of May 15 were also read publicly, apparently tried to get around the problem by beginning with "Forasmuch as" instead of "Whereas."[73] Jefferson's solution, as it emerged from the drafting committee, was far more successful:

> When in the course of human events it becomes necessary for one people to dissolve the political bands which have connected them with another, and to assume among the powers of the earth the separate and equal station to which the laws of nature & of nature's god entitle them, a decent respect to the opinions of mankind requires that they should declare the causes which impel them to the separation.[74]

That sentence—and it is a single sentence—immediately conveyed a sense of epic importance. It suggested, without saying so directly, that the emergence of the American people to a "separate and equal" station among "the powers of the earth" was an event of note "in the course of human events" on which, of course, mankind would have an opinion. That message must have offered some consolation to soldiers whose mole's-eye vision suggested they were caught in a rather grubby, hand-to-mouth defense effort, with insufficient guns, ammunition, or food, and would soon be thrown against the most impressive army and fleet they'd ever laid their eyes upon. The appeal to "the laws of nature and of nature's god"—a phrase whose rhythm adds grace to a sentence that would be prosaic without the redundant reference to "nature's god," whose laws were the same as the laws of nature—rather than to the "known laws and statutes" of Great Britain, to which the English Declaration of Rights had appealed, gave witness to the Independence that the Declaration announced. The opening sentence also announced a purpose of the document—to "declare the causes" of separation from Britain, the provocations that, indeed, had made Independence "necessary." That admirably introduced the rest of the Declaration and captured listeners' attention by intimating that an interesting story was about to be told.

The reference to Americans as "a people" has attracted some discussion of what might be described as a chicken-and-egg question: can a people issue a document that makes them a people?[75] That was, however, no problem for Jefferson, whose *Summary View* described the Americans as a people from the moment of settlement, one that had been divided and dismembered only by the unjust acts of seventeenth-century British kings.[76] As a practical matter, moreover, the colonists' consistent expression of respect and deference toward the Continental Congress demonstrated that they were in fact a people, with a sense of common identity and even established political bonds, well before July 1776. It is more important here to recognize that Jefferson achieved the clarity and power of his opening sentence through a series of editorial changes that were made either on his own initiative or on the suggestion of other committee members. In an earlier draft the opening began, "When in the course of human events it becomes necessary for a people to advance from that subordination in which they have hitherto remained, and to assume . . . ," which was more awkward and also harder to say than the revised version. The earlier draft also referred to an "equal & independent station" rather than a "separate and equal" one, and, after inserting the latter phrase, Jefferson changed the final word so the sentence concluded with a reference to "the separation" rather than, as originally, "the causes which impel them to the change."[77]

Jefferson—perhaps with some help from Franklin—made the same kind of careful editorial adjustments in the opening lines of the next paragraph, which, as an examination of successive drafts of the document reveals, were based upon the first three provisions of the Mason/committee draft of Virginia's Declaration of Rights. Jefferson began with Mason's statement "that all men are born equally free and independant," which he rewrote to say they were "created equal & independent," then (on his "original rough draft") cut out the "& independent." Mason said that all men had "certain inherent natural rights, of which they cannot, by any compact, deprive or divest their posterity," which Jefferson compressed marvelously into a statement that men derived from their equal creation "rights inherent & inalienable," then moved the noun to the end of the phrase so it read "inherent & inalienable rights." Among those rights, Mason said, were "the enjoyment of life and liberty, with the means of acquiring and possessing property, and pursuing and obtaining happiness and safety," which Jefferson again shortened first to "the preservation of life, & liberty, & the pursuit of happiness," and then simply to "life, liberty, & the pursuit of happiness."[78]

Again, scholars have devoted considerable effort to understanding where Jefferson picked up the phrase "pursuit of happiness," which, turns out, appeared with sufficient frequency in earlier European writings that Jefferson almost certainly encountered it "in his multifarious reading" and, because the phrase "caught his fancy," it "lingered in his memory." In fact, references to happiness as a political goal are everywhere in American political writings as well, as anyone can see who bothers to look. What did Jefferson mean? The obvious answer is that he meant to say more economically and movingly what Mason stated with some awkwardness and at considerably greater length. For Jefferson and his contemporaries, happiness no doubt demanded safety or security, which would have been in keeping with the biblical phrase one colonist after another used to describe the good life—to be at peace under their vine and fig tree with none to make them afraid (Micah 4:4). The inherent right to pursue happiness probably also included "the means of acquiring and possessing property," but not the ownership of specific things since property can be sold and is therefore alienable.[79] In this case, Jefferson perhaps sacrificed clarity of meaning for grace of language. In general, however, his rewriting of Mason produced a more memorable statement of the same content. Less was more.

Long essays have in fact been written on one phrase after another from the second paragraph of the Declaration. Unfortunately, no section of that document suffers more from a separation of parts from the whole, since its meaning lies in an escalating sequence of connected assertions. As reported by the Committee of Five, the paragraph began:

> We hold these truths to be self-evident; that all men are created equal; that they are endowed by their Creator with inherent and inalienable rights; that among these are life, liberty, and the pursuit of happiness; that to secure these rights, governments are instituted among men, deriving their just powers from the consent of the governed; that whenever any form of government becomes destructive of these ends, it is the right of the people to alter or to abolish it, and to institute new government, laying it's foundation on such principles, and organizing it's powers in such form as to them shall seem most likely to effect their safety & happiness.

This one long sentence, which was carefully worked over, asserted one right, the right of revolution, which was, after all, the right Americans were exercising in 1776. The point came at the end since, according to the historian Stephen Lucas, Jefferson used what the eighteenth century knew as the "Style Periodique," presenting a series of linked propositions in such a way that "the sense of the whole is not brought out till the close." That was considered an especially musical way of writing, notable for the dignity and gravity it conveyed.[80] If so, and Lucas's view accords well with what we know of Jefferson's fascination with the rules that governed harmonious uses of language, removing individual phrases or groups of phrases from their appointed place unravels Jefferson's artistry in composing the sequence.

In terms of substance, however, Jefferson's assertion of the right of revolution summarized succinctly ideas defended and explained at greater length by a long list of seventeenth-century writers that included such prominent figures as John Milton, Algernon Sidney, and John Locke, as well as a host of others, English and Scottish, familiar and obscure, who continued and, in some measure, developed that "Whig" tradition in the eighteenth century. By the time of the Revolution those ideas had become, in the generalized form captured by Jefferson, a political orthodoxy whose basic principles colonists could pick up from sermons or newspapers or even schoolbooks without ever reading a systematic work of political theory. The sentiments Jefferson eloquently expressed were, in short, absolutely conventional among Americans of his time.[81]

The opening assertions of "self-evident" truths concern men in a "state of nature" before government was established. That was even clearer in earlier drafts where the description of men as "equal & independent" echoed an opening reference to the Americans' collective assumption of an "equal & independent station" among "the powers of the earth." The equal status of separate nation-states, who lack any common superintending authority except for "the laws of nature and nature's god," is essentially the same as that of individuals in a state of nature, a point, incidentally, that John Locke made explicitly in his *Second Treatise of Government*. The equality asserted in the Declaration was therefore compatible with differences. France, Luxembourg, and Russia are, for example, equal in status as self-governing nations despite substantial differences in population, landmass, and wealth.[82] With regard to persons, equality meant simply that no one held authority over others by right of birth or as a gift of God.[83] The same idea appeared in many other contemporary writings, including *Common Sense*, which said that "all men being originally equals, no one by birth could have a right to set up his own family in perpetual preference to all others for ever."[84] Since no legitimate power came by right of inheritance, all rightful authority came from the people, who established and empowered governments to protect or "secure" their "inalienable rights" to life, liberty, and the pursuit of happiness. Those statements led directly to the "self-evident" point—and the term "self-evident" was perhaps Franklin's[85]—that the people had a right to reclaim that original grant of power and start over if the governments they created failed to serve the purpose those governments were meant to fulfill.

English and American defenders of "revolution principles"—that is, those who justified the English revolutions of the seventeenth century—were never at home with anarchy. From the beginning they explained at length the preconditions of legitimate popular resistance and revolution, which became increasingly elaborate and emphatic in the eighteenth century. Resistance and revolution could not be provoked by magistrates' casual errors or private immoralities, nor could force be used except as a last resort, after all the "peaceful means of redress" had been exhausted. Legitimate opposition had to answer acts of misrule so serious and so protracted that they aroused the "Body of the People," which was itself understood as a restraining factor since the people were hesitant to act. Only after a "long train of Abuses, Prevarications, and Artifices, all tending the same way," and making their "design visible to the People," Locke wrote, would the people "rouze themselves, and endeavour to put the rule into such hands, which may secure to them the ends for which Government was at first erected." These ideas Jefferson restated in his next sentences:

> prudence indeed will dictate that governments long established should not be changed for light & transient causes: and accordingly all experience hath shewn that mankind are more disposed to suffer while evils are sufferable than to right themselves by abolishing the forms to which they are accustomed. but when a long train of abuses & usurpations, begun at a distinguished period, & pursuing invariably the same object, evinces a design to reduce them under absolute Despotism, it is their right, it is their duty, to throw off such government, & to provide new guards for their future security.

The reference to "a long train of abuses" recalled Locke's phrase, but the same idea was stated in many other places by many other authors; and the phrase "begun at a distinguished period" had appeared earlier in Jefferson's *Summary View*.[86]

Jefferson's point was more important than the sources of his language: where abuses persisted and led toward the same objective, "absolute Despotism"—a term Franklin, or Adams and Franklin, substituted for Jefferson's "arbitrary power"[87]—it was not just the right but the duty of the people to "throw off such government" and establish another more likely to provide the security they sought. And that was precisely the situation of the Americans:

> such has been the patient sufferance of these colonies; & such now is the necessity which constrains them to expunge their former systems of government. the history of the present king of Great Britain is a history of unremitting injuries and usurpations, among which appears no solitary fact to contradict the uniform tenor of the rest, but all have in direct object the establishment of an absolute tyranny over these states. to prove this, let facts be submitted to a candid world, for the truth of which we pledge a faith yet unsullied by falsehood.

Here Jefferson revealed how he would fulfill his opening promise to explain what had impelled the colonists "to dissolve the political bands" connecting them to the British people, and assume a "separate and equal station" among the powers of the earth. His explanation—the story he set out to tell—was different from that in the state and local declarations of Independence, and perhaps different from what readers of the Declaration's first paragraph expected and, to some extent, still expect. State and local declarations told how and why the colonists had decided to abandon their longstanding bonds with Britain and accept Independence. A handful of events from 1775 and 1776, when their change of heart occurred, was enough for that, and enough to make the point that, without declaring Independence and seeking outside help, they faced imminent destruction. Like the state and local declarations, Jefferson's draft Declaration spoke of a "necessity" that constrained or forced the colonists to "expunge" British authority, but the necessity he described was firmly based on "Lockean" contract principles. The most recent state documents—especially those that called themselves "Declarations"—had, of course, moved in that direction, and for good reason. Major public pronouncements were appropriately founded on the grand principles that justified revolution. But in setting out to prove that George III had attempted to establish an "absolute tyranny" over the Americans and so forced them to go their separate way, Jefferson incurred, under the terms he stated, an obligation to demonstrate that they had suffered "a long train of abuses and usurpations" over an extended period of time.

In fact, Jefferson went further than he had to, asserting that George III's injuries were "unremitting," that there was "no solitary fact" that was not aimed at establishing tyranny. A kindly prayer for his American subjects, a token contribution to some colonial charity, any harmless or well-meaning act might derail that argument. Could Jefferson ever have cited facts enough to make his point? After stating all of its twenty-one charges, his draft Declaration concluded that

a prince whose character is thus marked by every act which may define a tyrant, is unfit to be the ruler of a people who mean to be free.

It was, it seems, not just the King's acts that were at issue—and under English Whig "revolution principles" they would have been enough to dissolve the Americans' contractual obligations to him and to the British state—but his character. Jefferson's draft Declaration of Independence did not, in short, blame the King merely because that was the English way of announcing that the state had forfeited its legitimacy, but because George III was personally responsible for the cruel acts attributed to him. "Future ages will scarce believe," Jefferson wrote, "that the hardiness of one man, adventured within the short compass of twelve years only, to build a foundation, so broad and undisguised for tyranny over a people fostered & fixed in principles of freedom." Here, it seems, John Adams differed with Jefferson: for

Adams (in 1822, at any rate) said that the King had acted outside the bounds of law on the basis of bad advice from his servants and so was cruel "in his official capacity only," without the private malevolence that would make him a tyrant "in disposition and in nature." On that point, however, Jefferson's lines echoed those state and local declarations of Independence that turned on the King not as a figurehead but as a man for whom the colonists had once held great affection, but who had forfeited their allegiance and their love by a persistent, personal hostility toward them.

It remained to explain why it had become necessary for the American people "to dissolve the political bands" that tied them to the British people. The "political bands" that bound the American and British peoples were severely limited under the theory of Empire that Jefferson and other colonists had espoused by 1776: both peoples were subject to the same King, and that was it. But those "bands" had been enough to bring together Englishmen—those of the City of London, for example—and colonists in a protracted effort to change the King's government and its policy toward America. Congress had appealed for support to the British people and so had the Massachusetts General Court, which sent its account of Lexington and Concord to England in the hope it would arouse the British people. There were also other, nonpolitical "bands"—of shared traditions, language, religion, and simple affection. But the support of the English people never emerged to the extent that the Americans had hoped. In recalling those ill-fated efforts to enlist the help of their fellow subjects in Britain, Jefferson further demonstrated that the Americans had not thrown off their ties with the Mother Country hastily or for "light and transient causes."

The penultimate section of the Declaration took up that subject. Garry Wills has attributed Jefferson's concern with the bands, above all of affection, that bound people together to the influence of eighteenth-century Scottish writers upon his thought. Wills's argument on the "influence" of the Scots, however, has been refuted by Ronald Hamowy;[88] indeed, since some changes that appear on the "original rough draft" in Jefferson's handwriting were suggested by other committee members, as Jefferson's "Friday morn" letter to Franklin testified, it is not absolutely certain that the phrase "political bands" in the Declaration's opening sentence was Jefferson's personal contribution. More important, his long paragraph on the British people emerged directly from the colonists' protracted efforts to coordinate opposition with the British people. Those fellow subjects "at home" could choose delegates to the House of Commons, but in 1774 they returned to power the same members of Parliament against whom the colonists had complained, and the British people seemed hopelessly passive thereafter as the Crown moved forcefully to suppress American opposition. The fact that no effective support for the colonists materialized in Britain served, as so many town, county, and state resolutions on Independence testified, to "alter" the deep feelings of affection Americans once felt for the British people, much as their "sentiments" toward the King had changed. In no part of the Declaration did Jefferson give expression to the minds and hearts of his countrymen more fully than in those that summarized the Americans' efforts to join hands with the British people and the implications of their failure:

> Nor have we been wanting in attention to our British brethren. we have warned them from time to time of attempts by their legislature to extend a jurisdiction over these our states. we have reminded them of the circumstances of our emigration & settlement here, no one of which could warrant so strange a pretension: that these were effected at the expence of our own blood & treasure, unassisted by the wealth or the strength of Great Britain: that in constituting indeed our several forms of government, we had adopted one common king, thereby laying a foundation for perpetual league & amity with them: but that submission to their parliament was no part of our constitution, nor ever in idea if history may be credited: and we appealed to their native justice & magnanimity as well as to the ties of our common kindred to disavow these usurpations which were likely to interrupt our connection & correspondence. they too have been deaf to the voice of justice & of consanguinity, & when occasions have been given them, by the regular course of their laws, of removing from their councils the disturbers of our harmony, they have by their free election reestablished them in power. at this very time too they are permitting their chief magistrate to send over not only soldiers of our common blood, but Scotch & foreign mercenaries to invade & destroy us. these facts have given the last stab to agonizing affection, and manly spirit bid us to renounce forever these unfeeling brethren.

There it was—Jefferson's claim that America had been settled with no help from Britain, sandwiched between an innocuous reminder that the colonists had addressed their "British brethren" and a statement of the empire's structure that had won wide acceptance among Americans. He slipped it in so inconspicuously that not every reader might catch its assertion that the colonists had settled America entirely at their own cost, "unassisted by the wealth or strength of Great Britain." The point was extremely important to Jefferson. He had written an entire treatise, which remained locked away in an unpublished notebook until the twentieth century, to refute a point in the speech on American affairs that George III delivered to Parliament on October 26, 1775. What had incensed Jefferson was not so much what incensed others, the King's assertion that American professions of loyalty and desire for reconciliation were only "meant to amuse," but his statement that the colonies had been planted by the British nation "with great industry, nursed with great tenderness," and, above all, "protected and defended at much expence and treasure." Against the "palpable untruth" that the colonies were established at British expense, Jefferson gathered an array of "facts" from Hakluyt's *Voyages*, then denounced a King who "can adopt falshood [*sic*], and solemnize it from the throne." Such an act, he ominously suggested, "justifies the revolution of fortune which reduces him to a private station."[89]

But had the colonists "reminded" the British people of the "circumstances of our emigration & settlement" as Jefferson understood them? Not in Congress's address to them of 1774, nor in that of 1775.[90] And yet Jefferson heaped on the British people an anger like that he had invested in the King, an anger that took form in a flood of words. The passage above is coherent and complete: it recalled American appeals to the British and, in remarkable detail, how those "brethren" had taken another course, then drew a conclusion that tied "these facts" to the document's overall subject, American Independence. But Jefferson, it seems, couldn't let it go at that. In lines full of passion he went on—it almost seems he couldn't stop—overleaping natural pauses, heaping one denunciation on another:

> we must endeavor to forget our former love for them, and to hold them as we hold the rest of mankind, enemies in war, in peace friends.

There was another natural ending. But no:

> we might have been a free & a great people together; but a communication of grandeur & of freedom it seems is below their dignity.

Done? Not quite, although anger was beginning to dissolve into melodrama:

> be it so, since they will have it: the road to happiness & to glory is open to us too; we will climb it apart from them and acquiesce in the necessity which denounces our eternal separation!

Then, finally, on the basis of all that came before, the Declaration arrived at its main business: "We therefore the representatives of the United States of America"—no longer the United Colonies—"in General Congress assembled do, in the name & by authority of the good people of these states, reject and renounce all allegiance & subjection to the kings of Great Britain & all others who may thereafter claim by, through, or under them," a passage that amounted to a rejection not only of George III but of his descendants and any other claimants to the throne, in effect, a rejection of monarchy, as well as of those public servants the King appointed. And more: "we utterly dissolve all political connection which may heretofore have subsisted between us & the parliament or people of Great Britain," a statement that strangely suggested there might once have been some political connection between Parliament and the "good people" of America; "and finally we do assert and declare these colonies to be free and independent states,"

> and that as free & independent states they have full power to levy war, conclude peace, contract alliances, establish commerce, & to do all other acts and things which independent states may of right do. And for the support of this declaration we mutually pledge to each other our lives, our fortunes, and our sacred honor.

The final sentence was particularly wonderful in that it took a commonplace—one community after another in Massachusetts and elsewhere had movingly committed their "lives" and "fortunes" to the cause—and, by adding to it "our sacred honor," gave the passage more power, since honor remained a force of considerable significance, as well as a dignity and a mellifluousness as pleasing to the mind as it is to the ear.

THE DECLARATION Jefferson and the Committee of Five delivered to Congress on June 28 was a mixture of beautifully crafted passages, some of which had begun with previously written prose, and others that remained overstated or overlong and so gave evidence of both its draftsman's feelings and the "haste" with which the draft had been written. No doubt it was a promising text, one that would have been easily improved if the author could have put it aside for two weeks, then looked at it afresh.

Jefferson didn't have two weeks. He had, however, the next best thing: an extraordinary editor.

4. Congress's Declaration

On July 2, after unanimously affirming that "these United Colonies are, and of right, ought to be, Free and Independent States," the Continental Congress resolved itself into a Committee of the Whole to consider the draft declaration of Independence submitted by the Committee of Five. At that point the official record of Congress's proceedings falls silent until the Committee of the Whole reported later in the day that it needed more time to complete its work. Congress agreed, took up one small piece of business, then adjourned.[91]

Each of the next two days began much the same, as Congress dispatched items of pressing business and routine administrative matters—receiving letters, many of which included information on the military situation, settling accounts, responding as best it could to the breaking crisis. Then, having made what provisions it could for holding off the enemy, Congress set the war temporarily aside and, "agreeable to the order of the day," again "resolved itself into a committee of the whole" to consider what it called the "declaration on independence."[92] Once again the curtain fell, concealing the delegates as they moved through the document, making changes as they went along, leaving no official record of their proceedings beyond its fruit—the Declaration that, reconstituted as the Continental Congress, they finally adopted. Even the private correspondence of delegates is remarkably silent on what the Committee of the Whole did and why. Only Jefferson's notes on Congress's proceedings discuss the subject in any detail, and Jefferson was anything but a dispassionate observer as the Committee of the Whole rewrote or chopped off large sections of his draft, eliminating in the end fully a quarter of his text.

How exactly did the Committee of the Whole execute its editorial work? Did one or two delegates take charge, or did many voices feed into the process? We will never know. If there was only one copy, the handwritten "fair copy" submitted by the Committee of Five, how could the delegates examine the text, propose changes, or even understand the revisions others proposed? To that question, at least, the historian Wilfred J. Ritz provides some answers. Unless its members were "dunderheads," he argues, Congress must have had the committee draft printed, and distributed copies to the delegates. None of those copies seems to have survived, and Congress's journal says nothing about having the draft printed—but then the journal made no pretense of offering a complete record of everything Congress did. Perhaps Congress gathered up all earlier printings and destroyed them once it decided upon the Declaration's final form. In working on the Articles of Confederation later in July, it openly followed a very similar procedure.[93] Ritz's theory makes sense, and allows us to imagine the delegates bent over their texts, marking changes, debating whether to move an adverb, change a word, delete a passage here or insert another there.

That Congress was willing to devote such efforts to the document should have been a cause of satisfaction for Jefferson. The draft Declaration submitted to Congress was, as the New Hampshire delegate Josiah Bartlett put it on July 1, "a pretty good one," unlike the initial draft of the Declaration on Taking Up Arms, which in June 1775 Congress sent back to a reconstituted drafting committee for a thorough reworking. Time was also a factor. Congress needed to announce its adoption of Independence as quickly as possible, and in an appropriate way. In short, the relatively obvious character of changes needed in Jefferson's draft, the urgency of issuing a Declaration, and the immediate importance of that document all suggested that Congress should itself take on the task of editing the text.[94]

Some of its changes were verbal. These are perhaps the most moving testament to the delegates' determination to make the Declaration as good as possible. They left most of the well-worked-over opening paragraphs untouched, except Jefferson's "inherent and inalienable rights" became "certain inalienable rights," which was better. ("Inalienable" seems to have become "unalienable" only later, in the course of printing the document.) At Jefferson's reference to "a long train of abuses and usurpations, begun at a distinguished period & pursuing invariably the same object," the delegates cut out "begun at a distin-guished period &," which was meant to emphasize that the King's ac-tions had occurred over a long period of time, and so probably seemed of substantive importance to Jefferson, but the phrase made the sen-tence cumbersome. The delegates were so attentive to detail that at one point they changed "neglected utterly" to "utterly neglected."

More often, however, the delegates cut back or eliminated the more extreme and untenable assertions in the committee draft. In the statement that necessity forced the Americans to "expunge" their for-mer systems of government, the delegates substituted "alter" for "ex-punge." There were, after all, some parts of their former governments worth keeping—representative assemblies, for example—so "alter" was more accurate. Where Jefferson had accused the King of "un-remitting" injuries, the delegates charged him with "repeated" injuries, which was easier to prove, and then cut out the assertion that there ap-peared in the King's conduct "no solitary fact to contradict the uni-form tenor of the rest." They also crossed out the phrase "for the truth of which we pledge a faith yet unsullied by falsehood" from the end of that paragraph, so it ended simply "to prove this let facts be submitted to a candid world." Did they dislike the tone of that assertion? Did they find it arrogant, or pretentious? Or was the problem that it in-vited silly quibbling over whether the colonists had ever said anything less than entirely truthful? In any case, the change made the connec-tion between that and the next section of document, and so the Decla-ration's overall structure, more emphatic, which was all to the good.

What adjustments the committee made in the individual charges against the King were, with one exception, of the same sort. The ex-ception concerned the King's "transporting large armies of foreign mercenaries" to America. There the delegates, reflecting the outrage of their constituents, made Jefferson's denunciation even harsher, de-scribing the act as "scarcely paralleled in the most barbarous ages" and inserting "totally" before Jefferson's statement that it was "unworthy the head of a civilized nation." Everywhere else they moderated Jeffer-son's claims. Where the draft declaration accused George III of dis-solving houses of representatives "repeatedly & continually," the delegates crossed out "& continually," which went too far. They tight-ened up the statement that the King "has suffered the administration of justice totally to cease in some of these states by refusing his assent to laws for establishing judiciary powers," so it said he "obstructed the administration of justice by refusing his assent . . ." The complaint, remember, was mainly North Carolina's, so the reference to "some of these states" served curiously not to modify the charge but to reduce its accuracy. And the administration of justice there had not "totally" ceased since a political compromise allowed the inferior courts to continue functioning; only the superior courts were closed. The revised text was nearer the truth.

The delegates took the "our" out of the charge that the King had made "our judges dependent on his will alone," perhaps again for accuracy's sake. Judges, after all, had been Crown appointees, and so servants of the King. The delegates also cut the words "and ships of war" from the charge that the King had kept armies in the colonies without the permission of their legislatures, probably because the jurisdiction of those legislatures over the sea was open to dispute. In the end, the King stood accused of depriving the colonists of trial by jury "in many cases," not universally; he was not charged with withdrawing governors who had in fact often been forced from office, and he was said simply to have abdicated government by declaring the colonists "out of his protection"—which recalled the Prohibitory Act—"and waging war against us."

Above all, however, the delegates eliminated entirely Jefferson's long passage on the slave trade. In the notes he kept of Congress's proceedings, Jefferson said that change was made "in complaisance to South Carolina & Georgia," which had never tried to restrain the slave trade and, indeed, wanted it to continue, with the consent of "Northern brethren" who had few slaves but were sensitive on the issue because they had been "pretty considerable carriers of them to others."[95] Maybe so, but the very acknowledgment that colonists had been in the past or were at present willing participants in the slave trade undermined the assertion that "the *Christian* king of Great Britain" was alone responsible for that outrage on humanity. The Americans were destined to receive criticism enough for asserting the "inalienable" rights to "life, liberty, and the pursuit of happiness" while themselves owning slaves. Some people recognized the contradiction and were ready to move toward greater consistency between principle and practice, but so monumental a change as the abolition of slavery could not be accomplished in a moment. For the time being, it was wise at least not to call attention to the persistence of the slave trade and to the anomaly of American slavery.

The delegates did not, however, eliminate all reference to Lord Dunmore's effort to turn slaves against their masters, which, as the state and local resolutions testified, had powerfully alienated many colonists from British rule, and to which Jefferson referred at the end of his long passage on the slave trade. After omitting that charge and another, which accused the King of inciting "treasonable insurrections of our fellow citizens," the delegates inserted into the seventeenth charge, which castigated the King for turning Indians against the people of the frontiers, an accusation that he had "excited domestic insurrections among us," which covered both slaves and Loyalists. The final Declaration therefore included not twenty-one but nineteen charges against the King—surely enough to demonstrate a "long train of abuses" and a "history of repeated injuries." Moreover, having eliminated the old eighteenth charge on "treasonable insurrections" with its reference to "our fellow citizens," the delegates were free to use that phrase in place of "others" in the next charge, so the King was accused of constraining "our fellow citizens taken captive [Jefferson had said "captives"] on the high seas to bear arms against their country. . . ."

By then the delegates seem to have built up steam, and really ripped into the rest of the document. And, indeed, it badly needed editing; Jefferson had probably lacked time to work over the final portions of the document with the same care he devoted to its opening. His reference to the Americans as "a people who mean to be free" became "a free people." Much better: Jefferson's words suggested that Americans aspired to freedom but were not yet free, which was far from the general sense of their situation, and had a certain unfortunate petulant tone as well. Then out went the strained assertion that "future ages will scarce believe" that one man had "in only twelve years" attempted to found so "broad and undisguised" a foundation for tyranny over a people "fostered and fixed in principles of freedom." Again, less was more.

On that same principle, Congress reduced Jefferson's overlong attack on the British people to a more lean and constrained statement. Out went his claim that the Americans had settled the country without any British help; the remaining assertion that "we reminded them of the circumstances of our emigration and settlement here" then became more justifiable. From the beginning of the conflict, the colonists had insisted that in coming to America their ancestors had yielded none of the rights of Englishmen. That could be construed as reminding the British people of the "circumstances of our emigration." Out went the detailed references to the British people's returning the parliamentary "disturbers of our harmony" to power and to their allowing the King to send mercenaries "to invade and destroy us." It was enough to say that they proved "deaf to the voice of justice and consanguinity," and that "we must therefore acquiesce in the necessity which denounces our separation"—cutting out the "eternal" before "separation"—to which the delegates added, "and hold them, as we hold the rest of mankind, enemies in war, in peace friends." Those words were Jefferson's, but their grace was lost in his own draft, buried as they were in the midst of false stops and restartings.

This was no hack editing job: the delegates who labored over the draft Declaration had a splendid ear for language. Jefferson, however, did not see it that way. The changes in the passages on the British people were made, he said, because "the pusillanimous idea that we had friends in England still keeping terms with, still haunted the minds of many."[96] But the rewritten section remained severely critical of the British people. The language, however, was more restrained, the conclusion more eloquent, and the whole more in keeping with the economy of Jefferson's opening paragraphs.

Finally, Congress substituted the words of its own July 2 resolution—the composition of another Virginian, Richard Henry Lee—for much of Jefferson's conclusion, and eliminated his troubling suggestion, so out of keeping with the increasingly orthodox American conception of the Empire as a collection of otherwise independent communities bound together under the Crown, that the Americans might once have had a more direct political connection with the people or Parliament of Britain. It also added two references to God, which were conspicuously missing in Jefferson's draft, where God appeared only as the author of nature's laws and the endower of natural rights, and honor alone was "sacred." At the start of the final paragraph Congress inserted an appeal "to the supreme judge of the world" to affirm "the rectitude of our intentions," which echoed similar provisions in several state and local resolutions on Independence, and nearer the end of the document it also referred to the delegates' "firm reliance on the protection of divine providence." Americans held strong religious beliefs in 1776, and the Declaration was meant to state the convictions of the country's "good people." The delegates retained, however, Jefferson's concluding sentences, including its memorable mutual pledge of "our lives, our fortunes, and our sacred honor."

The more alterations Congress made on his draft, the more miserable Jefferson became. He had forgotten, as has posterity, that a draftsman is not an author, and that the "declaration on independence," as Congress sometimes called it, was not a novel, or a poem, or even a political essay presented to the world as the work of a particular writer, but a public document, an authenticated expression of the American mind. Franklin, who was sitting nearby, "perceived that I was not insensible to these mutilations," Jefferson later recalled, and attempted to console him with the story of a young hatter, about to open his own shop, who proposed to have a fine signboard made with the words "John Thompson, Hatter, makes and sells hats for ready money" and the figure of a hat. First, however, he asked his friends for their advice. One proposed taking out "hatter" since it was redundant with "makes hats." Another recommended that "makes" be removed since customers wouldn't care who exactly made the hats. A third said "for ready money" was unnecessary since it was not the local custom to sell on credit. "*Sells* hats," a fourth commented; did Thompson suppose people thought he meant to give them away? In the end, the sign said simply "John Thompson," with a picture of a hat, which probably served its function quite well. Franklin said, however, that he had learned from that anecdote to avoid, "whenever in my power, . . . becoming the draughtsman of papers to be reviewed by a public body."[97] Did Franklin understand how much Congress, like the relentless editors in his story, was practicing a technique that Jefferson had himself used to good effect when he compressed Mason's language until it gained in power far more than it lost in length?

Others seem to have shared Jefferson's preference for the committee draft over the version Congress adopted. So strong was his conviction on that issue that Jefferson laboriously copied the earlier version several times over—by hand, of course, which made it a tedious, time-consuming task—and sent those copies to friends so they could judge for themselves, as he wrote Richard Henry Lee, "whether it is the better or worse for the Critics." Lee responded that he "sincerely" wished, "as well for the honor of Congress, as for that of the States, that the Manuscript had not been mangled as it is," and years later John Adams also said that Congress "obliterated some of the best" of the draft declaration "and left all that was exceptionable, if any thing in it was."[98] Obviously the two versions were strikingly different in the opinion of contemporary observers. And what generations of Americans came to revere was not Jefferson's but Congress's Declaration, the work not of a single man, or even a committee, but of a larger body of men with the good sense to recognize a "pretty good" draft when they saw it, and who were able to identify and eliminate Jefferson's more outlandish assertions and unnecessary words. So successful an exercise of group editing probably demanded a text that required cutting, not extensive rewriting. Congress's achievement was remarkable nonetheless. By exercising their intelligence, political good sense, and a discerning sense of language, the delegates managed to make the Declaration at once more accurate and more consonant with the convictions of their constituents, and to enhance both its power and its eloquence.

FINALLY, on July 4, the Committee of the Whole reported that it had agreed upon a Declaration. Congress's journal says that the text was then read and that Congress accepted it, ordered it to be authenticated and printed under the supervision of the drafting committee, and provided for its distribution and proclamation.[99] Jefferson's notes on Congress's proceedings for once added more detail. After devoting "the greater parts of the 2d. 3d. & 4th. July" in debating the declaration, he said, those deliberations were finally "in the evening of the last closed. the declaration was reported by the comm[itt]ee, agreed to by the house, and signed by every member present except Mr. Dickinson."[100] Careful research has been devoted to determining when exactly the Declaration was approved—late morning, not evening, seems most likely[101]—and whether the document was in fact signed on the 4th by anyone except Congress's President, John Hancock, whose name appeared as the sole signer on the published broadside. There remains a remote possibility that delegates signed a copy of the Declaration that has since been lost, but probably Jefferson was wrong there, too.[102] The Journals of the Second Continental Congress say only that on July 19, after New York's approval became known, Congress resolved "that the Declaration passed on the 4th, be fairly engrossed on parchment, with the title and stile of 'The unanimous declaration of the thirteen United States of America,' and that the same, when engrossed, be signed by every member of Congress," and that on August 2 "the declaration of independence being engrossed and compared was signed,"[103] although some members added their signatures at later times.

Why, however, was it signed at all? Only John Browne, Parliament's clerk, signed the English Declaration of Rights. Moreover, according to Lois Schwoerer, the members of England's seventeenth-century Parliaments did not customarily sign instruments they presented to the King, nor were declarations and petitions signed by their drafters elsewhere in Europe. "Of documents comparable to the Declaration of Rights," she says, "only the Declaration of Independence of the American colonies was signed by its framers."[104]

The Declaration of Independence was not the only Congressional document that was signed by the delegates. Members of the First Continental Congress had affixed their signatures to the Continental Association and to their petition to the King, but not to the addresses they sent the inhabitants of Great Britain and of the American colonies, "The Bill of Rights [and] a List of Grievances," or, finally, their letter to the inhabitants of Quebec, which was simply signed "By order of the Congress, Henry Middleton, President," on October 26, 1774. The Second Continental Congress signed its "Olive Branch Petition" to the King but no other document previous to the Declaration of Independence, although some were, again, signed by John Hancock as President of the Congress.[105]

In the absence of any direct testimony on why some documents were signed and others not, the answer or answers to that riddle must lie in the texts themselves. The Association set up a colony-wide nonimportation, nonexportation, and nonconsumption agreement. Since the First Continental Congress had no independent legislative authority, the document's binding character could come only from the consent of those who were parties to it. The text made that clear and also mandated that delegates sign: ". . . we do solemnly bind ourselves and our constituents," it said, ". . . to adhere to this association. . . ." The signing of petitions to the King, contrary as it was to Parliamentary practice, is somewhat more difficult to explain. Again, the documents were written in a way that made delegates' signatures necessary. "We your majesty's faithful subjects of the colonies of Newhampshire, Massachusetts-by, Rhode-island and Providence Plantations, Connecticut, New-York, New-Jersey, Pennsylvania, the counties of New-Castle Kent and Sussex on Delaware, Maryland, Virginia, North-Carolina, and South Carolina," began the petition of 1774, "in behalf of ourselves and the inhabitants of these colonies who have deputed us to represent them in General Congress, by this our humble petition, beg leave to lay our grievances before the throne." Its successor of 1775 began in an almost identical way, except that the opening statement entreated "your Majesty's gracious attention to this our humble petition."[106]

But why were the petitions written in that way? Probably out of respect for the King, and to enhance the petitions' persuasiveness. Unlike the convention Parliament of 1689, Congress had no place in British constitutional tradition. It was new, and the Crown did not recognize its legitimacy. By affixing their signatures, the delegates signaled that each of the colonies mentioned supported the petition, and also founded it upon their own personal authority and dignity. This was, they seemed to say, not the work of an inconsequential faction of colonists, as their critics in England so often alleged, but the voice of the American people and of the men of consequence they selected to speak for them. Since, moreover, the petitions were conspicuously loyal statements from the King's "faithful subjects," there was no particular reason not to sign.

The Declaration of Independence was altogether different. It was not loyal; it was an avowal of revolution. From the viewpoint of those who opposed its message, the Declaration was nothing less than a public confession of treason. And conviction for treason meant death and confiscation of estate. Surely there was cause enough for fear: opponents in England had long since begun urging the King to prosecute the colonists for treason. In 1776, the supporters of Independence suspected that some colonies had adopted a "settled policy to keep in the rear of the confederacy, that their particular prospect might be better even in the worst event."[107]

Signing the Declaration was no way "to keep in the rear." Nonetheless, the delegates adopted a document that, like the Association, and like the petitions to the King, mandated their signatures. "We, therefore, the Representatives of the United states of America," it concluded, ". . . do, in the name, and by the authority of the good people of these Colonies, solemnly publish and declare, that these united colonies are, and of right ought to be free and independent States." By eliminating from his draft conspicuous debts to the English Declaration of Rights, Jefferson had constructed a document that manifested the Independence it declared. In the same way, the signers, by affixing their names to the text, and so making their signatures part of that most hazardous of Congressional papers, mutually pledged to each other, "for the support of this Declaration" and "with a firm reliance on the protection of divine Providence," their lives, their fortunes, and their sacred honor.

They were not, however, given to throwing their fate into God's hands needlessly. Only on January 18, 1777, after the long, disastrous military campaign of 1776 was over and the Americans had won victories at Trenton and Princeton, did Congress send the states authenticated copies of the Declaration of Independence "with the names of the members . . . subscribing the same."[108]

CHAPTER IV

American Scripture

RESPONSIBILITY FOR DISTRIBUTING the Declaration of Independence fell to Congress's president, John Hancock. He executed that job with none of the anxiety that had gripped him a year earlier, as he and Samuel Adams set out for the Second Continental Congress. Fear of division haunted him then, fear that the other colonies would blame Massachusetts for the outbreak of war and leave it to face the British alone. But in July 1776 Congress managed to agree unanimously on Independence, a far harder decision than any that preceded it.[1] Britain's persistent, wrongheaded policy provoked that unity, but it also rewarded months of strenuous political maneuvering within Congress and throughout the country. Now it was necessary to tell the American people that they had assumed a "separate and equal station" among the "powers of the earth," and then, more difficult, to earn recognition of that status on the battlefield.

How the word went out is one story; what became of the Declaration afterward is another, more complex and of continuing significance. The Declaration was at first forgotten almost entirely, then recalled and celebrated by Jeffersonian Republicans, and later elevated into something akin to holy writ, which made it a prize worth capturing on behalf of one cause after another. The politics that attended its creation never entirely left its side, such that the Declaration of Independence, which became a powerful statement of national identity, has also been at the center of some of the most intense conflicts in American history, including that over slavery which threatened the nation itself. In the course of those controversies, the document assumed a function altogether different from that of 1776: it became not a justification of revolution, but a moral standard by which the day-to-day policies and practices of the nation could be judged.

The Declaration of Independence was in some ways the most unlikely of all documents to play such a role, one whose work was essentially done once it had successfully announced and justified Congress's decision to break with Britain and begin a new nation. Moreover, its assertion that "all men are created equal," which became a prominent part of the document's moral message, had originally referred to men in a state of nature, that is, before government existed. To accomplish so thorough a remaking of that eighteenth-century document went beyond the power of any one man. No less than its original creation, the redefinition of the Declaration was a collective work by Americans who struggled over several generations to establish policies consistent with the revolutionary heritage as they came to understand it in the only way open to them—through politics.

I.   Spreading the News

Hancock's prose was somewhat awkward; he was no Thomas Jefferson. The letters he sent to the states and to General Washington emphasized that Congress had acted cautiously. It was impossible "to foresee the Consequences of Human Actions," Hancock said, "yet it is nevertheless a Duty we owe ourselves and Posterity in all our public Counsels, to decide in the best Manner we are able, and to trust the Event to that *Being* who controuls both Causes and Events." With that thought in mind, and confident that American affairs might "take a more favourable Turn," Congress decided it was "necessary to dissolve all Connection between Great Britain & the American Colonies, and to declare them free and independent States, as you will perceive by the enclosed Declaration," which he was "directed by Congress to transmit to you, and to request you will have it proclaimed in your Colony in the Way you shall think most proper." Hancock's letter to Washington told him to proclaim the Declaration "at the Head of the Army," and omitted an important sentence that appeared in his letter to the states. "The important Consequences . . . from this Declaration of Independence, considered as the Ground & Foundation of Government," it said, "will naturally suggest the Propriety of proclaiming it in such a Manner, that the People may be universally informed of it."[2]

The Declaration could be "proclaimed" or made known in many different ways. The most common method was to read it before groups of people in a public and appropriately ceremonial manner. That was Washington's choice. On July 9 he ordered officers of the several Continental Army brigades stationed in New York City to pick up copies of the Declaration at the Adjutant General's Office. Then, with the British "constantly in view, upon and at Staten-Island," as one participant recalled, the brigades were "formed in hollow squares on their respective parades," where they heard the Declaration read, as the General had specified, "with an audible voice." The event, Washington hoped, would "serve as a free incentive to every officer, and soldier, to act with Fidelity and Courage, . . . knowing that now the peace and safety of his Country depends (under God) solely on the success of our arms: And that he is now in the service of a State, possessed of sufficient power to reward his merit, and advance him to the highest Honors of a free Country."[3] By raising the spirit of the people, the Declaration might also encourage men to join the army and so help American affairs "take a more favourable Turn," as Hancock and the Congress hoped. A call could finally go out for men to fight "for the Defence of the Liberties and Independence of the United States," as a recruiting poster of late 1776 put it. The conflicting loyalties that had weakened the American war effort during its first year were over. "Now we know what to depend on," wrote Joseph Barton from Sussex County, New Jersey, soon after learning of Congress's action. "For my part, I have been at a great stand: I could hardly own the King and fight against him at the same time; but now these matters are cleared up. Heart and hand shall move together."[4]

The Declaration was also read to largely civilian audiences, with rituals suited to the occasion, starting with the official events on July 8 at Philadelphia (or perhaps with an unofficial public reading there of a "leaked" copy of the Declaration four days earlier) and on the same day at Easton, Pennsylvania, and Trenton, New Jersey, on into August, when the document finally made its way to distant Georgia. The festivities at Philadelphia on July 8 began with members of the Committee of Safety and Committee of Inspection going "in procession" to the State House, where "the Declaration of Independency of the United States of America was read to a very large number of the inhabitants of the City and County," who responded, a newspaper account said, with "general applause and heart-felt satisfaction." John Adams recalled that "the Battalions paraded on the Common, and gave Us the Feu de Joie, notwithstanding the Scarcity of Powder. The Bells rang all Day and almost all night." In the evening, too, bonfires were lit and houses were "illuminated" by candles put in their windows, as colonists had done in earlier days to celebrate the King's birthday.[5]

Celebrations elsewhere were much the same; and everywhere the Declaration itself was the centerpiece of events. In Huntington, Long Island, it was read with the New York Provincial Congress's endorsement at "the several places of parade," probably to accommodate the large number of people who gathered from "the distant quarters of the district" and who indicated their approbation with "animated shouts." Similarly, in Williamsburg, Virginia, "the Declaration of Independence was solemnly proclaimed at the Capitol, the Court House, and the Palace." And in Savannah the document was read four times—in the Council Chamber by those officials who first received the letter from Hancock; in the square before the Assembly House "to a great concourse of people"; at the Liberty Pole, to which civil officials and local militiamen marched in a formal procession, and where, "after the reading of the Declaration," the Georgia battalion "discharged their field pieces, and fired in platoons"; then, finally, at the Trustees Gardens, "where the Declaration was read for the last time, and the cannon of the battery discharged."[6]

Independence was a beginning, and so over and over the festivities included the firing of thirteen musket rounds, or the offering of thirteen toasts, celebrating the number of states now bound together in the newborn nation. Independence was also an end. And in place after place—in Philadelphia, New York, Providence, Boston, Baltimore, as at Bridgeton, New Jersey, and Worcester, Massachusetts—all "portable signs of royalty" were destroyed with the declaring of Independence. The King's arms or pictures of the King or the Crown on public buildings, coffeehouse and tavern signs, even in churches, were ripped down, trampled, torn, or otherwise broken to pieces, then consumed in great bonfires before crowds of people who responded with "repeated huzzas." In New York City a crowd pulled down a gilded equestrian statue of George III that had been put up in 1770: "the IMAGE of the BEAST was thrown down," one observer reported, "and his HEAD severed from his Body." Later the monument was sent off to Litchfield, Connecticut, where local women converted its lead contents into bullets.[7]

There was no mistaking the meaning of these ritual acts. "Compelled by strong necessity," said the president of the local Committee of Safety in the town of Dover, Delaware, as he threw a picture of George III into the flames, "thus we destroy even the shadow of that King who refused to reign over a free people." Sometimes communities expressed their anti-monarchical convictions in other ways. The people of Huntington, Long Island, for example, ripped the name "George III" from a local flag, then hastily created "from base materials" an effigy of the King "with its face black like Dunmore's Virginia regiment, its head adorned with a wooden crown stuck full of feathers like . . . Savages," and its cloak "lined with gunpowder, which the original seems to be fond of." Finally, the effigy, with the flag fragment, was "hung on a gallows, exploded, and burnt to ashes." Georgians instead staged a mock funeral for the King. "Forasmuch as George the Third . . . hath most flagrantly violated his coronation oath, and trampled upon the constitution of our country, and the sacred rights of mankind," they declared, "we therefore commit his political existence to the ground, corruption to corruption, tyranny to the grave, and oppression to eternal infamy; in sure and certain hope that he will never obtain a resurrection to rule again over these United States of America. . . ."[8]

Such events occurred in out-of-the-way places as well as major towns and cities: to assure that the people were "universally informed" of the Declaration, as Hancock requested, provincial officials devised means of circulating the news through the rural countryside, where over nine out of every ten Americans lived. The way they did so varied according to the customs and political systems of the several states. Pennsylvania's Committee of Safety sent letters by an express rider "to the Counties of Bucks, Chester, Northampton, Lancaster, and Berks, Inclosing a Copy of the said Declaration, requesting the same to be publish'd on Monday next, at the places where the Election for Delegates are to be held."[9] There, it seems, the people of Pennsylvania would congregate in significant numbers. Virginia asked sheriffs to proclaim the Declaration each "at the door of his courthouse the first court day after he shall have received the same"; and Rhode Island had the Declaration read in the state's several towns "at their next stated meetings." Massachusetts not only told sheriffs to "proclaim Independency," but also ordered ministers in the parishes of every religious denomination to read the Declaration to their congregations "as soon as divine Service is ended . . . on the first Lord's-Day after they shall receive it," and then to deliver the document to the clerks of their towns or districts so it could be recorded in local records and remain there "as a *perpetual* Memorial thereof." The North Carolina Council of Safety let recipients in that colony's towns and counties decide how best to reach the people, asking only that the Declaration "be proclaimed in the most public Manner." The Maryland Council of Safety also told "the several committees of Observation in each County and District in this Province" to proclaim the Declaration in whatever manner seemed "most proper for the Information of the People." And so the grand events at Philadelphia or New York recurred, on a smaller scale but no less meaningfully, in communities throughout the country, including places such as Frederick, Maryland, or Amherst, Massachusetts, that had already formally committed their "lives and fortunes" to American Independence.[10]

The Declaration of Independence could also be "proclaimed" or "published" (i.e., made public) through print. The copies of the Declaration of Independence that Hancock sent out had been printed as broadsides—that is, on one side of a single sheet of paper—at Philadelphia by John Dunlap. Then they were reprinted in other cities and towns for mass circulation as broadsides or in newspapers, sometimes by order of an official body such as the provincial councils of Massachusetts and Virginia. The Declaration appeared in the *Pennsylvania Evening Post* on July 6, in the *Pennsylvanischer Staatsbote*—in German—on the 9th, and in no fewer than thirty other American newspapers before the month was over. In Connecticut, where a New London newspaper reprinted the full text of the document on July 12, the Declaration was apparently proclaimed only through the public press.[11] Although banner headlines remained far in the future, the Declaration was nonetheless generally "front page news." But New York's radical printer John Holt chose to publish the document on a page by itself, after the other news, to accommodate "a number of our Customers, who intend to separate it from the rest of the paper and fix it up, in open view, in their Houses, as a mark of their approbation of the INDEPENDENT SPIRIT of their Representatives." Broadsides could, of course, serve that same purpose. One such printed document, executed in Massachusetts "In the Name, and by Order of the Council" and now at the New York Public Library, "is torn . . . at the bottom, both on the right and left of the centre, and at the top—as if it had been nailed or pasted to something and torn loose."[12]

2.   An All-But-Forgotten Testament

What were Americans celebrating with their processions, their ceremonial bonfires, their "illuminations," the firing of guns and ringing of bells, the printed pages that they "fixed up" on the walls of their homes? The news, not the vehicle that brought it; Independence, the end of monarchy, and the assumption of self-government, not the document that announced Congress's decision to break with Britain. Considering how revered a position the Declaration of Independence later won in the hearts and minds of the American people, their disregard for it in the earliest years of the new nation verges on the incredible. One colonial newspaper dismissed the Declaration's charges against the King as another "recapitulation of injuries," one, it seems, in a series, and not particularly remarkable compared to the others. There's some evidence that when the Declaration was read listeners heard mainly what was already in their heads and what one state and locality after another had concluded over the previous few months, that Independence came because the colonists had no alternative: "the people are now convinced," reported a newspaper article on the July 8 festivities at Trenton, "that our enemies have left us no middle way between perfect freedom and abject slavery." Citations of the Declaration were usually drawn from its final paragraph, which said that the united colonies "are and of right ought to be free and independent states" and were "absolved of all allegiance to the British Crown," words that Congress had inserted into Jefferson's draft. Independence was new; the rest of the Declaration seemed all too familiar, a restatement of what had already been said time and again.[13]

The adoption of Independence was, however, from the beginning confused with its declaration and the document that officially performed that function. The various meanings of the word "declare" contributed to that confusion. Before the Declaration of Independence had been issued—while, in fact, Congress was still at work editing Jefferson's draft—Pennsylvania newspapers announced that on July 2 the Continental Congress had "declared the United Colonies Free and Independent States," by which they meant simply that it had officially accepted that status, and the news was repeated in other colonial papers.[14] In later years, moreover, the "Anniversary of the United States of America" came to be celebrated on the day Congress finally approved the Declaration of Independence. That custom began almost by accident. In 1776, John Adams—to the amusement of some later Americans—suggested that July 2 should be "celebrated by succeeding generations as the great Anniversary Festival" with "pomp and parade, shows, games, sports, guns, bells, bonfires, and illuminations, from one end of the continent to the other from this time forward, forever more." But in 1777, no member of Congress thought of marking the day until the 2nd of July, and no mention was made of it until the third. The first great "Anniversary of Independence" was therefore celebrated at Philadelphia—and, it seems, in a handful of other cities and towns—on the 4th, which thereafter became the tradition. One somewhat curmudgeonly Connecticut Congressman, who saw the festivities as little more than a waste of gunpowder and other scarce resources, described them as "celebrating the Anniversary of the Declaration of Independence," but then, and over the next few years, references to the "Anniversary of Independence" and to that of the Declaration seem to have been virtually interchangeable.[15]

Accounts of celebrations at Philadelphia on July 4, 1777, say quite a bit about the music played by a band of Hessian soldiers who had been captured at Trenton the previous December and the "splendid illumination" of houses by candles put in the windows, but little about the Declaration itself. The day ended with fireworks on the Commons, including the firing of thirteen "rockets"—one for each state in the union. All was conducted with the greatest order and decorum, the *Pennsylvania Evening Post* reported, and with universal joy and gladness. "Thus may the fourth of July, that glorious and ever memorable day, be celebrated through America, by the sons of freedom, from age to age till time shall be no more. Amen, and amen." In fact, celebrations were not held everywhere during the late 1770s and 1780s, and seem actually to have declined in popularity immediately after the war ended in 1783. Where the day was remembered, however, the rituals usually included a parading of troops, firing of guns and cannon, festive dinners where numerous toasts were offered, and, occasionally, fireworks, although they apparently became common only in the nineteenth century. Sometimes people attended religious services where patriotic sermons or orations were given, and the day might include nonmilitary processions, the ancestors of modern parades. At Philadelphia in 1783, for example, a "car" with portraits of military leaders was carried through the streets led by children dressed in white and carrying torches.[16]

But seldom if ever, to judge by newspaper accounts and histories of the celebrations, was the Declaration of Independence read publicly in the late 1770s and 1780s. It was as if that document had done its work in carrying news of Independence to the people, and neither needed nor deserved further commemoration. The festivities included no praise of Thomas Jefferson, whose authorship of the Declaration was not yet common knowledge, and no suggestion that the document itself was, as posterity would have it, unusually eloquent or powerful.[17] Perhaps the only public commentary of the time on the document's literary qualities came in the report of a speech in Parliament by the English radical John Wilkes that appeared in Dixon and Hunter's *Virginia Gazette* on April 25, 1777. Wilkes set out to answer an opponent who had attacked "the American declaration of independency . . . as a wretched composition, very ill written, drawn up with a view to captivate the people." But Wilkes, a longtime defender of the Americans, actually seemed to accept that description of the Declaration. Those supposed flaws in the document were, he said,

> the very reason why I approve it most as a composition, as well as a wise, political measure, for the people are to decide this great controversy. If they are captivated by it, the end is attained. The polished periods, the harmonious, happy expressions, with all the grace, ease, and elegance of a beautiful diction, which we chiefly admire, captivate the people of America very little; but manly, nervous sense they relish, even in the most awkward and uncouth dress of language.

The Declaration of Independence was, of course, more than a Congressional press release, or an effort to enlist popular enthusiasm with "awkward and uncouth" language. It performed a constitutional function in formally closing the previous regime and so provided, as Hancock noted, "the Ground and Foundation of a future Government." Colonists everywhere, children as they were of English tradition, understood the necessity of performing that task before new governments were begun. The two permanent state constitutions adopted before July 4, 1776, those of Virginia and New Jersey, both included preambles that formally ended British rule. Even the temporary constitutions that New Hampshire adopted in January and South Carolina in March 1776, both of which were meant to endure only until the conflict with Britain was settled, began by listing the provocations that forced them to establish new governments.[18] The obligation to explain how and why British authority had ended did not persist into future times: no such provisions were necessary in latter-day constitutions that did not establish new regimes, but revised the institutions of an already established government. The obligation rested only on Americans who lived through the Revolution and established the first governments of the American republic.

The state declarations of Independence issued after July 4, 1776, suggest again how relatively little esteem Congress's Declaration commanded at the time. Once Congress had declared Independence, the states, it seems, could simply have referred to Congress's Declaration and been done with that subject. Many state constitutions of late 1776 and 1777 did refer to Congress's Declaration, and in ways that recognized the Continental Congress's right to speak for the states. But those references gave no indication whatsoever that Congress's case for Independence was so compelling and its language so eloquent that no improvements were possible. The preamble to the New York Constitution of 1777 did repeat the entire Declaration of Independence, word for word, but it also repeated other documents relevant to the establishment of a new state government. The Declaration of Independence was just one among several resolutions of the state and Continental congresses by which "all power whatever . . . hath reverted to the people" so they could empower their representatives to "institute and establish such a government as they shall deem best calculated to secure the rights and liberties of the good people of this State."[19]

Other states preferred to explain the dissolution of British authority in their own words, and cited Congress's Declaration of Independence only briefly or in passing. Pennsylvania's constitution of 1776 began, in the time-tested way, with a set of "whereas" clauses that asserted the people's right to change their government when it failed to

promote their safety and happiness. After recalling the King's withdrawal of protection over the colonists and his waging of war against
them with the help of "mercenaries, savages, and slaves," it referred
to "many other acts of tyranny" that were "more fully set forth in
the Declaration of Congress." As a result of those acts, the Pennsylvania constitution said, "all allegiance and fealty to the said king and
his successors, are dissolved and at an end." North Carolina opened its
constitution in much the same way, except that it did not refer to
the grievance section of Congress's Declaration to explain why government under royal authority "hath ceased," but instead paraphrased
its concluding paragraph. The Continental Congress had declared,
North Carolina said, that "the Thirteen United Colonies are, of right,
wholly absolved from all allegiance to the British crown," and that "the
said Colonies now are, and forever shall be, free and independent
States."[20] Georgia's constitution of 1777 similarly noted in one of
several opening "whereas" clauses that Congress had declared American Independence, and that "all political connection" between the
United States "and the Crown of Great Britain is in consequence
thereof dissolved."[21] However, Maryland's constitution of 1776 made
no direct reference to Congress's Declaration of Independence in a
brief preface to its Declaration of Rights and Constitution, which restated the circumstances that had "constrained" the Americans to declare themselves Independent and "assume government under the
authority of the people." And Massachusetts—which in 1780 adopted
the last of the first state constitutions—ignored the Declaration of Independence altogether and, in fact, skipped any prefatory statement
on the causes of Independence as if the need for such justifications had
passed.[22]

The historian Philip F. Detweiler, who carefully studied the
changing reputation of the Declaration of Independence in its first
fifty years, looked for the Declaration's influence on the declarations or
bills of rights that eight states attached to their constitutions during
the revolutionary period. They, too, he noted, failed to use the language of the Declaration of Independence. Of course, the Declaration
of Independence was emphatically not a bill of rights in the American
sense, that is, a statement of fundamental rights that government must
honor and protect: it corresponded to the first, not the second part of
the English Declaration of Rights. There are, however, good historical
reasons why the Declaration of Independence is so easily confused

with a bill of rights. After all, the words from its second paragraph that are today remembered beyond all others—"that all men are created equal; that they are endowed by their Creator with certain unalienable rights; that among these are life, liberty, and the pursuit of happiness"—were originally adapted from a draft of the Virginia Declaration of Rights written by George Mason and amended by a committee of the Virginia convention.

In fact, the words of the Mason draft made their way into several other revolutionary state bills of rights, and seem to have had a far greater impact than either the Declaration of Independence or the Declaration of Rights that the Virginia convention finally adopted, both of which were themselves descended from the Mason draft.[23] What might seem to be minor differences of wording are critical in tracing its lineage. Where the Declaration of Independence said men were "created equal," the Mason/committee draft asserted

> that all men *are born* equally free and independant, and have certain inherent natural rights, of which they cannot, by any compact, deprive or divert their posterity; among which are the enjoyment of life and liberty, with the means of acquiring and possessing property, and pursuing and obtaining happiness and safety. [Italics added]

The Virginia convention changed the opening phrase to say "That all men *are by nature* equally free and independent and have certain inherent rights" (again, italics added), which had few if any echoes in the eighteenth century.[24] Those who drafted state bills of rights with assertions of human equality seem to have begun, like Jefferson, with the Mason/committee version either as they encountered it in the press or, later, as it appeared in some previous state bill of rights. But, again like Jefferson, they felt free to make adjustments in the text. Pennsylvania's 1776 "Declaration of the Rights of . . . Inhabitants," in whose creation Benjamin Franklin played a part, said "That all men are born equally free and independent," but changed the next phrase so it said that all men "have certain natural, inherent and inalienable rights," then completed the paragraph making further minor changes in the Mason text. Similarly, the Massachusetts "Declaration of the Rights of the Inhabitants," which John Adams drafted in 1780, said "All men are born free and equal," which was close to Mason, then rephrased the rest of the paragraph:

> and have certain natural, essential, and unalienable rights; among which may be reckoned the right of enjoying and defending their

THE DECLARATION OF INDEPENDENCE: A FAMILY TREE

THE ENGLISH DECLARATION OF RIGHTS, February 12, 1689

First Part, Ending the Reign
of James II

Second Part, Declaring *"Undoubted
Rights and Liberties"*

Thomas Jefferson's Preamble,
Virginia State Constitution,
June 1776
(Charges Against the King)

George Mason/Committee Draft of
the Virginia Declaration of Rights,
June 1776
(*"that all men are born equally free and
independant, and have certain inherent
natural rights"*)

The American Declaration of
Independence, July 4, 1776
(*"that all men are created equal; that
they are endowed by their Creator with
certain inalienable rights"*)

STATE DECLARATIONS or BILLS OF RIGHTS

Virginia 1776
(*"that all men are by nature equally
free and independent and have certain
inherent rights"*)

Massachusetts 1780

New Hampshire 1784

Pennsylvania 1776
(*"That all men are born equally
free and independent"* and have
*"certain natural, inherent and
inalienable rights"*)

Vermont 1777

The French Declaration of the
Rights of Man and Citizen, 1789
(*"Men are born and remain free and
equal in rights."*)

lives and liberties; that of acquiring, possessing, and protecting property; in fine, that of seeking and obtaining their safety and happiness. Vermont's 1777 Declaration of Rights followed the Pennsylvania model. And in 1784 New Hampshire said that "All men are born equally free and independent," then offered still another version of Mason's statement on rights:

> All men have certain natural, essential, and inherent rights; among which are—the enjoying and defending life and liberty—acquiring, possessing and protecting property—and in a word, of seeking and obtaining happiness.[25]

There, at least, and perhaps also in the Massachusetts document, was an answer to the much-asked question about what the "pursuit of happiness" meant in the revolutionary era. All of the above, New Hampshire seemed to say—life, liberty, and property.

In none of these documents is there any evidence whatsoever that the Declaration of Independence lived in men's minds as a classic statement of American political principles. Not one revolutionary state bill of rights used the words "all men are created equal." Nor, for that matter, did the Declaration of the Rights of Man and Citizen adopted by the French National Assembly on August 26, 1789, which is sometimes said to be a descendant of the American Declaration of Independence. The French seem, however, to have had high regard for the American Declaration. They were familiar with its text and also those of the American revolutionary constitutions and bills of rights, since those documents had been translated and published in France not once but several times. Indeed, the duc de La Rochefoucauld d'Enville, who sat in the National Assembly in 1789, had himself—with some help from Franklin—translated and published the *Constitutions des treize Etats-Unis de l'Amérique* (1783), which included not just the state constitutions and bills of rights but an array of charters, the Declaration of Independence, and the Articles of Confederation. The marquis de Lafayette, a veteran of the American revolutionary war who became the first person to propose that the National Assembly issue a declaration, had a particular affection for the Declaration of Independence. In the library of his Paris home he had hung a frame half-filled with a copy of that document. The remaining empty space, he explained to visitors, was reserved for the French Declaration of Rights that would one day be adopted. Lafayette tried his hand at drafting such a declaration in early January 1789, and submitted his manuscript for comment to Jefferson, who was in Paris as the American minister to France. Later, as the Declaration of the Rights of Man evolved, other members of the National Assembly also regularly consulted Jefferson.[26]

Lafayette's draft and the Declaration of the Rights of Man and the Citizen that the National Assembly finally adopted were, however, counterparts of the American declarations or bills of rights, not the Declaration of Independence. Unlike the English in 1688 or the Americans in 1776, the French in 1789 were not yet ready to end the old regime. They sought "to establish a new government inside the old one," to fix the legitimacy of the National Assembly while maintaining monarchy. Moreover, the circumstances of August 1789, in the wake of the July uprisings in Paris, and when the French countryside was in turmoil, virtually precluded the National Assembly from forcefully asserting the right and duty of the people to "throw off government" when subjected to "a long train of abuses & usurpations." Even compared to the American state bills of rights, moreover, the French Declaration was distinctive for reasons that were tied, as contenders of the time recognized, to that country's very different history and situation. Where English and American bills of rights were phrased as limits on government sanctioned by long tradition, the French Declaration was a "national catechism" designed to educate the people in both their rights and their duties since, as the preamble said, "ignorance, disregard or contempt of the rights of man are the sole causes of public misfortunes and governmental corruption." Only a handful of provisions—on freedom of religion, for example—recalled the American state bills of rights, and that of Pennsylvania was the most influential, in no small part because Benjamin Franklin had promoted its glories among French enthusiasts of America. As a result, the first numbered provision of the French Declaration of Rights, "Men are born and remain free and equal in rights," echoed the language of George Mason as it appeared in the Pennsylvania Declaration of Rights—not as Jefferson had revised it for the Declaration of Independence.[27]

DURING THE FIRST fifteen years following its adoption, then, the Declaration of Independence seems to have been all but forgotten, particularly within the United States, except as the means by which Americans announced their separation from Great Britain. The histories and political writings of the 1780s generally describe the document "primarily as the act of independence." Participants in the extensive debates over the creation and ratification of the federal constitution mentioned the Declaration, again, very infrequently and then generally cited its assertion of the people's right to "abolish or alter their governments" and to found new ones that "to them shall seem most likely to effect their safety and happiness."[28]

Indeed, the first twenty volumes of the comprehensive modern *Papers of Thomas Jefferson*, which cover the period to 1791, include few references to the Declaration of Independence after those of 1776 that concern its drafting, revision, and adoption. There are, however, at least two significant exceptions, one of which has more to do with Independence than its declaration. On August 29, 1787, after reading an article in the *Journal de Paris* that attributed the adoption of American Independence to the influence of John Dickinson, Jefferson wrote a long letter to the editor that summarized Congress's proceedings in detail, drawing upon his notes on Congress's proceedings and demonstrating that Dickinson was on the other side. Jefferson revealed no rancor toward Dickinson, who, he said, would himself have disavowed the error, nor did he mention the names of other delegates who were in fact responsible for Congress's adoption of Independence. He acted, Jefferson said, from a desire to "bear witness to the truth." If the living did not contradict falsehood about events they had witnessed, he asked, how could future histories be accurate? But, perhaps because he feared that his reply would in some way seem self-serving, he decided in the end against sending the letter, which at his death remained among his papers, unpublished.[29]

Then, on July 4, 1789, a group of Americans in Paris, including the poet Joel Barlow, sent a tribute to Jefferson that shows they knew he had written the Declaration of Independence, and contains some of the earliest praise of his prose. "As this is the anniversary of our Independence," they said, their pleasure was increased "from the idea that we are addressing ourselves to a man who sustained so conspicuous a part in the immortal transactions of that day—whose dignity energy and elegance of thought added a peculiar lustre to that declaratory act which announced to the world the existence of an empire."[30] That was a far cry from John Wilkes's description of the Declaration and its "awkward and uncouth dress of language." And it was a sign of things to come.

3. A Partisan Document

The modern reputation of the Declaration of Independence was born in the bitter partisan politics of the 1790s and reached a recognizably mature form, complete with quasi-religious attributes, thirty years later. The standard story goes like this: celebrations of the Fourth of July in the 1780s were controlled by nationalists who would later find a home in the Federalist Party. The festivities they held made few if any references to the Declaration of Independence itself, and that tendency became more conscious and rigid in the 1790s. The Declaration's anti-British character was an embarrassment to a party that sought economic and diplomatic rapprochement with the onetime Mother Country. Moreover, after the execution of Louis XVI and the onset of the Terror, the Federalists shed any enthusiasm they once felt for the French Revolution; and the assertions of equality and unalienable rights in the second paragraph of the Declaration of Independence, although different in formulation from the French Declaration of the Rights of Man, still seemed too "French" for the Federalists' comfort. They also understandably found it best to say as little as possible about a fundamental American text that had been drafted by Thomas Jefferson, a leader of the opposing Republican Party.[31]

It was, then, the Republicans—Joel Barlow among them—who began to celebrate the Declaration of Independence as a "deathless instrument" written by "the immortal Jefferson." The Republicans considered themselves defenders of the republic founded in 1776 against subversion by pro-British, "monarchist" opponents, and they hoped that by recalling the causes of Independence they would make Americans suspicious of further dealings with Britain. They were also delighted to identify the founding principles of the American Revolution with those of America's sister republic in France. In Republican hands, the attention that had focused first on the grievance section of the Declaration, and then on its conclusion, shifted toward the opening paragraphs as a statement of basic political principles that went beyond the right of revolution and had an enduring significance for established governments. The Declaration, as one Republican newspaper said, was not to be celebrated merely "as affecting the seperation of one country from the jurisdiction of another; but as being the result of a rational discussion and definition of the rights of man, and the end of civil government." At their Fourth of July festivities the Republicans publicly read the Declaration of Independence; their newspapers reprinted it; and they chided the Federalists for their unwillingness to do the same. Sometimes, however, even they got the text wrong: that "sublime instrument," the Declaration of Independence, according to Boston's Republican *Independent Chronicle* of July 6, 1797, said that " 'All men'... are born 'Free' and 'Equal.' "[32] Could it be that the words that lived on even in Republican hearts and minds were not Jefferson's but Mason's?

Federalists responded by insisting that Jefferson had not produced the Declaration alone. The Republicans, they said, "pretend that Mr. Jefferson is entitled almost exclusively to the credit of the declaration." He was, of course, a member of the Committee "appointed after the subject had been fully discussed in Congress . . . to draw up the *Declaration* of that question." But John Adams—a Federalist—was also on the Committee "and must have had his voice in the instrument," and Congress itself made changes before issuing the document. Indeed, Congress's vote for Independence on July 2 was far more important than the mere "penning a bill," and in that "glorious work" Adams was critical. The Federalists also argued that Jefferson's work as "the scribe who penned the declaration" was not so distinguished as his followers suggested. They rediscovered the similarities in phraseology between parts of the Declaration and Locke's *Second Treatise of Government* that Richard Henry Lee had noticed long before, and used them to argue that even the "small part of that memorable instrument" that could be attributed to Jefferson "he stole from *Locke's Essays*."[33]

After the War of 1812, the Federalist Party slipped from sight and, with it, public efforts to disparage the Declaration of Independence. When a new party system formed in the late 1820s and the 1830s, both Whigs and Jacksonians claimed descent from Jefferson and his party, which served to confirm and perpetuate the old Republican reverence for the Declaration of Independence and its emphasis upon Jefferson's role in its creation, which persists today, over a century and a half later.[34] In truth, however, Federalist reservations did not vanish altogether, nor have they been without their own lasting influence. In his 1823 Fourth of July oration, Timothy Pickering—as stolid an old Federalist as ever walked the earth—described the Declaration of Independence as "a compilation of facts and sentiments" previously stated by other defenders of colonial rights, and claimed that the excisions and other changes Congress made "manifestly improved" the text. Jefferson knew exactly where Pickering was coming from—the old, antirevolutionary, pro-British Federalist politics of the 1790s. Pickering, Jefferson said, would have been happier if everything in the Declaration had been cut out except the "single sentiment" recommending "friendship to his dear England, whenever she is willing to be at peace with us." For Pickering, Jefferson charged, the Declaration was "a libel on the government of England, composed in times of passion," which "should now be buried in utter oblivion, to spare the feelings of our English friends and Angloman fellow-citizens." But Jefferson failed to notice how different Pickering's comments were from those of Federalists in times past. Pickering had, after all, described the Declaration of Independence as a "celebrated paper" more distinguished than any other act of the Congress of the Thirteen United Colonies, and he actually read the Declaration to the crowd at Salem after completing his opening "observations," something no Federalist worth his salt would have done twenty years earlier.[35]

Partisan politics also played a role, along with regional rivalries, in one of the strangest episodes in the Declaration's history, the "discovery" of the so-called Mecklenburg Declaration of Independence, which was first published on April 30, 1819, in the *Raleigh Register and North Carolina Gazette* within an article by Dr. Joseph McKnitt Alexander. On hearing news of Lexington and Concord, Alexander said, representatives of militia companies in Mecklenburg County, North Carolina, met at Charlotte on May 20, 1775, and passed a set of resolutions that declared themselves "a free and independent People." They did so, moreover, using language amazingly like that of the Declaration of Independence. The Mecklenburg Resolutions referred, for example, to the "inherant and inalienable rights of man"; they spoke of dissolving the "political bands" that bound England and America; the militiamen said they were, "and of right ought to be, a sovereign and self-governing Association," and pledged "our mutual cooperation, our lives, our fortunes, and our most sacred honor" to the cause of Independence. Alexander's father, John McKnitt Alexander, who died at age eighty-four in 1817, had been clerk of the Mecklenburg meeting, and so kept its records; in later life he became a Federalist. The "original book" of accounts was destroyed in a fire of April 1800, but the version Dr. Alexander produced in 1819 was, he insisted, a "true copy of the papers on the above subject."[36]

John Adams encountered the Resolutions in June when they were republished in the *Essex Gazette*—an old Federalist paper—of Salem, Massachusetts, and sent a copy to Jefferson. Adams instinctively accepted the Resolutions as valid, if only because they seemed to support a view he had held for over forty years: "What a poor, ignorant, malicious, short-sighted, Crapulous mass is Tom Pain[e]'s Common Sense, in comparison with this paper," he commented. Although Paine was then ten years in his grave, Adams's enmity toward him was obviously alive and well. In truth, Adams was also miffed by all the glory conferred on Jefferson for having drafted the Declaration of Independence, and that resentment, too, fed into his delight with the Mecklenburg "Declaration of Independence" since it undercut Jefferson's celebrity as effectively as Paine's. Adams wrote the Reverend William Bentley in Salem that Jefferson must have seen the Mecklenburg Resolutions since he "copied the spirit, the sense, and the expressions of it *verbatim* into his Declaration of the 4th of July, 1776," and asked Bentley to have the printer of the *Gazette* send him a half dozen copies of the June 5 issue "whatever they may cost."[37]

But was the document what it pretended to be? Jefferson quickly pronounced it "spurious," since no one had apparently heard of the Mecklenburg "Declaration" until 1819, when the principal people mentioned were dead and the original version was in ashes. Adams wrote Jefferson that he agreed, but in fact, deep in his Federalist soul, he continued to believe that the Mecklenburg Declaration was legitimate. "I could as soon believe that the dozen flowers of the Hydrangia now before my Eyes were the work of chance," he wrote a friend, "as that the Mecklenburg Resolutions and Mr. Jefferson's declaration were not derived the one from the other."[38]

Today the preponderant opinion of "most sensible" modern historians, as Merrill Peterson put it, supports Jefferson's position. The author of Alexander's "true copy"—perhaps his father, writing after the fire of 1800—probably attempted to summarize from memory a set of resolutions that were actually adopted on May 31, 1775, and mistakenly incorporated the language of the Declaration of Independence (and, in the phrase "inherent and inalienable rights of man," curiously went back to both Jefferson's draft of the Declaration and the French Declaration of the Rights of Man). When compared to other documents of the time, the "Mecklenburg Declaration of Independence" supposedly adopted on May 20, 1775, is simply incredible. It makes the reaction of North Carolinians to Lexington and Concord more extreme than that of the Massachusetts people who received the blow. The resolutions of May 31, 1775, of which there is contemporary evidence, were also radical, but remain believable. They responded to an address Parliament sent the King in February 1775, which declared the colonies in a state of rebellion, by declaring "null and void" all American civil and military commissions granted by the Crown and initiating a temporary county government "independent of the Crown of Great-Britain." That ad hoc government would remain in place until the North Carolina Provincial Congress made other arrangements or Parliament gave up "its unjust and arbitrary pretentions with respect to America." Since the May 31 resolutions anticipated a possible reconciliation, they were not a "declaration of independence." Unfortunately, by 1838, when the archivist Peter Force discovered the May 31 resolutions in a newspaper of 1775, old political divisions and regional rivalries left little room for a simple mistake. The North Carolina legislature, anxious to confirm the state's claim as "first for independence," had already published a pamphlet that mobilized the testimony of aged revolutionaries to prove the document's authenticity, which certain "Federalist-minded" historians were inclined to accept. Meanwhile, latter-day Jeffersonians saw the supposed Mecklenburg "Declaration" of May 20, 1775, as another fraudulent effort to discredit their hero by accusing him of plagiarism.[39]

Behind the details of the controversy lay a more basic point: by 1819 the language of the Declaration of Independence was not just familiar, but sufficiently cherished that responsibility for it was worth fighting over. By then, too, for better or worse, the modern emphasis on individual creativity and novelty, so unlike the eighteenth century's respect for imitation and adaptation, had made its appearance. The origins of the new attitudes toward the Declaration and its author involved far more than the demise of the Federalist Party and the triumph of Jeffersonianism. After 1815, when the Treaty of Ghent ended a half century of Anglo-American conflict, the Declaration of Independence became the subject of massive public attention that crossed old partisan lines and was itself part of a widespread, intense interest in American history, particularly that of the Revolution, that appeared quite suddenly and reached a high point in 1826 with the fiftieth anniversary of Independence. In that critical period, members of the revolutionary generation were heroicized and the Declaration began to assume a certain holy quality. The reasons lay in the circumstances of the moment, above all in a remarkable confluence between the needs of young Americans and those of aged revolutionaries, particularly Jefferson himself. The results, however, stretched on into later times.

4. Sacred Text

As late as January 1817, John Adams said that his country lacked any interest in its past: "I See no disposition to celebrate or remember, or even Curiosity to enquire into the Characters, Actions, or Events of the Revolution," he wrote John Trumbull. But a little over a month later Congress commissioned Trumbull to produce four large paintings commemorating the American Revolution, which were to hang in the rotunda of the new American Capitol. For Trumbull the most important of the series, and the one to which he first turned, was the Declaration of Independence. He based the new work upon a smaller painting he had done between 1786 and 1793 that showed the drafting committee presenting its work to Congress and included portraits of forty-eight members of the Continental Congress, many of which had been painted from life. Trumbull's basic design was, like the Declaration itself, adapted from an earlier work—Benjamin West's painting of American and British diplomats signing a preliminary peace treaty on November 30, 1782. When the new twelve-by-eighteen-foot canvas was completed in 1818, Trumbull exhibited it to large crowds in Boston, Philadelphia, and Baltimore before delivering it in Washington: indeed, of all the paintings he completed for the Capitol, *The Declaration of Independence* was the greatest popular success.[40]

In 1818, too, Benjamin Owen Tyler published an engraved copy of the Declaration of Independence, which led to a heated controversy between Tyler and John Binns, who two years earlier had announced his intention of publishing a decorated copy of the Declaration. Binns finally brought out his print in 1819. Both the Tyler and Binns versions sold briskly, which perhaps inspired Secretary of State John Quincy Adams to have an exact facsimile of the Declaration made in 1823—the only one ever produced—which Congress decided to distribute widely throughout the country.[41]

Books also began to appear. In 1819, Joseph M. Sanderson published his *Proposals . . . for Publishing by Subscription a Biography of the Signers to the Declaration of Independence*, complete with plates and the Declaration itself "with Fac-Simile Engravings of the Signatures." That work finally appeared in nine volumes published between 1823 and 1827. If it was not to everyone's taste (one reviewer said the work was "too long and too diffuse" and included "much false taste of every kind"[42]), no problem; Charles A. Goodrich would soon produce a one-volume *Lives of the Signers to the Declaration of Independence* (New York, 1829). By then Hezekiah Niles had published his *Principles and Acts of the Revolution in America*, which its subtitle described as *an Attempt to Collect and Preserve Some of the Speeches, Orations, & Proceedings . . . Belonging to the Revolutionary Period in the United States; Which, Happily, Terminated in the Establishment of Their Liberties* (Baltimore, 1822), and which, as Niles explained in his "Prefatory," had first been proposed by a subscriber to the *Weekly Register* he edited in November 1816. By the time the last volume of Sanderson's biographies of the signers was published, Jared Sparks had begun reading and editing the papers of George Washington, which he published in twelve volumes in the 1830s, as well as a life of Gouverneur Morris, ten volumes of Franklin's works, and a ten-volume *Library of American Biography*. Meanwhile, Peter Force began editing the *American Archives*, a huge repository of historical documents that included many of the state and local declarations of Independence discussed earlier in this book.

Biographies of revolutionaries, often written by descendants, started to multiply. William Wirt's *Sketches of the Life and Character of Patrick Henry* (1817) claimed for its subject the honor of opening the American Revolution, and so began a controversy over which state led the movement toward Independence. It provoked North Carolina's

Senators to make inquiries about their state's revolutionary history that led directly to publication of the "Mecklenburg Declaration of Independence" two years later.[43] William Tudor made a pitch for Massachusetts in his *Life of James Otis* (Boston, 1823), which he wrote with the encouragement of John Adams. (And in a part of his famous 1822 letter to Pickering, which Pickering repeated in the 1823 Fourth of July oration that so riled Jefferson, Adams volunteered that the essence of the Declaration of Independence was "in a pamphlet voted and printed by the town of Boston before the first Congress met, composed by James Otis ... and pruned and polished by Samuel Adams.")[44] Other books followed, such as Josiah Quincy's *Memoir of the Life of Josiah Quincy, Junior* (Boston, 1825) and John Drayton's *Memoirs of the American Revolution ... as relating to the State of South Carolina* ... (Charleston, 1821), both of which were based on papers left by the authors' deceased fathers.

What happened, in short, was that a new generation of Americans turned its attention back in time, and made preservation of the nation's revolutionary history its peculiar mission. The revolutionaries themselves had little time to reflect on their history because they were so busy making it, a writer in the *North American Review* explained in 1826. After declaring Independence, they had a war to fight; and when peace returned, "the whole country was miserably exhausted by the exertions and sufferings incident to the arduous struggle, and all became earnestly engaged ... in repairing their wasted fortunes. ..." Then other pressing issues demanded attention: the reorganization of national government, the challenge of achieving domestic stability during the 1790s, when the French Revolution made "a recurrence to the principles of the revolution ... the instrument of party." For all those reasons, "we are not to look at the early years of our national progress ... for any very intense interest in the history of the revolution." But at last, after 1815 and the Treaty of Ghent, Americans had arrived at a period when "the principles, causes, events, and characters of the revolution" could claim "their just share of public attention."[45]

The task of collecting and preserving the nation's revolutionary history was urgent. Precious time had been lost; many documents remained in private hands, where they were gradually separated from one another and lost. Niles consoled himself that his *Principles and Acts of the Revolution,* however incomplete and imperfect, nonetheless would "rescue from oblivion" many items that were "hastening to it." Even worse, many members of the revolutionary generation had died, taking with them facts and memories that could no longer be recovered.[46] Never before was interest in the American past greater than in the decade before 1826, and never was the sense of impending loss more widespread.

In the course of recalling and recording the events of the Revolution, Americans of the 1820s remembered the revolutionaries as mighty fathers whose greatness threw into relief the ordinariness of their descendants. It wasn't the first time that Americans attributed superhuman characteristics to an earlier generation. New Englanders of the late seventeenth century had looked back at the Puritan founders of Massachusetts with a similar sense of awe. In both cases, moreover, the Americans who heroicized their ancestors had survived the uncertainties of a founding period and enjoyed at last the blessings of prosperity and a certain stability. The contemporaries of Hezekiah Niles lived in a nation that no longer needed to endure the hostility and insults of England. Once the world's lone republic, the United States in the 1820s witnessed efforts to establish sister republics in Europe and Latin America. Its western border stretched beyond the nation's first boundary, the Mississippi, and toward the Pacific; its population had quadrupled since 1776 and by the fiftieth anniversary of Independence was approaching 12 million.

Americans of the 1820s had also seen the beginnings of American industrialization and of the canal era, a first stage in the creation of a manmade domestic transportation system that would allow an astounding expansion of internal trade. Soon the railroad would appear. All these blessings were considered the fruits of Independence since they could hardly have happened under London's jealous rule. As a result, it seemed appropriate that work on the Ohio Canal, the Farmington Canal, and the Chesapeake and Ohio Canal should officially commence on July 4 in 1825 and 1828, or that on July 4, 1828, Charles Carroll of Carrollton, then the last surviving signer of the Declaration of Independence, should turn the first earth for the Baltimore and Ohio Railroad. In the midst of such material abundance, however, it seemed all the more important to recall and perpetuate the values of the Revolution. And so Niles characteristically dedicated his document collection to "the young men of the United States" in the hope that they would emulate the "noblest deeds" of their fathers "when the Liberties of their Country are Endangered, by Foreign Enemies or Domestic Encroachments; so that the blessings which these Patriots won may Descend to Posterity."[47]

The very appearance of revolutionary veterans—or even of small things saved from the past—awoke deep feelings among Americans of the time. In 1824, President James Monroe and Congress officially invited the marquis de Lafayette to visit the United States. It was the "ardent desire" of the "whole nation . . . once again to see you amongst them," they said; and Lafayette was celebrated by crowds throughout the nation during his triumphal tour of 1824 and 1825. The visit generated volumes of souvenirs, and also inspired Americans to exhibit and celebrate small artifacts of the Revolution such as "fragments of arms or projectiles," even "military buttons" saved from the 1770s. All such "monuments of the revolution" were preserved and revered, Lafayette's secretary noted: "every thing which recalls this glorious epoch, is to them a precious relic, which they regard almost with religious reverence" and use to feed "the sacred fire of love of liberty."[48]

Homegrown revolutionaries had much the same effect, and on through the 1850s communities paraded their octo- and nonagenarian veterans in numbers suspiciously large, as one historian has noted, given the meager size of the Continental Army. But Congress expanded its definition of revolutionary military service in 1832, when it offered pensions to those who served in the militia or some other capacity outside the regular army. Then the country watched as their numbers shrank, year by year, decade by decade. Of the many "venerable and now sacred men" who fought in the Revolutionary War, only seven survived in 1864, all but one of whom had lived more than a century. The Reverend Elias Brewster Hillard hurried to interview and photograph those "last survivors of our great national conflict" for the benefit of posterity. "The present is the last generation that will be connected by living link with the great period in which our national independence was achieved," he wrote in the introduction to his book, *The Last Men of the Revolution.* "Our own are the last eyes that will look on men who looked on Washington; our ears the last that will hear the living voices of those who heard his words. Henceforth the American Revolution will be known among men by the silent record of history alone." But while veterans were still around to break the silence, what they said was sometimes strikingly like what Niles said at the start of his *Principles and Acts of the Revolution in America.* Take the eighty-year-old Colonel John Franklin, who read the Declaration of Independence at Bradford County, Pennsylvania, on July 4, 1828. Franklin expressed hope that the sight of "a frail remnant of one of those who faced the British cannon" and "gained for you the liberty you have enjoyed for more than half a century" would "strengthen you with virtue to defend your inheritance against foreign invasion, as well as against domestic intrigue and military usurpation."[49]

THOMAS JEFFERSON actively fostered this newborn dedication to the past, while John Adams, true to his Puritan roots, played the iconoclast. Adams compared the idolization of Washington and other revolutionaries to the canonization of saints and other "corrupt" practices of a superstitious, hierarchical past, and told young Americans that his generation was no better than theirs. Such differences were, however, carefully set aside as these old warhorses of 1776, now retired from the demands of office, resumed their friendship and exchanged letters from 1812 through the rest of their lives. With the death of Robert R. Livingston in 1813, they became the last two survivors of the committee that drafted the Declaration of Independence. Franklin had been the first to go, in 1790, and was followed three years later by Roger Sherman. Now Jefferson and Adams watched as other onetime colleagues disappeared. "Of the signers of the Declaration of Independance I see now living not more than half a dozen on your side of the Potomak," Jefferson wrote Adams on January 21, 1812, "and, on this side, myself alone."[50]

Their minds, like all old men's, moved naturally toward the remote past, sidestepping the years of partisan conflict that had separated them, and settled comfortably on the fight for Independence during which their friendship was first formed. Frequently they shared memories and news of the people they knew then. A Fourth of July orator in Milford, Massachusetts, had given Samuel Chase credit for having "'started the cry of independance in the ears of his countrymen.' Do you remember anything of this?" Jefferson asked Adams. "I do not." Later Jefferson reported that "Genl. Starke is off at the age of 93," and that Congress's old secretary, Charles Thomson, "still lives at about the same age, chearful, slender as a grasshopper," but with so little memory that he had trouble remembering who he was and once told the same story four times in one hour. "Is this life?" he asked. When our faculties have left, the friends of youth are all in the grave, "and a generation is risen around us whom we know not, is death an evil?"[51]

In fact, Jefferson, who took pleasure in the company of his many grandchildren, knew the generation rising around him and understood its burgeoning historical consciousness. When his grandson, Thomas Jefferson Randolph, planned to visit Boston, he "would think he had seen nothing," Jefferson wrote Adams, "were he to leave it without having seen you. . . . Like other young people, he wishes to be able, in the winter nights of old age, to recount to those around him what he has heard and learnt of the Heroic age preceding his birth, and which of the Argonauts particularly he was in time to have seen. It was the lot of our early years," he went on, "to witness nothing but the dull monotony of colonial subservice, and of riper ones to breast the labors and perils of working out of it. Theirs are the Halcyon calms succeeding the storm which our Argosy had so stoutly weathered. Gratify his ambition then by recieving [*sic*] his best bow. . . ." Jefferson was, of course, another "Argonaut," one whom crowds of Americans, young and old, rich and poor, were desperate to see. Many such pilgrims flocked to Monticello, uninvited, hoping to catch a glimpse of him, making nuisances of themselves and disrupting his moments of tranquillity. One woman, it is said, even smashed a window with her parasol to improve her view of the old man. He knew, then, of what he spoke when he sympathized with Adams over "the trouble these interruptions give."[52]

Jefferson played a particularly important role in rescuing the Declaration of Independence from its early obscurity and making it the defining event of a "Heroic age." It was he who first suggested that the young artist John Trumbull paint *The Declaration of Independence.* Trumbull had planned to paint a series of exclusively military scenes before he met Jefferson during a trip to Paris in the spring of 1786, then stayed with him at the Hôtel de Langeac in Paris later that year and again in 1787–88. Trumbull's first sketch of his famous painting shares a piece of drawing paper with a sketch by Jefferson, done in Paris during 1786, of the assembly room in the Old Pennsylvania State House, now known as Independence Hall. Trumbull's first paintings of the scene carefully followed Jefferson's sketch, which unfortunately included architectural inaccuracies, as Trumbull later learned to his dismay.[53] In 1813, Jefferson also reviewed with approval the sketch of "ornaments" that William P. Gardner proposed to use in publishing a copy of the Declaration of Independence—a scheme that was subsequently carried out by John Binns. The composition, Jefferson said, seemed to him "judicious and well imagined." If, however, he were to "hazard a suggestion" it would be that John Hancock "should occupy the middle and principal place" in an engraving dedicated to the Declaration, and that no man merited "a most conspicuous place in the design" more than John Adams, who was the "pillar of its support" in Congress and the Declaration's "ablest advocate and defender against the multifarious assaults it encountered."[54]

Meanwhile, Jefferson spent hour after hour answering patiently and in longhand letters that numbered, as he calculated, some 1,267 in 1820, many of which asked historical questions that required "elaborate research" to answer. Fortunately, he had at hand certain critical documents—the rough draft of the Declaration "with the corrections of Dr. Franklin and Mr. Adams interlined in their own hand writings," as he described it for James Madison in August 1823, and also written notes on Congress's proceedings which were, he insisted, "taken by myself at the moment and on the spot."[55] For Joseph Delaplaine in 1817 he discussed the drafting of the Declaration, which, he said, he alone composed, although its "sentiments were of all America." He declined, however, to provide more personal information of a sort that might suggest he was "worthy to occupy the public attention." Two years later he gave Samuel Adams Wells information on Congress's debates of 1776 and the role of Wells's grandfather, Samuel Adams, for whom Jefferson had a deep and abiding affection.[56] He retold Benjamin Franklin's story about the hatmaker's sign for Robert Walsh in 1818, and sent George Otis his recollections about regional attitudes toward Britain before Independence in 1821. He recalled the drafting process, the purpose of the Declaration of Independence, and its relationship to other similar documents in letters of 1823 to Madison and also to Henry Lee in May 1825. George Mason, he told Judge Augustus B. Woodward, wrote Virginia's Bill of Rights and its constitution, and was "one of our really great men, and of the first order of greatness." He, Jefferson, had, however, written the preamble that "became tacked to the work of . . . Mason," and that preamble resembled the Declaration of Independence because both had the "same object, of justifying our separation from Great Britain," and so "used necessarily the same materials of justification." Five months later, in September 1825, he told John Vaughan, who wondered about the origins of a copy of the Declaration that Vaughan possessed, that he, Jefferson, had made a "fair copy" of the Declaration during the drafting process whenever the previous copy became "too marked up," and sent those rough drafts to friends who wanted to know what was happening. He was unsure how many he'd sent out, or to whom, but the copy Vaughan had "must be of great value," he suggested, "and until all these private hoards are made public, the real history of the revolution will not be known."[57]

That was a reasonable answer, but probably, like the sketch of Independence Hall Jefferson made for Trumbull, and like many of his gracious responses to inquiries, inaccurate in some details. The copies Jefferson sent out were clean copies made after Congress edited his draft; they were not earlier, "marked up" rough drafts. And the notes on Congress's proceedings that Jefferson consulted had not been taken "on the spot," but were compiled at some later time from what were probably more fragmentary records that Jefferson kept while the actual events occurred. Those "Notes" also contained errors, which Jefferson sometimes later repeated. The Declaration was probably not signed on July 4, and "by every member present except Mr. Dickinson," as Jefferson insisted to the end of his life: the story, as Garry Wills said, makes no sense at all; and the Declaration was probably approved by Congress not in the evening, as Jefferson said, but the morning of the Fourth.[58] Even Jefferson's account of sending his manuscript to John Adams and Benjamin Franklin for comments before submitting it to the committee as a whole, which assumed almost canonical authority in later histories of the Declaration, underplayed the role of the committee, as the note he sent to Franklin with the draft Declaration reveals. Jefferson's accounts were mistaken not from malevolence certainly, or from moral failure, or even for partisan reasons. The errors probably came from simple failures of memory, or, more exactly, from the way old memories are sharpened and shaped by the contexts in which they are awakened. And no fellow delegates of 1776 stood up to correct his accounts, which were, in any case, entrusted to private letters, or, with the exception of John Adams, to assert their own claims to fame—to take credit, for example, for Congress's magnificent editing job—because death had sealed their lips.

Jefferson did not consciously seek to exaggerate his own role. Indeed, he tried to avoid focusing attention on himself, readily acknowledging the contributions of Adams, Franklin, and Hancock, and, although he insisted that he alone was responsible for drafting the document, Jefferson cautioned Delaplaine against attributing too much significance to "mere composition." There Adams agreed: he had long since complained that celebrations of the Declaration's drafting let Jefferson run off with "all the glory" deserved by many. For Adams, the Declaration fell into a category he once described as "dress and ornament rather than Body, Soul, or Substance." And if Independence, the "Body, Soul, or Substance," was commemorated, not its Declaration, the limelight would naturally shift toward Adams. Where had Jefferson been, after all, while Adams and a few other committed Congressmen were organizing grass-roots movements for Independence, maneuvering to overturn the obstructionist government of Pennsylvania, debating furiously to convert wavering delegates to Independence? Jefferson was home at Monticello and then, when he finally returned to Congress, spent much of his time composing a constitution for Virginia, or sitting tongue-tied through debates on Richard Henry Lee's resolutions, taking notes on the arguments other people made. Would the "true history" of the Revolution ever be told? Adams, who craved the esteem but emphatically not the adoration of posterity, was pessimistic. Patriotic mythology would more likely prevail and undercut the self-confidence of young Americans who had, in fact, far more talent than the generation of 1776.[59]

Meanwhile, Jefferson, who suffered moments of self-doubt that Adams rarely experienced, found ever deeper consolation in the fact that he had composed the Declaration of Independence. The personal meaning of that act, and perhaps also a desire to meet contemporary conceptions of creativity with their emphases on individualism and novelty, probably influenced the way he remembered the drafting process, effacing recollections of the committee's role in framing and revising the document or, for that matter, of the documents that had inspired him. More than anything else he had done, writing the Declaration of Independence came to justify his life and helped save Jefferson from an acute despair he experienced during the Missouri Controversy of 1819–20, which seemed to jeopardize all that he and his generation had accomplished. The effort to ban Missouri's admission to the Union unless it abandoned its slave system or, later, opened its borders to free blacks and mulattos, was for Jefferson a violation of the federal bargain negotiated at the time of the Revolution by which the states retained their sovereign power to determine and regulate their domestic affairs. He denied that legitimate concern over the persistence of slavery—over the universal rights of men—prompted the effort to prevent its spreading to new states in the West. Pretensions of that sort were fraudulent, he said; the controversy did not arise over a "moral question," but "one merely of power." If Congress could exclude Missouri from the Union unless it abandoned its slave system and restrictions on migration into the state, it could end slavery itself. Jefferson insisted that he would welcome the emancipation of American slaves—but only if their owners were compensated and the freedmen moved to new homes outside the United States, which, he understood, was no longer practical, given the size of the slave population and a birthrate that kept it growing at a brisk pace. To prevent Missourians from having a slave system was, however, an illegitimate extension of federal power that would provoke state resistance and, Jefferson predicted, destroy the Union. Those who opposed the admission to the Union of a slaveholding Missouri were therefore not liberals but counterrevolutionary reactionaries, like his old Federalist enemies. "I regret that I am now to die in the belief," he wrote in April 1820, "that the useless sacrifice of themselves by the generation of 1776, to acquire self-government and happiness to their country, is to be thrown away by the unwise and unworthy passions of their sons."[60] Jefferson's dark mood did not entirely disappear once political compromise settled the Missouri conflict. In later years it fed on other causes—the plague of problems that beset the University of Virginia, the pet project of his old age, in its opening years; financial problems so severe that he feared the loss of his beloved home, Monticello; and his own deteriorating health.

Years earlier—maybe even as early as 1800—Jefferson had composed a memorandum asking "whether my country is the better for my having lived at all? I do not know that it is." Among the contributions he listed, many "would have been done by others; some of them, perhaps, a little better." He began with his effort to make the Rivanna River suitable for navigation, mentioned the Declaration of Independence and the achievement of religious liberty in Virginia along with some other legal reforms, but also included a miscellaneous set of other services, among them his importing olive trees from Marseilles and sending seed for upland rice to Carolina "in hopes it might supersede the culture of the wet rice, which renders South Carolina and Georgia so pestilential through the summer."[61]

By 1826, however, Jefferson had arrived at a "short list" of his life's achievements. His tomb, he proposed, should say:

Here was buried
Thomas Jefferson
Author of the Declaration of American Independance
of the Statute of Virginia for religious freedom
& Father of the University of Virginia.[62]

Author, not draftsman, of the Declaration of Independence. That contribution, even beyond the other two contributions he mentioned, had assumed preeminence in his writings and reflections, as the Declaration itself became a redemptive force. The Declaration was "the fundamental act of union of these States" and should be kept in mind, he wrote Madison in 1823, "to cherish the principles of the instrument in the bosoms of our own citizens." In 1824 Jefferson received "with pleasure" copies of the new facsimile edition of the Declaration of Independence sent him under a resolution of Congress because of the evidence that republication gave "of reverence for that instrument, and . . . view in it a pledge of adhesion to its principles and of a sacred determination to maintain and perpetuate them," which he described as a "holy purpose."[63]

The words he chose—"reverence," "sacred," "holy"—were words of religion. This, mind you, was the same Thomas Jefferson whose draft Declaration of Independence made no appeal to God, and who took pride in having written a vigorous, precedent-setting statute that totally separated church and state in Virginia. Now, however, he applied the language of religion not just to the Declaration, but to everyday objects associated with its creation. "Small things may, perhaps, like the relics of saints, help to nourish our devotion to this holy bond of Union, and keep it longer alive and warm in our affections," he noted in 1825 before telling Dr. James Mease about "the house of a Mr.

Graff, a new brick house, three stories high," on Philadelphia's Market Street where Jefferson had lodged in 1776, and where he drafted the Declaration. Even the "plain, neat, convenient" writing desk on which he had worked might merit special attention, like the chair on which William Penn sat that, he noted, had recently been gratefully received by a newly founded historical society in Pennsylvania. "If . . . things acquire a superstitious value because of their connection with particular persons," he suggested, "surely a connection with the great Charter of our Independence may give a value to what has been associated with that. . . ." When he proposed to give his desk to Joseph Coolidge, the husband of his beloved granddaughter, Ellen Wayles Randolph, he predicted that "its imaginary value will increase with years." And if Coolidge "lives to my age, or another half-century, he may see it carried in the procession of our nation's birthday, as the relics of the saints are in those of the Church."[64]

The sight of things—chairs, desks, buttons, even the published documents of the Revolution—was important because Jefferson and others of his time believed it could arouse in Americans, who knew the events with which they were associated, the deepest feelings and bring their minds "to a condition of moral sensitivity and reflection."[65] The emotions and commitments fostered in that way would, they hoped, save Americans from a shallow materialism and strengthen their determination to honor and preserve the accomplishments of the Revolution, including the federal union. But to describe the impulse simply as a conservative effort to strengthen the state would be misleading since the right of revolution held a prominent place among the "principles" of the Declaration of Independence that its devotees sought to reinforce. Recall that Hezekiah Niles hoped to encourage young Americans to emulate their ancestors in resisting foreign and domestic encroachments on their liberties; similarly, Joseph Sanderson's 1819 proposal for publishing biographies of the Declaration's signers stressed the transcendent importance of "resistance to tyranny and political oppression." American enthusiasm for revolution, which waned in the 1790s under the influence of the French Revolution, had recovered by the 1820s, when revolutionary movements swept through Spain, Portugal, Naples, Piedmont, Sicily, Greece, and Latin America. The revolutionaries of Latin America "adopt our principles, copy our institutions, and, in many instances," Henry Clay told Congress in

1818, "employ the very language of our revolutionary papers."[66] Clay was wrong; Latin American revolutionary documents were not copies or imitations of their North American counterparts.[67] The American Revolution seemed nonetheless to have begun a movement against repressive regimes and for enlightened, constitutional government that, for the moment at least, was spreading over much of the Western world.

Many of the new regimes were disappointingly short-lived, which led John Adams to conclude that no free government could be established where the Roman Catholic religion prevailed. Jefferson was more sanguine on that issue. "I will not believe our labors are lost," he wrote Adams. "I shall not die without a hope that light and liberty are on a steady advance." Even if "the cloud of barbarism and despotism" should "again obscure the science and liberties of Europe, this country remains to preserve and restore light and liberty to them. In short," he went on, "the flames kindled on the 4th of July 1776. have spread over too much of the globe to be extinguished by the feeble engines of despotism. On the contrary they will consume those engines, and all who work them."[68] In his last letter, Jefferson reaffirmed his belief in the world's future, a future that turned on a spreading fire of revolution that had been ignited in the United States. It was there that he borrowed the words of that old seventeenth-century English revolutionary, Colonel Richard Rumbold, much as he had once taken passages from George Mason, again reworking the text so thoroughly that it became his own. May the American example "be to the world," he said,

> what I believe it will be, (to some parts sooner, to others later, but finally to all,) the signal of arousing men to burst the chains under which monkish ignorance and superstition had persuaded them to bind themselves, and to assume the blessings and security of self-government. That form which we have substituted, restores the free right to the unbounded exercise of reason and freedom of opinion. All eyes are opened, or opening, to the rights of man. The general spread of the light of science has already laid open to every view the palpable truth, that the mass of mankind has not been born with saddles on their backs, nor a favored few booted and spurred, ready to ride them legitimately, by the grace of God. These are the grounds of hope for others. For ourselves, let the annual return of this day forever

refresh our recollections of these rights, and an undiminished devotion to them.[69]

Finally, on July 3, 1826, in brief moments of consciousness during his final hours, Jefferson spoke for the last time, asking family members if it was yet the Fourth.[70] He wanted to die on the anniversary of a day he had first suffered with the pain of wounded authorship, but which had come to be the defining event of his eighty-three years on earth. At his death on July 4, Thomas Jefferson was an old man, but as young and committed a revolutionary as he had ever been, bristling at unwarranted extensions of federal power, predicting the downfall of regressive regimes everywhere, celebrating the future triumph of man's rights and reason over the deadening force of worldly constraints.

5. Equality and Rights

Americans had scarcely ended their celebrations when they learned that not just Jefferson, but John Adams, too, had left this life on the fiftieth anniversary of the Declaration of Independence. With one voice those who gave eulogies interpreted God's taking together two of the last three signers of the Declaration not as a sign of His displeasure, but proof that the United States had a special place in His plans and affections. "Had the horses and the chariot of fire descended to take up the patriarchs, it might have been more wonderful," one speaker said, "but not more glorious."[71]

No less strange, the Protestant spokesmen for an increasingly evangelical nation, men who thrilled at Jefferson's execration of "monkish ignorance and superstition," and who readily attributed the failure of the French Revolution to a "catholic priesthood" that had thrown over the people a "pall of bigotry, through which no ray from above could penetrate," proved as ready as Jefferson to use religious, and often Catholic, terms in describing America's revolutionaries and their heritage. But then what other language could they use? Protestantism traditionally regarded the visual richness and material appurtenances of Catholic worship with deep suspicion. It therefore never developed a vocabulary that would be of use to Americans who discovered the importance of revolutionary artifacts and the superhuman virtues of their forefathers. And so the children of an American en-

lightenment enlisted the terminology of "monkish ignorance and superstition," and spoke of relics and altars, of saints and canonizations,
reconstructing a secular, eighteenth-century political tradition into a
functional Catholicism for a Protestant country.

Jefferson became a Christlike figure whose "disembodied spirit
was . . . upborne by the blessings of ten millions of Freemen" in a fan-
ciful Fourth of July ascension. Or was he a saint, like Washington,
whose death nearly three decades earlier had "left an admiring world
to canonize his memory"? Jefferson and Adams were "exalted individuals" who had "long since ceased to be regarded by the nation or by the
world at large, as living characters. The estimation in which they have
been held for the last ten years," as one eulogist put it, "has partaken
more of posthumous veneration than of co[n]temporary respect." Men
did not wait for death to "sanctify" their names; their homes became
"the shrines, to which the lover of liberty and the admirer of genius,
from every land, devoutly made his pilgrimage." Speakers referred to
the "altar of freedom" raised by the country's fathers, to the "sacred fire
they lighted upon it," and to the "sacred principles . . . solemnly inscribed upon the banner of the revolution" and "still borne aloft by the
strength of increasing millions." Adams won credit as the "bold and
eloquent debater" in the Continental Congress who "urged and defended the measure, big with the fate of empires," but "Jefferson's was
the unequalled skill, which embodied the principles of liberty in the
language of inspiration, as an eternal monument and landmark for the
guidance of posterity."[72]

The generation that discovered this holy greatness was ready and
willing to congratulate itself on that achievement. "Time was," a
speaker in Newburyport, Massachusetts, noted, when Jefferson's character, "seen through the distorted optics of party, was so grossly misrepresented, that men gravely denied him the capacity to compose the
consummately beautiful lines of that splendid manifesto to the nations
of the earth. But another generation has rightly appreciated his
deserts." By 1826, as Peleg Sprague in Hallowell, Maine, testified,
"every thing connected" with the Declaration of Independence "excites
deep and acute interest."[73] The eulogists continued to accept approv-
ingly Jefferson the revolutionary, "born to overturn systems and pull
down establishments," and, like him, to revere the Declaration as a
statement of the right of revolution: that manifesto awoke a "mighty

spirit" that "walks abroad upon the earth," and that "shall in its onward march overturn principalities and powers, and tramp thrones and sceptres in the dust."[74]

But the right of revolution was not, it seems, the only "principle of liberty" in the Declaration of Independence, or even the most important for the guidance of posterity. "The same venerated instrument that declared our separation from Great Britain," said John Sergeant in Philadelphia, "contained also the memorable assertion, that 'all men are created equal, that they are endowed by their Creator with certain unalienable rights, and that to secure these rights, governments are instituted among men, deriving their just powers from the consent of the governed.'" And that, he said, "was the text of the revolution—the ruling vital principle—the hope that animated the patriot's heart and nerved the patriot's arm, when he looked forward through succeeding generations, and saw stamped upon all their institutions, the great principles set forth in the Declaration of Independence." For Sprague, too, the Declaration of Independence was a "Declaration, *by a whole people*, of what before existed, and will always exist, *the native equality of the human race*, as the true foundation of all political, of all human institutions."[75]

By including human equality among the "great principles" that the Declaration stated and describing it as "the foundation of all political, of all human institutions," Sergeant and Sprague contributed to a modern reading of the document that had begun to develop among Jeffersonian Republicans in the 1790s but became increasingly common after the 1820s, and gradually eclipsed altogether the document's assertion of the right of revolution. It is important to understand, however, that the issue of equality had a place in American life and politics long before it was associated with the Declaration of Independence. In the eighteenth century, the republican form of government was commonly considered best suited to egalitarian societies, and Americans, conscious that they lacked the extremes of wealth characteristic of older European countries, generally accepted equality as a characteristic of their society and of the governments they were founding. The state and local declarations of Independence made that abundantly clear. Remember that on May 15, 1776, the Virginia convention authorized the drafting of a new state constitution that would "secure substantial and equal liberty to the people." Two months earlier Judge

William Henry Drayton praised South Carolina's new constitution for allowing voters to raise even the poorest Carolinian to the highest office in the state, while the Grand Jury at Charlestown took pleasure in the founding of a government whose benefits extended "generally, equally, and indiscriminately to all," and another grand jury in the Cheraws District took delight in the new constitution because under it "the rights and happiness of the whole, the poor and the rich, are equally secured." Meanwhile, Massachusetts coastal towns argued that the people's right to equal liberty and equal representation mandated a reallocation of legislative seats so they would be more closely keyed to population (which would, of course, shift power toward them). None of those references to equality had anything to do with the Declaration of Independence since they predated it. And together they suggested enough different meanings of the word "equality"—equal rights, equal access to office, equal voting power—to keep Americans busy sorting them out and fighting over practices that seemed inegalitarian far into the future. The equality mentioned, moreover, was generally between rich and poor white men, or those who lived in different geographical sections; its application to women or people of other races or persons with conflicting religious convictions would open whole new fields for conflict.

The Declaration of Independence was, in fact, a peculiar document to be cited by those who championed the cause of equality. Not only did its reference to men's equal creation concern people in a state of nature before government was established, but the document's original function was to end the previous regime, not to lay down principles to guide and limit its successor. True, the Declaration of Independence offered an implicit standard against which all governments could be compared and found wanting: unless they secured men's inalienable rights, the people could alter or abolish them and institute others "more likely to effect their safety and happiness." But the function of stating fundamental principles that established governments had to respect was normally entrusted to declarations or bills of rights like those attached to many state constitutions. Moreover, after an initial period of uncertainty, state bills of rights were recognized as legally binding parts of the states' fundamental laws. Their provisions could therefore be enforced in the courts, which was not true of the Declaration of Independence. And some of the earliest efforts to work out the meaning of American equality occurred in states whose bills of rights asserted a fundamental human equality with language derived, like that in the Declaration of Independence, from George Mason's draft of the Virginia Declaration of Rights. The arguments raised within the states are important here because subsequent debates based on the Declaration of Independence essentially reworked and extended positions first expressed on the state level.

Right away, in June 1776, the Virginia Convention confronted the fact that assertions of men's equal birth raised problems for a slave society. After several days of intense debate, the Convention finally amended the Mason draft so it said that "all men are by nature equally free and independent" and had "certain inherent rights" that they could not yield for posterity by any compact "when they enter into a state of society." The statement was not an entirely satisfactory compromise, but at least it freed the state of Virginia from an obligation to recognize and protect the inherent rights of slaves since—as even supporters of the Mason draft agreed—slaves had never entered Virginia's society, which was confined to whites.[76] Subsequent developments in Massachusetts demonstrated that the Virginians' fears were well founded. During the early 1780s, several slaves won their freedom by arguing before the Massachusetts Supreme Judicial Court that the provision in the state's bill of rights that all men were born free and equal made slavery unlawful. Later, in the famous case of *Commonwealth v. Aves* (1836), Justice Lemuel Shaw ruled that those words in the 1780 bill of rights were alone sufficient to end slavery in Massachusetts, indeed, that it would be difficult to find others "more precisely adapted to the abolition of negro slavery."[77]

White Americans also found the equality provisions in their state bills of rights useful in arguing for reforms that would benefit them. In the Virginia constitutional convention of 1829–30, for example, a delegate from the trans-Appalachian west, John R. Cooke, cited that "sacred instrument," the Virginia Declaration of Rights, in opposing the state's system of giving each county equal representation in the legislature regardless of population differences, and its imposition of a property qualification for the vote. Both of those measures served to enhance the power of Virginians in the Tidewater and Piedmont, where the bulk of the state's slaves and so most of its slave owners lived. Easterners insisted on retaining that advantage because they feared nonslaving Westerners might weaken or abolish Virginia's "peculiar institution," and their selfishness provoked outrage among white Virginians in the West. The Declaration's statement "that all men are, by nature, *equally* free" meant, Cooke said, that

> no *one* man is born with a natural right to control any *other* man; that no *one* man comes into the world with a mark on him, to designate him as possessing superior rights to any *other* man; that neither God nor nature recognize, in anticipation, the distinctions of bond and free, of despot and slave; but that these distinctions are artificial; are the work of man; are the result of fraud or violence.

The framers of Virginia's 1776 constitution allowed the freehold franchise and county representation system to continue despite their inconsistency with the Declaration of Rights, he said, because there were limits on how much they dared change "in the midst of war." They therefore left it for posterity to resolve the inconsistency "as soon as leisure should be afforded them," as Cooke claimed Thomas Jefferson had said in 1781, when he, too, urged an equalization in the power of white male voters throughout Virginia. In the hands of men like Cooke, the Virginia Declaration of Rights became not a statement of "mere abstract principle" but, as he insisted, a practical program of reform to be realized over time.[78] His position was essentially the same as one Abraham Lincoln would later take in describing the Declaration of Independence.

If, however, state bills of rights provided an effective foundation for egalitarian causes, why would contenders turn to the Declaration of Independence? Because not all states had bills of rights, and those that existed did not always assert the natural equality of men or mention their inalienable rights. Moreover, compared to the bills or declarations of rights in states such as Virginia, Pennsylvania, or Massachusetts, the federal Bill of Rights was a sorry specimen, a lean summary of restrictions on the federal government, tacked onto the end of the Constitution like the afterthought it was, with no assertion of fundamental revolutionary principles. Had the constitutional convention heeded George Mason's plea that it add to the constitution a bill of rights based on those of the states, the situation would probably have been different, but the convention brushed Mason's proposal aside.

Indeed, had Congress adopted the bill of rights James Madison proposed on June 8, 1789, the federal document would have looked more like those of the states. Madison moved that "a declaration" be "prefixed to the constitution" in the traditional manner, and that it assert

> That all power is originally vested in, and consequently derived from the people.

> That Government is instituted, and ought to be exercised for the benefit of the people; which consists in the enjoyment of life and liberty, with the right of acquiring and using property, and generally of pursuing and obtaining happiness and safety.

> That the people have an indubitable, unalienable, and indefeasible right to reform or change their government, whenever it be found adverse or inadequate to the purposes of its institution.

These provisions were essentially a pared-down version of the Virginia Declaration of Rights in which the original equality of men, their possession of inherent and unalienable rights, and their right to abolish government (as opposed to changing it) went unmentioned. Why they were excluded is a question easier asked than answered. Perhaps by 1789 Independence was so far in the past that Madison saw no need to restate the principles Jefferson wrote into the Declaration of Independence. Indeed, those principles might impede the foundation of a stable, effective national government. Perhaps, too, Madison feared alienating the support of slaveholders, who by 1789 recognized the disadvantage of building statements of men's equal birth and basic rights into constitutional documents. One delegate in the South Carolina ratifying convention, which was called to pass judgment on the federal constitution, warned against recommending a bill of rights because such documents "generally began with a statement that all men are born free and equal, which was not the case in South Carolina." After two hundred years, it's easy to forget what an uphill battle supporters of both the Constitution and the Bill of Rights faced in getting those documents ratified, and to what lengths they went to avoid alienating potential supporters unnecessarily. In any case, the "prefix" Madison proposed seems to have constituted what he called a "bill of rights."[79]

Madison also proposed a series of changes to the body of the Constitution. He would have inserted provisions protecting several basic civil rights—including freedom of religion, of speech, and of the press, the rights of assembly and of petition, and the right to bear arms—in

Article 1, Section 9, among other restrictions on Congress, and he proposed adding to Article 1, Section 10, a statement that "No state shall violate the equal rights of conscience, or the freedom of the press, or the trial by jury in criminal cases." Adoption of his proposal might have complicated later efforts to make binding on the states what were originally restrictions on Congress, but that was not a problem for Madison. He had no sense whatsoever of how important the federal Bill of Rights would later become. Such paper restrictions on power, he thought, were proven to be ineffectual during the 1780s, when state legislatures simply ignored them on one occasion after another. The best way to protect civil liberty, Madison believed, was by imposing structural limits on power such as those the Philadelphia convention had built into the federal Constitution. However, the Anti-federalist critics of the Constitution and several state ratifying conventions had insisted upon a bill of rights. Madison hoped to stem their discontent by providing innocuous assertions of uncontested rights while ignoring the substantial reductions in federal power, particularly the power to tax, that they also proposed. Contemporaries therefore described his proposal as "a tub to the whale," that is, a harmless way to divert the attention of a powerful outside force from a mission of destruction, like the barrels or tubs seamen sometimes tossed as playthings to whales in an effort to keep them from destroying their ships.[80]

The first federal Congress, which was dominated by Federalists, was even less convinced than Madison that the Constitution needed to be amended so soon after it went into effect, if at all, and so cut back and redefined his proposal. It eliminated the "prefix" and, in September 1789, sent to the states for ratification twelve amendments that were to be listed at the end of the Constitution. Of those twelve, the states accepted ten by December 15, 1791, eliminating one amendment that affected the allocation of representatives and another that required a new election before changes in compensation of Congressmen could go into effect.[81] Those ten amendments became the federal Bill of Rights. And in time that abbreviation of an abbreviation of an abbreviation—that is, the states' partial ratification of Congress's reduction of Madison's watered-down version of the more extensive bills of rights demanded by state ratifying conventions—became another of the nation's "vital documents." But because the federal Bill of Rights, like the Constitution, was unembellished by assertions of men's original equality or their unalienable rights or the fundamental power of the people or their right to change or replace their government, individuals who found it useful to cite those old revolutionary principles on behalf of some cause in national politics had to turn to the Declaration of Independence. It was all they had.

Moreover, the sacralization of the Declaration of Independence after 1815 made it a powerful text to enlist on behalf of any cause that might conceivably claim its authority. It could not, like the state bills of rights, be used in court cases to strike down institutions and practices that violated its principles, but the Declaration's newfound status as a sacred document made it extremely useful for causes attempting to seize the moral high ground in public debate. And so, starting in the 1820s, workers, farmers, women's rights advocates, and other groups continually used the Declaration of Independence to justify their quest for equality and their opposition to the "tyranny" of factory owners or railroads or great corporations or the male power structure. Frequently such contenders composed "alternative declarations of independence," the latter-day analogues of the "other" declarations of independence composed in the spring and early summer of 1776, to dramatize the connection between their causes and that of 1776. "We hold these truths to be self-evident," declared women at the Seneca Falls Convention of 1848, "that all men and women are created equal," and they went on to submit "facts" to a "candid world" to prove that "the history of mankind is a history of repeated injuries and usurpations on the part of man toward woman, having in direct object the establishment of an absolute tyranny over her."[82]

The opponents of slavery also cited the Declaration of Independence, and they had one advantage over the contenders for other causes: they did not need to rewrite the Declaration of Independence to enlist its authority on their behalf. If all men were created equal, if they were "born equally free and independent," and if those words meant that "no *one* man is born with a natural right to control any *other* man, . . . that neither God nor nature recognize, in anticipation, the distinctions of bond and free, of despot and slave"; if those distinctions were "artificial, . . . the work of man, . . . the result of fraud or violence," as John Cooke put it in the Virginia convention of 1829 (or if men were not "born with saddles on their backs, nor a favored few booted and spurred, ready to ride them legitimately, by the grace of God"), then a system of slavery in which men were born the subjects and, indeed, the property of others, was profoundly wrong. In short, the same argument that denied kings an inherited right to rule denied the right of masters to own slaves whose status was determined by birth, not consent.

The inconsistency between American principle and practice was recognized in the Northern states, which, one after another, ended their slave systems in the first decades after Independence, whether in the courts or the legislatures, immediately or over time. New York's gradual-emancipation act took effect appropriately on July 4, 1799, New Jersey's on the same day five years later.[83] The cause of emancipation also commanded substantial support in those Southern states that held the greatest concentrations of slaves as long as it included plans to "colonize" free blacks elsewhere, such as in the West Indies or Africa. So late as 1831–32, the Virginia legislature seriously debated an emancipation proposal submitted by Thomas Jefferson Randolph that would have freed slaves born after July 4, 1840. By then, however, reasons of security were as much a consideration as ideological consistency: Virginia was reeling under the impact of Nat Turner's slave uprising—which had been originally planned to begin on July 4, 1831.[84]

Later and more extreme opponents of slavery condemned the colonizers for their unwillingness to accept blacks into the society of free Americans, fought segregationist practices in the North, and, above all, insisted on the "immediate" emancipation of slaves, citing the Declaration of Independence on behalf of their cause. In 1829, William Lloyd Garrison, the New England–born, evangelistic founder of radical Abolitionism and future publisher of *The Liberator*, noted that every Fourth of July Americans read the Declaration of Independence and the evidence it offered of British tyranny. The grievances it listed were, however, "pitiful" compared with the wrongs slaves had to endure day after day. "I am ashamed of my country," he said, ashamed "of our unmeaning declamations in praise of liberty and equality—of our hypocritical cant about the inalienable rights of man." In later years Garrison continued to denounce the "vile hypocrisy," the "solemn, heaven daring mockery," the "horrible inconsistency" of self-professed "haters of tyranny . . . treading upon the necks and spilling the blood of more than two millions of human beings! . . . Heaping imprecations upon the heads of foreign despots, and yet keeping in chains one-sixth portion of our own countrymen!" Garrison and the most radical Abolitionists did not, however, cite the

Declaration as a would-be bill of rights—the "unalienable rights" it affirmed were universal, they said, and needed no documentary embodiment—but for what it originally was, a justification of revolution. In claiming their right to fight for liberty, Garrison wrote, the American people necessarily conceded that right to all mankind, including slaves. By 1847 he and his colleague Wendell Phillips were ready to call upon "every citizen . . . to devote himself to the destruction of the Union and the Constitution, which have already shipwrecked the experiment of civil liberty," in the hope that "out of the wreck" would arise a state more faithful to "the principles of the Declaration of Independence, whose promises made us once the admiration of the world."[85]

As the future of slavery emerged again as a critical issue in American politics, contenders repeatedly debated the meaning of the Declaration's assertions of human equality and unalienable rights, which, despite the contrary opinions that swirled around it, served to reinforce the Declaration's status as a national icon. Again, the effort to define exactly how far American equality went did not begin in the 1830s; it was well under way a half century earlier, and from the first years of the republic provoked passionate denials of human equality of a sort that would be repeated in later years by one self-styled iconoclast after another.[86] Now, however, contenders increasingly insisted that the Declaration's statement on equality was fundamentally inaccurate. In 1806, a Pennsylvania congressman, Joseph Clay, said that the Declaration's assertion on unalienable rights was not literally true, and during the Missouri debates of 1820 those who defended slavery again disputed the notion that all men were created equal. Surely they were not created equal in Virginia, insisted John Tyler; "no, sir, the principle, although lovely and beautiful, cannot obliterate those distinctions in society which society itself engenders and gives birth to." Six years later, the Virginian John Randolph, a self-styled aristocrat, called the notion of man's equal creation "a falsehood, and a most pernicious falsehood, even though I find it in the Declaration of Independence." Man was born "in a state of the most abject want, and a state of perfect helplessness and ignorance," and so necessarily subject to the control of others.[87]

There was "not a word of truth" in the notion that men were created equal, repeated South Carolina's Democratic senator John C. Calhoun in 1848. Born in 1782, named after an uncle who had been killed by Loyalists during the Revolutionary War, Calhoun had begun a long and distinguished public career (he served as a senator, secretary of war, secretary of state, and vice president of the United States) as an outspoken nationalist. Like Jefferson in 1820, he saw Northern efforts to interfere with Southern slavery as a standing threat to the Union. Now, in the final years of his life, Calhoun's effort to defend Southern rights and preserve the nation brought him up against the document in whose drafting Jefferson had taken such deep pride. In 1776, he argued, the Declaration's assertion of human equality was a "hypothetical truism" about man in a state of nature taken from writers whom the revolutionaries admired such as John Locke and Algernon Sidney, but even then it was wrong. Men could not survive, much less develop their God-given talents, alone. The political state, in which some had authority and others were obliged to obey, was man's "natural state" and the "one in which he is born, lives and dies." For a long time the "false and dangerous" notion that men were created equal "lay dormant; but in the process of time it began to germinate, and produce its poisonous fruits." By the late 1840s Americans had begun "to experience the danger of admitting so great an error . . . in the declaration of our independence," where it had been inserted "without any necessity" since separation from Britain could have been justified without it.[88]

Where would it end, this justification of authority at the hands of Calhoun and others, this emphasis on subjection as natural to man, but in tyrannies worse even than those whose disappearance from the earth had been the dream of men like Jefferson and Thomas Paine and Samuel Adams? And what, then, had the Revolution accomplished except the creation of another nation like all that preceded it? The issue emerged again in 1853 during Senate debates of the Kansas-Nebraska Act, in which opponents of that measure such as the Ohio senators Salmon P. Chase and Benjamin Wade invoked the Declaration of Independence, "that immortal document," and its "sublime creed of human rights" against the extension of slavery into the free territories of Kansas and Nebraska. There, too, Indiana's John Pettit pronounced his widely quoted statement that the supposed "self-evident truth" that "all men are created equal" was in fact a "self-evident lie" with "no truth in it. . . . The negro in Africa and the free-born American are not created equal," he said, and "the serf of Russia, under the Autocrat, is not the equal of his master. . . ." If the Declaration had said that men "ought to have been created equal," he would have no argument with it, "but it is utterly false that men are, either mentally, morally, physically, or politically, created equal."[89]

The "great declaration cost our forefathers too dear" to be so "lightly . . . thrown away by their children," argued Benjamin Franklin Wade, an outspoken opponent of slavery known for his vituperative style and intense patriotism. Perhaps Wade's name gave him a special bond with the Declaration, its creators, and those who adopted it, all of whom became a powerful presence in his oratory. To vindicate the "great truths" in that "immortal instrument," he recalled, the fathers had pledged their lives, fortunes, and sacred honor. Without "the influence of those soul-inspiring principles it would not have been possible for the patriots of that day to have achieved our independence," he said; those principles were in their eyes "worth the sacrifice of all else on earth, even life itself." How exactly were men created equal? "Not in physical power; certainly not. Not in point of intellect; nobody pretends it." The "good old Declaration" said "that all men are created equal, and have inalienable rights; that is, [they are] equal in point of right; that no man has a right to trample upon another." The serfs of Russia and slaves of the South "have precisely the same rights as he who has trampled them down," and where those rights were wrested from them by force or fraud, justice demanded that they be "restored without delay." To deny that principle—to say that the Revolution was unconcerned with "personal rights," that it involved nothing more than, as Pettit said, an assertion that Americans had the right to be "a free and independent nation, and to fix our domestic and home institutions as we pleased"—was to make a lie of the Americans' boast that their fathers had discovered "a new principle of government," which the present generation was "to impart to all who come after us." Pettit's position implied, Wade said, that force, not consent, conferred authority, which vindicated the rights of kings and of privileged orders everywhere. In short, Pettit's argument robbed the Revolution of all meaning beyond Independence alone and denied its heirs the mission that inspired their political lives.[90]

ABRAHAM LINCOLN, a little-known forty-four-year-old lawyer in Springfield, Illinois, who had served one term in Congress as a member of the Whig Party before being turned out of office by voters unhappy with his opposition to the Mexican War, read these de-

bates, was aroused by the controversy as by nothing before, and began
to pick up the lost threads of his political career. Like Wade and others of his time, Lincoln idealized the men who had participated in the
Revolution: they were for him "a forest of giant oaks," "pillars of the
temple of liberty," "a fortress of strength," "iron men." He also shared
the deep feelings of his contemporaries as the numbers of living veterans of the Revolution gradually shriveled. In 1838 he had expressed fear
that, as the "silent artillery of time" removed them and the "*living history*" they embodied from the world, memories of the Revolution
would necessarily fade, and with them the passion that had done so
much to maintain the institutions and the freedom they established.[91]
Before the 1850s, however, Lincoln seems to have had relatively little
interest in the Declaration of Independence. Then, suddenly, that
document, and, above all, its assertion that all men were created equal,
became his "ancient faith," "the father of all moral principles," an
"axiom" of free society. He was provoked, it seems, by the attacks on
the Declaration of Calhoun, Pettit, and Rufus Choate of Massachusetts, who called its affirmations of natural rights "glittering and
sounding generalities." Lincoln recalled each of those denunciations of
the Declaration, always with regret. And he made the arguments of
those who defended the Declaration his own, much as Jefferson had
done with the texts upon which he drew in drafting that document, reworking the ideas from speech to speech, pushing their logic, and
eventually arriving at a simple statement of profound eloquence. Later
Lincoln would say that he "never had a feeling politically that did not
spring from the sentiments embodied in the Declaration of Independence." His understanding of the document became in time that of the
nation.[92]

　　Lincoln's position emerged most fully and powerfully during his
debates with Illinois' Senator Stephen Douglas, a Democrat who had
proposed the Kansas-Nebraska Act. Lincoln ran for the Senate against
Douglas in 1858 as a member of the new Republican Party—whose
first national convention, which convened at Philadelphia on June 17,
1856, the anniversary of the Battle of Bunker Hill, adopted a platform
that described maintaining "the principles promulgated in the Declaration of Independence" and embodied in the Constitution as "essential to the preservation of our republican institutions."[93] Lincoln and
Douglas were another of history's odd couples, the one uncommonly
tall (six foot four), gangly, with rough facial features and deep hollows

in his cheeks, the other short (at full height Douglas came only to Lincoln's shoulder), rotund, with regular facial features and chubby cheeks. What differences nature did not supply, the contenders cultivated: Douglas, a two-term senator anxious to convey his power and respectability, dressed in well-tailored, immaculate clothes and traveled with his elegant wife in a special train; Lincoln's clothes did not quite cover his large frame, and he sat in ordinary passenger cars, mixing with the people, having left his well-bred, socially conscious wife at home with their small children. Douglas was in general a more polished speaker than Lincoln, who could ramble on, losing his point and his audience. But Lincoln told stories well, had a sharp sense of humor, and, particularly with a worked-over text in hand, could achieve impressive oratorical power.[94]

The most important difference between the two contenders, however, lay in the positions they took on the issue that preoccupied them, the future of slavery. Lincoln's attacks on Douglas began in 1854, the year after Douglas had steered the Kansas-Nebraska Act through Congress, and concluded four years later with the formal Lincoln-Douglas debates, which won national attention and put Lincoln on the road to the presidency. Throughout those debates the contenders founded their arguments on the authority of the Revolution and the Declaration of Independence, which they explained in different ways. Lincoln carried to each event a small leather notebook in which he pasted for quick reference some newspaper articles, often accounts of his own earlier speeches, from which he frequently read publicly, and a handful of basic documents, including the second paragraph of the Declaration of Independence and part of an 1842 speech by Henry Clay in which Clay described the phrase "all men are created equal" as a "great fundamental principle" of significance both "in the original construction of society, and in organized societies."[95]

Douglas defended the Kansas-Nebraska Act, which allowed the people of those states to decide whether to allow slavery within their borders, as perfectly consistent with the principles and practices of the Revolution. While instructing their Congressional delegates to vote for Independence in 1776, Douglas recalled correctly, one state after another had explicitly retained the exclusive right of defining its domestic institutions. The Kansas-Nebraska Act only confirmed that right, he said. Moreover, the Declaration of Independence carried no implications whatsoever with regard to slavery since the signers referred to white men only, to "men of European birth and European descent, when they declared the equality of all men." In fact, Douglas asserted, the equality they asserted was between American colonists and British subjects in Great Britain, both of whom had equal rights and neither of whom could be justly held subject to the other. The signers were not thinking of "the negro or . . . savage Indians, or the Feejee, or the Malay, or any other inferior or degraded race." Had they meant to include blacks, the signers would have been honor-bound to go home and immediately free their slaves, which not even Thomas Jefferson did. To say that "every man who signed the Declaration of Independence declared the negro his equal" was therefore to call the signers hypocrites. The Declaration had one purpose and one purpose only: to explain and justify American Independence from the British Crown.[96]

To Lincoln, Douglas's argument left a "mere wreck," a "mangled ruin," of the Declaration of Independence, whose "plain, unmistakable language" said "*all* men" were created equal, which meant "there can be no moral right in connection with one man's making a slave of another." In affirming that government derived its "just powers from the consent of the governed," the Declaration said that no man could govern another without his consent, which was "the leading principle— the sheet anchor of American republicanism." If, then, "the negro is a man," was it not a "total destruction of self-government, to say that he too shall not govern *himself*?" To govern another man without his consent was "despotism." Like Benjamin Wade and others before him, Lincoln understood that it was impossible to separate the Declaration's condemnation of monarchy from a condemnation of slavery. To deny that kings can justly rule by right of birth was to deny that anyone could rule another, of any race or creed or national origin, without his or her consent. Moreover, to confine the Declaration's significance to the British peoples of 1776 meant that the document lost significance not only for Douglas's "inferior races," but for the French, Irish, German, Scandinavian, and other immigrants who came to America after the Revolution (and who were well represented among Illinois voters). For them the promise of equality for all men was a moral sentiment that linked newly arrived Americans with the founding generation, an "electric cord" that bound them into the nation "as though they were blood of the blood, and flesh of the flesh of the men who wrote that Declaration," and so made one people out of many. "I had thought the Declaration contemplated the progressive improvement in the condition of all men everywhere," Lincoln said, but if, instead, it was simply a justification of American Independence, the document was "of no practical use now—mere rubbish—old wadding left to rot on the battle-field after the victory is won," nothing more than "an interesting memorial of the dead past . . . shorn of its vitality, and practical value," without "the *germ*, or even the *suggestion* of the individual rights of man in it."[97]

Again like Wade, Lincoln denied that the signers of the Declaration meant that men were "equal *in all respects*. They did not mean to say all were equal in color, size, intellect, moral development, or social capacity. They defined with tolerable distinctness, in what respects they did consider all men created equal." He, too, made sense of the Declaration's assertion of man's equal creation by eliding it with the next, separate statement on rights. The signers, he insisted, said that men were equal in having "'certain inalienable rights. . . .' This they said, and this they meant." They had no intention of affirming the "obvious untruth, that all were then enjoying that equality," nor to confer it on them immediately.[98] Like Virginia's John Cooke and his own "beau ideal of a statesman," Henry Clay,[99] Lincoln thought that the founders allowed the persistence of practices at odds with their principles for reasons of necessity. To establish the Constitution demanded that slavery be allowed to continue within those original states that chose to keep it. "We could not secure the good we did secure if we grasped for more," but that did not "destroy the principle that is the charter of our liberties." And if, as Douglas said, the states that made up the Union in 1776 reserved power over their domestic institutions, that did not mean slavery had to be allowed in states not yet organized in 1776, such as those in the Northwest Territory, or Kansas and Nebraska.[100]

Lincoln saw the Declaration of Independence's statements on equality and rights as setting a standard for the future, one that demanded the gradual extinction of conflicting practices as that became possible, which was the way Cooke had interpreted the opening section of Virginia's Declaration of Rights. The authors of the Declaration of Independence, Lincoln said, meant

> simply to declare the *right* so that the *enforcement* of it might follow as fast as the circumstances should permit. They meant to set up a standard maxim for free men which should be familiar to all, and revered

by all; constantly looked to, and constantly labored for, and even though never perfectly attained, constantly approximated and thereby constantly spreading and deepening its influence, and augmenting the happiness and value of life to all people of all colors everywhere.[101] He was therefore able to agree with Calhoun that the assertions of human equality and inalienable rights were unnecessary in the Declaration of Independence: the Americans could have declared their Independence without them. But that made their inclusion even more wonderful. "All honor to Jefferson," Lincoln wrote in a letter of 1859,

—to the man who, in the concrete pressure of a struggle for national independence by a single people, had the coolness, forecast, and capacity to introduce into a merely revolutionary document, an abstract truth, applicable to all men and all times, and so to embalm it there, that to-day, and in all coming days, it shall be a rebuke and a stumbling-block to the very harbingers of re-appearing tyranny and oppression.[102]

JEFFERSON AND THE MEMBERS of the Second Continental Congress had not understood what they were doing in quite that way on July 4, 1776. For them, it was enough for the Declaration to be "merely revolutionary." Their text would not risk becoming wadding left to rot on the battlefield until the war with Britain was over, a memorial to the dead past until time had silenced the contests of their day. They sought to extend support for their cause and enhance the chances of victory; more they did not ask. In many ways, Douglas's history was more faithful to the past and to the views of Thomas Jefferson, who to the end of his life saw the Declaration of Independence as a revolutionary manifesto, and who understood that slavery violated the values of the Revolution but saw federal coercion of Western slaveholders in exactly the same way. Lincoln's view of the past, like Jefferson's in the 1770s, was a product of political controversy, not research, and his version of what the founders meant was full of wishful suppositions.

But Lincoln was the greater statesman. By the mid-nineteenth century, when the standard of revolution had passed to radical Abolitionists and Southern secessionists who wanted to dismember the Union, the Declaration of Independence was in need of another reading. In Lincoln's hands, the Declaration of Independence became first and foremost a living document for an established society, a set of goals to be realized over time, and so an explanation less of the colonists' decision to separate from Britain than of their victory in the War for Independence. Men would not fight and endure "as our fathers did," Lincoln wrote in a fragment probably composed early in 1861, "without the promise of something better, than a mere change of masters." He understood the Northern cause in the Civil War in much the same way: the North fought not only to save the Union, but to save a form of government, as Lincoln told Congress on July 4, 1861, "whose leading object is to elevate the condition of men; to lift artificial weights from all shoulders—to clear the paths of laudable pursuit for all—to afford all, an unfettered start and a fair chance in the race of life." The rebellion it opposed was at base an effort "to overthrow the principle that all men were created equal."[103]

The deaths of Adams and Jefferson on the Fourth of July in 1826 had reinforced belief that the United States held a special place in God's plans for the world. Surely Divine Providence was again at work when the turning point of the Civil War, the Northern victory at Gettysburg—as well as that at Vicksburg in the West—coincided with the celebration of Independence Day in 1863, six months after Lincoln issued the Emancipation Proclamation, freeing the slaves in rebel states. In Lincoln's hands that Union triumph became a vindication of the "proposition that all men are created equal" to which the new nation's "fathers" had committed it in 1776, "four score and seven years ago," and a challenge, as he said in dedicating the cemetery at Gettysburg the following November, to complete the "unfinished work" of the Union dead and bring to "this nation, under God, a new birth of freedom."[104]

In time, Lincoln's Gettysburg Address became itself an American sacred text. It stated briefly and eloquently deep convictions that he had developed over the previous decade, convictions that on point after point echoed earlier Americans—the eulogists Peleg Sprague and John Sergeant in 1826, John Cooke in the Virginia constitutional convention a few years later, Henry Clay in 1842, Benjamin Wade in Senate debates on the Kansas-Nebraska bill, and others who had also struggled to understand the practical implications of their revolutionary heritage, some of whose remarks Lincoln knew as well as many whose arguments were unknown to him but who had followed the same logic to the same conclusions. No less than Thomas Jefferson, then, Abraham Lincoln gave expression to a powerful strain in the American mind, not what all Americans thought but what many did. The values he emphasized—equality, human rights, government by consent—had in fact been part and parcel of the Revolution, and as much the subject of controversy then as later. Lincoln and those who shared his convictions did not therefore give the nation a new past or revolutionize the Revolution. But as descendants of the revolutionaries and of their English ancestors, they felt the need for a document that stated those values in a way that could guide the nation, a document that the founding fathers had failed to supply. And so they made one, pouring old wine into an old vessel manufactured for another purpose, creating a testament whose continuing usefulness depended not on the faithfulness with which it described the intentions of the signers but on its capacity to convince and inspire living Americans.

The Declaration of Independence Lincoln left posterity, the "charter of our liberties," was not and could not have been his solitary creation. It was what the American people chose to make of it, at once a legacy and a new conception, a document that spoke both for the revolutionaries and for their descendants, who confronted issues the country's fathers had never known or failed to resolve, binding one generation after another in a continuing act of national self-definition.

Reflecting at the Memorials

DOWN THE MALL from the nation's Capitol, past the 555-foot-high needle that commemorates George Washington and at the far end of the Reflecting Pool, sits Abraham Lincoln, enclosed in his memorial. Moving words from his Second Inaugural Address are engraved to one side, the Gettysburg Address on the other, decisively refuting his prediction in November 1863 that the world would "little note, nor long remember what we say here."

The Jefferson Memorial, of more recent construction, is south of the mall, beside the Tidal Basin. The seated Lincoln seems painfully human despite his statue's massive proportions, but Jefferson stands, towering above visitors, his back to the Potomac, his face looking past the Washington Monument toward the White House, surrounded by four panels with passages from his writings that seem in their way as monumental as his 10,000-pound bronze image. One panel is dedicated to Jefferson's most famous composition, the Declaration of Independence, which Lincoln made the moral text of his politics.

Unfortunately, designers told the Jefferson Memorial Commission that it could put no more than 325 letters on a panel. A section from the document's second paragraph seemed perfect, so the commission proposed the following inscription:

> WE HOLD THESE TRUTHS TO BE SELF-
> EVIDENT THAT ALL MEN ARE CREATED
> EQUAL: THAT THEY ARE ENDOWED BY
> THEIR CREATOR WITH CERTAIN IN-
> ALIENABLE RIGHTS: THAT AMONG
> THESE ARE LIFE, LIBERTY AND THE
> PURSUIT OF HAPPINESS: THAT TO SE-
> CURE THESE RIGHTS GOVERNMENTS ARE

INSTITUTED AMONG MEN, DERIVING
THEIR JUST POWERS FROM THE CON-
SENT OF THE GOVERNED.
WHENEVER ANY FORM OF GOVERNMENT
BECOMES DESTRUCTIVE OF THESE ENDS
IT IS THE RIGHT OF THE PEOPLE TO
ALTER OR ABOLISH IT.

That wasn't an exact version of the official Declaration. The punctuation was changed; "unalienable" went back to "inalienable," a "that"
was removed so the last statement became a separate sentence, and the
final phrase of what was in the original a linked sequence—"and to institute new Government, laying its foundation on such principles and
organizing its Powers in such form, as to them shall seem most likely
to effect their Safety and Happiness"—was eliminated altogether. The
proposed inscription still had too many letters, but in May 1941 it was
sent to President Franklin Roosevelt for final approval. Excellent, he
said, except that he missed the last paragraph of the Declaration.
Couldn't it be condensed and included? Roosevelt submitted a sample
text to show how that might be done, complete with ellipses to indicate where words had been cut—something the Commission did not
usually bother to include.[1]

The Commission went back to work, whittling away parts of the
passage it had first proposed. Another "that" was removed, and with it
the assertion that governments derived their just powers from the consent of the governed, which was critical to Lincoln's understanding of
the document. The Commission also eliminated the passage on the
people's right to alter or abolish their government when it failed to
protect their rights, that is, on the right of revolution, which was the
point of the original sequence and essential to the meaning of the
Declaration as Jefferson understood it down to the final weeks of his
life. As finally engraved on the Memorial, that part of the citation says:

WE HOLD THESE TRUTHS TO BE SELF-
EVIDENT: THAT ALL MEN ARE CREATED
EQUAL, THAT THEY ARE ENDOWED BY THEIR
CREATOR WITH CERTAIN INALIENABLE
RIGHTS, AMONG THESE ARE LIFE, LIBERTY
AND THE PURSUIT OF HAPPINESS, THAT
TO SECURE THESE RIGHTS GOVERNMENTS
ARE INSTITUTED AMONG MEN.[2]

Then, in deference to the president, the Commission added words from the document's final paragraph in a form much like what he proposed. Because the passage was then far too long, the architects removed a few more words without inserting ellipses, and someone—maybe a clerk—changed "honor" to "honour," so the final part of the inscription reads:

> WE . . .
>
> SOLEMNLY PUBLISH AND DECLARE, THAT
> THESE COLONIES ARE AND OF RIGHT
> OUGHT TO BE FREE AND INDEPENDENT
> STATES . . . AND FOR THE SUPPORT OF THIS
> DECLARATION, WITH A FIRM RELIANCE
> ON THE PROTECTION OF DIVINE
> PROVIDENCE, WE MUTUALLY PLEDGE
> OUR LIVES, OUR FORTUNES AND OUR
> SACRED HONOUR.

Again, the passage differed from the official Declaration.[3] The real problem, however, is that most of those words were written by Richard Henry Lee or by some anonymous Congressmen between July 2 and 4, 1776, and inserted by Congress in place of Jefferson's prose. Did no one have the nerve to tell the President? Or were they unaware that much of the above quotation, now permanently inscribed on the Jefferson Memorial, was not of Jefferson's composition? Jefferson became very upset by the way Congress "mutilated" his draft. What would he have said about the Jefferson Memorial Commission?

THE CHANGES the Commission made tell more than the obvious, that pleasing the President was a high priority. The right of revolution was easily sacked, and with it all the punctuation and the "thats" that made clear how all previous assertions—of equality, of inalienable rights, of the purpose and nature of government—had led to the Declaration's assertion of the people's right to abolish their government and replace it with another. Revolutionary documents are always uncomfortable for established governments. Even nations founded in revolutions quickly become conservative, if only to preserve the advances that revolution has brought. Once Americans had won their Independence, many leaders of the resistance to Britain condemned the followers of Daniel Shays and other domestic insurgents, insisting that in a republic, where oppressive rulers could be removed through the ballot box, there could be no rightful resistance to government outside the ordinary procedures of politics and law. Revolution was for other people, for those who had yet to establish their republic, such as the French, whose revolution awoke widespread American enthusiasm in its opening years, or the European and Latin American revolutionaries of the 1820s.

The predicament of preserving a nation that formally began with a revolutionary manifesto in a world torn by revolution fell to the Federalists in the 1790s. Their solution was to forget the Declaration of Independence. In 1861 Lincoln inherited the problem of preserving the Union; but by then he had already redefined the Declaration as a treatise for established societies whose function as a revolutionary manifesto was part of the dead past. Once again in the twentieth century it became necessary to explain away the Declaration of Independence as Jefferson understood it. Consider the problem of Archibald MacLeish, the poet who, as Librarian of Congress, had to compose a foreword for Julian Boyd's *The Declaration of Independence: The Evolution of the Text* . . . in 1943—the two-hundredth anniversary of Jefferson's birth and the year the Jefferson Memorial was dedicated—when the United States was an ally of Britain in a great war against fascism. "It is not to wound our English friends and Angloman fellow citizens that we publish at this time a study of the evolution of the Declaration's text," he said, but, borrowing from an 1823 statement of Jefferson, "to cherish the principles of the instrument in the bosoms of our own citizens." The Declaration, he went on, was negative and divisive in denouncing British rule and setting Englishmen and Americans against each other, but it remained nonetheless "creative and unifying" in declaring "the basic principles of human liberty" and in "its proposal for the future of a society in which human liberty could flourish." In that positive role, the Declaration, like Magna Carta, was part of the tradition of liberty among English-speaking peoples and "as such is a part of the British inheritance as it is of ours." Time had canceled the Declaration's negative aspects, MacLeish said, "but never at any time in the history of either country was the affirmative and creative significance of the Declaration of Independence more living than it is today."[4]

No less than Lincoln, and probably with more self-consciousness

than the Jefferson Memorial Commission, MacLeish transformed a
historical embarrassment into a living document. To do that, he had
to turn history upside down: just imagine George III's amazement at
learning that the Declaration of Independence would one day become
a constructive part of the British heritage! Yet MacLeish was right in
describing the Declaration of Independence as part of a political tradition that united the British and American peoples. Even the sacralization of the Declaration of Independence has analogues in British
history. In 1895, F. W. Maitland, the great British legal historian, referred to Magna Carta as "a sacred text, the nearest approach to an ir-
repealable 'fundamental statute' that England has ever had." Like the
Declaration of Independence, Magna Carta began in 1215 as a political
document, negotiated between the King and a group of barons. The
"great charter"—whose greatness at first rested in its physical size, not
its importance—was reissued repeatedly in the thirteenth century (as,
for example, by the charter of 1297 on display in the rotunda of the National Archives), then reinterpreted by Parliamentary statutes of the
fourteenth century. Three hundred years later the document was rediscovered by Sir Edward Coke and his legal colleagues, who saw it as
an affirmation of fundamental law and England's "ancient liberty."
Many parts of the document were quietly forgotten along the way.
Other clauses were recalled and developed in both Britain and America because they proved useful. For example, the provision in Magna
Carta that no one could be deprived of liberty except by the "judgment
of peers" became in time trial by jury, something that existed "only in
embryo in 1215" but which in March 1776 was for South Carolina's
Judge William Henry Drayton a basic right that the Crown had violated in contempt, as he put it, of Magna Carta. The document's continuing power depended on its adaptability and on the mythic qualities
it assumed: Magna Carta "not only survived but it became a sacred
text, glossed, interpreted and extended. . . ."[5]

Americans are accustomed to having the federal Constitution and
Bill of Rights reinterpreted and adapted to changing circumstances;
we have, in fact, institutionalized that process in the Supreme Court.
But the Declaration of Independence has been no less "glossed, interpreted and extended" over time. MacLeish, like Lincoln, relegated the
bulk of its words to the dead past and emphasized a handful of passages, most of which are on the Jefferson Memorial. There the open-

ing sentence of the Declaration's second paragraph leads to only three self-evident truths: that all men are created equal, that they have certain inalienable rights, including the rights to life, liberty, and the pursuit of happiness, and that governments are created to protect those rights. Those are the lines most Americans remember (indeed, memories tend to fade after "life, liberty, and the pursuit of happiness"). They are also the lines that Lincoln emphasized, but their implications have shifted since his time. In 1858 he wrote a correspondent that the language of the Declaration of Independence was at odds with slavery but did not require political and social equality for free black Americans.[6] Few disagreed then. How many would agree today?

The gradual reinterpretation of the Declaration of Independence has not, however, been institutionalized. To be sure, the character of that process of change was affected by the passage of the Thirteenth, Fourteenth, and Fifteenth amendments to the Constitution, which ended slavery and involuntary servitude, precluded states from depriving anyone of "life, liberty, or property, without due process of law" or denying them the equal protection of the laws, and assured that the right to vote would not be denied because of race, color, or previous condition of servitude. Those amendments, which emerged from the caldron of idealism and resentment that was Reconstruction politics, have served in some measure to read into the Constitution principles in the Declaration of Independence and so provide a legal foundation for equality and equal rights. Today the pursuit of gender or age equality is, as a result, often carried out in the courts. The ultimate authority of the Declaration itself nonetheless rests, as it always has, less in law than in the minds and hearts of the people, and its meaning changes as new groups and new causes claim its mantle, constantly reopening the issue of what the nation's "founding principles" demand.

In 1963, a century after Lincoln issued the Emancipation Proclamation and presented his Gettysburg Address, Martin Luther King stood beside the Lincoln Memorial and called for the new birth of freedom that Lincoln had promised, a freedom that for King meant an end to the poverty, discrimination, and segregation that left black citizens "languishing in the corners of American society," exiles in their own land. His dream, that one day the sons of former slaves and former slaveholders would be able to "sit together at the table of brotherhood," and that his children would be judged by the quality of their character, not the color of their skins,[7] was beyond anything Thomas Jefferson could imagine. It was also beyond what Lincoln believed possible in his own day, although it fit Lincoln's conception of a Declaration of Independence whose maxims would be applied ever more broadly over time "as circumstances should permit," that is, as the people became more accepting. No less than Lincoln's vision, moreover, King's was an old American dream with legitimate roots in the American Revolution and its insistence that people should be judged for what they were and not by the accident of birth.

AND THE SHRINE up the mall at the National Archives, with its curious altar, which would seem more at home in a Baroque church somewhere in Rome? Understand it, if you will, as a reminder of what happened in the 1820s, or, better yet, as a monument to the issues and peculiarities of the twentieth century, but not to the heritage of the American Revolution. Why should the American people file by, looking up reverentially at a document that was and is their creation, as if it were handed down by God or were the work of superhuman men whose talents far exceeded those of any who followed them? The symbolism is all wrong; it suggests a tradition locked in a glorious but dead past, reinforces the passive instincts of an anti-political age, and undercuts the acknowledgment and exercise of public responsibilities essential to the survival of the republic and its ideals.

Debate whether affirmative action is an anti-egalitarian bestowal of special privilege or a necessary remedy for centuries of unequal opportunity; ask whether the "individualistic character" of those passages from the Declaration of Independence on the Jefferson Memorial has helped liberate the human spirit or fostered a self-centered culture of rights at odds with the public good. Let interests clash and argument prosper. The vitality of the Declaration of Independence rests upon the readiness of the people and their leaders to discuss its implications and to make the crooked ways straight, not in the mummified paper curiosities lying in state at the Archives; in the ritual of politics, not in the worship of false gods who are at odds with our eighteenth-century origins and who war against our capacity, together, to define and realize right and justice in our time.

Appendixes

Appendix A
STATE AND LOCAL DECLARATIONS OF INDEPENDENCE:
A LOG: April–July 1776

STATES

North Carolina
Instructions   12 April 76   Peter Force, ed., *American Archives*,
                                               4th Series (Washington, D.C.,
                                               1833–46), V: 859–60 and 1322
                                               (henceforth "Force").

Rhode Island
Act repealing another   4 May 76   John R. Bartlett, ed., *Records of the
securing allegiance   Colony of R.I.*, VII (Providence,
                                               1862), 522–27.

Virginia
Instructions   15 May 76   Force VI: 461–62 and 1524.
Preamble, constitution   29 June 76   Julian Boyd, ed., *The Papers of
                                               Thomas Jefferson*, I (Princeton,
                                               1950), 377–79.

Connecticut
Instructions   14 June 76   Force VI: 867–68.

New Hampshire
Instructions   15 June 76   Force VI: 1030.

Delaware
Instructions   15 June 76   George Herbert Ryden, ed., *Letters
                                               to and from Caesar Rodney*
                                               (Philadelphia, 1933), 92.

New Jersey
    Instructions   22 June 76   Force VI: 1628–29; Larry Gerlach, ed., *New Jersey in the American Revolution* (Trenton, 1975), 211.

    Preamble, constitution 2 July 76   Ibid., 213.

Pennsylvania
    Instructions: Assembly 8 June 76   Force VI: 755, *Pennsylvania Gazette*, June 12.

    Instructions: Provincial 24 June 76   Force VI: 962–63.
      Conference

Maryland
    Instructions   28 June 76   Force VI: 1491.
    "A Declaration"   6 July 76   Force VI: 1506–07.

COUNTIES

(Instructions to Provincial Conventions or Assemblies)

Virginia:
    Cumberland   22 April 76   *Virginia Magazine of History and Biography*, XXXIV (1926), 184–86.

    Charlotte   23 April 76   Force V: 1034–35; *Virginia Gazette* (Purdie), 10 May 1776; Brent Tarter and Robert Scribner, eds., *Revolutionary Virginia* (Charlottesville, 1973–83), VI: 447–48.

    James City   24 April 76   Force V: 1046–47; Tarter and Scribner, eds., *Revolutionary Virginia*, VI: 458.

    Buckingham   n.d. (13 May 76?) Force V: 1206–09; *Virginia Gazette* (Purdie) 14 June 76; Tarter and Scribner, eds., *Revolutionary Virginia*, VII: 109–13.

Maryland
    Frederick   17 June 76   Force VI: 933.
    Anne Arundel   22 June 76   Force VI: 1017–18.
    Charles   n.d.   Force VI: 1018–19.
    Talbot   n.d.   Force VI: 1019–21.

GRAND JURY PRESENTMENTS

Charlestown, S.C.	23 April 76	Force V: 1032–34.
Judge Drayton's charge to the above		Force V: 1025–32.
Georgetown, S.C.	6 May 76	Force V: 1205–06.
Cheraws District, S.C.	20 May 76	Force VI: 514–15; Alexander Gregg, *History of the Old Cheraws* (Columbia, S.C., 1925), 264–66.

PRIVATE AND QUASI-PUBLIC GROUPS

N.Y. Mechanics in Union 29 May 76   Force VI: 614–15.

See also the resolutions of various militia companies in Pennsylvania, including:[1]

Associators, 4th Battalion, City and Liberties of Philadelphia	n.d. (10 June 76?)	Force VI: 784–85.
Associators of 5th Battalion, City and Liberties of Philadelphia	n.d. (10 June 76?)	Force VI: 785.
Associators, 1st Battalion of Chester County	10 June 76	Force VI: 785–86; *Pennsylvania Gazette*, June 12, 1776.
Elk Battalion Militia, Chester County	n.d.	Force VI: 786; *Pennsylvania Gazette*, June 19, 1776.
Associators of Col. Crawford's Battalion, Lancaster County	10 June 76	Force VI: 786–87; *Pennsylvania Gazette*, June 19, 1776.

[1]For other sets of Pennsylvania resolves, which speak somewhat less directly on the issue of Independence, see the Associators of the 2nd Battalion, Northampton County, 27 May, Force VI: 567–68, and Colonel Bartraim Galbraith's Battalion, Elizabethtown, 27 May, p. 568. Also the York County Committee, 30 May, pp. 620–21.

TOWNS

MASSACHUSETTS (County in Parentheses[2]):

Chelmsford (Middlesex)	13 (?) May	Rev. Wilson Waters, *History of Chelmsford* (Lowell, 1917), 209.
Lynn (Essex)	21 May 76	*Records of ye Towne Meetings of Lyn* (Lynn, 1971), 38–39.
Plymouth (Plymouth)	20 May 76	*Records of the Town of Plymouth*, III, *1743 to 1783* (Plymouth, 1903), 315.
Watertown (Middlesex)	20 May 76	*Watertown Records*, VI (Newton, 1928), 139.
Brookline (Suffolk)	20 May 76	John G. Curtis, *History of . . . Brookline* (Boston, 1933), 164–65.
Rowley (Essex)	22 May 76	Thomas Gage, *History of Rowley*, (Boston, 1840), 252.
Plympton (Plymouth)	23 May 76	Henry S. Griffith, *History of . . . Carver* (New Bedford, 1913), 96.
Billerica (Middlesex)	23 May 76	Force VI: 556.
Boston (Suffolk)	23 May 76	Force VI: 556–58; Hezekiah Niles, ed., *Principles and Acts of the Revolution* (Baltimore, 1822), 132–33; *Boston Gazette*, June 10, 1776.
Dedham (Suffolk)	27 May 76	Erastus Worthington, *The History of Dedham* (Boston, 1827), p. 67.
Malden (Middlesex)	27 May 76	Force VI: 602–03; Niles, ed., *Principles and Acts of the Revolution*, 131–32.

[2]Eighteenth-century counties identified from maps in Lester J. Cappon, ed., *Atlas of Early American History* (Princeton, 1976), 2, 3, 37, or from the county designations in Force. See also the *Journals of Each Provincial Congress in Massachusetts in 1774 and 1775 . . .* (Boston, 1838), 7–15, and n. 1 at p. 10. A more exhaustive survey of town records, many of which remain within individual towns, would no doubt expand this list, which, although substantial, includes a minority of the roughly 200 town seats mentioned in the records of the first Provincial Congress. Until a more thorough survey is made, it is difficult to draw conclusions with regard to the relative strength of support for Independence in the counties or regions of Massachusetts, although it's worth noting that a majority of Essex's town seats appear on the list. The absence of any returns from Duke County, or from Nantucket Island, which was known as a Loyalist enclave, and the relative lack of resolutions from Barnstable County, which covered Cape Cod, is also striking.

Brunswick (Bristol)	31 May 76	Force VI: 603–04.
Newburyport (Essex)	31 May 76	Force VI: 649.
Newbury (Essex)	31 May 76	Joshua Coffin, *A Sketch of the History of Newbury* . . . (Boston, 1845), p. 253.[3]
Stockbridge (Berkshire)	n.d.	Force VI: 649.
Pittsfield (Berkshire)	n.d.	Force VI: 649.
Taunton (Bristol)	3 June 76	Force VI: 698–99.
Scituate (Plymouth)	4 June 76	Force VI: 699.
Wrentham (Suffolk)	5 June 76	Force VI: 699–700.
Hanover (Plymouth)	6 June 76	Force VI: 700.
Tyringham (Berkshire)	7 June 76	Force VI: 700.
Alford (Berkshire)	7 June 76	Force VI: 701.
Norwich (Hampshire)	7 June 76	Force VI: 701.
Ipswich (Essex)	10 June 76	Thomas F. Waters, *Ipswich* . . ., II (Ipswich, 1917), 336.
Salem (Essex)	12 June 76	Joseph B. Felt, *Annals of Salem* . . . (Salem, 1827), 499.
Andover (Essex)	12 June 76	Abiel Abbot, *History of Andover* . . . (Andover, 1829), 61.
Beverly (Essex)	13 June 76	Edwin M. Stone, *History of Beverly* (Boston, 1843), 67–68.
Amherst (Essex)	13 June 76	Town Records in *History of* . . . *Amherst* (Amherst, 1896), Pt. II, p. 75.
Topsfield (Essex)	14, 21 June 76	Force VI: 703–04; George Francis Dow, *History of Topsfield* (Topsfield, 1946), 178.[4]
Acton (Middlesex)	14 June 76	Force VI: 702; Lemuel Shattuck, *History of* . . . *Concord* (Boston, 1835), 282.

[3] On May 27, Newbury "voted to instruct their representatives, 'that they after having seriously weighed the state and case of independence, act their best judgment and prudence respecting the same.'" But on the 31st it voted affirmatively on the proposition put by the assembly, committing its people to support Independence with their lives and fortunes.

[4] Topsfield affirmed its willingness to support Independence on 14 June and set up a committee of three to draft instructions to that effect. It adopted those instructions on 21 June.

Hubbardston (Worcester) 14 June 76   J. M. Stowe, *History of . . .*
Hubbardston (Hubbardston, 1881), 43.

Palmer (Hampshire)   17 June 76   Force VI: 701–02.

Bedford (Middlesex)   17 June 76   Force VI: 702.

Murraysfield
(Hampshire)   17 June 76   Force VI: 702–03.
(Name subsequently changed to Chester.)

Marblehead (Essex)   17 June 76   Joseph S. Robinson, *Story of*
Marblehead (n.p., 1936), 36.

Boxford (Essex)   17 June 76   Sidney Perley, *History of Boxford*
(Boxford, 1880), 227.

Weston (Middlesex)   18 June 76   Town of Weston, *Records . . .*
1754–1803 (Boston, 1893), 222.

Leverett (Hampshire)   18 June 76   Force VI: 703.

Danvers (Essex)   18 June 76   J. W. Hanson, *History of . . .*
Danvers (Danvers, 1848), 95–96.

Gageborough (Bristol)   19 June 76   Force VI: 703.
(Name subsequently changed to Windsor.)

Natick (Middlesex)   20 June 76   Force VI: 703.

Bradford (Essex)   20 June 76   Gardner B. Perry, *History of*
Bradford (Haverhill, 1872), 26–27.

Southampton
(Hampshire)   21 June 76   Force VI: 704.

Gloucester (Essex)   24 June 76   John J. Babson, *History of*
. . . Gloucester (Gloucester, 1860), 408.

Williamstown
(Berkshire)   24 June 76   Force VI: 705.

Northbridge (Worcester)   25 June 76   Force VI: 704–05.

Haverhill (Essex)   25 June 76   B. L. Mirick, *History of Haverhill*
(Haverhill, 1832), 174.

Sturbridge, (Worcester)   27 June 76   Force VI: 706.

Ashburnham,
(Worcester)   28 June 76   Ezra S. Stearns, *History of*
Ashburnham, I (Ashburnham, 1887), 146.

Hanover (Plymouth)	30 June 76	John S. Barry, *Historical Sketch of . . . Hanover* (Boston, 1853) 119.
Amesbury (Essex)	1 July 76	Joseph Merrill, *History of Amesbury* (Haverhill, 1880), 261.
Fitchburg (Worcester)	1 July 76	Force VI: 706; Walter A. Davis, ed., *Old Records of . . . Fitchburg . . .*, I (Fitchburg, 1898), 127.
Ashby (Middlesex)	1 July 76	Force VI: 706.
Greenwich (Hampshire)	1 July 76	Force VI: 706.
Bellingham (Suffolk)	4 July 76	George F. Partridge, *History of . . . Bellingham* (Bellingham, 1919), 126.
Winchendon (Worcester)	4 July 76	Force VI: 706.
Eastham (Barnstable)	n.d.	Force VI: 706.

For a Massachusetts town that voted against endorsing Independence, See:

Barnstable (Barnstable)	25 June 76	Force VI: 705–06.

NEW YORK (County in Parentheses):

King's District (Albany)	24 June 76	Force VI: 1056; *Massachusetts Spy*, July 5, 1776.
Spencer-Town (Albany)	24 June 76	Force VI: 1056; *Massachusetts Spy*, July 5, 1776.

Appendix B

LOCAL RESOLUTIONS ON INDEPENDENCE: SOME EXAMPLES

What follows are not so much "representative" local declarations as a sampling of those documents for the benefit of readers who would like a closer look. I have skipped the state resolutions in part because the most important of them are quoted or described quite fully in Chapter II. The resolutions of counties and towns and grand juries also came from nearer the "grass roots," often had a more open and informal character, and are, as documents, even more obscure than the state pronouncements.

These local instructions or presentments speak to many issues, from the obvious—Independence—to others on which their comments are sometimes indirect, such as the relationship of constituents to their elected delegates. The instructions in particular show, I think, a respect for the men the voters chose to represent them—and so a readiness to let their judgment have some free rein—along with a strong sense (stronger in some than others) that representatives' actions should be guided if not determined by their constituents' views. As such, the instructions give a good sense of "attorneyship representation" and popular politics in America at the time of the Revolution. Several documents also demonstrate how powerfully interested the people were in the reconstitution of political institutions. If we are to understand Americans of the eighteenth century, we have to shed our preoccupations and understand theirs. Nothing spurs historical understanding in that sense more powerfully than sources such as these.

Each of the documents is distinguished in some way. The Buckingham County, Virginia, instructions are long and maybe even garrulous; however, they review the entire conflict with Britain in a way that, I think, describes well the road toward Independence as the colonists experienced it. The grand jury presentment from South Carolina's Cheraws District, after explaining the reasons for Independence, reveals how deeply moving the jurymen found the inauguration of self-government under South Carolina's "temporary" constitution of March 1776. Charles County, Maryland, instructed its representatives to the Maryland Convention how to vote on Independence as well as how to act on several other issues. Its justification for Independence singled out for criticism not just the government of Great Britain, but the British people. The townsmen of Natick, Massachusetts, confidently asserted what was, it seems, a quite recent discovery, that Americans were better qualified to govern America than were the British (and on that point their instructions resemble the presentment of the Cheraws District's Grand Jury); those of Topsfield expressed in a direct and memorable way their amazement at the issue they were asked to debate.

The resolution of Ashby, Massachusetts, was less unusual; in fact, it resembled the resolutions of several other Massachusetts towns in both content and length. So brief a statement obviously covered less than did the instructions of Buckingham County, Virginia. But Ashby managed to say a lot, and to suggest even more, in a few words. From a literary point of view, perhaps again less was more.

BUCKINGHAM COUNTY, VIRGINIA.
[May 13, 1776?] Peter Force, ed., *American Archives*, 4th Ser.
(Washington, D.C., 1833–46), V: 1206–08

To *CHARLES PATTERSON* and *JOHN CABELL*, Gentlemen
Delegates for the County of *BUCKINGHAM*, now in General
Convention:

The Address and Instructions of the Freeholders of the said County.

As you were elected and deputed by us to fill the most difficult and important places that the Representatives of this County were ever appointed to act in, we cannot, in justice to ourselves and posterity, forbear to give some instructions concerning the discharge of your great trust. In this we have the example of many; but would not tie you down in a manner too strict and positive. Though a general confidence in your honesty and wisdom may be required; yet, in some great and leading questions, it may not be unnecessary to take the sense of your constituents: we give you ours in the plainest, easiest, and best method it can be collected. If it does not agree with the general opinion, we trust, at least, it will be pardonable. Actuated by a warm and sincere regard for the interests and rights of mankind, [1206/1207] and a deep sense of our present situation, we wish to think and proceed aright in the affairs of such great consequence; and are willing, therefore, to submit our opinions to the candid judgment of the publick.

The unhappy dispute between *Great Britain* and these United Colonies seems now arrived to a crisis, from whence events ought to take place which, at the beginning, we believe, were in contemplation of but few, and even by them viewed at a much greater distance. When dissensions first arose, we felt our hearts warmly attached to the King of *Great Britain* and the Royal family; but now the case is much altered. At that time we wished to look upon the Ministry and Parliament as the only fountains from which the bitter waters flowed, and considered the King as deceived and misguided by his counsellors; and were therefore led to think that he might, in a proper time, open his eyes, and become a mediator between his contending subjects. The measures, however, still pursued against *America* leave no room to expect such an interposition from motives of goodness and affection, or with concessions, which may be justly required. Our enemies denounce our ruin, from the whole tenour of their conduct; and the King's speeches, and addresses, resolutions, and acts of Parliament, are evidently concerted to carry their great favourite point. Prospects of a reconciliation have opened themselves to some; but they, we fear, were only the ignorant, credulous, and unwary; and even to them they must, ere this, have closed with more threatening appearances. The gracious receipt of a Continental petition, and the bare mention of Commissioners, have been severally construed good marks of reconcilement and peace, by those who too fondly hoped what was generally desired.

When the *British* Parliament assumed an absolute power over us, and attempted to exercise that power, an opposition was formed in the United Colonies, the most pacifick which could be adopted, with any probability of success, in the last resort, should our enemies persist in their measures, and endeavour to drive us into submission by force. This opposition became a great offence in their eyes: our petitions were treated with contempt, our actions termed rebellious, and arms used to subdue us. As the Colonies seemed determined, from the first, to maintain their rights, and the rights of a free people, they were obliged to repel force by force; and, for the effectual purpose thereof, as occasions required, to take into their own hands the Legislative, Executive, and Judicial powers of Government. This was a necessary consequence, and no settled and permanent opposition could be made without it. They violated the faith of Charters, the principles of the Constitution, and attempted to destroy our legal as well as natural rights. We could do nothing without forming at least a temporary Government of our own, by laying aside that part, and dispensing with those forms, of the old Constitution, which were incompatible with our safety or success. They have broken through positive laws, and express acts of Assembly, as well as the ties which unite man to man in general affection; by which means they have become felons and enemies under those laws. In the struggle, the lives of hundreds have been destroyed; flourishing towns burnt down and demolished; property seized and taken, secretly and openly; thousands reduced from easy and affluent circumstances to poverty and distress; and all the horrors of an expensive and dreadful war experienced. We have opposed with arms, and persevered in our measures, with a resolution to maintain our rights, and regarded no law heretofore made but as it was found consistent with such a laudable design. Both sides grew every day more and more incensed, from circumstances which always arise in such contests; and that general confidence, so necessary to the support of every kind of Government, seems entirely annihilated, without a prospect of reunion of affections sufficient to restore it; it becomes daily more out of their power and farther from their inclinations to put us on the footing we stood at the close of the last war, or repair the great damages we have sustained; which, if they should ever confess their errors, and desire to close with us on the terms we have hitherto offered, they must, in justice and reason, agree ought to be done.

Besides, the welfare of ourselves and future generations obliges us to turn matters over in every point of view, and consider what has been the issue of contests most similar to our own. As virtue or publick spirit cannot be thoroughly [1207/1208] lost in any country, but must survive in the breasts of many individuals, so it would be too sanguine to imagine that any country is without some men of ambitious and selfish views, who, taking the advantage of favourable opportunities and an unsettled state, turn the scale too much to their own side, and destroy the liberty or fix the chains of their country. This evil we find generally arises in or after civil broils, when the people have no established Government, or are led, from a sense of danger or unlimited confidence, to give themselves up blindly to their leaders. This misfortune, we hope, will never happen among us; nor do we believe that, at this time, there is any influence or inclination to effect or desire it. However, it is better to prevent evils than have them to remedy; and no precaution can be too great for the attainment of every valuable end to mankind. When things are fixed in a point beyond the present, many advantages may probably accrue; we, therefore, your constituents, recommend and instruct you, as far as your voices will contribute, to cause a total and final separation from *Great Britain* to take place as soon as possible; or, as we conceive this great point will not come within your immediate province, that, as far as in your power, you cause such instructions to be given to the Delegates from this Colony to the Continental Congress; that you weigh well the importance of the matter, and endeavour to lodge power in the hands of those whose honesty, wisdom, and love for their country, will direct them to use it for the publick good; that, as far as you conceive are admitted, you cause a free and happy Constitution to be established, with a renunciation of the old, or so much thereof as has been found inconvenient and oppressive; and that you endeavour to fix a publick jealousy in this Constitution, as an essential principle of its support.

In the present unsettled state of affairs, when the Government erected among us is confessed on all hands to be only temporary, for the immediate purpose of opposing the arbitrary strides of *Great Britain,* and effecting a reconciliation with the mother country; when the contest is between subject and subject, with the established power of peace and war at the head of our enemies, and our professions and actions tend only to bring about a reconciliation, we have not the least room to believe that any foreign nation will espouse our cause in an open and avowed manner; but when we lay aside these considerations, and bid the last adieu, some foreign power may, for their own interest, lend an assisting hand, settle a trade, and enable us to discharge the great burdens of the war, which otherwise may become intolerable.

Here, again, we would direct you, as far as relates to your Province, to beware of any other than commercial alliances with foreigners; and to keep their armies off your shores, if possible. We ask for a full representation; free and frequent elections; and that no standing armies whatever should be kept up in time of peace. We trust you will use your utmost care and circumspection at this trying crisis, that, as *America* is the last of the world which has contended for her liberty, so she may be the most free and happy. She has many advantages which others in nearly her circumstances have not known, arising from her situation and strength, and the experience of all before to profit by. View well the defects in other Governments, and consider the visible causes which reduced them from freedom to slavery, or raised them from slavery to liberty; and learn by these examples. It was by a Revolution, and the choice of the people, that the present Royal family was seated on the Throne of *Great Britain*; and we conceive the Supreme Being hath left it in our power to choose what Government we please for our civil and religious happiness; and when that becomes defective, or deviates from the end of its institution, and cannot be corrected, that the people may form themselves into another, avoiding the defects of the former. This we would now wish to have effected, as soon as the general consent approves, and the wisdom of our councils will admit; that we may, as far as possible, keep up our primary object, and not lose ourselves in hankering after a reconciliation with *Great Britain.*

Good Government alone, and the prosperity of mankind, can be in the Divine intention; we pray, therefore, that under the superintending providence of the Ruler of the Universe, a Government may be established in *America,* [1208/1209] the most free, happy, and permanent, that human wisdom can contrive, and the perfection of man maintain.

Published by order of the Committee:

ROLFE ELDRIDGE, *Clerk.*
[May 13, 1776?]

CHERAWS DISTRICT, SOUTH CAROLINA.
May 20, 1776. Force, ed., *American Archives,* VI: 514-15

At a Court of General Sessions of the Peace, Oyer and Terminer, Assize and General Jail Delivery, begun to be holden in and for the said District, at *Long-Bluff,* in the Colony aforesaid, on *Monday,* the 20th day of *May,* in the year of our Lord one thousand seven hundred and seventy-six: The Presentments of the Grand Jury of and for the said District:

I. When a people, born and bred in a land of freedom and virtue, uncorrupted by those refinements which effeminate and debase the mind, manly and generous in their sentiments, bold and hardy in their nature, and actuated by every principle of liberality, from too sad experience are convinced of the wicked schemes of their treacherous rulers to fetter them with the chains of servitude, and rob them of every noble and desirable privilege which distinguishes them as freemen,—justice, humanity, and the immutable laws of *God,* justify and support them in revoking those sacred trusts which are so impiously violated, and placing them in such hands as are most likely to execute them in the manner and for the important ends for which they were first given.

II. The good people of this Colony, with the rest of her sister Colonies, confiding in the justice and merited protection of the King and Parliament of *Great Britain,* ever signalized themselves by every mark of duty and affection towards them, and esteemed such a bond of union and harmony as the greatest happiness. But when that protection was wantonly withdrawn, and every mark of cruelty and oppression substituted; when tyranny, violence, and injustice, took the place of equity, mildness, and affection; and bloodshed, murder, robbery, conflagration, and the most deadly persecution, stamped the malignity of her intentions; self-preservation, and a regard to our own welfare and security, became a consideration both important and necessary. The Parliament and Ministry of *Great-Britain,* by their wanton and undeserved persecutions, have reduced this Colony to a state of separation from her, unsought for and undesired by them; a separation which now proves its own utility, as the only lasting means of future happiness and safety. What every one once dreaded as the greatest misery, they now unexpectedly find their greatest advantage. Amidst all her sufferings, and manifold injuries which have been done her, this Colony was ever ready, with her sister Colonies, to ask for that reconciliation which showed every mark of forgiveness and promise of future harmony. But how were they treated? Each token of submission was aggravated into usurpation; humbled petitions styled insults; and every dutiful desire of accommodation treated with the most implacable contempt. Cast off, persecuted, defamed, given up as a prey to every violence and injury, a righteous and much injured people have at length appealed to *God!* and, trusting to his divine justice and their own virtuous perseverance, taken the only and last means of securing their own honour, safety, and happiness.

III. We now feel every joyful and comfortable hope that a people could desire in the present Constitution and form of Government established in this Colony; a Constitution founded on the strictest principles of justice and humanity, where the rights and happiness of the whole, the poor and the rich, are equally secured; and to secure and defend which, it is the particular interest of every individual who regards his own safety and advantage.

IV. When we consider the publick officers of our present form of Government now appointed, as well as the method and duration of their appointment, we cannot but declare our entire satisfaction and comfort; as well in the characters of such men, who are justly esteemed for every virtue, as their well-known abilities to execute the important trusts which they now hold.

V. Under these convictions, and filled with these hopes, we cannot but most earnestly recommend it to every man, as essential to his own liberty and happiness, as well as that [514/515] of his posterity, to secure and defend with his life and fortune a form of Government so just, so equitable, and promising; to inculcate its principles to their children, and hand it down to them unviolated, that the latest posterity may enjoy the virtuous fruits of that work, which the integrity and fortitude of the present age had, at the expense of their blood and treasure, at length happily effected.

VI. We cannot but declare how great the pleasure, the harmony, and political union which now exists in this District affords; and having no grievances to complain of, only beg leave to recommend that a new Jury list be made for this District, the present being insufficient.

And lastly, we beg leave to return our most sincere thanks to Mr. Justice *Matthews*, for his spirited and patriotic charge; at the same time requesting that these our presentments be printed in the publick papers.

> PHILIP PLEDGER, *Foreman.*

ABEL EDWARDS,	BENJAMIN JAMES,
JOHN HEUSTES,	MAGNUS CORGELL,
CHARLES MACCALL,	THOMAS BINGHAM,
JOHN WILD,	PETER KOLB,

THOMAS LIDE,   BENJAMIN RODGERS,
MARTIN DEWITT,   THOMAS ELLEBREE,
JOHN MIKELL,   MOSES SPRIGHT.

CHARLES COUNTY, MARYLAND.
[June 1776]. Force, ed., *American Archives,*
VI: 1018-19

To *JOSIAH HAWKINS, THOMAS STONE, ROBERT T. HOOE,*
JOSEPH H. HARRISON, and *WILLIAM HARRISON,* Esqs.

We, the subscribers, freemen of *Charles* County, in the Province of *Maryland,* taking into our most serious consideration the present state of the unhappy dispute between *Great Britain* and the United Colonies, and the very great distress and hardships they have brought upon us thereby, think proper to deliver you our sentiments, and to instruct you in certain points relative to your conduct in the next Convention, as Representatives of this County. Reasons for the mode of voting, and determining questions, by a majority of Counties, have not appeared to us to exist since the last general election; therefore, we charge and instruct you to move for, and endeavour to obtain a regulation for voting individually, and determining questions by a majority of members, and not of Counties, in future. And as we know we have a right to hear, or be informed what is transacted in Convention, we instruct you to move for, and endeavour to obtain, a resolve for the doors of the House to be kept open in future, and that, on all questions proposed and seconded, the yeas and nays be taken, and, together with every other part of your proceedings, published, except such only as may relate to military operations, questions which ought to be debated with the doors shut, and the determinations thereon kept secret.

The experience we have had of the cruelty and injustice of the *British* Government, under which we have too long borne oppression and wrongs, and notwithstanding every peaceable endeavour of the United Colonies to get redress of grievances, by decent, dutiful, and sincere petitions and representations to the King and Parliament, giving every assurance of our affection and loyalty, and praying for no more than peace, liberty and safety under the *British* Government, yet have we received nothing but an increase of insult and injury, by all the Colonies being declared in actual rebellion; savages hired to take up arms against us; slaves proclaimed free, enticed away, trained and armed against their lawful masters; our towns plundered, burnt, and destroyed; our vessels and property seized on the seas, made free plunder to the captors, and our seamen forced to take arms against ourselves; our friends and countrymen, when captivated, confined in dungeons, and, as if criminals, chained down to the earth; our estates confiscated, and our men, women and children robbed and murdered: and at this time, instead of Commissioners to negotiate a peace, as we have been led to believe were coming out, a formidable fleet of *British* ships, with a numerous army of foreign soldiers, in *British* pay, are daily expected on our coast, to force us to yield the property we have honestly acquired, and fairly own, and drudge out the remainder of our days in misery and wretchedness, leaving us nothing better to bequeath to posterity than poverty and slavery:—we must, for these reasons, declare, that our affection for the people, and allegiance to the Crown of *Great Britain*, so readily and truly acknowledged till of late, is forfeited on their part. And as we are convinced that nothing virtuous, humane, generous, or just, can be expected from the *British* King or nation, and that they will exert themselves to reduce us to a [1018/1019] state of slavery, by every effort and artifice in their power, we are of opinion that the time has fully arrived for the Colonies to adopt the last measure for our common good and safety, and that the sooner they declare themselves separate from, and independent of the Crown and Parliament of *Great Britain*, the sooner they will be able to make effectual opposition, and establish their liberties on a firm and permanent basis. We, therefore, most earnestly instruct and charge you to move for, without loss of time, and endeavour to obtain, positive instructions from the Convention of *Maryland* to their Delegates in Congress, immediately to join the other Colonies in declaring that the United Colonies no longer owe allegiance to, nor are they dependant upon, the Crown or Parliament of *Great Britain*, or any other power on earth, but are, for time to come, free and independent States; provided that the power of forming Government, and regulating the internal concerns of each Colony, be left to their respective Legislatures; and that said Delegates give the assent of this Province to any further confederation of the Colonies for the support of their union, and for forming such foreign commercial connections as may be requisite and necessary for our common good and safety. And as the present Government under the King cannot longer exist with safety to the freemen of this Province, we are of opinion a new form of Government, agreeable to the late recommendation of the honourable Continental Congress to all the United Colonies, ought immediately to be adopted.

NATICK, MASSACHUSETTS.
June 20, 1776. Force, ed., *American Archives*, VI: 703

At a meeting of the town of *Natick, June* 20, 1776, legally warned, in consequence of a resolve of the late House of Representatives being laid before the Town, setting forth their sense of the obligations that lie upon every town in this Colony solemnly to engage to support with their lives and fortunes the honourable Continental Congress, should said Congress, for the safety of the Colonies, come into the measure of declaring themselves independent of the Kingdom of *Great Britain*, it was unanimously

Voted, That, in consideration of the many acts of the *British* Parliament, passed at divers sessions of the same, within about thirteen years past, relating to said Colonies, especially those within the two or three last years, by which every idea of moderation, justice, humanity, and Christianity are entirely laid aside, and those principles and measures adopted and pursued which would disgrace the most unenlightened and uncivilized tribe of aboriginal natives in the most interior parts of this extensive continent; and, also, in consequence of the glaring impropriety, incapacity, and fatal tendency, of any State whatever, at the distance of three thousand miles, to legislate for these Colonies, which at the same time are so numerous, so knowing, and capable of legislating; or to have a negative upon those laws which they, in their respective Assemblies, and by their united representation in General Congress, shall, from time to time, want and establish for themselves; and upon divers other considerations, which, for brevity's sake, we omit to mention,—we, the inhabitants of *Natick*, in town-meeting assembled, do hereby declare, agreeable to the tenor of the aforementioned resolve, that, should the honourable Continental Congress declare these *American* Colonies independent of the Kingdom of *Great Britain*, we will, with our lives and fortunes, join with the other inhabitants of this Colony, and with those of the other Colonies, in supporting them in such measure, which we look upon to be both important and necessary, and which, if we may be permitted to suggest our opinion, the sooner it is come into the fewer difficulties we shall have to contend with, and the grand objects of peace, liberty, and safety, will be more likely speedily to be restored and established in our once happy land.

TOPSFIELD, MASSACHUSETTS.
June 21, 1776. Force, ed., *American Archives*, VI: 703-04

At a legal Town-meeting held in *Topsfield*, by adjournment, *June* 21, 1776, the Town voted the following Instructions:

To Mr. JOHN GOULD, *Representative of Topsfield*.

SIR: A resolution of the honourable House of Repre- [703/704] sentatives, calling upon the several towns in this Colony to express their minds with respect to *American* independence of the Kingdom of *Great Britain*, is the occasion of our giving you instructions; this being the greatest and most important question that ever came before this town. A few years ago, sir, such a question would have put us into a surprise, and, we apprehend, would have been treated with the utmost contempt. We then looked on ourselves happy in being subjects of the King of *Great Britain*. It being our forefathers' native country, we looked up unto them as our parent State; and we have always looked upon it as our duty, as well as our interest, to defend and support the honour of the Crown of *Great Britain*, and we have always freely done it, both with our lives and fortunes—counting ourselves happy when in the strictest union and connection with our parent State. But the scene is now changed; our sentiments are now altered. She who was called our mother country and parent State, has now, without any just cause, or injury done by these Colonies, become their greatest enemy. The unprovoked injuries these Colonies have received; the unjustifiable and unconstitutional claims that have been made on the Colonies by the Court of *Great Britain*, to force us, and take away our substance from us, and that at any time, or for any use, that they please, without our consent, and the prosecuting these their claims, have been cruel and unjust to the highest degree.

The whole conduct of the Court of *Great Britain*, and the fallacious conduct of their Governours appointed and sent into these Colonies, are so well known, and have been, by much abler hands, set forth in such a clear, plain, and true light, we think it needless to enumerate any further particulars. For these reasons, sir, as well as many others that may be mentioned, we are confirmed in the opinion that the United Colonies will be greatly wanting in their duty, both to the great Governour of the Universe, to themselves, and posterity, if independence of the Kingdom of *Great Britain* is not declared, as soon as may be; these being our sentiments—but we would not be understood that we mean to dictate. Leaving that momentous affair to the well-known wisdom, prudence, justice, and integrity, of that honourable body the Continental Congress, under whose direction it more immediately belongs, and in respect to a form of government for the future, we take it that belongs to an after question; and we could wish that no Court nor Congress on this continent might spend their time in debating about forms and ceremonies, equal or unequal representation in Court, at present. As innovations are always dangerous, we heartily wish that the ancient rules in the Charter, which this Province has been so much contending for, might be strictly adhered to, until such time as the whole of the people of this Colony have liberty to express their sentiments in respect to that affair as fully as they have in the case of independence; for we are full in the opinion that the sentiments of the people in general are never fully collected by the vote or opinion of a few persons met together, appointed, when they descend into matters of great importance that are wholly new, especially when the whole of the people are concerned therein.

Having thus freely spoken our sentiments in respect to independence, &c., we now instruct you, sir, to give the honourable the Continental Congress the strongest assurance that if, for the safety of the United Colonies, they shall declare *America* to be independent of the Kingdom of *Great Britain*, your constituents will support and defend the measure with their lives and fortunes, to the utmost of their power.

ASHBY, MASSACHUSETTS.
July 1, 1776. Force, ed., *American Archives*, VI: 706.

Agreeable to a Resolve of the late honourable House of Representatives, passed on the 10th of *May* last, the inhabitants of this town being assembled for that purpose, on the 1st day of *July* instant, and unanimously voted as follows, viz: That should the honourable Congress, for the safety of the Colonies, declare them independent of *Great Britain*, the inhabitants of *Ashby* will solemnly engage with their lives and fortunes to support them in the measure.

Appendix C
THE DECLARATION OF INDEPENDENCE: THE JEFFERSON DRAFT WITH CONGRESS'S EDITORIAL CHANGES

Of the various efforts to show just what additions and excisions Congress made in the draft Declaration of Independence submitted by the Committee of Five, the most accurate and easiest to understand, to my mind, is in Carl Becker's The Declaration of Independence *(New York, 1942), pp. 174–84. Becker began with the transcript that Jefferson sent Richard Henry Lee on July 8, 1776, which probably replicates most faithfully the Committee's long-lost "fair copy." He then added Congress's changes, which he determined by examining the text of the Declaration in Congress's Rough Journal, onto a typescript of the Lee copy, crossing out deleted parts and inserting new words and phrases above the lines. Twenty-one years later, Julian Boyd, in* The Declaration of Independence: The Evolution of the Text. . . . *listed Congress's changes, making a few minor adjustments in Becker's conclusions as to what Congress did. For this purpose, see the revised edition published by Princeton University Press (Princeton, N.J., 1945), pp. 31–37. What follows is closely modeled on Becker, with a little updating. I consulted Boyd's work, and also made a few minor adjustments in Becker's transcription of the Lee draft—a photograph of which is conveniently reproduced in Boyd's* Declaration of Independence. *In short, I restored Jefferson's spelling (he generally used the spelling "independant," and "it's" for the possessive form of "it"). I also added an "s" to "domestic insurrection," eliminated Becker's mistaken crossing-out of a pronoun that in fact Congress kept (i.e., the "his" in "declaring us out of his protection. . . ."), and reversed his listing of "parliament or people." Spelling and capitalization in the document as it emerged from Congress underwent further adjustments before the document was published.*

Inevitably, human error crept into the various transcriptions of the document, making each different from the others. Often the differences are of little substantive significance. The Becker version (which remains very useable) and the amended Becker version included here are nonetheless preferable to the copy of the committee report with indications of Congress's changes that Jefferson included in his "Notes" on Congress's proceedings, from which Jefferson probably copied the document he sent James Madison in 1783. The text as it appears in Jefferson's "Notes" is frequently reproduced, but, as Boyd noted in the first volume of The Papers of Thomas Jefferson, *Jefferson's notations "were not exact or comprehensive" (416). The same can be said of Jefferson's effort to indicate what changes Congress made to the committee draft on the copy of the Declaration he sent to Richard Henry Lee. His summary of Congress's editorial work there was good enough for Jefferson's purposes at the time, but it is nonetheless inexact and incomplete.*

A Declaration by the Representatives
of the UNITED STATES OF AMERICA
in General Congress assembled.

When in the course of human events it becomes necessary for one people to dissolve the political bands which have connected them with another, and to assume among the powers of the earth the separate and equal station to which the laws of nature and of nature's god entitle them, a decent respect to the opinions of mankind requires that they should declare the causes which impel them to the separation.

We hold these truths to be self-evident; that all men are created equal; that they are endowed by their Creator with ~~inherent and~~ certain inalienable[1] rights; that among these are life, liberty, and the pursuit of happiness; that to secure these rights, governments are instituted among men, deriving their just powers from the consent of the governed; that whenever any form of government becomes destructive of these ends, it is the right of the people to alter or to abolish it, and to institute new government, laying it's foundation on such principles, and organising it's powers in such form as to them shall seem most likely to effect their safety and happiness. prudence indeed will dictate that governments long established should not be changed for light & transient causes. and accordingly all experience hath shewn that mankind are more disposed to suffer, while evils are sufferable, than to right themselves by abolishing the forms to which they are accustomed. but when a long train of abuses and usurpations, ~~begun at a distinguished period,~~ & pursuing invariably the same object, evinces a design to reduce them under absolute despotism, it is their right, it is their duty, to throw off such government, & to provide new guards for their future security. such has been the patient sufferance of these colonies; & such is now the necessity which constrains them to

---

[1] In the printed version, "inalienable" became "unalienable." Becker, n. 1 at p. 175, suggests that "unalienable" might have been "the more customary form in the eighteenth century."

<ins>alter</ins>
~~expunge~~ ^their former systems of government. the history of the present king of

<ins>repeated</ins>
Great Britain, is a history of ~~unremitting~~ ^injuries and usurpations, ~~among which~~

<ins>having</ins>
~~appears no solitary fact to contradict the uniform tenor of the rest; but~~ all ^~~have~~

in direct object the establishment of an absolute tyranny over these states. to

prove this let facts be submitted to a candid world, ~~for the truth of which we~~

~~pledge a faith yet unsullied by falsehood~~.

He has refused his assent to laws the most wholesome and necessary for the

public good.

he has forbidden his governors to pass laws of immediate & pressing impor-

tance, unless suspended in their operation till his assent should be obtained; and

<ins>utterly</ins>
when so suspended, he has ^neglected ~~utterly~~ to attend to them.

he has refused to pass other laws for the accomodation of large districts of

people, unless those people would relinquish the right of representation in the

legislature; a right inestimable to them, & formidable to tyrants only.

he has called together legislative bodies at places unusual, uncomfortable, &

distant from the depository of their public records, for the sole purpose of fatigu-

ing them into compliance with his measures.

he has dissolved Representative houses repeatedly ~~& continually,~~ for oppos-

ing with manly firmness his invasions on the rights of the people.

he has refused for a long time after such dissolutions to cause others to be

elected whereby the legislative powers, incapable of annihilation, have returned

to the people at large for their exercise, the state remaining in the mean-

time exposed to all the dangers of invasion from without, & convulsions within.

he has endeavored to prevent the population of these states; for that purpose

obstructing the laws for naturalization of foreigners; refusing to pass others to

encourage their migrations hither; & raising the conditions of new appropria-

tions of lands.

<ins>obstructed</ins>
he has ~~suffered~~ ^the administration of justice ~~totally to cease in some of these~~

<ins>by</ins>
~~states,~~ ^ refusing his assent to laws for establishing judiciary powers.

he has made ~~our~~ judges dependent on his will alone, for the tenure of their

offices, and the amount & paiment of their salaries.

he has erected a multitude of new offices ~~by a self-assumed power,~~ & sent hither swarms of officers to harrass our people, and eat out their substance.

he has kept among us, in time of peace, standing armies ~~and ships of war,~~ without the consent of our legislatures.

he has affected to render the military independant of, & superior to, the civil power.

he has combined with others to subject us to a jurisdiction foreign to our constitution*s* and unacknoleged by our laws; giving his assent to their acts of pretended legislation

for quartering large bodies of armed troops among us;

for protecting them by a mock-trial from punishment for any murders which they should commit on the inhabitants of these states;

for cutting off our trade with all parts of the world;

for imposing taxes on us without our consent;

for depriving us ^*in many cases*^ of the benefits of trial by jury;

for transporting us beyond seas to be tried for pretended offences;

for abolishing the free system of English laws in a neighboring province, establishing therein an arbitrary government and enlarging it's boundaries so as to render it at once an example & fit instrument for introducing the same absolute rule into these states.[2]

for taking away our charters abolishing our most valuable laws, and altering fundamentally the forms of our governments;

for suspending our own legislatures, & declaring themselves invested with power to legislate for us in all cases whatsoever.

he has abdicated government here, ~~withdrawing his governors, &~~ ^*by*^ declaring us out of his ~~allegiance and~~ protection ^*and waging war against us*^.

---

[2]Boyd, in *The Declaration of Independence: The Evolution of the Text* . . . (revised edition, Princeton, N.J., 1945), argues that Congress substituted "states" for "colonies," and so restored Jefferson's original wording, which had been changed either by Jefferson or the drafting Committee (p. 30 and n. 57, p. 33 and n. 61). Becker did not include this among Congress's changes, nor have I, since the Lee copy says "states."

he has plundered our seas, ravaged our coasts, burnt our towns, & destroyed the lives of our people.

he is at this time transporting large armies of foreign mercenaries, to compleat the works of death, desolation & tyranny, already begun with circum- *scarcely paralleled in the most barbarous ages and totally* stances of cruelty & perfidy ₐunworthy the head of a civilized nation.

excited domestic insurrections amongst us and has
he has ₐendeavored to bring on the inhabitants of our frontiers the merciless Indian savages, whose known rule of warfare is an undistinguished destruction of all ages, sexes & conditions ~~of existence.~~

~~he has incited treasonable insurrections of our fellow citizens, with the al-~~
~~lurements of forfeiture & confiscation of property.~~

our fellow citizens
he has constrained ₐ~~others,~~[3] taken ~~captives~~ on the high seas to bear arms against their country, to become the executioners of their friends & brethren, or to fall themselves by their hands.

~~he has waged cruel war against human nature itself, violating it's most sacred~~
~~rights of life & liberty in the persons of a distant people, who never offended~~
~~him, captivating and carrying them into slavery in another hemisphere, or to~~
~~incur miserable death in their transportation thither. this piratical warfare, the~~
~~opprobrium of *infidel* powers, is the warfare of the *Christian* king of Great~~
~~Britain. determined to keep open a market where MEN should be bought &~~
~~sold, he has prostituted his negative for suppressing every legislative attempt to~~
~~prohibit or to restrain this execrable commerce: and that this assemblage of hor-~~
~~rors might want no fact of distinguished die, he now is now exciting those very~~
~~people to rise in arms among us, and to purchase that liberty of which *he* has de-~~
~~prived them, by murdering the people upon whom *he* also obtruded them: thus~~
~~paying off former crimes committed against the *liberties* of one people, with~~
~~crimes which he urges them to commit against the *lives* of another.~~

[3]Boyd, *Declaration of Independence,* 33, does not seem to include this among Congress's changes. I have followed Becker, who explained his position in n. 2 at p. 166. The change is clearly shown on the Lee draft. The Lee copy is now in the possession of the American Philosophical Society, which published it, with background information on the manuscript by I. Minis Hays, in its *Proceedings,* Vol. XXXVII (1898), pp. 88–107 (mss. on 103–107).

In every stage of these oppressions, we have petitioned for redress in the most humble terms; our repeated petitions have been answered only by repeated injury. a prince whose character is thus marked by every act which may define a tyrant, is unfit to be the ruler of a ~~free~~ people ~~who mean to be free. future ages will scarce believe that the hardiness of one man adventured within the short compass of twelve years only, to build a foundation, so broad and undisguised, for tyranny over a people fostered and fixed in principles of freedom~~.

Nor have we been wanting in attentions to our British brethren. we have warned them from time to time of attempts by their legislature to extend ~~a~~ *an unwarrantable* jurisdiction over ~~these our states.~~ *us.* we have reminded them of the circumstances of our emigration and settlement here, ~~no one of which could warrant so strange a pretension: that these were effected at the expence of our own blood and treasure, unassisted by the wealth or the strength of Great Britain: that in constituting indeed our several forms of government, we had adopted one common king, thereby laying a foundation for perpetual league and amity with them: but that submission to their parliament was no part of our constitution, or ever in idea, if history may be credited: and~~ we *have* appealed to their native justice & magnanimity, ~~as well as to~~ *and we have conjured them by* the tyes of our common kindred, to disavow these usurpations, which ~~were likely to~~ *would inevitably* interrupt our connection~~s~~ & correspondence. they too have been deaf to the voice of justice and of consanguinity; ~~and when occasions have been given them, by the regular course of their laws, of removing from their councils the disturbers of our harmony, they have by their free election re-established them in power. at this very time too, they are permitting their chief magistrate to send over not only soldiers of our common blood, but Scotch and foreign mercenaries to invade and destroy us. these facts have given the last stab to agonizing affection; and manly spirit bids us to renounce forever these unfeeling brethren.~~ we must *therefore* ~~endeavor to forget our former love for them, and to hold them, as we hold the rest of mankind, enemies in war, in peace friends. we might have been a free & a great people together; but a communication of grandeur and~~

~~of freedom, it seems, is below their dignity. be it so, since they will have it. the~~

~~road to happiness and to glory is open to us too; we will climb it apart from them~~
and hold them, as we hold the rest of mankind, enemies in war, in peace friends.
~~and~~ acquiesce in the necessity which denounces our ~~eternal~~ separation.ᴬ↓

We therefore the Representatives of the United states of America, in Gen-
appealing to the supreme judge of the world for the rectitude of our intentions,
eral Congress assembled,ᴬ do, in the name and by authority of the good people of
colonies, solemnly publish and declare, that these united colonies are and of right ought to be
these ~~states, reject~~ᴬ ~~and renounce all allegiance and subjection to the kings of~~
free and independent states; that they are absolved from all allegiance to the British Crown, and that
~~Great Britain, & all others who may hereafter claim by, through, or under them;~~

~~we utterly dissolve~~ all political connection ~~which may heretofore have subsisted~~
them *state* *is & ought to be totally dissolved;*
between ~~us~~ᴬ and theᴬ ~~parliament or people~~ of Great Britain;ᴬ ~~and finally we do as-~~

~~sert~~ [~~and declare~~]⁴ ~~these colonies to be free and independant states,~~ & that as free

& independant states, they have full power to levy war, conclude peace, contract

alliances, establish commerce, & to do all other acts and things which indepen-
with a firm reliance on the protection of divine providence,
dant states may of right do. And for the support of this declaration,ᴬ we mutually

pledge to each other our lives, our fortunes, and our sacred honor.

---

⁴Becker added the words "and declare" from Jefferson's "Rough Draft," assuming that Jefferson had mistakenly left it out of the Lee copy. Becker also reversed "parliament or people" in conformance with the Rough Draft. There I chose to remain consistent with the Lee copy. See Becker 170, n.1.

Notes

KEY TO ABBREVIATIONS

Boyd Julian P. Boyd, ed., *The Papers of Thomas Jefferson*, Volume I, *1760–1776*. Princeton, 1950.

Becker Carl Becker, *The Declaration of Independence: A Study in the History of Political Ideas*. New York, 1942 (original publication 1922).

Decent Respect James H. Hutson, ed., *A Decent Respect to the Opinions of Mankind: Congressional State Papers, 1774–1776*. Washington, D.C., 1975.

Force Peter Force, ed., *American Archives*, 4th Series, Volumes I–VI. Washington, D.C., 1833–1846.

Hazelton John Hazelton, *The Declaration of Independence: Its History*. New York, 1906.

JCC Worthington Chauncey Ford, ed., *Journals of the Continental Congress, 1774–1789*, Volumes I–V, Washington, D.C., 1904–1906.

LDC Paul H. Smith, ed., *Letters of Delegates to Congress, 1774–1789*, Volumes I–IV, Washington, D.C. (Library of Congress), 1976–79.

LMCC Edmund C. Burnett, *Letters of Members of the Continental Congress*, Volumes I and II, Washington, D.C., 1921–1923.

Thorpe Francis Newton Thorpe, *The Federal and State Constitutions, Colonial Charters, and Other Organic Laws of the States, Territories, and Colonies, Now or Heretofore Forming the United States of America*. Seven Volumes; Washington, D.C., 1909.

WMQ The *William and Mary Quarterly*.

INTRODUCTION

1.   Warren E. Leary, "Nation's Vital Documents Get Checkups," *New York Times*, February 14, 1995, pp. C1, C14; "Welcome to the National Archives Rotunda," General Information Leaflet No. 18, 1995, National Archives and Records Administration, Washington, D.C.

2.   Leary, "Nation's Vital Documents."

3.   Ibid.

4.   The account of the physical history of the Declaration of Independence here and in the following paragraphs is based on the *Annual Report of the Librarian of Congress for the Fiscal Year Ending June 30, 1949* (Washington, 1950), pp. 36–55 (quotation at 52), which was later reprinted as David C. Mearns, *The Declaration of Independence: The Story of a Parchment* (Washington, D.C. [Library of Congress], 1950), and Verner Clapp, "The Declaration of Independence: A Case Study in Preservation," *Special Libraries*, LXII (December 1971), 503–08, quotation at 503. I am indebted for these references to Elissa O'Loughlin, Senior Conservator, Document Conservation Branch, Preservation Policy and Services Division of the National Archives in Washington, D.C.

5.   *Annual Report of the Librarian of Congress for 1949*, esp. 41 (quotation from the report of a committee of the National Academy of Sciences, 1903), 46 (statement of the Librarian of Congress, Herbert Putnam, January 16, 1922), and 46–47.

6.   Clapp, "Declaration of Independence," 505.

7.   See esp. *Annual Report of the Librarian of Congress for 1949*, 48–51, which includes passages from the journal of the 1942 restoration team (which, incidentally, questioned whether the ink used in writing the main text was iron-based), and also the description of what the author calls a "reliquary" on pages 47–48: the Declaration and Constitution were removed from the "Shrine," put between sheets of acid-free manila paper, "then wrapped in a container stiffened at top and bottom with all-rag, neutral millboard and secured by scotch tape, and inserted in a specially designed bronze container, which had been scrupulously cleaned of other possible harmful elements, and heated for some six hours to a temperature of about 90° F. to drive off any moisture. Empty space was then filled with sheets of all-rag, neutral millboard, and the top of the container was screwed tight over a cork gasket and locked with padlocks on each side." Later, "under the constant surveillance of armed guards, the bronze container was removed to the Library's carpenter shop, where it was sealed with wire and a lead seal, . . . and packed in rock wool in a heavy metal-bound box measuring forty by thirty-six inches, which, when loaded, weighed approximately one hundred and fifty pounds."

8.   Dr. Norbert S. Baer in Leary, "Nation's Vital Documents," C14.

9.   *Annual Report of the Librarian of Congress for 1949*, 51.

10.   Elissa O'Loughlin to author, May 17, 1995. The discovery of the document as a physical artifact coincided with a more general "discovery" of the Bill of

Rights in 1939–41, which, along with its "rediscovery" in 1955–56, Michael Kammen described in *A Machine That Would Go of Itself: The Constitution in American Culture* (New York, 1987), 336–56.

11.   Morton White, *The Philosophy of the American Revolution* (New York, 1978), and Garry Wills, *Inventing America: Jefferson's Declaration of Independence* (Garden City, N.Y., 1978), both focus on Jefferson's draft. Fliegelman's book, *Declaring Independence: Jefferson, Natural Language, and the Culture of Performance* (Stanford, Cal., 1993), also focuses on Jefferson's draft and interprets it in the context of European rhetorical theory, and I. B. Cohen's *Science and the Founding Fathers: Science in the Political Thought of Jefferson, Franklin, Adams and Madison* (New York, 1995) fits the general tendency by seeing the Declaration as a Newtonian document. There is, however, another, less well established tendency to see the document as a legal text rather than an intellectual treatise with which I feel more kinship. See John Philip Reid, "The Irrelevance of the Declaration," in Hendrik Hartog, ed., *Law in the American Revolution and the Revolution in Law* (New York and London, 1981), 46–89, Peter Hoffer, *The Law's Conscience: Equitable Constitutionalism in America* (Chapel Hill, 1990), esp. 67–76, and, above all, the work of Stephen Lucas, of which I became aware only when this book was almost completed. Lucas approaches the Declaration of Independence as a student of rhetoric, but sees it as part of a long Anglo-American constitutional tradition. Our analyses coincide on point after point. See esp. his essay "Justifying America: The Declaration of Independence as a Rhetorical Document," in Thomas W. Benson, ed., *American Rhetoric: Context and Criticism* (Carbondale, Ill., 1989), 67–130, and also "The *Plakkaat Van Verlatinge:* A Neglected Model for the American Declaration of Independence," in Rosemarijn Hoefte and Johanna C. Kardux, *Connecting Cultures: The Netherlands in Five Centuries of Transatlantic Exchange* (Amsterdam, 1994), 187–207.

12.   Jefferson to Henry Lee, Monticello, May 8, 1825, in Paul Leicester Ford, ed., *The Writings of Thomas Jefferson*, X (New York and London, 1899), 343. On the ideas that shaped the revolutionary movement see Pauline Maier, *From Resistance to Revolution: Colonial Radicals and the Development of American Opposition to Britain, 1765–1776* (New York, 1972), ch. 2, pp. 27–48; Bernard Bailyn, *Ideological Origins of the American Revolution* (Cambridge, 1967), and, on Loyalists, Mary Beth Norton, "The Loyalist Critique of the Revolution," in *The Development of a Revolutionary Mentality: Papers Presented at the First [Library of Congress] Symposium, May 5 and 6, 1972* (Washington, D.C., 1972), 127–48.

13.   See particularly Merrill D. Peterson, *The Jefferson Image in the American Mind* (New York, 1960), which is as fresh and insightful today as when it was first published, and also, more recently, Joseph J. Ellis, "American Sphinx; The Contradictions of Thomas Jefferson," in *Civilization: The Magazine of the Library of Congress,* I (November/December 1994), 34–45, and Gordon S. Wood, "The Trials and Tribulations of Thomas Jefferson," in Peter S. Onuf, ed., *Jeffersonian Legacies* (Charlottesville, 1993), 395–417.

14.   Introduction of 1941 to Carl Becker, *The Declaration of Independence; A Study in the History of Political Ideas* (New York, 1953; orig. 1922), vi.

15.   M. E. Bradford, "The Heresy of Equality: A Reply to Harry Jaffa," in *A Better Guide than Reason: Studies in the American Revolution* (La Salle, Ill., 1979), 29–57, esp. 44, and see also Willmoore Kendall, *The Conservative Affirmation* (Chicago, 1963), 17–18, 252, and Kendall and George W. Carey, *The Basic Symbols of the American Political Tradition* (Baton Rouge, 1970), ch. 5, esp. 88ff. Bradford and Kendall wrote in part to contest the position of Harry Jaffa in *Crisis of the House Divided* (New York, 1959). Garry Wills, *Lincoln at Gettysburg: Words That Made American History* (New York, 1992), 38.

CHAPTER I:
INDEPENDENCE

1.   Records of the First Continental Congress (September 5–October 26, 1774) in JCC I, esp. 102, 53, 39, 57–62 (quotations), 55; *Decent Respect*, 79.

For an account of the beginning of the Anglo-American conflict, see Edmund S. and Helen M. Morgan, *The Stamp Act Crisis; Prologue to Revolution* (1953); and, on its development, Pauline Maier, *From Resistance to Revolution: Colonial Radicals and the Development of American Opposition to Britain, 1765–1776* (New York, 1972).

2.   Samuel Adams Wells, *The Life and Public Services of Samuel Adams* (2nd ed., Freeport, N.Y., 1969; orig. 1865–88), II, 296–97, including Hancock to the Committee of Safety, Worcester, April 24, 1775, of which I have used here and in the succeeding paragraph a somewhat fuller text from *Journals of the Provincial Congress of Massachusetts in 1774 and 1775, and of the Committee of Safety* . . . (Boston, 1838), 170n. The Committee of Safety was an executive body of the Provincial Congress established in October 1774 and charged with responsibility for the defense of the colony. It had power to mobilize, dispatch, and discharge the militia: see ibid., 32. It continued to sit when the Provincial Congress was out of session. The Provincial Congress, which Adams and Hancock had been attending at Concord, adjourned on April 15, then reassembled at Watertown on the 22nd (ibid., 146–47, and n. 3 at 147) .

3.   Wells, *Samuel Adams*, II, 297–301; Edmund C. Burnett, *The Continental Congress* (New York, 1941), 63–64; and Silas Deane to his wife, n.d. [New York, May 7?, and Philadelphia, May 12, 1775] in *Collections of the Connecticut Historical Society*, II (Hartford, 1870), 221–24, 226–28, and a newspaper account at 226n.

4.   Deane to his wife, May 12, 1775, in ibid., 226–28, and LDC I: 345–47; Samuel Curwen's Journal for 10 May quoted in Wells, *Samuel Adams*, II: 299–300; Caesar to Thomas Rodney, Philadelphia, May 11, 1775, LDC I: 343.

5.   John Adams to William Tudor, September 29, 1774, LDC I: 130–31; Samuel Adams to Joseph Warren, Philadelphia, September 25, 1774, in Harry Alonzo Cushing, ed., *Writings of Samuel Adams* (Boston, 1904–08), III: 158–59, and [September; misdated as May 21,] 1774, in *The Warren-Adams Letters*, I (Boston, 1917), 25–26; Richard Henry Lee to William Lee, Philadelphia, May 10, 1775, in LDC I: 337. Also Jack N. Rakove, *The Beginnings of National Politics: An Interpretive History of the Continental Congress* (New York, 1979), 45–49.

6. Massachusetts Provincial Congress to the Continental Congress, Watertown, May 3, 1775, JCC II: 24–25.

7. Massachusetts Provincial Congress to the Inhabitants of Great Britain, Watertown, April 26, 1775, in JCC II: 42–44; First Continental Congress's Address to the Inhabitants of Great Britain, September 5, 1774, in *Decent Respect*, esp. 31. The events mentioned in the Massachusetts letter were not entirely fictional, since atrocities were committed by both sides on April 19: see Don Higginbotham, *The War of American Independence: Military Attitudes, Policies, and Practice, 1763–1789* (New York, 1971), esp. 62–63. The Provincial Congress's account of the battle was sent to England on a ship that sailed from Salem in ballast four days after Governor Thomas Gage had sent his dispatches, but managed to arrive at Southampton first. As a result, the provincials' version of the event, which seemed to Lord Dartmouth "plainly made up for the purpose of conveying every possible prejudice & Misrepresentation of the Truth," began to circulate through England at the end of May before the ministry had any official knowledge of the battle, which left it bewildered and not a little annoyed. Dartmouth to Gage, June 1, 1775, Gage papers, English Series 29, Clements Library, Ann Arbor, Michigan.

8. JCC II: 14, 18–19, and see 13–21 for the instructions or "credentials" of other delegations presented on May 11, 1775.

9. Rakove, *Beginnings of National Politics*, 72–73, on the position of that quintessential Congressional moderate, John Dickinson; Resolution of October 8, 1774, in JCC I: 58.

10. JCC II: 55–56.

11. JCC II: 11–21, 49–52, 59–61. On Congress's assumption of military authority, see also Jerrilyn Greene Marston, *King and Congress: The Transfer of Political Legitimacy, 1774–1776* (Princeton, 1987), esp. 145–49.

12. JCC II: 78–79, 91, and passim; Higginbotham, *War of American Independence*, 65–77.

13. *Decent Respect*, 59–69, 83–87, and JCC I: 105–13, II: 66–70; Christopher Ward, *The War of the Revolution*, ed. John Richard Alden (New York, 1952), I: 138–39.

14. JCC II: 75, 104, 109–10, and Ward, *The War of the Revolution*, I: 139–40.

15. Allen's plea for an attack on Canada to the New York Provincial Council, June 2, 1775, cited in ibid., I: 139; Charles R. Ritcheson, *British Politics and the American Revolution* (Norman, Okla., 1954), 200.

16. John Adams to James Warren, May 21, 1775, LMCC I: 95; JCC II: 77, 83–84, and III: 319, 326–27, 403–04 (resolutions of November 3, 4, and December 4, 1775). See also Marston, *King and Congress*, 253–80.

17. JCC III: 269. The report of the committee on trade was not adopted at that time, but referred to the Committee of the Whole for further consideration. See also Marston, *King and Congress*, 171–72, 224–50.

18. JCC III: 374.

19. Merrill Jensen, *The Founding of a Nation: A History of the American Revolution, 1763–1776* (New York and London, 1968), 632 and n. 1. For a fuller

discussion of the Continental Congress's committee system, see Calvin Jillson and Rick K. Wilson, *Congressional Dynamics: Structure, Coordination, and Choice in the First American Congress, 1774–1789* (Stanford, 1994), esp. 91–131.

20. Ibid., esp. 99–106 on standing committees, which were not entirely successful in making Congress more efficient; Rakove, *Beginnings of National Politics*, esp. 193–98; Marston, *King and Congress*, 305–06, and JCC II: 259, III: 438, and passim.

21. Deane to his wife, June 3, 1775 (and see also 6 June, where he notes that he was up with a committee "almost the whole of last [night] on business"), LDC I: 437–38.

22. Rakove, *Beginnings of National Politics*, 79, 71, and also 202 (at times in the course of the war Congress consisted of "between two and three dozen members"), 218–24; on absenteeism, Jillson and Wilson, *Congressional Dynamics*, 157–58.

23. Ibid., 116–22; Samuel Adams to his wife, February 26, 1776, in LDC III: 304; Hewes to Samuel Johnson, Philadelphia, July 8, 1776, LDC IV: 410.

24. Deane to his wife, June 3, 1775, LMCC I: 111.

25. John Adams to James Warren, June [July] 6, and to Abigail Adams, June 17, 1775, LMCC I: 152, 132. In Connecticut, all officials, including the governor, were elected.

26. Rakove, *Beginnings of National Politics*, 71–73, and Deane's notes for May 16 and 23, 1775, in LDC I: 351–52 (quotation), 371, and see also John Dickinson's notes on speeches he made and resolutions he proposed, 371–91.

27. The Second Continental Congress's "Declaration . . . Seting [*sic*] forth the CAUSES and NECESSITY of their taking up ARMS," July 6, 1775, and the First Continental Congress, "To the People of Great-Britain," October 27, 1774, in *Decent Respect*, 91, 28.

28. Ibid., 34, 51.

29. Boyd I: 187, 170–74 (quotations at 171 and 174n), 225–33; *Decent Respect*, 118; Marston, *King and Congress*, 46–47, 207–09. On proposals for settling the conflict that were suggested in England early in 1775—including those of Edmund Burke, Lord Chatham, and North—see Ritcheson, *British Politics*, 178–91. Richeson notes that Lord North's proposal was probably the work of the Secretary for the American Colonies, Lord Dartmouth, who favored conciliation, but that neither North nor the King was optimistic that it would bring peace. They did, however, as the colonists suspected, hope it would destroy American unity.

30. Boyd I: 187–92 (quotations at 188, 192), 202, 203, 211, 212, 217–18.

31. *Decent Respect*, 103–04, 142, 145, 113–14, 115.

32. Jefferson to John Randolph in Boyd I: 242; "Hampden," Williamsburg, May 1, 1776, in Force V: 1158.

33. American "Bill of Rights," 1774, in *Decent Respect*, 54. Jefferson's position was stated at length in his *Summary View*, 1774, in Boyd, I: 121–37, and see also Wilson, *Considerations on the Nature and Extent of the Legislative Authority of the British Parliament* (Philadelphia, 1774). Behind the controversy lay a difference in the nature of representation in England and its colonies. Representation

in the House of Commons had no relationship to population since the right to elect members of Parliament rested on ancient claims of an extraordinarily diverse sort. In the 1770s, defenders of Parliament described its system as one of "virtual representation," by which delegates, however chosen, thought of the good of Englishmen everywhere, not only of their immediate constituents. In the newer governments of the American colonies, however, representation did have at least a rough connection with population levels, and the colonists had come to think of representation in a different way, with representatives speaking first and foremost for their constituents. That system of "real" or "attorneyship representation" precluded colonial acceptance of English claims that they were represented in Parliament, whose members considered their good as well as that of people within England or Scotland. If we don't elect members of Parliament, the colonists said, they are not our representatives. Indeed, the contrary interests of British and American people on issues such as Parliamentary taxation of colonists, and the proven ignorance of Members of Parliament on American circumstances and even American geography, made assertions of "virtual representation" untenable.

34.   *Decent Respect*, 93, and n. 7 at 97–98; W. Brodham Donne, ed., *The Correspondence of King George the Third with Lord North from 1768 to 1783*, I (London, 1867), 215. See also Marston, *King and Congress*, chapter 1, esp. 39–49, which notes that the order in which news of the First Continental Congress's acts arrived in England served to undermine its conciliatory efforts. The radical Suffolk Resolves, which, she argues, Congress endorsed quickly as a means of expressing support for Massachusetts and not as a more general policy statement (84–86), arrived before its more carefully considered declaration of rights and petition to the King. The effect, however, was not to change British policy, but to broaden support for the King's policy of using force to bring colonial submission, which he had decided upon long before learning about the Suffolk Resolves.

35.   *Decent Respect*, 31, 97 n. 6 (quoting the King's speech); Maier, *From Resistance to Revolution*, 236–37; Jensen, *Founding of a Nation*, 578–82, and, for the New England Restraining Act, also William MacDonald, ed., *Select Charters and Other Documents Illustrative of American History, 1606–1775* (New York, 1904), 368–74.

36.   Richard Penn and Arthur Lee to the President of Congress, London, September 2, 1775, in Force III: 627 (and also 1792, 1851–82). That letter, and its news of the petition's fate, was read in Congress on November 9, and Congress ordered that "the substance of said letter" be published. The version in the *Pennsylvania Packet* printed the statement that no answer would be given in capital letters. See JCC III: 343, and n. 1. See also *Decent Respect*, 97 n. 5, 126–27, and, on the maneuverings behind the petition, Rakove, *Beginnings of National Politics*, 71–72, 78; Maier, *From Resistance to Revolution*, 213–14 n. 39, 238–39, and Marston, *King and Congress*, 58–59, 210–14.

37.   MacDonald, ed., *Select Charters*, 389–91, and Force III: 240–41. The King's Proclamation of Rebellion was a de facto rather than an intentional answer to the American petition since it had been drawn up before Dartmouth re-

ceived a copy of the petition from Penn and Lee: see Marston, *King and Congress*, 58. The text of the proclamation suggests it was prompted by American military actions, including no doubt Lexington and Concord, Ticonderoga, and Bunker Hill, and by Congress's further military preparations: the Americans proceeded to open rebellion, it said, "by arraying themselves in a hostile manner, to withstand the execution of the law, and traitorously preparing, ordering and levying war against us." For Congress's answer to the proclamation, rejecting the charge of rebellion but promising retaliation for any punishments imposed on America's friends in England, see JCC III: 409–12 (for December 6, 1775).

38.   Force VI: 1–2.

39.   Ibid., esp. 12–13.

40.   Ibid., 186–237; MacDonald, ed., *Select Charters*, 391–96; Jensen, *Founding of a Nation*, 649–50; Marston, *King and Congress*, 60–62.

41.   JCC III: 372; Marston, *King and Congress*, 55–57.

42.   Boyd I: 217, 219 n. 6. For critical assessments of this charge, see Marston, *King and Congress*, 55 ("the British did not use their Indian allies for offensive action until the colonists had begun to do so"), and Jack M. Sosin, "The Use of Indians in the War of the American Revolution: A Re-Assessment of Responsibility," *Canadian Historical Review*, XLVI (1965), 101–21. Which side actually first used Indians against the other, and whether for offensive or defensive purposes, is not entirely clear, nor were all initiatives to enlist Indians done under the direction of the King's government or of Congress. Canada's Governor Guy Carleton, the target of many colonial suspicions, seems to have been particularly resistant to turning Indians against colonists. On the other hand, the British commander Sir Thomas Gage began making inquiries about the availability of Canadian and Indian allies "should matters come to extremities" in 1774, and later ordered Carleton to raise Indian troops on the pretext that the colonists had already done so (107, 110). Rumors were, it seems, as upsetting to colonists as hard facts, and British actions gave reason enough for rumors to circulate.

43.   Jensen, *Founding of a Nation*, 645; Jefferson to John Randolph, November 29, 1775, in Boyd, I: 269.

44.   Smith diary, January 8, LMCC I: 302–03; on the burning of Norfolk, see Jensen, *Founding of a Nation*, 645, and John E. Selby, *The Revolution in Virginia, 1775–1783* (Williamsburg, 1988), 80–84. On January 1 the British opened fire on Norfolk, but the subsequent destruction of the town was mainly the work of colonists. That, however, would not be publicly known for sixty years, and it took another century for historians to note the fact.

45.   Smith diary, January 9 and February 13; Samuel to John Adams, January 15, 1776, in LMCC I: 302–03, 348, n. 4 at 348, 311. The position of moderates like Wilson and Dickinson was weakened, it seems, not only by the news of the King's speech and the burning of Norfolk, but by the almost simultaneous publication of *Common Sense*. The mood of Congress was also affected by the American defeat at Quebec in late December, of which it learned on January 17. See LDC III: n. 1 at 63–64.

46.   Diary of Richard Smith, January 9, 1776, LMCC I: 304.

47.   Hancock to Thomas Cushing, February 13; Adams to Horatio Gates,

March 23, 1776, and Morris to Robert Herries, February 15, LDC III: 244, 431, 258. See also Jensen, *Founding of a Nation*, 655–56.

48.   Hewes to Samuel Johnson, March 20, 1776, LDC III: 416–17.

49.   Ibid.

50.   On colonial fears of being partitioned like Poland, which came into debates as early as 1774, see James Hutson, "Formulating an American Foreign Policy," in Hutson, *John Adams and the Diplomacy of the American Revolution* (Lexington, Ky., 1980), esp. 13–14, 17–20, 22–24, and 27 for the Dickinson quotation. Hutson also emphasizes how belief in the balance of power and international interest politics shaped early American foreign policy.

51.   Dickinson, *Letters from a Farmer in Pennsylvania . . .* (New York, 1903), 33 (from letter III); "Hampden," Williamsburg, May 1, 1776, in Force V: 1158.

52.   Ibid., and Maryland instructions in Force VI: 463–64.

53.   Jensen, *Founding of a Nation*, 641–43, which quotes state instructions.

54.   "Hampden" in Force V: 1158; Maier, *From Resistance to Revolution*, passim, on the process of disillusionment with Britain and on attitudes toward the British constitution, Bernard Bailyn, *Ideological Origins of the American Revolution* (rev. ed., Cambridge and London, 1992), esp. 67–77, 129–30.

55.   On Paine, see the introduction to Philip S. Foner, ed., *The Complete Writings of Thomas Paine* (New York, 1969), I: ix–xlvi; David Freeman Hawke, *Paine* (New York, 1974); Eric Foner, *Tom Paine and Revolutionary America* (New York and London, 1976), and John Keane, *Tom Paine; A Political Life* (Boston, 1995).

56.   Adams's Autobiography, in L. H. Butterfield, ed., *Diary and Autobiography of John Adams* (New York, 1964 [orig. Boston, 1961]), III: 333.

57.   "Common Sense" in Foner, ed., *Paine Writings*, I: 6–16.

58.   Ibid., 6, 27–29, 45, 3.

59.   Ibid., 18, 30–31, 40, 20–25.

60.   Adams's Autobiography, in Butterfield, ed., *Diary and Autobiography*, III: 333; Maier, *From Resistance to Revolution*, 287–95.

61.   Bartlett to John Langdon, Philadelphia, January 13, 1776, LDC III: 88; Paine, autobiographical sketch enclosed in a letter to Henry Laurens, January 14, 1779, in Foner, ed., *Paine Writings*, II: 1163; *The Life of Ashbel Green* (New York, 1849), 47.

62.   Bartlett to Langdon, January 1, 1776; Samuel Ward to Henry Ward, February 19, 1776, and John Adams to James Warren, April 20, 1776, in LDC III: 88, 285, 558, and see also Henry Wisner to John McKesson, [January 13?] 1776, a brief letter scribbled on the first page of *Common Sense*, which Wisner was sending to New York, at 90–91.

63.   Adams to James Warren, May 12, 1776, LDC III: 661, and see also Butterfield, ed., *Diary and Autobiography*, III: 331–32.

64.   [Braxton,] "Address to the convention of the Colony and Ancient Dominion of VIRGINIA, on the subject of Government . . . ," in Force VI: 748–54, esp. 751–52.

65.   Ibid.; Braxton to Landon Carter, Philadelphia, April 14, 1776, LDC

III: 522. See also "A.B." to Mr. Alexander Purdie (publisher of the *Virginia Gazette*), Williamsburg, April 12, 1776, in Force V: 860–61, which observed that for many the word "Independence" still brought "the terrifying ideas of an everlasting separation from Great Britain, of the destruction of the finest Constitution in the world, . . . and of the substitution of Republican Governments in the Colonies," which would lead to "a dreadful train of domestick convulsions . . . of jealousies, dissensions, wars, and all their attendant miseries."

66. Adams to Horatio Gates, Philadelphia, March 23, 1776, LMCC I: 406.

67. Jensen, *Founding of a Nation,* 662–65; Carter to General Washington, Sabine-Hall, May 9, 1776, in Force VI: 390, and Braxton to Carter, Philadelphia, April 14, 1776, LMCC I: 421.

68. Adams to Archibald Bullock and to Samuel Chase, July 1, 1776, in Force VI: 1193–95; and see also his letter to Abigail Adams, July 3, at 1232.

69. Maryland Convention, May 15, 1776, in Force VI: 462.

70. JCC IV: 342, 357–58.

71. On the vote, see Carter Braxton to Langdon Carter, Philadelphia, May 17, 1776, LDC IV: 19, and also n. 3 at 20–21. Braxton said, somewhat tentatively, that he thought the vote was six to four, but a diary entry by James Allen, a Philadelphia lawyer, said it was seven to four. There were twelve colonies represented, since the Georgia delegation arrived only on May 20.

72. John Adams's Notes of Debates, [May 13–15, 1776,] LDC III: 668–70 and n. 1 at 670; Rakove, *Beginnings of National Politics,* 97; John to Abigail Adams, May 17, 1776, in Force VI: 488 and LDC IV: 17, and see also Butterfield, ed., *Diary and Autobiography,* III: 386: "Mr. Duane called it, to me, a Machine for the fabrication of Independence. I said, smiling, I thought it was independence itself: but We must have it with more formality yet." (Entry in Autobiography for May 15, 1776.) Probably because the resolutions were not a formal declaration of Independence, some delegates could still cling to their hopes of reconciliation. Braxton insisted the preface was not understood within Congress as a resolution for Independence, "but I find those out of doors on both sides the question construe it in that manner." To Landon Carter, May 17, 1776, LDC IV: 19. John Dickinson, who was not present when the resolution and preface were adopted, apparently thought, somewhat strangely, that Congress's call for establishment of regular American governments would actually "promote a more speedy reconciliation" by goading the British to offer terms before those governments were in place. Thomas to Caesar Rodney, May 19, in LDC IV: 62–63n.

73. Lee to Samuel Purviance, May 6, 1776, LDC III: 632 and see also 33, 564, 625–26, 669; Hancock to the Massachusetts Assembly, May 16, in LDC IV: 7; Josiah Bartlett to John Langdon, May 21, 1776, LMCC I: 458 and n.5 and LDC IV: 55 and n. 2; Caesar Rodney to Thomas Rodney, May 22, 1776, LDC IV: 62. See also JCC IV: 369–70 (May 21).

74. For accounts of the Canadian campaign, see Higginbotham, *War of American Independence,* 106–15, and also Ward, *War of the Revolution,* which tells the tale for the spring of 1776 in useful detail, 135–201, esp. 195 for casualty figures from the battle at Quebec.

75.   Hancock to John Thomas, Philadelphia, May 24, 1776, and also to Philip Schuyler, May 24, LDC IV: 68, 67, and Ward, *War of the Revolution*, esp. 200–01 for quotations.

76.   London petition and the King's reply in Force V: 462–63; Morris to Silas Deane, June 5, 1776, in LDC IV: 146–47, and also Rakove, *Beginnings of National Politics*, 97–99.

77.   JCC V: 424–26; Jefferson's "Notes of Proceedings" in Boyd, I: 309.

78.   Ibid., 309–11, and Hutson, *John Adams and the Diplomacy of the American Revolution*, esp. 26–28.

79.   Boyd I: 311–13. John Adams was as suspicious of France as the moderates in Congress. He reflected carefully on what connection with France the Americans could safely enter, and decided it could be neither political—the Americans would "submit to none of her Authority" by receiving governors or other civil officers—nor military: in the spring of 1776 he did not anticipate the use of French troops on American soil. Adams sought a commercial alliance that would open French ports to American ships and allow France to supply the Americans with arms and other materials necessary to carry out the war. Moreover, under the Model Treaty that Adams helped draft, and which was submitted to Congress on July 18, 1776, France was explicitly precluded from taking possession of territories in North America. Marston, *King and Congress*, 222–23; JCC V: 579. Hutson notes that not even the commercial provisions were designed to weaken Britain significantly. The Model Treaty, he says, sought to maintain a balance of power, leaving "Britain and France strong enough to prevent each other from destroying American independence, which each would do, Americans believed, if they could." In *John Adams and the Diplomacy of the American Revolution*, 31.

80.   Ibid., 313–14; JCC V: 428–29, 431, 491; Jensen, *Founding of a Nation*, 688–96.

81.   Washington to Colonel James Clinton, June 29, and to General Ward, New York, July 1, 1776, Force VI: 1135, 1196; Hancock to certain colonies, June 11, 1776, and Josiah Bartlett to John Langdon, Philadelphia, July 1, 1776, in LDC IV: 189–90, 350–51.

82.   In Force VI: 1131.

83.   JCC V: 504; Adams to Samuel Chase, July 1, and the notes for Dickinson's speech in LDC IV: 347, 351–58; Boyd I: 314.

84.   JCC V: 506–07, 434; Boyd I: 314, and see the New York resolution of June 9 in *Journals of the Provincial Congress, Provincial Convention, Committee of Safety and Council of Safety of the State of New York, 1775–1777*, Vol. I (Albany, 1842), 518: "*Resolved Unanimously,* That the reasons assigned by the Continental Congress for declaring the United Colonies free and independent States are cogent and conclusive; and that while we lament the cruel necessity which has rendered that measure unavoidable, we approve the same, and will, at the risk of our lives and fortunes, join with the other Colonies in supporting it." The state's Congressional delegates were also authorized "to consent and adopt all such measures as they may deem conducive to the happiness and welfare of the United States of America."

85.   JCC V: 507–09; and, on the military crisis, Gen. Livingston to Gen. Mercer, Elizabethtown, N.J., July 3, 1776, and Washington to Hancock, New York, July 4, 1776, in Force VI: 1233–34, and Committee of Congress to the Lancaster Associates, Philadelphia, July 4, 1776, LDC IV: 379–81, and notes, 381–82. Both Congress and its committees acted with a sense of great urgency since without Pennsylvania's "timely" help, as the letter to Lancaster put it, New Jersey would be "defenceless." The people in New Jersey, Livingston observed, were "greatly dispirited" by their situation. See also Washington to Hancock, July 3, 1776, in W. W. Abbot and Dorothy Twohig, eds., *The Papers of George Washington, Revolutionary War Series*, V (Charlottesville, 1993), 191–93.

CHAPTER II:
THE "OTHER" DECLARATIONS OF INDEPENDENCE

1.   Jefferson to Thomas Nelson, Philadelphia, May 16, 1776, in Boyd I: 292.

2.   Boyd I: 345n and also, more generally, 329–37.

3.   Jefferson to Judge Augustus B. Woodward, Monticello, April 3, 1825, in Paul Leicester Ford, ed., *The Writings of Thomas Jefferson*, X, *1816–1826* (New York and London, 1899), 341–42; Boyd I: 331, 384n–86n.

4.   In Ibid. I: 356–57, 377–79.

5.   For a list of these documents that indicates where they can be found, see "State and Local Declarations of Independence April–July 1776: A Log," Appendix A. Adams's statement appeared in a letter to James Warren, May 20, 1776, LDC IV: 41.

6.   Lois G. Schwoerer, *The Declaration of Rights, 1689* (Baltimore and London, 1981), 14–15 and 315 n. 10; Elizabeth Read Foster, "Petitions and the Petition of Right," *Journal of British Studies*, XIV (1974), 21–45.

7.   Schwoerer, *Declaration of Rights*, 16–17. I am also grateful to Morton Horwitz and Hiller Zobel for help in defining legal "declarations."

8.   *Decent Respect*, 91.

9.   William Huse Dunham, Jr., and Charles T. Wood, "The Right to Rule in England: Depositions and the Kingdom's Authority, 1327–1485," *American Historical Review*, LXXXI (1981), 738–61 (quotation at 757).

10.   Samuel Rawson Gardiner, ed., *Constitutional Documents of the Puritan Revolution, 1625–1660* (Oxford, England, 1958 [reprint; orig. 1889; 3d ed., 1906]), esp. 357–58, 371–80, 384–88, quotations at 357, 375, 388. The "Act Abolishing the House of Lords" simply said that "too long experience" had show that "the House of Lords is useless and dangerous to the people of England" (March 19, 1649; p. 387), but the case against monarchy was more extensive. It "is and hath been found by experience," the Commons asserted, "that the office of a King in this nation and Ireland, and to have the power thereof in any single person, is unnecessary, burdensome, and dangerous to the liberty, safety, and public interest of the people, and that for the most part, use hath been made of the regal power and prerogative to oppress and impoverish and enslave the subject; and that usually and naturally any one person in such power makes it his interest to incroach

upon the just freedom and liberty of the people, and to promote the setting up of their own will and power above the laws, that so they might enslave these kingdoms to their own lust." (The Act abolishing the Office of King, March 17, 1649, p. 385.)

11.   Schwoerer, *Declaration of Rights*, passim.

12.   The text summarized here and in later paragraphs is the "presentation copy" discovered in the House of Lords Record Office by Schwoerer and reprinted as Appendix I in ibid., 295–98.

13.   Ibid., esp. 24–29. Most Whigs, it should be noted, assumed that James II's son was not in fact his child, but an infant who had been smuggled into the Queen's birthing room, and so had no legitimate claim to the throne.

14.   In Edmund S. Morgan, ed., *Stamp Act Congress Declarations and Petitions October 1765*, published by the Old South Association as Old South Leaflet No. 223 (Boston, 1948); "A State of the Rights of the Colonists and of this Province in particular," 1772, in Merrill Jensen, ed., *Tracts of the American Revolution* (Indianapolis, 1977), 233–55.

15.   In *Decent Respect*, 49–57. See also Jerrilyn Greene Marston, *King and Congress: The Transfer of Political Legitimacy, 1774–1776* (Princeton, 1987), esp. p. 81, which argues that the First Continental Congress understood itself as modeled after English extralegal conventions that met in earlier constitutional crises, and "referred to their body as 'the Convention' before formally voting to call themselves 'the Congress.'"

16.   Boyd I includes the various drafts of this preamble; my quotations are from the third draft, which Jefferson sent to the Virginia Convention. See esp. 356–57.

17.   Boyd I: 357, 379. Note that, as in the passages quoted here, Jefferson frequently used "it's" for "its." That error is, in fact, one way of identifying passages or documents he composed.

18.   Compare the document in Schwoerer, *Declaration of Rights*, 295–98, esp. provision 10 at 297, with the Virginia Declaration of Rights in Thorpe VII: 3812–14, esp. provision 9 at 3813.

19.   From Jefferson's "Notes of Proceedings" in Boyd I: 309.

20.   Ibid., 312.

21.   *Journals of the House of Representatives*, Vol. LI, Part III, *1776* (Boston, 1984), 254.

22.   See, for example, the item in the warrant for a meeting of the town of Needham, Massachusetts: "To See if it be the mind of the Inhabitants of the town to Instruct, and advise their Present Representative, that if the Honorable Congress for the Safety of the United Colonies Declare them Independent of the Kingdom of Great Britain, that they the Said Inhabitants will Solemnly Engage with their Lives and fortunes to Support them in ye Measure." In George Kuhn Clarke, *History of Needham Massachusetts 1711–1911* (privately printed at Cambridge, 1912), p. 465, which goes on to say that "Presumably this vote passed, but the record does not indicate it," which, Clarke suggests, might reflect the "prudence" of the town clerk.

23.   Vote of the Council and House of Representatives, January 18, 1776, in

Journals of the House of Representatives., Vol. LI, part II, *1775–1776* (Boston, 1983), 165.

24. Gerry to Warren, Philadelphia, March 26, 1776, LMCC I: 410 and also LDC III: 441–42.

25. Warren to Adams, April 3, and Adams to Warren, April 22, 1776, in Robert J. Taylor, ed., *Papers of John Adams*, IV (Boston, 1979), 96–97, 136.

26. *Journals of the House of Representatives*, LI, Part III, pp. 244, 252; on Cushing's resentment and the enmity between members of the previous Massachusetts delegation, see Stephen E. Patterson, *Political Parties in Revolutionary Massachusetts* (Madison, Wisc., 1973), 132–35, and also LDC III: 6–8 and n. 1, 104–06 and n. 1.

27. *Journals of the House of Representatives*, Vol. LI, Part III, p. 254, and Vol. LII, Part I (Boston, 1985), 19, 21, 47, 58–59; Joseph Hawley to Elbridge Gerry, Watertown, June 13, 1776, in Force VI: 844–45. The provision in the House vote of June 6 that towns debate Independence "whether they are represented or not" served to expand the number of persons whose opinion was solicited. The town of Fitchburg, for example, had the town clerk forward its resolution of July 1 that the inhabitants of that town would support Independence with their "lifes and fortains" because they had decided on May 23 not to send a representative to the assembly that year. See Walter A. Davis, ed., *Old Records of the Town of Fitchburg*, I (Fitchburg, 1898), 127, 125.

28. Francis Tiffany Bowles, *The Loyalty of Barnstable in the Revolution* (Cambridge, Mass., 1924); Topsfield and Acton, Mass., in Force VI: 703–04, 702. Patterson, *Political Parties in Revolutionary Massachusetts*, pp. 139–52, argues that the delay of towns in debating Independence, particularly in the eastern part of the state, turned on concern over the distribution of power after Independence. Towns in Essex County had proposed changing the allocation of seats in the legislature so it would reflect more closely population levels. The effect of its proposal would be to transfer power from western communities toward the more densely populated East, and towns in Essex County, Patterson said, "seemed reluctant to vote for Independence until they were sure that the maritime towns would control the new state government" (146). Suggestions that towns failed to respond to the General Court's request because they never saw the newspaper notices are, he argues, "fallacious" because after passing the resolution members of the General Court went home between sessions and so could have "informed their constituents what was expected of them" (147). His account suggests, however, that the legislature approved the change in representation on May 6, before it called on the towns to debate Independence (see pp. 143–44), which makes it difficult to see how the representation issue could have inhibited action on Independence, at least in the East. Moreover, if, as Patterson says, members had probably "already begun to depart" at the end of the session, they could hardly have carried home news that the legislature had called on towns to debate Independence. In short, the towns' responses (or lack thereof) are not so easily explained.

29. Cooke to Congressman Stephen Hopkins, May 7, 1776, and instruc-

tions of May 4 in Hazelton, 55–56, and also John Russell Bartlett, ed., *Records of the Colony of Rhode Island and Providence Plantations*, VII (New York, 1968 [reprint of Providence, 1862]), 522–27, for the act on allegiance and commissions, the instructions, and also Hopkins to Cooke, Philadelphia, May 15, 1776, in which Hopkins says the instructions and act of assembly "leave me little room to doubt what is the opinion of the colony I came from." The new instructions "authorized and empowered" delegates Stephen Hopkins and William Ellery "to consult and advise" with the delegates of other colonies in Congress "upon the most proper measures for promoting and confirming the strictest union and confederation between the said United Colonies, for exerting their whole strength and force to annoy the common enemy, and to secure to the said colonies their rights and liberties, both civil and religious; whether by entering into treaties with any prince, state, or potentate; or by such other prudent and effectual ways and means as shall be devised and agreed upon."

30. James City County and Virginia instructions in Force V: 1046–47; Cumberland County instructions in *Virginia Magazine of History and Biography*, XXXIV (1926), 184–86; Carter to George Washington, cited in Hazelton, 75–76.

31. Force VI: 1524; JCC V: 425.

32. Force VI: 867–68, and 902 for Connecticut's Gov. Trumbull's reply to the Virginia Convention, Hartford, June 14, 1776.

33. Meshech Wear to the New Hampshire delegates, Exeter, June 18, 1776, and New Hampshire instructions of June 15, 1776, in Force VI: 1029–30. Note that the instructions referred specifically to the creation of one State, not several independent states. Delaware instructions in George Herbert Ryden, ed., *Letters to and from Caesar Rodney, 1756–1784* (Philadelphia, 1933), 92. Delaware was probably less influenced by Virginia than by Congress's resolutions of May 10 and 15, which Thomas McKean had set before it on June 14th. Virginia's influence on New Hampshire might have been somewhat indirect: its Congressional delegates asked for new instructions after the Virginians laid their new instructions before Congress on May 27. See Merrill Jensen, *The Founding of a Nation* (New York and London, 1968), 692.

34. Records of the New Jersey Provincial Congress and its instructions of June 22, 1776, in Force VI: 1618, 1623–29, and Larry R. Gerlach, ed., *New Jersey in the American Revolution, 1763–1783: A Documentary History* (Trenton, 1975), 211; Jensen, *Founding of a Nation*, 692–93.

35. Instructions in Hazelton, 17, and Jensen, *Founding of a Nation*, 641; Gerry to Warren, May 20, 1776, in LDC IV: 42–43.

36. For an account of Pennsylvania events, see Richard Alan Ryerson, *The Revolution Is Now Begun; The Radical Committees of Philadelphia, 1765–1776* (Philadelphia, 1978), esp. pp. 207–40; and Jensen, *Founding of a Nation*, 681–87.

37. John Adams to James Warren, May 20, 1776, in LDC IV: 41; Force VI: 755, 951–67, esp. "Declaration" at 962–63.

38. Adams to James Warren, LDC IV: 41; Force VI: 462–64.

39. Maryland Delegates to the Maryland Council of Safety, Philadelphia, June 11, 1776, LDC IV: 192–93; Chase to Adams, June 21 and 28, 1776, in Taylor,

ed., *Papers of John Adams*, IV: 322–23, 351. Before changing its instructions, the Maryland convention had also learned—via a letter from John Adams to Chase—that Delaware and New Jersey had authorized their Congressional delegates to vote for Independence, and received a copy of the "Declaration of the Deputies of Pennsylvania, Met in Provincial Conference." That meant only Maryland and possibly New York remained on the other side. See Herbert E. Klingelhofer, "The Cautious Revolution: Maryland and the Movement Toward Independence, 1774–1776," *Maryland Historical Magazine*, LX (1965), 261–313, esp. 294–304.

40.   Address of the New York Mechanics in Union and votes of King's District and Spencer-Town in Force VI: 614–15, 1056; *Journals of the [New York] Provincial Congress*, I (Albany, 1842), 474 (for the Congress's answer to the Mechanics, June 4), 516, 518; Hazelton, 181–87. The Spencer-Town vote resembled those of many Massachusetts towns: "The town of *Spencer-Town* . . . in a full meeting, unanimously agreed, that as soon as the honourable Continental Congress should see fit to declare the *American* Colonies independent of *Great Britain*, they would support and defend the same with their lives and fortunes."

41.   On Adams and Young, see Pauline Maier, *The Old Revolutionaries: Political Lives in the Age of Samuel Adams* (New York, 1982), esp. chs. 1 and 3; David Hawke, *In the Midst of a Revolution* (Philadelphia, 1961), esp. 112–13; Ryerson, *The Revolution Is Now Begun*, 211–12.

42.   In Force V: 1025–32.

43.   Drayton attributed the English Revolution to 1688, as participants would have done, since under the "old style" calendar of the seventeenth century the new year began on March 25, not January 1. In fact, he probably took the date, and perhaps also at least part of the text he used in quoting the Declaration of Rights, from Sir William Blackstone's *Commentaries on the Laws of England*, of which I have used the fourth edition (Oxford, England, 1770), where the quotation from the Declaration of Rights is at I: 212. Why Blackstone cited the text as of February 7, 1688/89, rather than the final text as adopted on February 12, is more difficult to explain. Clearly he sensed nothing odd about the earlier version, which conformed nicely with his "Lockean" understanding of the Glorious Revolution.

44.   Blackstone, *Commentaries*, Vol. I, Book I, Chapter III, "Of the King," and Chapter VII, "Of the King's Prerogative," esp. pp. 212, 244–45 in the 1770 Oxford edition. The Blackstone passage cited by Drayton is also, in context, more ambiguous: "The facts themselves thus appealed to, the king's endeavour to subvert the constitution by breaking the original contract, his violation of the fundamental laws, and his withdrawing himself out of the kingdom, were evident and notorious; and the consequences drawn from these facts (namely, that they amounted to an abdication of the government; which abdication did not affect only the person of the king himself, but also all his heirs, and rendered the throne absolutely and completely vacant) it belonged to our ancestors to determine" because decisions concerning society at large and any magistrate with powers delegated by that society "must be decided by the voice of the society itself," and "our

ancestors" accordingly came to their decision "in a full parliamentary convention representing the whole society" (212). Gerald Stourzh discussed the section of Blackstone's *Commentaries* in which these passages appear, and demonstrates its impact on a South Carolina newspaper essay of 1769, written only four years after the relevant Blackstone volume was published, as well as on other American political writings in "William Blackstone: Teacher of Revolution," *Jahrbüch für Amerikastudien*, XV (Heidelberg, 1970), 184–200.

45.   Force V: 1047; 1034–35; VI: 1019; Klingelhofer, "The Cautious Revolution," 298. On Buckingham County, see Brent Tarter and Robert L. Scribner, *Revolutionary Virginia: The Road to Independence . . . A Documentary Record* (7 volumes, Charlottesville, 1973–83), VII: n. 1 at 112, and also 458 and n. 5 at 462 on the signatures to the James City County instructions. The printed notation that those instructions were signed "by a majority of the freeholders living in the county, whose names may be seen," was apparently inserted by the printer of the *Virginia Gazette*, who chose not to print all the names but was willing to show readers the original, signed copy, which was kept at the printer's office.

46.   Force V: 1206–09; VI: 699–700, 706.

47.   In this regard, the instructions are like the patriotic sermons of the mid-1770s examined by Patricia U. Bonomi, who found their content virtually identical regardless of the preacher's denomination or the region from which he came. See Bonomi, *Under the Cope of Heaven: Religion, Society, and Politics in Colonial America* (New York, 1986), 212.

48.   Force VI: 704, 702, 700, 1018, and see also 603 (Malden), 557 (Boston), and Plymouth, May 20, 1776, in *Records of the Town of Plymouth*, III, *1743 to 1783* (Plymouth, 1903), 325.

49.   Force V: 860; VI: 868, 1507; and Ryden, ed., *Rodney Letters*, 92.

50.   Force VI: 705, 933, 785, 786, 1018.

51.   Force VI: 867, 704.

52.   Force VI: 786, 704, 701, 1506; and also, for Congress's Declaration on Taking Up Arms, *Decent Respect*, 93.

53.   Force VI: 755, 701, 1018, 461, 557, 614, and see also Wrentham, Mass., 700; V: 461, for the Virginia instructions, and 1034 for those of Charlotte County, Virginia.

54.   Force V: 859; VI: 603.

55.   Force V: 1207, 860; VI: 963, and see also Charlotte County's charge that the British had encouraged, "by every means in their power, our savage neighbours, and our more savage domesticks, to spill the blood of our wives and children," in V: 1034. On British use of Indians, and the danger they posed particularly to American prisoners taken at the Cedars near Montreal, see Force VI: 595–99.

56.   Force VI: 1524, 755, and, for the other instructions mentioned, 963; V: 859; VI: 867, 1506, and also V: 1034 (Charlotte County, Va.); VI: 1018 (Charles County, Md.), 1020 (Talbot County, Md.), 785 (First Battalion, Chester County, Pa.).

57.   Force VI: 755, 557, 1506, and see also Wrentham, Mass., 700.

58. Force VI: 1018; V: 1208.

59. Force V: 1034; VI: 732–33, and, for an excellent account of the incident and the repercussions of the letters in Maryland, Ronald Hoffman, *A Spirit of Dissension: Economics, Politics, and the Revolution in Maryland* (Baltimore and London, 1973), 157–63.

60. London address and reply in Force V: 462–63; VI: 1506 (Maryland), 963 (Pennsylvania Conference), 755 (Pennsylvania Assembly), and see also Talbot County, 1020.

61. Force V: 1207; VI: 557, 603, and see also Wrentham, 700: "A reconciliation has become as dangerous as it is absurd. A recollection of past injuries will kindle and keep alive the flames of jealousy. We, your constituents, therefore, think that to be subject to or dependant on the Crown of *Great Britain* would not only be impracticable, but unsafe and dangerous to the State."

62. Force V: 859; VI: 461, 1030. Regarding the colonists' earlier modus operandi, see Pauline Maier, *From Resistance to Revolution: Colonial Radicals and the Development of American Resistance to Britain, 1765–1776* (New York, 1972).

63. Force VI: 867–68.

64. Ibid., VI: 962–63, 1506–07, and see also Boyd I: 377, and Gerlach, ed., *New Jersey in the American Revolution*, 213. Recall that the English Declaration of Rights said, "Whereas the late King James the second, by the Assistance of divers Evil Counsellors, Judges, and Ministers, imployed by him did endeavour to Subvert and extirpate the Protestant Religion, and the Lawes and Liberties of this Kingdome" (Schwoerer, *Declaration of Rights*, 295) and that Congress's preamble of 15 May began, "Whereas his Britannic Majesty, in conjunction with the lords and commons of Great Britain, has . . ." (JCC IV: 357).

65. Force VI: 614–15. See also the instructions of Cumberland County, Virginia, which not only advocated Independence but asked that references to the King in church liturgy be deleted "since we can neither love, honor nor esteem, but must detest the Wretch who hath brought Fire and Sword into our Country." *Virginia Magazine of History and Biography*, XVII (1946), 186.

66. Force VI: 1020, 700, 557; V: 1207, 1035.

67. Force VI: 704, 602.

68. In Boyd I: 203. See also the Congress's Address to the British people, which said the British government prosecuted its measures against America "with a design, that by having our lives and property in their power, they may with the greater facility enslave you." Address adopted September 5, 1774, in *Decent Respect*, 23.

69. On American hopes in and disillusionment with the British people, see Maier, *From Resistance to Revolution*, 234–35, 247–55, 260–63, 269–70; Bartlett quoted in Maier, *The Old Revolutionaries*, 145.

70. Force VI: 557, 1018, 963.

71. Ibid., VI: 1524; V: 8560; VI: 8687; V: 1028.

72. See Bonomi, *Under the Cope of Heaven*, 212–13 (includes quotation on self-preservation as a God-given instinct), and also the Rev. Samuel West, "A Sermon Preached Before the Honorable Council, and the . . . House of Repre-

sentatives of . . . Massachusetts-Bay, . . . May 29th, 1776" (orig. pub. Boston, 1776), in John Wingate Thornton, ed., *The Pulpit of the American Revolution* (Boston, 1860), 279–80: ". . . when a people find themselves cruelly oppressed by the parent state, they have an undoubted right to throw off the yoke, and to assert their liberty, if they find good reason to judge that they have sufficient power and strength to maintain their ground . . . ; for, in this case, by the law of self-preservation, which is the first law of nature, they have not only an undoubted right, but it is their indispensable duty, if they cannot be redressed any other way, to renounce all submission to the government that has oppressed them, and set up an independent state of their own. . . ." For another reference to "the first law of nature," see the Charlotte County, Virginia, instructions, in Force V: 1035.

73.   Blackstone, *Commentaries,* I: 213; Ronald Hamowy, "Jefferson and the Scottish Enlightenment: A Critique of Garry Wills's *Inventing America: Jefferson's Declaration of Independence,*" *William and Mary Quarterly,* 3d Ser., XXXVI (1979), 505–06, 508–09, and Thad W. Tate, "The Social Contract in America, 1774–1787, Revolutionary Theory as a Conservative Instrument," ibid. XXII (1965), 375–91.

74.   Force VI: 933. The statement, of course, also echoed Congress's resolves of May 10–15, 1776.

75.   Rhode Island law in Bartlett, ed., *Records of R.I.,* VII: 522. See also the similar presentment of a grand jury at Georgetown, South Carolina, May 6, 1776, which managed to cite both inherent rights and compact theory, but again concluded by justifying resistance in terms of self-preservation: "When a People, ever dutiful and affectionate to that system of Government formed for their happiness, and under which they had long lived, find that, by the baseness and corruption of their rulers, those laws which were intended as the guardians of their sacred and unalienable rights are impiously perverted into instruments of oppression; and, in violation of every social compact, and the ties of common justice, every means is adopted by those whom they instituted to govern and protect them, to enslave and destroy them; human nature and the laws of *God* justify their employing those means for redress which self-preservation dictates." In Force V: 1205. Locke spoke of self-preservation as a law of nature, but said the right to do whatever was necessary to preserve the self and the rest of mankind could be regulated and so modified by the laws of society. *Second Treatise,* Ch. 2, para. 6–7, and Ch. IX, para. 129. For other references, see, for example, John Trenchard and Thomas Gordon, *Cato's Letters,* Ronald Hamowy, ed. (Indianapolis, 1995), I: 492, 408.

76.   Force VI: 962–63, 1506–07.

77.   "A.B.," Williamsburg, April 12, 1776, from the *Virginia Gazette* (Purdie), in Force V: 862, and VI: 1019 for Charles County.

78.   Ibid., VI: 603, V: 1047. Paine's words were " 'Tis time to part," but the debt is nonetheless clear.

79.   Force VI: 603, 963, and also 1135–36, for a statement on American virtue in an address of officers and soldiers of several regiments stationed in and near New York City, June 29, 1776.

80. Ibid., V: 1031; VI: 603.

81. Pittsfield "Petition Remonstrance and Address" to the General Court, December 26, 1775, and Proclamation of the General Court, January 23, 1776, in Oscar and Mary Handlin, *The Popular Sources of Political Authority: Documents on the Massachusetts Constitution of 1780* (Cambridge, 1966), 63–64, 67; Force VI: 703.

82. Force V: 1031.

83. Force V: 1033.

84. Force VI: 514–15. The presentment is also reprinted, again with signatures, in the Right Reverend Alexander Gregg, *History of the Old Cheraws* (Spartanburg, S.C., 1975; orig. pub. 1925), 264–66. The presentment concluded with a request that it be "printed in the public papers." See also Judge Drayton's charge of November 15, 1774, to the Cheraws District Grand Jury, the response of the Petit Jury on November 18, and that of the Grand Jury, November 19, 1774, pp. 211–18, including the Grand Jury's statement of its determination to defend the "right of being exempted from all laws but those enacted with the consent of Representatives of our own election . . . at the hazard of our lives and fortunes" (218). The Court ordered all of these statements to be published "in the several *Gazettes* of this Province" (pp. 218–19). For further information on grand jury presentments in the revolution, see Richard D. Younger, *The People's Panel: The Grand Jury in the United States, 1634–1941* (Providence, R.I., 1963), ch. 3, esp. pp. 34–36.

85. Force VI: 702 (Acton), 603 (Malden), and 649 (Pittsfield); "Call for Political Convention to be held at Ipswich, April 25, 1776," a broadside issued in Essex County, Massachusetts, April 17, 1776, in *Essex Institute Historical Collections*, XXXVI (1900), 104.

86. Force V: 1322.

87. Force VI: 1018, 1020, 557, 962; "Call for a Political Convention at Ipswich," 104; Paine, "The Rights of Man," second part (1792) in Philip S. Foner, ed., *The Complete Writings of Thomas Paine* (New York, 1969), I: 354.

CHAPTER III:
MR. JEFFERSON AND HIS EDITORS

1. Boyd I: 313–14, and 308 on dating Jefferson's "Proceedings."

2. JCC V: 431; Adams to Timothy Pickering, August 6, 1822, in Charles Francis Adams, ed., *The Works of John Adams*, II (Boston, 1850), 514n: "I think he [Jefferson] had one more vote than any other, and that placed him at the head of the committee."

3. In L. H. Butterfield, ed., *Diary and Autobiography of John Adams*, III (Cambridge, 1961), 336, and also Adams, ed., *The Works of John Adams*, II: 512–15.

4. In Adams, ed., *The Works of John Adams, II:* 512–14n, esp. 514n.

5. Jefferson to James Madison, Aug. 30, 1823, in Paul Leicester Ford, ed., *The Writings of Thomas Jefferson*, X (New York and London, 1899), 267–69, esp. 267.

6.   On the dating of the notes Jefferson kept on the proceedings of Congress, see Boyd I: 299–308. In short, Boyd argues that the notes were probably written in the late summer and early fall of 1776, and certainly before June 1, 1783.

7.   Butterfield, ed., *Diary and Autobiography of John Adams*, II: 392.

8.   Franklin to Washington, Philadelphia, June 21 (his gout "has kept me from Congress and Company almost ever since you left us," that is, on June 4), and to Benjamin Rush, from "Mr. Duffield's" at Moreland (outside Philadelphia), June 26, 1776, in William B. Willcox, ed., *The Papers of Benjamin Franklin*, XXII (New Haven and London, 1982), 484–85 and n.7 at 485, 491, and editorial comment at 485–86.

9.   Boyd I: 413–17, and Becker, ch. IV, pp. 135–93, which includes various versions of the document with insertions and identifies, insofar as possible, who made those changes. Becker assumed that the "original rough draft" was in fact Jefferson's original draft. Boyd subsequently identified two earlier compositions—Jefferson's first draft of the Virginia constitution and a fragment of the declaration's section on the British people. Becker, however, did the basic groundwork of separating out the generations of changes recorded on the "original rough draft" by comparing the Adams copy with the versions Jefferson sent Richard Henry Lee and other correspondents, which were probably copied from the "fair copy," incorporating all the committee's amendments, that was presented to Congress on 28 June. Those efforts were necessary because the original "fair copy" has been lost. See also Julian Boyd, *The Declaration of Independence: The Evolution of the Text as Shown in Facsimiles of Various Drafts by its Author* (Washington, D.C., 1943). Both Becker and Boyd accepted uncritically Jefferson's 1823 version of the drafting process. Boyd even said that "there appears to be no known documentary evidence to prove Jefferson wrong in the statement made to Madison" with regard to the drafting process, and cites Becker to the same effect (p. 28).

10.   Jefferson to Franklin, "Friday morn," in Boyd I: 404–06; Willcox, ed., *Papers of Benjamin Franklin*, XII: 486.

11.   JCC V: 429, 433, 438; on the Board of War, see Robert J. Taylor, ed., *Papers of John Adams*, IV (Cambridge, Mass., and London, 1979), 252–53.

12.   Boyd I: 404–05n. The calculation was made for a select period of six months in which both Jefferson and Franklin were in Congress.

13.   JCC V: 446, 448–58, and n. 1 on 458; Boyd I: 389–404.

14.   JCC V: 473, 468, 474.

15.   See *Col. Pickering's Observations Introductory to Reading the Declaration of Independence, at Salem, July 4, 1823* (Salem, Mass., 1823), 8–9. The assertion that Jefferson produced a draft in two days appeared in Adams's autobiography but not in the Pickering letter.

16.   See Stephen E. Lucas, "The *Plakkaat Van Verlatinge*: A Neglected Model for the American Declaration of Independence," in Rosemarijn Hoefte and Johanna C. Kardux, *Connecting Cultures: The Netherlands in Five Centuries of Transatlantic Exchange* (Amsterdam, 1994), 187–207, esp. 203–07, which includes the quotation from Malone's *Jefferson the Virginian* (Boston, 1948), 148. With regard to the values and educational methods of the eighteenth century, note that

Jefferson himself kept a "Commonplace Book." Its pedagogical purpose was suggested by Jefferson's teacher, the Rev. James Maury, who instructed his own son "to reflect, and remark on, and digest what you read," and "to dwell on any remarkable beauties of diction, justness or sublimity of sentiment, or masterly strokes of true wit which may occur in the course of your reading." Cited in Douglas L. Wilson, ed., *Jefferson's Literary Commonplace Book* (Princeton, N.J., 1989), 7.

The Lucas essay also argues that the *Plakkaat Van Verlatinge*, a document the States General of the United Provinces of the Low Countries issued on July 26, 1581, to justify their independence from Spanish rule, provided a model for the American Declaration of Independence. The Dutch document, which in English is referred to as the Act of Abjuration, does seem to have striking similarities with the Declaration, but I find Lucas's argument unpersuasive with regard to its influence and have myself encountered no evidence that the *Plakkaat Van Verlatinge* provided a model for Jefferson or other members of the drafting committee. It could conceivably have had a secondary (or tertiary) influence, however, if it provided a model for the English Declaration of Rights of 1688/89.

17. Boyd I: 332, 415–20.

18. Becker, 203–05.

19. Malcolm Freiberg, ed., *Thomas Hutchinson's Strictures upon the Declaration of the Congress at Philadelphia; In a Letter to a Noble Lord, &c.* (London, 1776), which was published by the Old South Association as Old South Leaflet No. 227 (Boston, 1958), 3, 5.

20. Ibid., 5, 11; and Hazelton, 233.

21. See Becker's version of that report, based on the copy Jefferson sent R. H. Lee, pp. 160–71, and also the "original rough draft" in Boyd I: esp. 424–26. I am counting the statement that American petitions were "answered only by repeated injury," which appeared in the paragraph after the list of "he has" or "he is" statements.

22. Garry Wills, in *Inventing America: Jefferson's Declaration of Independence* (Garden City, N.Y., 1978), instead divided them into four parts: see his chapter 5, pp. 65–75. So did Stephen E. Lucas in "Justifying America: The Declaration of Independence as a Rhetorical Document," in Thomas W. Benson, ed., *American Rhetoric: Context and Criticism* (Carbondale, Ill., 1989), 67–130, esp. 96 and ff.

23. At this point Jefferson apparently wrote onto his first draft of the Virginia constitution phrases that appeared in an expanded version in his "original rough draft" of the Declaration of Independence. See Boyd I: 418 and 419, n. 5 and 6.

24. In ibid., 338–39 and 417–19.

25. The phrase "in the legislature" was apparently crossed out in copying the "rough draft" for Congress's "fair copy": see ibid., 428, n. 6. It remained, however, in the copy Jefferson prepared for Richard Henry Lee: see Becker, 177.

26. In Becker, 162–64. The "original rough draft" in Boyd's *Jefferson Papers* does not include clause 4 and differs also in other relatively minor details.

27.   Herbert Friedenwald, *The Declaration of Independence: An Interpretation and an Analysis* (New York, 1974; orig. 1904), 230–33. William L. Saunders, ed., *The Colonial Records of North Carolina*, IX (Raleigh, 1890), xx–xxvi, offers a more detailed account of the court controversy, and see also Jack P. Greene, *The Quest for Power: The Lower Houses of Assembly in the Southern Royal Colonies, 1689–1776* (Chapel Hill, N.C., 1963), 337–42, 420–24. Lucas, "Justifying America," 98–99, says colonial assemblies had been moved from their usual meeting places in Virginia and South Carolina, but that had happened more than once only in Massachusetts. Greene, *Quest for Power*, 451–52, notes that the fourth charge could apply to the royal governor's calling the South Carolina assembly to meet at Beaufort in 1772 "in an attempt to force the Commons to accept the royal instruction of April 1770 prohibiting the issuance of money from the treasury without executive consent. . . ."

28.   Bernard Bailyn, *Ideological Origins of the American Revolution* (Cambridge and London, 1992; orig. pub. 1967), 105–08, and *Pamphlets of the American Revolution, 1750–1776*, I (Cambridge, 1965), 249–55 (quotation of George III at 250). On the ninth charge, see also Friedenwald, *The Declaration of Independence*, 233–36. In assuming responsibility for judicial salaries, the Crown would at once increase its power and reduce those of the legislatures, which had traditionally been paymaster of judges in America.

29.   Freiberg, ed., *Hutchinson's 'Strictures,'* 19, 14, and, on John Adams's probable responsibility for adding the clause on calling legislative bodies at unusual places, Becker, 173. [John Lind,] *An Answer to the Declaration of the American Congress* (London, 1776), esp. 29–31.

30.   For two particularly heroic efforts to explain the events behind Jefferson's charges, see Friedenwald, *Declaration of Independence*, and Edward Dumbauld, *The Declaration of Independence and What It Means Today* (Norman, Okla., 1950).

31.   Compare Jefferson's draft 1774 instructions and draft preamble for the Virginia constitution in Boyd I: 129–34, and 417–18. The draft instructions Boyd chose to reprint are not identical with the printed pamphlet, but the differences are relatively minor. See editorial notes at 135–37. The quoted passages are on pp. 121, 134.

32.   Jefferson's 1774 draft instructions in Boyd I, esp. 121–23, 129.

33.   Ibid., 129–30. On colonial efforts to tax the slave trade, see Bailyn, *Ideological Origins*, 245, which notes that a Massachusetts effort had been nullified by the royal governor's veto in 1771 and 1774, and that similar efforts were made elsewhere. In Virginia, taxing slave imports would have hurt both slave traders and those poor but ambitious colonial planters who were still acquiring slaves, and it would have benefited established planters, who controlled the House of Burgesses, and whose slaves would increase in value as imports declined. There was, in other words, some limited justification for the Crown's position.

It is, of course, possible to find instances in which the colonists thought the King had, through his governors, vetoed other laws necessary for the public good. Friedenwald, *Declaration of Independence*, 214–19, also cites the Crown's thwarting of efforts to block the transportation of convicts to the colonies, to issue legal tender bills of credit, and to naturalize aliens.

34.   Ibid., 219–222; citations in text are from Boyd I: 130.

35.   Boyd I: 131–32.

36.   Ibid., 132–33. On "the little known affairs of land grants and naturalization," see Friedenwald, *Declaration of Independence*, 226–29. In November 1773, royal instructions were issued "prohibiting absolutely the naturalization of any aliens, and the passage of any acts to that end," which was "a heavy blow to the prosperity of the larger land-holding colonies, Virginia, New York, New Jersey, and Pennsylvania. . . ." See also Dumbauld, *The Declaration of Independence*, 105–08.

37.   Boyd I: 133–34.

38.   Boyd I: 135. The 1774 pamphlet, however, also referred to "a series of oppressions, begun at a distinguished period, and pursued unalterably thro' every change of ministers," which suggested that the King—who, of course, alone persisted through "every change of ministers"—was himself a party to what Jefferson described as a "deliberate, systematical plan" for reducing the Americans to "slavery" (125).

39.   Freiberg, ed., *Hutchinson's 'Strictures'*, 27–28. Virginia, for example, petitioned the King to approve laws that would discourage the slave trade, and Massachusetts remonstrated against the act setting up the commissioners of customs. Dumbauld, *The Declaration of Independence*, 89, 117. See also JCC I: 116, for the Congress's address to the King of October 1774, which complained that judges had been made dependent "on one part of the legislature for their salaries, as well as for the duration of their commissions," that "new, expensive and oppressive offices have been multiplied," and that a standing army had been stationed in the colonies since the "conclusion of the late war, without the consent of our assemblies," and, with "a considerable naval armament," was used to enforce tax collections, which reappeared as items nine, ten, and eleven in the Declaration of Independence. Two other charges not mentioned by Hutchinson—the fifth and twelfth—also appeared in Congress's 1774 address to the King (but not the sixth and eighth, despite the contrary suggestion in Wills, *Inventing America,* 69). Hutchinson implied that the existence of rebellion justified the presence of troops; however, the colonists strenuously denied that they were involved in a rebellion, which in Lockean terms connoted opposition to lawful authority. Congress's "Olive Branch Petition" of July 1775 did not list grievances: see JCC II: 158–62.

40.   Boyd I: 338, and also, with Jefferson's markings as he moved toward adapting it for the Declaration of Independence, 418.

41.   From Becker, 164–65.

42.   Ibid., 19–20.

43.   Cf. Friedenwald, *Declaration of Independence*, 240–54, and Dumbauld, *The Declaration of Independence*, 119–41. Also, with regard to trials in England, *A Decent Respect*, 31–32 n. 8.

44.   Boyd I: 200. The charges he reversed were numbers seven and eight,

so in the Declaration of Independence Parliament's "abolishing the free system of English laws in a neighboring province" comes before its "taking away our charters, abolishing our most valuable laws, and altering fundamentally the forms of our governments." *A Summary View* mentioned fewer charges against Parliament, and arranged them differently. Cf. ibid., 123–29.

45.   Ibid., 200–02.

46.   Ibid., 338–39.

47.   Ibid., 418–19; Becker, 165–67, 179–81.

48.   Becker, 214.

49.   Ibid., 216–18.

50.   Wills, *Inventing America*, 74.

51.   Adams to Pickering, August 6, 1822, in Adams, ed., *Works of John Adams*, II: 514n; Becker, 151.

52.   For example, later, in his "Notes on the State of Virginia," Jefferson argued that the thrust of colonial policy under George III left the Americans "no alternative . . . but resistance, or unconditional submission. Between these could be no hesitation. They closed in the appeal to arms. They declared themselves independent states." In Paul Leicester Ford, ed., *The Works of Thomas Jefferson*, IV (New York, 1904), 16.

53.   There was, however, a Dutch precedent: the *Plakkaat Van Verlatinge*, issued by the United Provinces of the Low Countries in 1581 to justify their independence from Spain, argued that Philip II of Spain was a tyrant, and in ways that resemble the American Declaration of Independence. See Lucas, "The *Plakkaat Van Verlatinge*," esp. 187, 191–95, which notes that the Dutch document differed in that way from "any other British deposition apologia" (191). American state and local "declarations" on Independence did, it should be said, frequently refer to British policy as tyrannic or despotic, but they seemed simply to assume that the designation was appropriate given the outrageous recent actions that they mentioned.

54.   Lind, *An Answer*, 119; Freiberg, ed., *Hutchinson's 'Strictures,'* 10–11.

55.   (New York, 1978), 3–4.

56.   Jefferson to Madison, Monticello, August 30, 1823, in Ford, ed., *The Writings of Thomas Jefferson*, X: 267–68; Adams to Pinckney, August 6, 1822, in Adams, ed., *The Works of John Adams*, II: 514n. Lucas, "The *Plakkaat Van Verlatinge*," 196, notes that Jefferson's statement to Madison that he had turned to neither book nor pamphlet in composing the Declaration can be read to mean only that he had not turned to Locke's "Second Treatise of Government" or James Otis's *The Rights of the Colonies Asserted and Proved* (Boston, 1964). See also Jacques Derrida, "Declarations of Independence," *New Political Science*, XV (1986), 8–9: Jefferson "was not responsible for *writing*, in the productive or initiating sense of the term, only for drawing up, as one says of a secretary that he or she draws up a *letter* of which the spirit has been breathed into him or her, or even the content dictated."

57.   In Boyd I, 106n. The reference is to John Rushworth's *Historical Collections of Private Passages of State, Weighty Matters in Law, Remarkable Proceed-*

ings in Five Parliaments beginning the Sixteenth Year of King James, anno 1618, and ending . . . with the death of King Charles the First, 1648, 8 volumes (London, 1659–1701).

58.   Adair, "Rumbold's Dying Speech, 1685, and Jefferson's Last Words on Democracy, 1826," *WMQ*, 3d. Ser., IX (1952), 521–31, esp. 525–26, 530, and see notes 10 and 11 at pp. 530–31, which suggest that parts of Rumbold's speech might themselves have been borrowed from still earlier sources.

59.   The committee version of the Virginia Declaration of Rights had been published earlier—it appeared, for example, in the *Pennsylvania Evening Post* on June 6, and later in the *Pennsylvania Ledger*—but the *Gazette* republication seems especially important since it coincided with the appointment and early meetings of the drafting committee. The kinship with Mason's Declaration was noted in John C. Fitzpatrick, *The Spirit of the Revolution* (Boston and New York, 1924), 2–3, 5–6, and more recently in Lucas, "Justifying America," 87, which, however, claims that it is impossible to know how much Jefferson was influenced by the Mason document. Boyd, in his *Declaration of Independence*, 21–22, insisted that Jefferson was "a recognized master, not an imaginative imitator," and dismissed Jefferson's debt to the Mason/committee draft as "not yet proved" and something that will "in all probability remain a matter of opinion." However, a careful comparison of the various drafts of the Declaration, which Becker sorted out, with the Mason/committee draft makes it clear that Jefferson began with that draft and gradually altered it. Such a comparison will be made later. It is, however, impossible to know whether the idea of using the Mason/committee draft came out of the Committee of Five or, as Fitzpatrick assumed, "the clarion note of liberty in [the draft Virginia Declaration's] first three sections found sympathetic echo" in Jefferson's "brain; he seized upon them and, with the artist's perfect judgment, commenced the Declaration with the trumpet blast of their bold principles" (6). See also Robert A. Rutland, ed., *The Papers of George Mason, 1725–92* (Chapel Hill, 1970), I, 275–91, for drafts of the document and a brief discussion of its evolution and influence.

60.   Congressional vote of 11 June in JCC V: 428–29; Hancock to Certain States, Philadelphia, July 6, 1776, in LDC IV: 396.

61.   From the *Pennsylvania Gazette*, June 12, 1776.

62.   Compare the draft Virginia Declaration in the *Pennsylvania Gazette* for June 12, 1776, with the Declaration as finally adopted in William W. Hening, ed., *Laws of Virginia*, IX (Richmond, 1821), 109–112, and the English Declaration in Schwoerer, *Declaration of Right*, esp. 296–97. Note, for example, that the 8th provision of the English Declaration, "That Elections of Members of Parliament ought to be free," is restated and extended in the sixth provision of both the draft and final Virginia Declaration, which begins, "That elections of members to serve as representatives of the people, in assembly, ought to be free." Similarly, the draft Declaration's eighth (and final version's seventh) provision, against suspending laws, echoes the first and second clauses in the English Declaration. Both the draft and final versions of the Virginia Declaration of Rights say "that standing armies, in time of peace, should be avoided, as dangerous to liberty," while the sixth provision of the English Declaration said "That the raiseing or

keeping a Standing Army within the Kingdom in time of Peace unless it be with the consent of Parliament is against Law." On the development and influence of the Virginia Declaration, see John Selby, *The Revolution in Virginia, 1775–1783* (Williamsburg, 1988), 101–04, 106–10. The committee draft, it seems, was far more widely circulated and more influential than that finally adopted by the Virginia Convention, which, Selby says, was virtually lost for some forty years. The final quotation appears in John Trenchard and Thomas Gordon, *Cato's Letters*, Ronald Hamowy, ed. (Indianapolis, 1995; orig. pub. 1720–23), I: 406.

63.   Boyd I: 357, 363. Selby, *Revolution in Virginia*, 103, says that Pennsylvania, Massachusetts, and four of the other five states that adopted bills of rights in the next decade drew on the Mason/committee draft (Delaware, Maryland, Vermont, and New Hampshire), and that North Carolina seems to have been more influenced by the final version as adopted by the Virginia convention—which, of course, was itself based on the Mason draft. On the use specifically of Mason's language on equality and natural rights, see Chapter IV, below.

64.   Boyd I: 413; Dumbauld, *The Declaration of Independence*, 54 (and see also 77); D.W. Brogan quoted in Philip F. Detweiler, "The Changing Reputation of the Declaration of Independence: The First Fifty Years," *WMQ*, 3d Ser., IXX (1962), 557.

65.   Boyd I: 213, and *Decent Respect*, 91.

66.   JCC II: 129, and Boyd I: 199.

67.   Committee of Secret Correspondence to Silas Deane, Philadelphia, July 8 and August 7, 1776, in LDC IV: 405, 635–36; Deane to "Gentlemen," Paris, November 28, 1776, in "Letter of Silas Deane," *Pennsylvania Magazine of History and Biography*, XI (1887), 199–200.

68.   JCC V: 516. Note that Jefferson's draft of the Declaration on Taking Up Arms also aspired to make the justice of the American cause known "to the world, whose affections will ever take part with those encountering oppression." But the Declaration was "to be published by General Washington, upon his arrival at the camp before Boston" mainly, it seems, for domestic consumption. That declaration did make some effort to reassure the friends of America in Britain and other parts of the empire—which constituted, in any case, a small part of "the world"—but that function was served more directly by Congress's address to the Inhabitants of Great Britain, which it approved two days after the Declaration on Taking Up Arms. See JCC II: 129 and n. 1, 138–39, 162.

69.   Instruction on Independence of Buckingham County in Force V: 1208. On American assumptions about international affairs, see James Hutson, "Formulating an American Foreign Policy," in Hutson, *John Adams and the Diplomacy of the American Revolution* (Lexington, Ky., 1980), 1–32.

70.   See Hancock to Certain States, Philadelphia, July 6, 1776, in LDC IV, 396: "I am directed by Congress to transmit [the enclosed Declaration] to you, and to request you will have it proclaimed in your Colony in the Way you shall think proper." Hancock's letter to Washington of the same date also asked to have the Declaration "proclaimed at the Head of the Army in the Way you shall think most proper" (397).

71.   Jay Fliegelman, *Declaring Independence: Jefferson, Natural Language, &*

the Culture of Performance (Stanford, 1993), 5; JCC V: 491, and "Proceedings" in Boyd I, 313: "I reported [the Declaration] to the house on Friday the 28th. of June when it was read. . . ."

72.   On "Jefferson's Pauses," see Fliegelman, *Declaring Independence*, 4–15, and esp. 11, where he presents a passage from the declaration "as Jefferson rhythmically set it forth." The rhythm is, however, more singsong than pleasing. For a clear and succinct summary of Jefferson's rhetorical strategies, see Lucas, "Justifying America," 83–85.

Becker ingeniously linked Jefferson's strengths as a writer with his weaknesses as an orator: "one who in imagination hears the pitch and cadence and rhythm of the thing he wishes to say before he says it, often makes a sad business of public speaking because, painfully aware of the imperfect felicity of what has been uttered, he forgets what he ought to say next. He instinctively wishes to cross out what he has just said, and say it over again in a different way—and this is what he often does, to the confusion of the audience" (195). It is not, however, altogether clear that what Becker described was Jefferson's problem as a speaker. Gilbert Chinard said that "His voice, pleasant and modulated in ordinary conversation, 'sank in his throat', if raised higher, and became husky." *Thomas Jefferson, The Apostle of Americanism* (2nd ed., Boston, 1939), 36–37.

73.   Selby, *Revolution in Virginia*, 97; Force VI: 1524.

74.   References to the Declaration as it emerged from the committee here and in the immediately subsequent pages are taken from Becker, 160–71, which reproduces Jefferson's rough draft "as it probably read when Jefferson made the 'fair copy' which was presented to Congress as the report of the Committee of Five," and indicates changes made after Jefferson first submitted the draft to fellow committee members, and also another version of the committee draft on pp. 177–84. (An earlier version is presented on pp. 141–51.)

75.   See esp. Derrida, "Declarations of Independence."

76.   See Boyd I: 122–23.

77.   See Becker's version of the draft with editorial changes made before the document was submitted to Congress, p. 160.

78.   Ibid., 142–43 and 160–61, and the committee draft of the Virginia Declaration in the *Pennsylvania Gazette*, June 12, 1776.

79.   Herbert Lawrence Ganter, "Jefferson's 'Pursuit of Happiness' and Some Forgotten Men," *WMQ*, 2d Ser., XVI (1936), 422–34, and, more important here, 558–85, and n. 30, pp. 559–60. Also Hamowy, "Declaration of Independence," in Jack P. Greene, ed., *Encyclopedia of American History*, I (New York, 1984), pp. 459–60, esp. 459. Hamowy discussed and rejected interpretations of the phrase that say Jefferson was abandoning property rights. The Declaration, Hamowy argued, does not impose on government an obligation to maximize the people's happiness, but only to see that their rights are respected and so "to provide the framework in which each person may pursue his own happiness as he individually sees fit." See also Hamowy, "Jefferson and the Scottish Enlightenment: A Critique of Garry Wills's *Inventing America: Jefferson's Declaration of Independence*," *WMQ*, 3d Ser., XXXVI (1979), 503–23, esp. 517, 519: "When Jefferson

spoke of an inalienable right to the pursuit of happiness, he meant that men may act as they choose in their search for ease, comfort, felicity, and grace, either by owning property or not, by accumulating wealth or distributing it, by opting for material success or asceticism, in a word, by determining the path to their own earthly and heavenly salvation as they alone see fit. Governments may infringe this right only at the peril of violating the social contract on which their legitimacy ultimately rests" (519).

80.   Lucas, "Justifying America," 84, quoting Hugh Blair's *Lectures on Rhetoric and Belles Lettres* (London, 1783), I: 206–07; at 259, Blair also noted that "when we aim at dignity or elevation, the sound should be made to grow to the last; the longest members of the period, and the fullest and most sonorous words, should be reserved to the conclusion." Lucas shows that Jefferson's preamble also conformed with that rule, ending all but one sentence with a word of three or four syllables.

81.   Pauline Maier, *From Resistance to Revolution: Colonial Radicals and the Development of American Opposition to Britain, 1765–1776* (New York, 1972), ch. 2, pp. 27–48; Bailyn, *Ideological Origins*; and, on Loyalists, Mary Beth Norton, "The Loyalist Critique of the Revolution," in *The Development of a Revolutionary Mentality: Papers Presented at the First [Library of Congress] Symposium, May 5 and 6, 1972* (Washington, D.C., 1972), 127–48. For an example of another publication that stated with remarkable fidelity the ideas in this part of the Declaration of Independence, and before that document was written, see the Reverend Samuel West, "A Sermon Preached Before the Honorable Council and the Honorable House of Representatives of . . . the Massachusetts–Bay, . . . May 29th, 1776," in John Wingate Thornton, ed., *The Pulpit of the American Revolution* (Boston, 1860), esp. 279–82. In discussing the origins of government, West began with the fact that "all men" were "by nature equal" (279), and stated that, "if magistrates have no authority but what they derive from the people; if they are properly of human creation; if the whole end and design of their institution is to promote the general good, and to secure to men their just rights,—it will follow, that when they act contrary to the end and design of their creation they cease being magistrates, and the people which gave them their authority have the right to take it from them again." West also stated that people had a right to form new governments, and emphasized, like Jefferson, that the "unhinging a people from a form of government to which they had been long accustomed" was only to be undertaken in the most extreme cases of oppression because it risked throwing people into "such a state of anarchy and confusion as might terminate in their destruction, or perhaps, in the end, subject them to the worst kind of tyranny" (281).

82.   See paragraph 14 of Locke's "Second Treatise of Government" in Peter Laslett, ed., *Two Treatises of Government* (Cambridge, England, and New York, 1965; orig. pub. 1960), p. 317: ". . . since all *Princes* and Rulers of *Independent* Governments all through the World, are in a State of Nature, 'tis plain the World never was, nor ever will be, without Numbers of Men in that State."

83.   Again, Locke made the same point in ibid., paragraph 4, p. 309, where he described men in a state of nature as in a state of equality in terms of power re-

lationships: there "all the Power and Jurisdiction is reciprocal, no one having more than another: there being nothing more evident, than that Creatures of the same species and rank promiscuously born to all the same advantages of Nature, and the use of the same faculties, should also be equal amongst another without Subordination or Subjection, unless the Lord and Master of them all, should by any manifest Declaration of his Will set one above another, and confer on him by an evident and clear appointment an undoubted Right to Dominion and Sovereignty."

84. In Philip Foner, ed., *The Complete Writings of Thomas Paine* (New York, 1969), I: 13.

85. Becker, n. 1 at 142; Boyd I: 427–28, n. 2.

86. Paragraph 225 of Locke's "Second Treatise" in Laslett, ed., *Two Treatises*, 463–64; Boyd I: 125.

87. Becker, 161. Boyd, *Declaration of Independence*, 25–26, suggests that the phrase "under absolute" was Adams's suggestion, and that Franklin then substituted "Despotism" for Jefferson's "power."

88. Hamowy, "Jefferson and the Scottish Enlightenment," 503–23; Becker, 160.

89. Boyd I: 277–85, quotations at 283.

90. *Decent Respect*, 21–32, 99–108.

91. JCC V: 507.

92. Ibid., 507, 510.

93. Ritz, "From the *Here* of Jefferson's Handwritten Rough Draft of the Declaration of Independence to the *There* of the Printed Dunlap Broadside," the *Pennsylvania Magazine of History & Biography*, CXVI (1992), 499–512. Ritz also argues that a printed fragment of the Declaration at the Historical Society of Pennsylvania, which earlier scholars described as a "proof" for the broadside published by John Dunlap after Congress approved the Declaration, was in fact "a distinct printing . . . made between the (now lost) first printing of Jefferson's draft Declaration and the final printing known as the *Dunlap Broadside*" (504).

94. Bartlett to John Langdon, Philadelphia, July 1, 1776, in LDC IV: 351. The discussion that follows draws upon the version of the document in Becker, 174–84, which shows the changes Congress made in the committee draft, and the slightly amended rendition of the document as Becker presented it below, in Appendix C.

95. Boyd I: 314–15.

96. Ibid., 314.

97. Printed with Jefferson's letter to Robert Walsh, Monticello, December 4, 1818, in Ford, ed., *The Writings of Thomas Jefferson*, X: 120n.

98. Lee to Jefferson, Chantilly (his plantation in Virginia), July 21, 1776, in Boyd I: 471; Adams to Pickering, August 6, 1822, in Adams, ed., *Works of John Adams*, II: 514n.

99. JCC V: 510–16.

100. Boyd I: 315.

101. Cf. LDC IV, editorial note at 381–82.

102.   The cases for and against a signing on July 4 are summarized in Boyd I: 304–08, which also refers to other discussions of the subject.

103.   JCC V: 590–91, 626. The copy reprinted, with signatures, under the entry for July 4 on pp. 510–15 was taken from "the engrossed original in the Department of State," and so is of a later date. A printed broadside from Congress's "Rough Journal" is reproduced in Boyd, *Declaration of Independence: The Evolution of the Text*, plate X.

104.   Schwoerer, *The Declaration of Rights, 1689* (Baltimore and London, 1981), 13.

105.   *Decent Respect*, passim.

106.   Ibid., 13, 75, 127.

107.   On invocations of 35 Henry VIII, c. 2, with regard to treason or misprision of treason committed outside the realm, see *Decent Respect*, p. 32, n. 8; Jefferson's notes on Congress's proceedings in Boyd I: 312.

108.   Hazelton, 284.

CHAPTER IV:
AMERICAN SCRIPTURE

1.   Hancock to General George Washington, Philadelphia, July 6, 1776, LDC IV: 397.

2.   Ibid., and Hancock to Certain States, Philadelphia, July 6, 1776, LDC IV: 396 and notes, 396–97, on when the letter was sent to which states. Another was sent to General Artemas Ward "or Officer Commanding the Continental Troops at Boston" with instructions for proclaiming the Declaration there (n. 2).

3.   Washington's Orders of July 9 and other recollections quoted in Hazelton, 252–53.

4.   Recruiting poster of 1776 in Charles Evans, *American Bibliography*, V, (New York, 1941; orig. pub. 1909), 282 (No. 15103); Barton to Henry Wisner (his cousin), Newton, N.J., July 9, 1776, in Charles S. Desbler, "How the Declaration Was Received in the Old Thirteen," *Harper's New Monthly Magazine*, LXXXV (July 1892), 169. He added that "We have had great numbers who could do nothing until we were declared a free State, who are now ready to spend their lives and fortunes in defence of our country. I expect a great turn one way or the other before I see you again."

5.   The account here and in the succeeding paragraph draws heavily upon Hazelton's Chapter XI, "The Fireworks of 1776," 240–81, which summarizes the celebrations colony by colony. The Adams account, in a letter to Samuel Chase of July 9, is quoted at p. 242 (and see also LDC IV: 414), and the account of the celebration at Savannah on August 10, from the *Pennsylvania Gazette* of October 9, 1776, is at pp. 280–81. See also Desbler, "How the Declaration Was Received in the Old Thirteen," 165–87, which includes quotations from contemporary accounts of the celebrations, including some cited in the text on those at Philadelphia at pp. 166–67. For evidence that the Declaration was first read publicly on July 4 to a small audience that included few "respectable" people, see Wilfred J.

Ritz, "From the 'Here' of Jefferson's Handwritten Rough Draft of the Declaration of Independence to the 'There' of the Printed Dunlap Broadside," *Pennsylvannia Magazine of History & Biography,* CXVI (1992), esp. 507–10.

6. Contemporary accounts quoted in Desbler, "How the Declaration Was Received," 178–79, 186–87.

7. Ibid., esp. 172–74, and Hazleton, esp. 266–68, 253, and 561 n. 53.

8. Desbler, "How the Declaration Was Received," esp. 170 (Dover), 179 (Huntington), 186–87 (Savannah); Hazelton, 280–81.

9. In Henry D. Biddle, "Owen Biddle," *Pennsylvania Magazine of History and Biography,* XVI (1892–93), 308–09.

10. Hazelton, 259, 263, 270–74. In Amherst, for example, the sheriff and other county magistrates, militamen, and several hundred spectators gathered on August 1 at the town's Meeting House. After "attending prayer," they drew into a circle, with the sheriff in the center "on horse back, with a drawn sword in his hand: The Declaration was read from an eminence on the parade, ... three cheers were given, colours flying, and drums beating; the militia fired in thirteen divisions attended with universal acclamations" (270–71).

11. *A Rising People: The Founding of the United States, 1765 to 1789* (Philadelphia, 1976), 70–75. This useful book draws on the valuable collections of the American Philosophical Society, the Historical Society of Pennsylvania, and the Library Company of Philadelphia. Hazelton also contains substantial information on the publication of the document, much of which is in the notes to Ch. XI, and see also Charles Warren, "Fourth of July Myths," *WMQ,* 3d Ser., II (1945), 242, n. 8. For the Virginia Council's order of July 20 that the colony's two printers publish the Declaration in their gazettes, see the *Virginia Gazette* (Dixon and Hunter), July 29 and also (Purdie), July 26. For Connecticut, and some speculation on why the Declaration was apparently not sent to towns for public readings as was done elsewhere despite the state's strong support for Independence, see Desbler, "How the Declaration Was Received," 176–78.

12. Hazelton, pp. 560–61, n. 50, and p. 570, n. 87.

13. *Virginia Gazette* (Purdie), July 19 and, on Trenton (Dixon and Hunter), July 29, 1776. See also Philip F. Detweiler, "The Changing Reputation of the Declaration of Independence: The First Fifty Years," *WMQ,* 3d Ser., XIX (1962), p. 558 and n. 2; and Desbler, "How the Declaration Was Received," 176–77, for resolutions of the Rhode Island General Assembly, July 20, and of Connecticut, October 1776.

14. *Pennsylvania Post,* July 2, and *Pennsylvania Gazette,* July 3, 1776, cited in Warren, "Fourth of July Myths," 240 and n. 5.

15. John to Abigail Adams, July 3, 1776, and to his daughter, July 5, 1777, and William Williams to Governor Jonathan Trumbull, Philadelphia, July 5, 1777, cited in ibid., 240–41, 255–56, references from 1780 at 257 and, for an account of the tradition's establishment, 254–72. See also Diana Karter Appelbaum, *The Glorious Fourth: An American Holiday, An American History* (New York, 1989), esp. 16–21.

16. *Pennsylvania Post,* July 5, 1777; July 8, 1778, and July 5, 1783 (account of

the "car"); the *Freeman's Journal*, July 7, 1784 (which again refers to a "display of the most elegant fire works"), and Appelbaum, *Glorious Fourth*, esp. 16–33.

17.   On this point, see also Detweiler, "Changing Reputation of the Declaration of Independence," 559–61.

18.   Thorpe VII: 3814–15 (Virginia); V: 2594–95 (New Jersey); IV: 2451–52 (New Hampshire), and VI: 3241–43 (South Carolina).

19.   Ibid., V: 2623–28.

20.   Ibid., V: 3081–82 and 2789–90. The North Carolina preamble said that the Continental Congress, "having considered the premises, and other previous violations of the rights of the good people of America, have therefore declared, that the Thirteen United Colonies are, of right, wholly absolved from all allegiance to the British crown, or any other foreign jurisdiction whatsoever: and that the said Colonies now are, and forever shall be, free and independent States."

21.   Ibid., II: 777.

22.   Ibid., I: 1686, 1888–89. On the other hand, Vermont's constitution of 1786 once again began with an explanation of how Vermont's obligation of allegiance to the Crown had ended: see ibid., VI: 3749–50.

23.   Detweiler, "Changing Reputation of the Declaration of Independence," 561–62. Detweiler says the Wisconsin constitution—or, more exactly, its declaration of rights—of 1848 was the first to use the wording of the Declaration, but in fact the first provision of that document was a hybrid. It began, again, with Mason's language, saying "all men are born equally free and independent," but used Jefferson's formulation in saying that among their "inherent rights" were "life, liberty, and the pursuit of happiness" and that "to secure these rights governments are instituted among men, deriving their just powers from the consent of the governed." Thorpe VII: 4077. See also John E. Selby, *The Revolution in Virginia, 1775–1783* (Williamsburg, 1988), 103–04, and R. Carter Pittman's discussion of the importance of the Mason/committee draft declaration in the *Virginia Magazine of History and Biography*, LXVIII (1960), 109–11.

24.   *Pennsylvania Gazette*, June 12, 1776, for Mason/committee draft; Virginia Declaration in Thorpe VII: 3813.

25.   Thorpe V: 3082; III: 1889, VI: 3739, and IV: 2453–54. On Franklin's role at the Pennsylvania constitutional convention of 1776, see Carl Van Doren, *Benjamin Franklin* (New York, 1938), 554, and also Allan Nevins, *The American States During and After the Revolution, 1775–1789* (New York, 1924), 149–52. Franklin served as the convention's president, but was also a member of the Continental Congress, which kept him from serving on the convention's drafting committee. He presided over only some sessions, Van Doren says, and was "chiefly an absentee adviser to the convention," but one who managed to get some of his favorite ideas adopted. Nevins, who devoted more attention to the subject, says that "all the evidence points to Franklin, [George] Bryan, [James] Cannon, and [Timothy] Matlack as the foremost contributors to this remarkable instrument," and that "the Constitution bears several of Franklin's hallmarks." Franklin took great pride in the Pennsylvania constitution, of which he

carried a copy to France "and exhibited it to Turgot, La Rochefoucauld, Condorcet, and other admirers." See also William B. Willcox, ed., *Papers of Benjamin Franklin,* XXII (New Haven and London, 1982), 512–15, which suggests that his influence was more on the shape of the government than on the Declaration of Rights. John Adams's role at the Massachusetts convention is clearer. He was appointed to a subcommittee of the convention's drafting committee, which then essentially left to him the task of drafting a Declaration of Rights and Constitution. See Gregg L. Lint et al., eds., *Papers of John Adams,* VIII (Cambridge, Mass., 1989), 230–31. Adams understood that Massachusetts could and should not act without consulting the work of states that had already drafted declarations of rights and constitutions. He in fact borrowed from those and other earlier state documents freely, having written Benjamin Rush that it was impossible for Massachusetts to "acquire any Honour, as so many fine Examples have been so recently set Us; altho We shall deserve some degree of Disgrace if We fall much short of them." September 10, 1779, ibid., 140.

Since both Adams and Franklin were on the Congressional committee responsible for drafting the Declaration, it is tempting to suggest that their use of the Mason/committee draft gives further evidence that the committee itself was taken with the Mason draft and instructed Jefferson to adopt some of its language. However, Franklin's absence from committee meetings due to illness weakens that argument significantly: if he came to appreciate the Mason draft, he probably did it alone, not in consultation with other members of the Declaration's drafting committee.

26.   Marcel Gauchet, "Rights of Man," and Philippe Raynaud, "American Revolution," in François Furet and Mona Ozouf, eds., *A Critical Dictionary of the French Revolution* (Cambridge, Mass., 1989), 818–28 (esp. 818–22), 593–604; Olivier Bernier, *Lafayette: Hero of Two Worlds* (New York, 1983), esp. 149–50, 190–91. For French enthusiasm for the American Revolution and an account of the various translations of American documents—often done with help from Franklin—see Durand Echeverría, *Mirage in the West: A History of the French Image of American Society to 1815* (Princeton, N.J., 1957), esp. 55–56, 70–72, 162–66. For another evaluation of the importance of the American example for the French Declaration of the Rights of Man and of the historical controversy that raged over that issue in the early twentieth century, see Stéphane Rials, *La Declaration des Droits de l'Homme and du Citoyen* (Paris, 1988), 355–69.

27.   Gauchet, "Rights of Man," esp. 822 and 820, and Georges Lefebvre, *The Coming of the French Revolution: 1789* (Princeton, N.J., 1947), esp. 174, on how provisions of the Declaration of Rights condemned practices of the Old Regime, and 221–23 for a translated text of the Declaration of the Rights of Man and Citizen.

28.   Detweiler, "Changing Reputation," 562–65.

29.   In Boyd, ed., *Jefferson Papers,* XII (Princeton, N.J., 1955), 61–65.

30.   Ibid., XV (Princeton, 1958), 239–40 and see also 240–41n.

31.   The account here and in succeeding paragraphs follows that in Detweiler, "Changing Reputation of the Declaration of Independence," but also

draws upon Warren, "Fourth of July Myths," esp. 254–72, and Appelbaum, *Glorious Fourth.*

32. Quotations from the *Independent Chronicle* (Boston) for July 19, 1792, and July 6, 1797, in Detweiler, "Changing Reputation," 565, 569; and see also Warren, "Fourth of July Myths," 263–68.

33. Citations from the Federalist press in Warren, "Fourth of July Myths," 269–71, and Detweiler, "Changing Reputation," 569–70.

34. Merrill D. Peterson, *The Jefferson Image in the American Mind* (New York, 1960), 69–87, 99–111.

35. Pickering, *Col. Pickering's Observations Introductory to Reading the Declaration of Independence, at Salem, July 4, 1823* (Salem, Mass., 1823), esp. 7, 10, 12, and Adams to Pickering, August 6, 1822, and editorial comment in Charles Francis Adams, ed., *The Works of John Adams,* II (Boston, 1850), 512–14n. Jefferson to Madison, Monticello, August 30, 1823, in Andrew A. Lipscomb and Albert Ellery Berg, eds., *The Writings of Thomas Jefferson,* 20 vols. (Washington, D.C., 1903–04), XV: 460–64, esp. 463.

36. The original publication is reprinted in William Henry Hoyt, *The Mecklenburg Declaration of Independence: A Study of Evidence Showing That the Alleged Early Declaration of Independency by Mecklenburg County, North Carolina, on May 20th, 1775, Is Spurious* (New York, 1907), 3–7, which summarizes the controversy that followed in Chapter 1. For a succinct account of the incident, see Peterson, *Jefferson Image,* 140–44. On John McKnitt Alexander, see V.V. McNitt, *Chain of Error and the Mecklenburg Declaration of Independence. A New Study of Manuscripts: Their Use, Abuse, and Neglect* (Palmer, Mass., and New York, 1960), 66–67, and also George W. Graham, *The Mecklenburg Declaration of Independence. . . . and Lives of Its Signers* (New York, 1905), 114: "He was quite a politician in his day, of the old Federal school. . . ."

37. Adams to William Bentley, Quincy, July 15, 1819, in Adams, ed., *Works of John Adams,* X (Boston, 1856), 381. Adams had made his resentments clear in letters to Benjamin Rush, September 30, 1805, and June 21, 1811, on reel 118 of the Adams papers, both of which letters are cited by Joseph Ellis in his biography of Jefferson, *American Sphinx*—which Ellis kindly allowed the author to read in manuscript before its publication—and in Ellis, *Passionate Sage: The Character and Legacy of John Adams* (New York and London, 1993), 64–65.

38. The correspondence between Adams and Jefferson on the subject, including Adams's letter of June 22, Jefferson's reply of July 9, and Adams's subsequent letters of July 21 and 28, 1819, are in Lester J. Cappon, ed., *The Adams-Jefferson Letters* (Chapel Hill, 1959), 542–46. Also Adams to Francis Vanderkemp, August 21, 1819, from reel 124 of the Adams Papers on microfilm, cited in Ellis, *Passionate Sage,* 121.

39. Peterson, *Jefferson Image,* 142–44, which also points out that North Carolina celebrators of the Mecklenburg Declaration in 1835 tended to be conservative Whigs and Nullifiers, who had joined in opposing Jackson. See also Hoyt, *Mecklenburg Declaration,* esp. 22–26 for the resolutions of May 31, 1775, and, for a modern defense of the "Mecklenburgh Declaration of Independence," McNitt,

Chain of Error, which provides a complex, not to say bewildering, analysis of the various documents at issue.

40.   Adams to Trumbull, January 1, 1817, quoted in Irma B. Jaffe, *Trumbull: The Declaration of Independence* (New York, 1976), 95, and see also 15, 69–70, 78–79, and passim. The Washington, D.C., rendition of the painting includes forty-seven portraits, all in the earlier version except Thomas Nelson, Jr. (p. 78). Trumbull worked on the first painting, which is now at Yale, between 1786 and 1793. The Washington version awoke controversy over the people he chose to include, which Trumbull explained, along with the means he used in assembling portraits, in an exchange with "Detector" published in the *Port-Folio* (1819), which has been reprinted in Charles L. Sanford, ed., *Quest for America, 1810–1824* (New York, 1964), 155–62. On Trumbull's debt to West, see Garry Wills, *Inventing America: Jefferson's Declaration of Independence* (New York, 1978), 345–48.

41.   John C. Fitzpatrick, *The Spirit of the Revolution: New Light from Some of the Original Sources of American History* (Boston and New York, 1924), 16–18, 20–22.

42.   *North American Review,* XVI (1923), 184–85.

43.   Hoyt, *Mecklenburg Declaration of Independence,* 1–3.

44.   Thomas N. Brown, "Some Uses of History in the Early Republic," in *Witness to America's Past: Two Centuries of Collecting by the Massachusetts Historical Society* (Boston, 1991), 13, and Pickering, *Observations,* 9–10.

45.   *North American Review,* XXII (1926), 176–78, 219–20.

46.   Niles, *Principles and Acts,* iv, and see also iii, where the subscriber who in 1816 suggested that Niles compile a collection of revolutionary documents notes that the opportunity is "transient, as but six Americans who witnessed the great debate [on Independence] remain."

47.   Appelbaum, *Glorious Fourth,* 51, 52; Niles, *Principles and Acts,* ii, and see also Brown, "Some Uses of History," 10.

48.   Marian Klamkin, *The Return of Lafayette, 1824–25* (New York, 1975), quotation from Monroe's letter of February 24, 1824, at p. 10; A. Levasseur, *Lafayette in America in 1824 and 1825* (Philadelphia, 1829), esp. quotation at I: 67, and see also J. Bennett Nolan, *Lafayette in America Day by Day* (Baltimore, 1934).

49.   Appelbaum, *Glorious Fourth,* 51–52, where she quotes *Niles Weekly Register* for August 16, 1828. Hillard, *The Last Men of the Revolution,* ed. Wendell D. Garrett (Barre, Mass., 1968; orig. pub. Hartford, 1864), 23. It seems that the "last soldier of the Revolution" was Daniel T. Bakeman of Freedom, Cattaraugas County, N.Y., who died on April 5, 1869. Ibid., 115.

50.   Adams to Benjamin Rush, March 14, 1809, cited in Ellis, *Passionate Sage,* 67, and see also 66–68, 99–101; Jefferson letter in Cappon, ed., *Adams-Jefferson Letters,* II, 292, and see also n. 38, which notes that there were actually ten surviving "signers" at the time.

51.   To Adams, September 12, 1821, and June 1, 1822, in ibid., 575, 577–78.

52.   Jefferson to Adams, March 25, 1826, ibid., 613–14; Saul K. Padover, *Jefferson* (New York, 1942), 380. The word "Argonaut" comes from Greek mythology, and referred originally to a band of heroes who sailed to Colchis in the ship *Argo* with Jason in search of the Golden Fleece.

53. Jaffe, *Trumbull: The Declaration of Independence*, 61–72. The painting was also historically inaccurate in other ways: see Wills, *Inventing America*, 348, and John Adams's criticisms in Ellis, *Passionate Sage*, 100.

54. Jefferson to Gardner, Monticello, Feburary 19, 1813, in Paul Leicester Ford, ed., *The Works of Thomas Jefferson* (Federal Edition: New York and London, 1904–05), XI: 280–81 (and Jefferson asked "permission to become a subscriber for a copy when published"), and, on Gardner's relationship with Binns, Fitzpatrick, *Spirit of the Revolution*, 16–17.

55. Jefferson to Adams, June 27, 1822, in Cappon, ed., *Adams-Jefferson Letters*, 581; Jefferson to Madison, August 30, 1823, in Lipscomb and Berg, eds., *Jefferson Writings*, XV: 460–61.

56. To Delaplaine—who published *Delaplaine's Repository of the Lives and Portraits of Distinguished American Characters* (Philadelphia, 1815–16)—April 12, 1817, and to Wells, May 12, 1819, in Lipscomb and Berg, eds., *Jefferson Writings*, XIX: 246–47, XV: 191–202, esp. 195–202.

57. "Anecdotes of Benjamin Franklin," written for Walsh and sent December 4, 1818, in ibid., XV: 175–77; to Otis, February 15, 1821; to Madison, August 30, 1823; to Lee, May 8, 1825; to Woodward, April 3, 1825, and to Vaughan, September 16, 1825, in Paul Leicester Ford, ed., *The Writings of Thomas Jefferson*, X (New York and London, 1899), 187–88, 266–69, 342–43, 341–42, 345–46.

58. Wills, *Inventing America*, 341–44. On the signing issue, and also the dating of the "Proceedings," see Boyd I: 299–308. On when Congress approved the Declaration, see LDC IV: n. 2 at 381–83.

59. Ellis, *Passionate Sage*, 64–65 (quotation), 99–101, 58, 81–83; Adams to Jefferson, November 12, 1813, and July 30, 1815, in Cappon, ed., *Adams-Jefferson Letters*, II: 393, 451.

60. Peter S. Onuf, "Thomas Jefferson, Missouri, and the 'Empire for Liberty,'" unpublished manuscript made available by its author, with citations at pp. 6 and 5 from Jefferson's letters to the marquise de LaFayette, December 26, 1820, and to John Holmes, April 22, 1820, from Lipscomb and Berg, eds., *Jefferson Writings* XV: 301, 250. See also the splendid discussion of Jefferson's and Adams's response to the Missouri Crisis in Ellis, *Passionate Sage*, 138, 140–41. Adams, in short, thought the controversy was over a moral issue and, like Abraham Lincoln later, saw reason for preventing slavery's spread to the West, while understanding and sympathizing with the dilemmas slavery raised for Southerners.

61. "A Memorandum (Services to My Country)" in Merrill D. Peterson, ed., *Thomas Jefferson. Writings* (New York [Library of America], 1984), 702–04.

62. In ibid., 706.

63. From the Minutes of the Board of Visitors, University of Virginia, for March 4, 1825, in ibid., 479. The minutes also state as a duty of the University its inculcating "principles of government" fundamental to the United States, and mention the Declaration of Independence as a basic text to be studied. Jefferson to Madison, August 30, 1823, and to John Quincy Adams, July 18, 1824, in Lipscomb and Berg, eds., *Jefferson Writings*, XV: 464, XIX: 278.

64. To Mease, September 26, 1825, and to Ellen W. Coolidge, November 14, 1825, in ibid., XVI: 122–23, XVIII: 348–50.

65. Brown, "Some Uses of History," 9–14, esp. 12, which observes that revolutionary artifacts took on particular significance because of the associationalist psychology prevalent at the time: "A glove, a gorget, a lock of hair, a battle map connected by memory with great men or great deeds could trigger in the imagination of those so instructed a chain of associated images, arousing thereby the appropriate emotion of awe and bringing the mind to a condition of moral sensitivity and reflection." Thus documents "were collected and published for the general reader, who pursued them with feelings of awe and wonder" (10). On the associationalist ideas of the time, see also Robert E. Streeter, "Association Psychology and Literary Nationalism in the *North American Review*, 1815–1825," *American Literature*, XVII (1946), 243–54. The prevalence of these ideas helps explain how so Protestant a society as that of the United States in the 1820s could have taken to "relics."

66. Joseph M. Sanderson, *Proposals . . . for Publishing by Subscription A Biography of the Signers to the Declaration of Independence . . .* (Philadelphia, 1819), 4; Clay, cited in George Dangerfield, *The Awakening of American Nationalism, 1815–1828* (New York, 1965), 166, and also 39–40, 164–65. On the revolutions of the 1820s and their fates, see Frederick B. Artz, *Reaction and Revolution, 1814–1832* (New York and London, 1934), esp. 149–83.

67. For example, Mexico's Grito de Dolores of September 16, 1810, whose anniversary is celebrated as Mexico's Independence Day, was issued in the names of the Virgin of Guadalupe and Spain's Ferdinand VII, and the later Plan de Iguala of February 24, 1821, which included both a declaration of independence from Spain and a brief sketch of government, was the work of an individual, Agustín de Iturbide: "At the head of a determined and valiant army," it said, "I have proclaimed the independence of Mexico." Edwin Williamson, *The Penguin History of Latin America* (London, 1992), 215, and William Spence Robertson, *Rise of the Spanish-American Republics* (New York and London, 1918), 118–120, which describes the Plan of Iguala and notes its differences from the American Declaration of Independence: "it did not present an indictment of the mother country. Neither did it contain a philosophy of the revolution." The great liberator of South America, Simón Bolívar, not only decided that Latin American republicanism could not follow the North American model, but adopted the British system as a constitutional model. See Williamson, *Penguin History of Latin America*, 221–22. Artz, *Reaction and Revolution*, 90, says that European constitutionalists of the time also preferred earlier European models, which set up limited monarchies, to the American constitution of 1787, which, of course, established a republic. The influence of American revolutionary and constitutional documents outside the United States will be traced in detail by George Billias in a forthcoming book.

68. Adams to Jefferson, February 3, 1821, and Jefferson to Adams, September 12, 1821, in Cappon, ed., *Adams-Jefferson Letters*, 571, 574–75.

69. To Roger O. Weightman, June 24, 1826, in Peterson, ed., *Jefferson*, 1516–17. In this frequently quoted letter Jefferson declined an invitation to participate in the celebrations at Washington, D.C., on July 4, 1826.

70.   Among other places, the story is told in Dumas Malone, *Jefferson and His Time*, Vol. VI, *The Sage of Monticello* (Boston, 1981), 497.

71.   Caleb Cushing, Newburyport, Massachusetts, July 15, 1826, in *A Selection of Eulogies, Pronounced in the Several States, In Honor of Those Illustrious Patriots and Statesmen, John Adams and Thomas Jefferson* (Hartford, 1826), 24, and see also John A. Shaw at Bridgewater, Massachusetts, August 2, 1826, at p. 163: "When was the hand of Providence more clearly seen than in the close of their eventful lives? . . . When centuries shall have rolled away, and the mists of time shall have shed around our revolutionary conflict the guise of a romantic age— when the fancies of the poet shall have mingled with the truths of history, scarcely will the world refrain from classing this act of heaven with the prodigies and marvels of a fabled era."

72.   Peleg Sprague, Hallowell, Maine, July 1826; John Tyler, Richmond, Virginia, July 11, 1826; the Cushing eulogy cited above, and also John Sergeant, Philadelphia, July 24, 1826, in ibid., 145–46, 7, 20, 48 , 100, 106, and 29.

73.   Ibid., 28, 143.

74.   Tyler in ibid., 8, and see also William Alexander Duer, Albany, New York, July 31, 1826, at pp. 122–23.

75.   Ibid., 105, 145.

76.   See Selby, *Revolution in Virginia*, 106–08, and Robert A. Rutland, ed., *The Papers of George Mason, 1725–92* (Chapel Hill, N.C., 1970), I: 287, 289.

77.   Arthur Zilversmit, *The First Emancipation: The Abolition of Slavery in the North* (Chicago and London, 1967), 112–15. Zilversmit notes that the provision was used in this way in the 1780s although the state's constitutional convention apparently had no intention of abolishing slavery. Also, on *Commonwealth v. Aves*, Octavius Pickering, *Reports of Cases Argued and Determined in the Supreme Judicial Court of Massachusetts*, XVII (Boston, 1840), 210. The case decided that a slave owner who brought a slave to Massachusetts on a visit for business or pleasure "cannot restrain the slave of his liberty during his continuance here, and carry him out of this state against his consent" (193). The case concerned the fate of a six-year-old child named Med.

78.   *Proceedings and Debates of the Virginia State Convention, of 1829–30* (Richmond, 1830), esp. 54–57. Cooke's argument was part of a fascinating discussion over the nature of the Declaration of Rights and its practical implications. See, for example, John Randolph, 317: "I subscribe to every word in the Bill of Rights. . . . The Bill of Rights contains unmodified principles. The declarations it contains are our lights and guides, but when we come to apply these great principles, we must modify them for use; we must set limitations to their operation, and the enquiry then is, *quousque?* How far? It is a question not of principle, but of degree. The very moment this immaculate principle of their's is touched, it becomes what all principles are, materials in the hands of men of sense, to be applied to the welfare of the Commonwealth." I have been unable to locate the precise quotation that Cooke attributed to Jefferson, but Cooke probably referred to Jefferson's *Notes on the State of Virginia*, which were composed in 1781, and included severe criticisms of the Virginia constitution of 1776 and its system of

county representation by which "every man in Warwick has as much influence in the government as 17 men in Loudon." Jefferson was not, however, as kind as Cooke in explaining inconsistencies as the result of wartime necessity—indeed, he made the point that Virginia was not threatened by invasion at the time—nor did he cite the state Declaration of Rights. He did, however, urge Virginians to "apply, at a proper season, the proper remedy" for their government's defects, and call a constitutional convention "to fix the constitution." Jefferson, *Notes on the State of Virginia*, ed. William Peden (Chapel Hill, N.C., 1955), esp. 118–20, 128–29, and see also Alison Goodyear Freehling, *Drift Toward Dissolution; The Virginia Slavery Debate of 1831–1832* (Baton Rouge and London, 1982), 36–81.

79.   Helen E. Veit et al., eds., *Creating the Bill of Rights: The Documentary Record from the First Federal Congress* (Baltimore, 1991), esp. xii–xvii for a general account of the document's development, 11–14 for Madison's proposal, and p. x for the S.C. quotation. See also Madison's speech to Congress of June 8, 1789, with his proposal, in Charles F. Hobson, et al., eds., *The Papers of James Madison*, XII (Charlottesville, 1979), 196–210, and note esp. 203: "The first of these amendments [i.e., the provisions to be "prefixed" to the constitution], relates to what may be called a bill of rights." For further discussions of Madison and the federal bill of rights, see James H. Hutson, "The Bill of Rights and the American Revolutionary Experience," and Jack N. Rakove, "Parchment Barriers and the Politics of Rights," in Michael J. Lacey and Knud Haakonssen, *A Culture of Rights: The Bill of Rights in Philosophy, Politics, and Law—1791 and 1991* (New York and Cambridge, England, 1991), 62–97 (esp. 87–91) and 98–143; and Herbert J. Storing, "The Constitution and the Bill of Rights," in Joseph M. Bessette, *Toward a More Perfect Union: Writings of Herbert J. Storing* (Washington, D.C., 1995), 108–28.

80.   Kenneth R. Bowling, "'A Tub to the Whale': The Founding Fathers and Adoption of the Federal Bill of Rights," *Journal of the Early Republic*, VIII (1988), and Rakove, "Parchment Barriers."

81.   Veit et al., *Creating the Bill of Rights*, pp. 47–50 for the version Congress finally adopted. The second of the amendments that the states at first failed to ratify became in 1992 the 27th amendment to the constitution.

82.   Philip S. Foner, ed., *We the Other People: Alternative Declarations of Independence by Labor Groups, Farmers, Women's Rights Advocates, Socialists, and Blacks, 1829–1975* (Urbana, Ill., 1976), esp. introduction, 1–38, and Seneca Falls "Declaration of Sentiments and Resolves," 78–79.

83.   Zilversmit, *First Emancipation*, 182–83, 213, and passim. In 1817, New York decided to hasten the process of abolition by declaring all slaves born before July 4, 1799, free as of July 4, 1827 (213).

84.   Freehling, *Drift Toward Dissolution*, 132–37, 2, and passim.

85.   Garrison to the *Boston Courier*, July 9, 1829; to Henry Brougham, Boston, August 1, 1832; to the *Boston Courier*, March 18, 1837, and to the *Liberator*, New York, [May] 22, 1847, in Walter M. Merrill and Louis Ruchames, eds., *The Letters of William Lloyd Garrison*, Vols. I–III (Cambridge, Mass., 1971–73), I: 85–86, 160; II: 226, and III: 478.

86.   For example, in 1785, when John Smilie stated in the Pennsylvania assembly that "a democratic government like ours, admits of no superiority" between honest men, the conservative jurist James Wilson dissented. "Surely," he insisted, "persons possessed of knowledge, judgment, information, integrity, and having extensive connections, are not to be classed with persons void of reputation or character—with criminals who infringe the laws, &c. &c." In Mathew Carey, ed., *Debates and Proceedings of the General Assembly of Pennsylvania, on the Memorials Praying a Repeal of the Law Annuling the Charter of the Bank [of North America]*, (Philadelphia, 1786), 21, 38. See also Jack P. Greene, "All Men Are Created Equal," in Greene, *Imperatives, Behaviors, and Identities: Essays in Early American Cultural History* (Charlottesville, N.C., 1992) esp. 238–46.

87.   Clay, Tyler, and Randolph quotations in William Sumner Jenkins, *Pro-Slavery Thought in the Old South* (Chapel Hill, N.C., 1935), 59–60. See also Larry E. Tise, *Proslavery: A History of the Defense of Slavery in America* (Athens, Ga., and London, 1987), esp. 39, 248, 342.

88.   Calhoun, speech on the Oregon Bill, June 27, 1848, in Calhoun, *Liberty and Union: The Political Philosophy of John C. Calhoun*, ed. Ross M. Lence (Indianapolis, 1992), 565–70.

89.   *Appendix to the Congressional Globe,* 33d Congress, First Session, ed. John C. Rives, new series Vol. XXXI (Washington, D.C., 1854), 137, 310.

90.   Ibid., 310–11.

91.   Merrill D. Peterson, *"This Grand Pertinacity": Abraham Lincoln and the Declaration of Independence*, the Fourteenth Annual R. Gerald McMurtry Lectures (Fort Wayne, Ind., 1991), esp. 5–7; Lincoln's Address to the Young Men's Lyceum of Springfield, Illinois, January 27, 1838, and his reply to Stephen Douglas at Chicago, July 10, 1858, in Roy P. Basler, ed., *The Collected Works of Abraham Lincoln* (New Brunswick, N.J., 1953–55), I: 114–15, II: 499.

92.   Lincoln's speech at Peoria, Illinois, October 16, 1854; reply to Douglas at Chicago, July 10, 1858; Letter to J. N. Brown, October 18, 1858; letter to H. L. Pierce and others, April 6, 1859, and address at Independence Hall in Philadelphia, February 22, 1861, in ibid., II: 266, 499; III: 327; IV: 375; V: 240, and see also his references to Calhoun's and Pettit's statements in his reply to Douglas at Alton, Illinois, October 15, 1858, in Harry Holzer, ed., *The Lincoln-Douglas Debates: The First Complete, Unexpurgated Text* (New York, 1993), 344–45. Choate made his statement in a letter to the Maine Whig State Central Committee, Boston, August 9, 1856, in *The Works of Rufus Choate*, 2 vols. (Boston, 1862), I: 215.

93.   John Tweedy, *A History of the Republican National Conventions from 1856 to 1908* (Danbury, Conn., 1910), 16, and see also pp. 43–45, for debates in 1860 over the party's platform, which in the end said "That the maintenance of the principles promulgated in the Declaration of Independence and embodied in the Federal Constitution, 'That all men are created equal; that they are endowed by their Creator with certain inalienable rights; that among these are life, liberty and the pursuit of happiness; that to secure these rights, governments were instituted among men, deriving their just powers from the consent of the governed,' is essential to the preservation of our Republican institutions. . . ."

94.   David Herbert Donald, *Lincoln* (New York, 1995), esp. 214–15.

95.   Holzer, ed., *Lincoln-Douglas Debates*, 17, 317–18; Lincoln to J. N. Brown, October 18, 1858, in Basler, ed., *Collected Works of Lincoln*, III: 327–28. The Clay speech, given at Richmond, Indiana, in response to a Mr. Mendenhall and others who petitioned him to free his slaves, was in general a statement on the impracticality of abolitionist demands. After making the statement Lincoln quoted, Clay went on to say that in acceding to the Declaration of Independence, the states had no intention "that it should be tortured into a virtual emancipation of all the slaves within their respective limits," and if extreme abolitionist arguments had been seriously promulgated at the time of the revolution "our glorious independence would never have been achieved." Moreover, "in no society that ever did exist, or ever shall be formed, was or can the equality asserted among the members of the human race, be practically enforced and carried out," and large portions of it, including "women, minors, insane, culprits, transient sojourners"—an interesting catch-pot of groups quite characteristic of the time—were likely always to remain subject to "another portion of the community." Obviously, Lincoln cited Clay selectively. Daniel Mallory, ed., *The Life and Speeches of the Hon. Henry Clay*, II (4th ed., New York, 1844), 595–600, esp. 596–97.

96.   Speech in Senate, March 3, 1854, in *Appendix to the Congressional Globe*, 33d Congress, 1st Session, XXXI: 337; quotation of a Douglas speech by Lincoln at Springfield, Illinois, June 26, 187, in Basler, ed., *Collected Works of Lincoln*, II: 406, and Douglas at Ottawa, August 21, and Jonesboro, Illinois, September 15, 1858, in Holzer, ed., *Lincoln-Douglas Debates*, 53, 57, 149 (and note that in these passages Douglas continually refers to the revolutionaries as "our fathers"), and esp. 151–52, 154–55, and also at Galesburg, Illinois, October 7, 1858, 247–48.

97.   Lincoln's replies to Douglas at Springfield, June 26, 1857; Peoria, October 16, 1854; and Chicago, July 10, 1858, in Basler, ed., *Collected Works of Lincoln*, II: 405–07, 266, 499–500. At Chicago, Lincoln also said that the argument that the principles of the Declaration of Independence do not apply to blacks was identical to "the arguments that kings have made for enslaving the people in all ages of the world. You will find that all the arguments in favor of king-craft were of this class." Douglas's argument was like that of "the same old serpent" who says "you work and I eat, you toil and I will enjoy the fruits of it. Turn it whatever way you will—whether it come from the mouth of a King, an excuse for enslaving the people of his country, or from the mouth of men of one race as a reason for enslaving the men of another race, it is all the same old serpent. . . ." Ibid., II: 500.

98.   At Springfield, June 26, 1857, in ibid., II: 405–06.

99.   Lincoln at Ottawa, August 21, 1858, and to J. N. Brown, October 18, 1858, ibid., III: 29, 327.

100.   At Chicago, July 10, 1858, to J. N. Brown, October 18, 1858, and at Peoria, October 16, 1854, ibid., II: 501, III: 327–28, II: 266–67.

101.   At Springfield, June 26, 1857, ibid., II: 406 (and repeated at Alton, October 15, 1858, in Holzer, ed., *Lincoln-Douglas Debates*, 344–45).

102.   Fragment on the Constitution and the Union, ca. January 1861, and

Lincoln to H. L. Pierce and others, April 6, 1859, in Basler, ed., *Collected Works of Lincoln*, IV: 168–69, III: 376.

103.   Fragment on the Constitution, ca. January 1861; Message to Congress, July 4, 1861; and "Response to a Serenade," July 7, 1863, ibid., IV: 169, 438; VI: 320.

104.   "Response to a Serenade," July 7, 1863, and Address at Gettysburg, November 19, 1863, ibid., VI: 319–20, VII: 23.

EPILOGUE

1.   Frank Whitson Fetter, "The Revision of the Declaration of Independence in 1941," *WMQ*, 3d Ser., XXI (1974), 133–38, esp. 134–35.

2.   This and the following passage from the Jefferson Memorial are taken from "Thomas Jefferson Memorial: Chamber Inscriptions," kindly supplied to the author by Gerry Gaumer of the National Park Service, and Tescia Ann Yonkers, *Shrine of Freedom: Thos. Jefferson Memorial* (Springfield, Va. [ARK Printing and Graphics], 1991 [orig. 1983]), which includes a photograph of the inscribed panel.

3.   The words excised by the associate architects include "UNITED" before "COLONIES," and "TO EACH OTHER" after "we mutually pledge." See Fetter, "Revision of the Declaration," 135–37.

4.   In Boyd, *The Declaration of Independence: The Evolution of the Text . . .* (Washington, D.C. [Library of Congress], 1943), 9.

5.   J. C. Holt, *Magna Carta* (2nd ed.; Cambridge, England, 1992), esp. 1–22, quotations at 3 (Maitland), 10 (trial by jury), 21.

6.   Lincoln to J. N. Brown, October 18, 1858, in Roy P. Basler, *Abraham Lincoln: His Speeches and Writings* (Cleveland and New York, 1946), 479.

7.   From Stephen B. Oates, *Let the Trumpet Sound: The Life of Martin Luther King, Jr.* (New York, 1982), 259–62.

Acknowledgments

The greater part of this book was written in summers and on two terms of paid leave from the Massachusetts Institute of Technology. Moreover, virtually all the expenses incurred were covered by an M.I.T. research fund attached to the William Rand Kenan, Jr., Professorship, to which John Deutch, then M.I.T.'s Provost, and the late Dean Nan Friedlaender appointed me several years ago. It would be nice if acknowledging M.I.T.'s generous support for my research would dent its misleading public image as a school of engineering and not much more, but that's probably too much to ask.

I should add that the book draws substantially on research done under earlier grants from the National Endowment for the Humanities and the John Simon Guggenheim Foundation to write a book that was supposed to be on the "revolutionary tradition in America." Projects don't always turn out the way writers anticipate at their outset, and a study of the Declaration provided a more workable way to explore several themes I had planned to discuss in that other book. I am grateful to the NEH and the Guggenheim Foundation for their support and also for their patience.

Only a very small part of *American Scripture* depends upon archival work. That segment was done at the University of Michigan's Clements Library, where John Dann and his staff were more open and helpful than any archivists with whom I have ever worked anywhere else. Otherwise, except for a few extraordinarily helpful consultations with Peter Drummy at the Massachusetts Historical Society, research was done at Harvard University's magnificent Widener Library, my "lab," as I tell my M.I.T. colleagues, my home away from home, and one of the greatest joys of my life. I am immensely grateful to all staff members at Widener who have facilitated my use of its rich resources over many years.

Historians, unlike scientists and engineers, characteristically work alone, not in teams or laboratories. We are nonetheless heavily dependent on others. Every endnote is a note of thanks to someone who told me something I needed to know, made assertions that got me thinking, or provided the text of a document I needed to examine. Several people contributed more actively to the book's completion. Greg Clancey, an M.I.T. graduate student, helped discover where I would and would not find more state and local "declarations" on Independence than those I'd already discovered. Jessica Maier, then a Brown undergraduate, used her well-honed research skills to find a remarkable number of additional

Massachusetts resolutions on Independence in Widener's collection of local histories, and later helped check endnotes with awesome efficiency. Eric Foner and Bernard Bailyn read what I now think of as an embarrassingly crude early version of the first three central chapters of the book and made extremely useful suggestions for their revision. Richard D. Brown, Ronald Hamowy, Joseph Ellis, and Jack Rakove examined all but the epilogue of a penultimate version and saved me from several errors and infelicities of language. Jill Kneerim was more than my agent: a Radcliffe classmate, friend, splendid editor, and spokeswoman for the "lay reader," she helped make the book more coherent and, I hope, more interesting and easier to follow for readers who have not had the pleasure of spending their working lives studying the American eighteenth century. I also want to thank Jane Garrett, now my editor for the third time, for her personal support and for making the task of shepherding a book through the works at Knopf seem almost easy; and Melvin Rosenthal, a production editor whose meticulous work on my manuscript was in keeping with his reputation as a legendary practitioner of his craft. My single greatest debt, however, goes to Thomas N. Brown, a longtime colleague, mentor, and friend, who saw the promise in this project before I did, and not only offered unfailing encouragement, but heroically read draft after draft, generously giving me the benefit of his broad historical knowledge and keen aesthetic sensitivities.

Finally, I am grateful to my husband, the historian Charles S. Maier, for reading the manuscript and offering both advice and reassurance when I most needed them, but even more for understanding when I preferred staying in the library to coming home for dinner (in part, I suspect, because he, too, was finishing a book). Now let us feast.

P.M.

Index